From a Minyan
to a Community

The line drawing of the Temple of Concord on the cover shows it as it appeared in 1851 when it was completed and dedicated. Five years later a wind storm blew down the cupola and it was never replaced.

From a Minyan
to a Community

A HISTORY OF
THE JEWS OF SYRACUSE

B. G. RUDOLPH

SYRACUSE UNIVERSITY

F
129
.S8
R8

DEDICATED

To my parents
   with reverence
To my wife and children
   with love

BERNARD G. RUDOLPH was a retail jeweler in Syracuse, New York, for more than half a century. He has been deeply involved in civic, charitable, and religious activities in Syracuse during the past six decades. His positions of responsibility have been many and varied: president, campaign chairman, and long-time member of the board of the Jewish Welfare Federation; president of the Western New York Zionist Region; member and president of the advisory board of St. Joseph's Hospital; president of the Retail Jewelers of America; service with the Food Rationing Board in World War I, and with the Civil Air Warning 1st Interceptor Command in World War II.

Mr. Rudolph has established an annual lectureship in Judaic Studies at Syracuse University, and a similar series at New College in Sarasota, Florida. His first literary venture was a brief account of his early life, *Tell Me More*, privately issued in 1966, and his interest in the origins of Syracuse Jewry led him to spend three years in research on the present volume.

Foreword

Writing this book on the development of the Jewish community in Syracuse has been a labor, but a labor of love. I have enjoyed the work, I have been stimulated by the subject matter, and I have discovered the joy and excitement of gathering facts, stories, and anecdotes and weaving them together into this book. The idea for such a book came to me from reading similar books on Utica, Milwaukee, Charleston, and Rochester, among others. Syracuse, too, needed its history recorded, and there were no scholars or rabbis with the time or the urge. And I, being retired, had both the time and inclination. That is why this book is the work of a layman, a layman who wanted to see that Syracuse had its Jewish beginnings set down on paper.

The Founding Fathers of the Syracuse Jewish community—who were they? Where did they come from? When did they arrive? How well did they lay the foundation on which the Syracuse Jewish community was built? That is what this book is all about.

In doing the research, I have come across many manuscripts and newspaper reports. Rather than try to rewrite them in the language of today, when we are prone to be sparing in our words and terse in our remarks, I have included many copies of the originals just as they were written. There is a charm and nostalgia in the expanse of words and the flowery phrases of the olden days. I have also included many photographs. The old proverb that a "picture is worth a thousand words" can be especially true when one tries to describe something that is no longer in existence. I have tried as much as possible to record the events through the eyes of the people who lived in the community, to describe the happenings as they occurred, and to limit the use of charts and dry statistics.

vii

The thickly settled Jewish neighborhood bordered by East Genesee, Adams, and Montgomery Streets and Irving Avenue is no longer
there. The area in which our first Jewish settlers chose to live close to
one another, that enclave known for over a hundred years as the Jewish neighborhood, has been demolished to make way for urban renewal. The synagogues, the temples, the halls where the weddings
and Purim balls were held—those monuments of the old Jewish community—are gone.

The Grape Street Shul, which stood near Harrison Street for more
than seventy years, is now Temple Beth El, located on the outskirts of
the city. The Jewish grocery stores, the kosher butcher shops, the fish
market, the delicatessen—all are gone. As early as 1900 the Jewish
population began moving eastward and upward, toward the hills that
lie east of the original Jewish neighborhood.

It is obvious that there is need for a recorded history of the Syracuse Jewish community. Inadequate though my efforts may be, it is
time—and long past—that a book of this kind be written and published.

I have endeavored not to go too far afield, limiting myself to accounts of the earliest settlers, their families, and a few of the important leaders who arrived later, but whose contributions to the building
of the Jewish community were notable. Inadvertently, someone may
have been overlooked who belongs in the above categories; if so, I ask
your forbearance in advance.

It is my hope that this volume will manifest to the reader that Syracuse's Jewish community *did not just happen*. It was the result of the
dedication of our Founding Fathers to a continuation of the value of
Jewish existence, and this took courage and forethought. Not all of
them were leaders. The peddlers and small merchants gave of their
hard-earned dollars to build the temples, the synagogues, and other
institutions. They were the warp and woof of what has come to be the
Jewish community of Syracuse, New York.

BERNARD G. RUDOLPH

Acknowledgments

The limitations and shortcomings of this book are my own responsibility, but I wish to publicly acknowledge my appreciation of and the debts I owe to many individuals and especially to those without whose help this book would not have been possible.

I owe my greatest debt to Professor A. Leland Jamison, Willard Ives Professor of the Bible at Syracuse University, whose experience in reviewing and editing manuscripts has been a bulwark of strength in guiding me in the right direction, and to Mrs. Carolyn Wright of the Onondaga Historical Society, who supplied me with much original material and who spared no time and effort in culling out items from old newspapers and periodicals. Without these two people, this book could not have arrived at publication. It is even more remarkable when I stop to remember that neither one is Jewish.

I am very grateful to Dr. Isidore S. Meyer, Editor Emeritus of the *American Jewish Historical Quarterly,* whose comments and correction of the manuscript at various stages of its preparation were most helpful.

I am deeply obligated to Chancellor William P. Tolley of Syracuse University for his interest and encouragement during the writing of my manuscript. He read the chapter on Syracuse University and offered constructive suggestions; he reviewed the manuscript when complete and approved it.

His offer to have Syracuse University sponsor the publication honored and sustained me greatly in my endeavors.

I owe many debts to others: to Rabbi Benjamin Friedman, of Temple of Concord, for his cooperation in providing material and many personal reminiscences; to Mr. Oscar Golden, for reading and translating for me items about Syracuse from Hebrew into English; to Dr. Gladys Rosen, of the American Jewish History Center; and to Dr. Jacob R. Marcus, Director of the American Jewish Archives, who read my manuscript and made many valuable suggestions.

My thanks to Frank J. Early, who edited the Syracuse Centennial Edition of the *Syracuse Herald-American* for Sunday, August 15, 1948. This edition contained a wealth of material of which I was able to make good use. In addition, Frank Early, now retired from newspaper reporting, took a personal interest in my manuscript, for all of which I am very grateful.

To Samuel Marcus, of Sarasota, Florida, who was beside me during much of the writing of the manuscript, and who has a good understanding of literary values from a layman's point of view, I owe a great debt.

I was fortunate in approaching Louis Stolz before he passed away at the age of ninety; when I first spoke to him in 1966, his mind was clear and he remembered well the early days going back to 1890 and before. He supplied me with much information about the Stolz family. I also received valuable material from his nephew, Max Stolz.

Many more people assisted me in rounding up material and from personal participation in creating Jewish history in Syracuse, just to name a few—Rabbi Samuel Yalow, Rabbi Jacob Epstein, Rabbi Theodore Levy, David Altfield, Cantor Harold Lerner, Isidore Shapiro, Harris Pine, Mrs. Julius Kelson, Mrs. Evelyn Nesbit, Mrs. Gerald Pliskin, Myron Small, Mrs. Frances Moss, and Max Rosenbloom.

I owe thanks to the ladies who did the typing and made many valuable suggestions while doing so—Miss Katherine Niles of Syracuse and Mrs. Pearl Hight of Sarasota, and above all, to Mrs. Ann Janks who was my right hand toward the last period when I was beginning to tire and needed a reliable and loyal helper and friend.

Introduction

What is past is but prologue and in his volume, *From a Minyan to a Community,* the author, a concerned observer of the development of the Jewish community of Syracuse, New York, for over six decades, endeavors to recount the history of that community from its modest beginnings down to the present day. In his dedicated task of assembling the data and documents pertaining to this history, one discerns that Bernard G. Rudolph has touched upon virtually every aspect of Jewish communal and civic experience, together with the multi-faceted reactions of the immigrants and their offspring during the past two generations to the challenges of the day, both as Americans and as Jews.

In addition to the events of the past two generations, the author has sought to garner and gather together information anteceding the period of his advent upon the Syracuse scene. He depicts the beginnings of the early settlement of the first German Jewish pioneers in that city and of their establishing there of the first *minyan,* and the groundwork they laid in bringing into being the earliest Jewish congregation in that city, the Society of Concord, in 1839, which was the foundation for the future development of the *Kehillah* (community). The author then continues the story from the fourth decade of the nineteenth century through the period of the initiation of East European Jewish mass immigration to the United States of America during the last two decades of the nineteenth century and the early decades of the twentieth, down to the era that followed. Thus, we have herein reflected a panorama of Jewish communal and general American civic history, touched upon sometimes peripherally, as it affected the Jews in Syracuse for almost four generations, including the periods before World War I and World War II and the more recent postwar period.

The structure of this volume relates to the various phases of Jewish communal endeavor over a century and a quarter. It deals with the growth of the Jewish community of Syracuse and its reaction toward events in this country and abroad as they impinged upon the Jewish inhabitants of Syracuse and upon their coreligionists residing in this country and in the Old World. It also describes the role of the Jewish citizens in the Syracuse community at large. For the local Jewish community, here and elsewhere, is a microcosm within a social macrocosm and must be understood as such. The chapters outlined may serve, therefore, as a guide to other dedicated Jewish laymen in detecting and collecting the literary sources, the historical memorabilia, and oral historical records and reminiscences in their own respective communities, as has been done with such perspicacity and warmth by Mr. Rudolph.

In emulating the author of this book, one might be mindful of the statement of Rabbi Tarphon in the *Ethics of the Fathers* (2:31):

It is not thy task to complete the work, but neither art thou free to desist from it.

To which, the late British Chief Rabbi, Dr. Joseph H. Hertz—the first graduate of the Jewish Theological Seminary of America, whose first position as a rabbi was that of the Adath Yeshurun Congregation of Syracuse—adds his commentary:

To complete the work. It may not be given thee to complete the task called for, but that is no reason why it should not be attempted. Be not disheartened by the greatness and difficulty of what is before thee. Do as much as is in thy power.[1]

For before the definitive history of the Jews of the United States of America is to be written, so that it can be objectively evaluated, the lacunae of local, communal, and regional histories must be written— the empty gaps must be filled in. Such endeavors must include the literary efforts of those who shared in the budding and flowering of the Jewish community, and whose views about it must be reflected as participant observers and as interested laymen. They may not complete the task; they may be circumscribed in their outlook, deal with it at times tangentially, and not carry it out in an organic totality in all of its aspects. But the fruits of such labors may induce the professional scholar to pursue the enterprise further in the production of various studies and monographs in depth that will touch upon the variegated facets of Jewish life and culture in the manifold areas of the social sciences and the humanities. It will beckon the historian, the sociologist, the economist, the social worker, the psychologist, the educator, the theologian, and the philosopher toward the further investigation and interpretation of the Jewish scene on American soil.

When one views the output of American Jewish historiography, one readily discovers that although considerable work has been done on the colonial and Civil War periods, only the surface has been touched in the ante-bellum and post-bellum periods. The lack is particularly felt in regard to the latter period, which witnessed the mass migrations of Jews from Eastern Europe, down to the present. It was then that the great institutions of Jewish higher learning and communal and philanthropic agencies came into being, matured, and bore fruit, and showed their response to the dire needs of Jews abroad and also met the requirements of the Jewish communities themselves. It was also the time when, as Americans, they fulfilled their duties and responsibilities together with their American compatriots on a local, state, and national level.

It was, therefore, most fortunate that not so long ago Dr. Benjamin Friedman, Senior Rabbi of the Temple of Concord, wisely counseled the author, shortly after the latter had completed a book of personal reminiscences, that in his retirement he should undertake the writing of the history of the Jews of Syracuse. In carrying this suggestion forward, Mr. Rudolph, who is not a professional historian, realized that such a venture would require preparation on his part. He thereupon secured and read diligently copies of all local and regional American Jewish histories that were available to him. He carefully read the volumes on Charleston, South Carolina; Rochester, Buffalo, and Utica, New York; and Milwaukee, Wisconsin.[2] He consulted guides for research in the areas of local and of regional history.[3] He consulted local records and interviewed the older settlers and their contemporaries, as well as some of their descendants.

Mr. Rudolph has, in his own modest way, fulfilled the proposal of Dr. Clifford K. Shipton, Custodian of the Archives of Harvard University, who until recently was the Director of the American Antiquarian Society in Worcester, Massachusetts. At a joint meeting of the American Jewish Historical Society and the American Historical Association at the latter's annual meeting on December 28, 1966, Dr. Shipton delivered an address titled "An Americanist Looks at American Jewish History," in which he alluded to two significant elements in determining American culture today: the Puritan version of the Hebraic contribution, and that of the modern Jewish immigrants.[4] In this address, he also emphasized the point that "Civilization is, of course, a record of communities." [5] The American Antiquarian Society, it may be noted parenthetically, also specializes in collecting histories of local communities and church bodies, and has one of the finest collections in this area. But reverting to his sagacious counsel on the preservation of the records of modern Jewish immigrants, whose reminiscences expressing their hopes and fears, their resentments and joys, will supply us with the raw materials of history, Dr. Shipton has this to say:

The first and most essential thing to do in the study of the Jewish community and its influence is to get down immediately on paper the recollections of the survivors of the immigrant generation.[6]

In evaluating the contributions of Jewish immigrants to American life and culture, to American medicine and science, to the arts and to the humanities, Dr. Shipton further stated that it derives from their intellectual energy—their vocation—from their cultural heritage.[7]

The author has long been interested in both the Jewish past and present. In a short account of his family's migration to America from Lithuania and of his own early life, privately printed under the title *Tell Me More*,[8] he recounts with reverence that he drew inspiration from his father, who imparted to him a knowledge of Talmudic and biblical lore. With affectionate warmth, he describes his mother, Jeanette, and her philanthropies. It was they who taught to their son the Lithuanian Jewish ethos of respect for learning, and of participation in all worthwhile community endeavors, of *Zedakah* (charity) and of *gemilut hasadim* (acts and deeds of loving kindness). It was they who imbued him with an empathy for everything constructively Jewish, and a love for humanitarian ideals.

As an early Zionist and as a leader of the Zionist movement in Syracuse, as a president of the Syracuse Jewish Welfare Federation, and as a campaign chairman for many years of Jewish philanthropic endeavors for local causes, for European Jewish relief, and for Israel, Mr. Rudolph has actively served the community. In all these he has been and continues to be a participant and an observer. For ten years, he was a member of the board of St. Joseph's Hospital, and for two years, chairman of its board. He maintains membership in and contributes to many national and international organizations whose aims and objectives are the furtherance of good human relations among men.

At Syracuse University, so dear to him, he endowed a lectureship in Judaic Studies for the purpose of bringing an eminent scholar for a period of three days to that seat of higher learning. The lectures that have been delivered by the visiting scholars are published and widely distributed to those in search of authentic Jewish knowledge. Thus, another link in the chain of the tradition of Judaic learning is being forged and continued on an academic level in the community so close to Mr. Rudolph's heart.

In his farewell song to the Israelites before their entrance into the Promised Land of Canaan, Moses counseled them:

Remember the days of old, consider the years of many generations; Ask thy father and he will declare unto thee; thy elders and they will tell thee. (Deuteronomy 32:7.)

The French Jewish medieval exegete, the Rashbam, grandson of Rashi, asks what this positive biblical commandment comes to teach us, this imperative to remember; and his answer to this query is that it comes to teach us to remember that

Before you were born, the Holy One blessed be He, prepared your legacy for you.

Memory therefore serves as an act of thanksgiving and gratitude by the children and grandchildren. They are commanded to remember and to record the words and deeds, the thoughts and the acts of the progenitors of the American Jewish community, to recall how they met the problems of Jewish association with American life—how the pioneers adjusted themselves in their new homeland; how they and their progeny became American citizens; how they and their descendants entered into the mainstream of American life; and how the descendants of peddlers in a later generation gained entrance into various businesses, the arts and professions, and other callings once the opportunity was granted them, and thus were able to contribute and to continue to contribute to the welfare and well-being of the budding city of Syracuse in previous years and down to the present day. And what happened in Syracuse also happened in other communities throughout the length and breadth of this land in various degrees, in parallel and in dissimilar circumstances.

One of the founders of the American Jewish Historical Society, a distinguished American and a devout Jew, Dr. Cyrus Adler once declared:

No body of people can ever have a secure future or a self-respecting present who do not understand and reverence their own past.

Mr. Rudolph, in this book, *From a Minyan to a Community: A History of the Jews of Syracuse,* has endeavored to meet this challenge. May this volume serve as a prolegomenon to that history and inspire others to continue to delve in depth into the various phases of Syracusan Jewish history. May it also encourage others to initiate the story of the immigrants and their descendants in their respective communities, so that questing spirits may learn to appreciate the legacy of their forebears and to transmit that heritage enhanced by act and thought, by deed and word, to those who will follow them in the years that lie ahead.

ISIDORE S. MEYER
Editor Emeritus
American Jewish Historical Society

*New York, New York
Summer, 1969*

Contents

From a Minyan
to a Community

CHAPTER I

The Founding Fathers

The First Minyan

The recorded history of a Jewish community usually begins after there are enough men who are mindful of the virtues and sacredness of worshiping together as a *minyan* (a quorum of ten). When these men meet, their first thought is to find a private and convenient place to worship. Temporarily, it might be in a home or in the back of a store. Later, when they find a permanent place, a congregation is formed, records are kept, and thereafter it becomes possible to trace the history of a Jewish community.

The foundation for the Jewish community of Syracuse was laid in 1839, when an assemblage of twelve newcomers joined the few Jewish families already here. Together they formed the first congregation, the Keneseth Sholom (Society of Concord).

The one-hundredth anniversary of the establishment of this congregation was formally and fittingly celebrated in Syracuse on December 1 and 2, 1939. In a brochure published for the occasion, Benjamin Friedman, rabbi of the Society of Concord, wrote an account of the founding of this first congregation in Syracuse:

The Society of Concord, the oldest Jewish congregation in Syracuse, was established in 1839 and incorporated under the laws of the State of New York on February 24, 1842.

In 1839, Syracuse had a population of about eleven thousand inhabitants. It was growing in importance as a distributing center and as a source of supply for the salt industry. Overland, and by way of the Erie Canal—"Clinton's Ditch"—pioneer tradesmen from New York City were arriving to establish themselves in business and industries.

1

Among these pioneers who were moving out of New York City to villages and cities along the Hudson-Erie waterway there were also men and women of the Jewish faith. Early in the year 1839, a group of Jews met in the home of a Mr. H. Weiksheimer in New York City. They decided to settle in Syracuse because they had heard favorable reports concerning its advantages from some of their co-religionists who had travelled through Syracuse and obtained their information at Bernheim[er] and Block's notion store.

Soon after docking at Canal Street on the Erie Canal, this group of twelve Jews proceeded to Bernheim[er] and Block's wholesale notion store. They made arrangements to buy merchandise and to start out as pack peddlers. They studied the topography of central New York over which they were to carry their wares. Their business transacted, they retired to the rear of the store to hold Divine services. From that time on, these industrious Jewish itinerant merchants met regularly on Friday nights to usher in the holy Sabbath. Services were held in Bernheim[er] and Block's notion store which was situated on the present site of the State Tower building.[1]

Another account of the founding of the Syracuse Jewish community can be found in Dwight H. Bruce's *Memorial History of Syracuse*. He differs from Rabbi Friedman's account in the matter of dates. He states that: "On September 26, 1841 in New York City 12 gentlemen met at the house of H. Weiksheimer and decided to remove to Syracuse." [2] These men, according to Bruce, were the founders of the Society of Concord. "The first meeting was held on November 21, 1841 at the residence of Jacob Garson, Mulberry Street." [3]

Rabbi Adolph Guttman, in *The Jewish Encyclopedia* (1905), and Rabbi Irwin Hyman, in *The Universal Jewish Encyclopedia* (1941), in their articles on Syracuse hardly differ, in the main, from the narrative of Rabbi Friedman and Dwight Bruce. Inasmuch as these accounts give no source for their material, it is assumed that the information was gathered orally from the founders or their descendants at the time the articles were written.

The *minyan*, augmented by more immigrants, moved its meeting place from the rear of Bernheimer and Block's to the upper floor of Jacob Garson's home on Mulberry Street (now State Street). The Garson home also served as a kosher boardinghouse. While there, the *minyan* organized a congregation and elected officers; president, Max Thalheimer; treasurer, Joseph Schloss; trustees, Hessel Rosenbach and Samuel Manheimer; and secretary, E. Rothchild.

The congregation selected the name *Keneseth Sholom,* translated into English as the "Society of Concord." In 1841 a spiritual leader, Rabbi Abraham Gunzenhauser, was engaged. In 1842 the Society of Concord was incorporated according to the laws of New York State. The incorporation papers list Max Thalheimer, Samuel Bernheimer and Joseph Wiseman as trustees.[4]

Samuel Bernheimer, one of the trustees, was a part-owner of Bernheimer and Block's peddler's exchange where the first *minyan* gathered. This store was a branch of a larger establishment based in New York, the firm of H. Bernheimer and Brothers.

Later that year the partnership between Samuel Bernheimer of Syracuse and his brothers in New York was dissolved. A notice, dated November 2, 1842, revoked Samuel Bernheimer's power as agent for the firm of H. Bernheimer and Brothers:

. . . Whereas Samuel Bernheimer and Jacob Block, constituting the firm of S. Bernheimer & Co. of Syracuse, have this day assigned to H. Bernheimer & Brothers of New York, all the goods, debts and demands of each description; therefore, all persons are hereby forbidden to pay any debts to S. Bernheimer & Co. or either of said firm after this date.[5]

The notice requested debtors to settle their accounts with the brothers Herman, Emanuel, or Simon Bernheimer, one of whom would be in Syracuse to accept payment. The same issue of the *Onondaga Standard* advertised the opening of another store by H. Bernheimer and Brothers.

The new store, called the New Peddler's Exchange, formerly occupied by N. Stephans—reopened again by subscribers with stock of Fancy Dry Goods. Subscribers can sell cheaper than any merchant in the place, on account of having a large wholesale establishment in the City of New York—will supply county merchants and peddlers—also fine jewelry for Christmas and New Year's presents.

November 29, 1841   H. Bernheimer & Brothers
                                       of Syracuse and New York

Nine months later a notice in the *Onondaga Standard* announced that the store on the corner of Genesee and Warren Streets would thereafter be operated by the partnership of M. L. Hellman and Bernard Cohen, as the New Peddler's Exchange. Since the names of Hellman and Cohen do not appear in any later city directories or as members of any Jewish society, it is probable that they did not remain long in Syracuse. However, the needs of peddlers were soon supplied by two local merchants, Morris Thalheimer and Joseph Wiseman, who opened a store on Cedar Street.

In 1842, Congregation Keneseth Sholom held services in the Townsend Block on Water Street. In the same year, the growing congregation bought a tract of land on Lodi Street to serve as a cemetery. The Rose Hill Cemetery, still in existence but no longer in use, now is in the center of the city.

In August, 1846, Rabbi Joseph Goodman was elected to succeed Rabbi Gunzenhauser, and Isaac H. Bronner was elected president. The Society of Concord was again ready to move to larger quarters. A house was purchased for $800 on the corner of Mulberry and Madison Streets. After extensive remodeling, the house was converted into a synagogue. Rabbi Isaac Mayer Wise was invited to deliver the dedication sermon.[6]

When Rabbi Wise came to dedicate the new house of worship he had been in this country only two months. At the age of twenty-seven he was an energetic young man, whose aim and purpose was to organize and lead American Jewry along the path to Reform Judaism. The Reform movement was emerging in Germany when Wise left for the United States. First in Albany, then as rabbi of Bene Yeshurun in Cincinnati, Ohio, he continued to advocate Reform.[7]

In his memoirs he recalled his visit to Syracuse in 1846.

These gentlemen, who had been delegated by the congregation to call upon me, took me to Gerson's kosher hotel [Jacob Garson's boardinghouse], where I spent two weeks. I can recall the name of one of them, a Mr. Henochsberg [Aaron Henocksburg]. The builder had not finished the synagogue at the promised time, and the dedication had to be postponed one week.

During my stay in Syracuse I learned much of importance, for it was my first opportunity for intimate contact with the people among whom I was to live and work, and I had ample time to observe and study them. It did not take me long to view the salt-works, the Indians, the canal, and other sights. . . . I found there several people of culture, notably a Mr. Stein [Jacob Stone], a most intelligent man who explained the situation thoroughly. He was as witty as he was intelligent; he was well read, and understood human nature. He took charge of me, introduced me to the people, called my attention to their merits and their faults, so that I began to comprehend the lay of the land.

The dedication took place on the Friday and Saturday preceeding the Jewish New Year in 1846, and was a great and joyous festival for the Jews of Syracuse. Everything passed off well, and the newspapers teemed with praise. All my instructions had been obeyed with one exception, viz; to omit a certain prayer on Sunday morning, called *Makhnise Rachamin*. I was completely satisfied with Syracuse, and contributed, to the best of my ability, to the success of the celebration and the organization of the congregation.[8]

Up to this time the services of the congregation were conducted according to the Orthodox tradition. The men who organized the *minyan*—and later the congregation—though most of them came from western Europe, knew nothing of Reform Judaism. It was not until this visit of Rabbi Isaac Mayer Wise that the seed of Reform was planted among the members of the Temple of Concord, and with it came discord and strife that were to last for decades.

SYRACUSE IN 1839

What was the village of Syracuse like in 1839, when the twelve Israelites disembarked from the packet boat at Clinton Square? It was still a village. Humpback bridges riding high above the canal stood out sharply at crossings over Clinton, Salina, and Warren Streets. The hub of the town was the junction of East Genesee and Salina Streets, the spot which for years was referred to as "Bogardes Corners." Clinton Square, north of the canal, was the farmers' market. It is said that even from across the canal one could hear the pigs squealing and the sheep bleating. On the south side, facing the canal, was Water Street, which had a row of stores that catered to the carriage trade.

Business centered around Bogardes Corners. On the southeast corner stood the town's popular tavern, The Syracuse House. This was the terminal for the stagecoaches, where the leading citizens and politicians often met for talk and refreshment.

The first block on South Salina Street had a few brick business buildings, but farther down the street one could see the steeple of the First Presbyterian Church rising above the one-and-a-half-story white houses which lined both sides of Salina Street from Washington Street south to Jefferson Street. That block and Water Street, where the leading stores stood, had recently been paved with cobblestones. All the other streets were ordinary dirt roads. Occasionally one would seē a stray farm animal wander across the streets.

Farther down East Genesee Street, at the junction with Water Street, was the hay market. Opposite the hay market was Bernheimer and Block's store, where the first *minyan* met.

Salina was then, as it is now, the main street. It was the only road that went all the way from the town of Salina in the north, through the village of Syracuse, and on to Onondaga Valley in the south. On the north side of the canal there were a few stores and businesses. The first block of James Street was full of taverns. Farther up the hill, James Street had begun to take on the character of a beautiful residential area.

Besides Salina Street, the two principal streets running north and south which were important to the village were Warren and Clinton Streets. These contained the blacksmith shops, the carriage and harness makers' establishments, the livery stables, and more of the one-and-a-half-story wood frame houses.

The two foremost citizens of the village were Judge Joshua Forman, who came to Onondaga Valley in 1800 and established a law office, and John Wilkinson, an attorney who came to Syracuse in 1819. Wilkinson had the distinction of having given the name of "Syracuse" to the village in 1825; Joshua Forman was looked upon as one of the best educated and most influential of its citizens.

Syracuse was a busy village, and the outlook for it was promising. The Erie Canal (which had taken almost twenty years to build) was now completed all the way from Albany to Buffalo. Syracuse, halfway between the two cities, was about to benefit greatly from the trade generated from what people at first had called "Clinton's Folly," but which later made Syracuse an important industrial center.

The first train to enter Syracuse was drawn by horses and ran on wooden tracks. This was the Auburn and Syracuse Railroad, built in 1838. Not until June 4, 1839, did this new line have a locomotive. The Syracuse and Binghamton Railroad was completed in the same year.

In the building of this road, some of the swamps to the south of the city were fortunately drained, and the threat of epidemics was averted.

Syracuse had the distinction of being one of the first cities in the country to build plank roads. Forests were abundant in the area, so trees were cut and plank roads were built to Central Square, Manlius, and other points. Stagecoaches used these roads to Watertown, Manlius, Phoenix, and Cazenovia, connecting with other stagecoaches to more distant places.

Beyond Division Street on the north was the village of Salina. It was there, on the shores of Lake Onondaga in 1630, that the French missionary, Father Le Moyne, had learned about the salt springs from the Indians. The extraction and refining of salt as an industry was not developed until late in the eighteenth century. Then the industry grew rapidly. Truly it can be said that salt built Syracuse. Newcomers could see miles of salt vats. The salt industry required many laborers, most of whom were crude and rude but had money to spend. They frequently came to the adjoining village of Syracuse to patronize the saloons on lower James Street, and the popular name for that block became "Robber's Row." They also often stopped to trade at the stores on the north side of the canal, and it was there that many of our Jewish immigrants opened their small dry goods and clothing stores.

At a spot where West Genesee Street crosses Onondaga Creek, the old red mill was still standing, and farmers brought their wheat to be ground into flour. On the east the village spread as far as Irving Avenue, which was only a lane at the time, and beyond were the forests. To the south, the village extended as far as Jefferson Street, and beyond that were swamps, creeks, and ponds.[9]

THE HARDSHIPS AND DANGERS OF TRAVEL

At a time when it takes about half an hour to go from New York to Syracuse by jet plane, it is hard to imagine the difficulty of such a journey in the 1830's. One descendant wrote about his grandfather: "It took my grandfather Salic seven weeks to come from New York to Syracuse by stage coach in 1824." [10] Later, after the Erie Canal was opened from Albany to Buffalo, one could make the same trip in about ten days, and traveling by water was cheaper and more comfortable.

There was also danger attached to a trip inland from New York. There were "runners and man-catchers," as they were called in those days, waiting for the immigrant the moment he stepped off the gangplank in New York. These runners and man-catchers would often mislead unwary passengers. As soon as they found out where the newcomer wanted to go, they would lead him to a boarding house for a meal and a place to stay overnight, and the runners would get a kickback from the landlord. The next day the immigrant would be taken to a train or boat. In many cases the runners would overcharge him on his tickets and would even steal some of his luggage, if he had anything worth taking.[11]

There were Jewish runners, too, who could speak Yiddish. Some of these were equally unscrupulous, and would take advantage of poor Jewish immigrants.

The *New York Tribune* of July 31, 1851, published "Advice to Immigrants," warning them that they were the "constant prey of sharpies and rascals of all sorts." The article indicated the "Principal Routes to the Interior," with prices charged. Steamer from New York to Albany was the most popular means of transportation. Fares ranged from twenty-five to fifty cents. The steamer also carried freight and stopped at all the towns along the Hudson River. As the *Tribune* further stated, "From Albany there are two modes of conveyance to Buffalo, one by canal, which takes from seven to ten days, at one dollar and a half, the other by railroad, going through in 36 hours at $4.00, and no higher prices should be paid." [12] The time and cost to Syracuse were less, since Syracuse was halfway between Albany and Buffalo on the Erie Canal.

ETHNIC GROUPS AMONG THE EARLY SETTLERS

The earliest settlers in Syracuse were primarily English. They came chiefly from the New England States, looking for greener pastures toward the west. The digging of the canal and the building of the railroad brought a considerable number of German and Irish immigrants. In those early days it was natural that the people of different ethnic groups desired to live close to one another. The Germans settled on the north side of the canal, the Irish toward the south. The Jewish immigrants looked for homes on the east side along Jefferson, Cedar, and Mulberry Streets. It was along these streets that the Jewish immigrants settled and formed the enclave which for more than a hundred years was known as "the Jewish Neighborhood," often referred to by non-Jews as "Jew Town."

After the city charter was granted in 1847, Syracuse grew at a phenomenal rate. More immigrants were coming in daily—more Irish, more Germans, and also more Jews.

The railroad depot was located on what is now Vanderbilt Square on Washington Street. Watching the trains arrive afforded considerable interest when railroads were new, and the early settlers had few places to go except for a walk about town. The trains coming from the east usually had one or two cars painted yellow; these were known as "immigrant cars" and were filled with newcomers on their way west. Each of the immigrants had a tag tied to his lapel, indicating his name and destination. Often some Jewish immigrants would be dropped off in Syracuse, either because they had been sent for by a relative or friend, or because they had been directed here by one of the immigration aid societies in New York. These societies were organized not only to help the immigrants as they arrived, but also to prevent them—as far as possible—from remaining in the large seaport cities of New York, Boston, or Philadelphia.

BRIEF SKETCHES OF EARLY SETTLERS

In the nineteenth century America was constantly on the move, pushing the frontier always westward. The country was young, cities and towns were being created, opportunities were seemingly unlimited. Jews, too, were on the move. When a man did not prosper in one place, he headed for new territory that was just being opened for settlement and business. On the other hand, if one found success and accumulated wealth, he might turn to larger metropolitan centers in which there were even greater opportunities to put his money to work. So it was with the Jews of Syracuse—many stopped briefly in the city and then went elsewhere, leaving few traces of their presence.

Here is an example of the mobility of Jews in the early days of Syracuse. We came across a notice of A. M. Cohen in the dyeing and cleaning business. It appeared in the form of an advertisement in the weekly newspaper, *The Onondaga Chief,* of August 30, 1837.

OLD CLOTHES MADE NEW

The subscriber respectfully informs his friends and the public that he had commenced the Dying and Scouring business at his stand in the SHADES, on the corner of Warren (& James) Sts where he will be glad to attend those who may favor him with their custom. ☞ all work not done to the satisfaction of his patrons will not be charged for.

A. M. Cohen   Syracuse   Aug. 30, 1837

It seems quite evident that there was a Jew by the name of A. M. Cohen in Syracuse on August 30, 1837, but nowhere else did we come across his name. Although the directories in those days were not very reliable, his name does not appear in any of them, before or after. Neither does his name show up in association with any other Jew, or in the founding of the first synagogue. Here is a man whose shop was the forerunner of the extensive dyeing and cleaning businesses of today, and he disappeared from Syracuse completely.

Others remained, however, and their names should not be forgotten. A community is like an army. The rank and file constitute the body of the community, and their efforts make affairs move. Although these deserve the major share of credit for the total accomplishments of the group, it is unfortunate that their names and deeds are not preserved in written records. Such records tell, rather, of the leaders— presidents, trustees, and other officials of the temples, societies, and lodges. To these our history gives major attention, mostly because we know so little about the others. But tribute ought to be paid to all the men and women who set their roots deeply here, shared in the growth of Syracuse from a village to a city, built their homes, raised their families, established synagogues and charitable institutions—in short, those who became an integral part of the land and city of their choice.

Among those who formed the substance of the Jewish community within the larger body of the citizens of Syracuse were men of stature and vision. We should recall the origins and further achievements of a few of those men and their families about whom we have authentic information, and whose participation in Jewish affairs continued for many years.

We have good reason to believe that the Rosenbach, Garson, and Sloss families were here before the *minyan* of Jews who arrived in Syracuse by way of the Erie Canal in 1839.

Hessel Rosenbach claimed that he was the first Jew in what is now Syracuse. We believe him to be the one his grandson claimed had arrived by stagecoach in 1824. He took an active part in forming the first congregation, and he was named a trustee when the Society of Concord was incorporated.

It is not known just when Joseph Sloss (Schloss) arrived in Syracuse, but he, too, was active in organizing the first congregation in 1841, and was elected treasurer. Joseph came from Bavaria, his wife, Nanette, from Prague. Schloss is one of the few pioneer families whose descendants remained in Syracuse and have been active in the Society of Concord to this day.[13]

THE GARSONS. Even before the first *minyan* arrived in 1839, the Garson family had settled in Syracuse. Jacob Garson owned a meat market and provisions store at 78 Towpath, catering to the canalers, while Henry Garson operated a tavern on Mulberry Street. It was in an upstairs room of Jacob's house, also on Mulberry Steet, that the Society of Concord was formally organized in 1841.

When Rabbi Isaac Mayer Wise visited Syracuse in 1846 for the purpose of dedicating the first house of worship, he lodged at Henry Garson's tavern, as he relates in his memoirs. On September 5, 1854, the *Standard* reported that Garson's Tavern was the scene of a robbery in which a peddler named Grosse lost $4,000 worth of jewelry. Although a reward of $500 was offered by Grosse, it is not known whether the thief was apprehended.[14]

At least two other Garsons lived in Syracuse, Isaac and Moses (sometimes referred to as Morris). In 1849 Isaac gave important testimony in the Nathan Adler murder trial. Records of 1851 and 1854 show that Isaac served as a trustee of the Temple of Concord and as president of the Mutual Aid Society. Both Isaac and Morris are listed in the 1855 city directory as being in the clothing business at 2 Franklin Block. The Garson name appears frequently in the early history of the Jewish community in Syracuse.

THE BONDYS. Gabriel Bondy and his first wife arrived in Syracuse from Prague, Bohemia, in the early 1840's. They were then in their twenties.

In the city directory of 1851, Bondy is listed as a peddler.[15] Jacob Marshall and David Stolz, when they first came to Syracuse in about 1852, boarded with the Bondys on East Jefferson Street. In later directories, Gabriel is recorded as a tailor and dealer in secondhand clothing at 79 Grape Street.

Bondy's wife passed away early in life, and he was left a widower with three children. Later he married Miriam Kohn, and they had two children, Yetta and Joseph.

In those days, Bondy was considered an educated man. He was an ardent reader and well versed in Hebrew. In 1854 he was a leader in the formation of the second Jewish synagogue in Syracuse, the Beth Israel Shul. For a number of years he acted as the *hazzan* (reader), and led the congregation in prayers.

Bondy outlived his second wife, Miriam, and on his retirement lived with his daughter, Yetta Bondy Bernstein in Ithaca, New York. He died in 1903 and is buried in the Old Beth Israel cemetery on Colvin Street.[16]

THE WISEMAN FAMILY. In the early records the name appears as "Weissmann," as it was spelled in Germany. Later we find that one "n" and one "s" were dropped, and the name was recorded as "Weisman." Still later it was changed to a more anglicized form of spelling—"Wiseman."

Joseph Wiseman and his wife Sarah, came to Syracuse in 1840 [17] and, although Sarah was then only twenty-two years old, they brought with them two infant children, Gates and Bertha. There is a good possibility that Joseph did not arrive penniless, for nowhere is it indicated that it was necessary for him to go out peddling. He immediately went into the dry goods business. He had a strong religious feeling, and he soon assisted in the establishment of the first Jewish house of worship in Syracuse. When the Society of Concord was incorporated in 1842, Joseph Wiseman was made a trustee.[18] In 1864 he was one of the leaders who broke away from the Temple of Concord, and he became vice-president of Adath Jeshurun.

Joseph and Sarah settled down, bought a house at 27 Cedar Street, and lived there until the end of their days. Sarah passed away on August 7, 1877, at the age of sixty-two, and Joseph died three years later in 1880.[19] His son, Gates, who remained with the Temple of Concord, became one of its foremost leaders.

MEYER AND MARY WEISMAN. Meyer, Joseph's brother, who spelled his name "Weisman," came to Syracuse in 1843. Meyer and Mary, who had lived in New York City for three years, brought with them a family of five children. Four more were born in Syracuse. The 1857 city directory listed Meyer Weisman as owning a clothing store at 101 North Salina Street, and the 1874 directory listed him as operating a jewelry store at 10 East Washington Street and living at 32 Mulberry Street. Mary, whose maiden name was Doppelmayer, made it her first order of business to bring over more Doppelmayers. Three sisters came to Syracuse: Babette, who married David Oberdorfer; Yetta, who married a Silberberg and moved to Niagara Falls; and Sophia, who married Isaac Wolf. A brother, Daniel Doppelmayer, came to Syracuse but did not stay long. He and Isaac Wolf left for Texas in the late 1850's, and started a settlement of former Syracusans in Marshall, Texas. Their relatives—the Weismans, the Wolfs, and the Exsteins—followed them during and soon after the Civil War. They grew with the state and all prospered. Now their descendants are spread throughout Texas.

Meyer Weisman died on July 15, 1887. Mary, his wife, became the matriarch of the Weisman, Exstein, and Wolf families. She was called "Aunt Mary" by most of the Jewish population in Syracuse. She lived in Syracuse until 1910 and then moved with the family of her daughter, Yetta Exstein, to New York City. So strong was her sense of responsibility for her family that, when she learned in 1912 that her last sister, Yetta Silberberg, had died, she was heard to remark that now her work in this world was done. She died three weeks later at the age of ninety.[20]

THE OBERDORFERS. David Oberdorfer arrived in New York City in the early 1840's from Bavaria, but the exact date is unknown. Learning of a fellow townsman who was living in Syracuse, he sent word to him that he was in America. His friend advised him to come to Syracuse, and he arrived by packet boat on the Erie Canal.

His friend took him to the peddler supply store. There he was fitted out with a pack and a stock of merchandise and was advised to go to Red Creek, New York, about one hundred miles north, because the immediate territory around Syracuse was already sufficiently covered by other peddlers.

Red Creek proved to be all right for a starter, since a peddler had to operate on foot and carry his store on his back, but Oberdorfer soon saved enough money to purchase a horse and wagon and was ready to conquer new worlds. Besides, there was no Jewish community in Red Creek, and he did not feel at home there. He moved back to Syracuse about 1845, married Babette Doppelmayer, one of Mary Weisman's sisters, and rented a home on North Salina Street. Their son, Moses, was born in that home on May 30, 1850.

While David Oberdorfer was busy peddling he had a desire to open a peddler supply store, but there was no room in Syracuse for another such business. Rome, New York, forty-one miles east of Syracuse, was enjoying a boom because of its iron rolling mill, and he decided to go there. He opened a store in Rome and did well until the Panic of 1857, when the mill failed and many people were out of work. He did not have the patience to wait for recovery, nor did he know that within a few years the mill was to take on the rolling of a new metal, copper, and that Rome was to enjoy a real boom and become known the country over as the "Copper City."

Meantime, Seneca Falls, New York, forty-seven miles west of Syracuse, was prospering through the industry of the Gould family. The Goulds had built an immense pump manufacturing business, which today continues as the Gould Manufacturing Company. So to Seneca Falls journeyed Oberdorfer with his wife, two sons—Moses and Joseph, the latter born in Rome—and all their possessions packed in a horse-drawn wagon.

The Seneca Falls general store proved a good venture—in fact, too good. The town was busy; it was the time of the Civil War, and prices and profits spiraled. Money was scarce, but what of it! The factories were paying in scrip, and everyone was accepting it at face value. Soon, however, the pump factories (there were several of them) closed because they could not obtain cash for their goods. Some failed and left the holders of their scrip with so much waste paper. Oberdorfer was one of those so caught, and one who became bankrupt. Not only had he a wife and two sons to care for, but also two brothers. Like many others at the time, he had sent for his brothers, bringing them over from the "Old Country," that they might not only enjoy the prosperity of America, but also avoid compulsory military service in Europe.

Back to Syracuse in the same old wagon went David Oberdorfer, his wife, two sons, two brothers, and all their worldly goods. They settled down in the old Seventh Ward, near the corner of Harrison and Grape Streets.

The country was now in the midst of the Civil War, and the two Oberdorfer brothers, who had fled Europe to avoid military service, enlisted in the Union Army, marched off to the South, and did not come back to Syracuse.[21]

MORRIS THALHEIMER. In 1845 from Württemberg, Germany, to Syracuse came Morris Thalheimer, brother of Max. As a young man full of energy and determination, he wasted no time and started right out peddling with a pack on his back. Morris was industrious and frugal; it did not take long to save enough so that he could fulfill his ambition and establish himself in business.

In partnership with Joseph Wiseman, he opened a dry goods and peddler supply store on Cedar Street. They were busy, mostly fitting out new immigrants with packs of dry goods and notions and sending them on their way to peddle. Sunday was the busiest day of all, for that was when the peddlers, who came in from the country to rest and worship on the Sabbath, would stop to replenish their stock of dry goods. Partnerships do not always run smoothly: there were disagreements and unpleasantness between the partners. After being in business together for a number of years, the Thalheimers and the Wisemans separated, and for a long time the two families did not mix socially.

Morris Thalheimer took his share of the business in cash and opened a grocery store in the Barton Block, later known as the Grand Theater Building, on East Genesee Street. Operating a grocery store was not easy: it meant hard work and long hours, and the whole family pitched in. Gates, the eldest of five children, often told how he used to deliver orders of groceries in a wheelbarrow to his father's customers. The business grew and prospered, until Thalheimer's grocery store was the finest and largest of its kind in Syracuse.

His family was growing up, and Papa Thalheimer was able to take it easier. He spent much time in the synagogue. Learned in Hebrew, he was able and well pleased when he had the opportunity to lead the congregation at regular prayer services.

He retired from active business five years before he passed away on October 12, 1890. At the time of his death he enjoyed the respect of the entire community. He was a congenial and friendly person and had many fine qualities. He was vice-president of Adath Jeshurun Synagogue, and treasurer of Cynosure Encampment, Independent Order of Odd Fellows. He was survived by his wife and five children: Gates, Max, Abraham, Mannie, and Carrie.[22]

JACOB MARSHALL. The patriarch of the Marshall family, after a rough crossing of the Atlantic in a sailing vessel from Germany, arrived in New York on September 1, 1849, at the age of nineteen. With only five francs (amounting to ninety-five cents in American money) in his pocket, it was necessary that he find work at once. He was young, strong, and did not mind manual labor. Like the Irish and German immigrants, he secured a job with a construction gang on the Erie Railroad, and later with the Central Railroad, working his way up to the Mohawk Valley. It was hard work, but he had a goal in mind. It was not for him to be a day laborer long. He was saving what little money he earned and wanted to settle in a community where he could live among other Jews.

Unfortunately, while he was working on the railroad he contracted typhoid fever. While he was lying ill, someone stole what little money he had saved. He recovered and started all over again. This time he was sent to Canandaigua, and worked his way south on the Northern New York Railroad. The construction gangs were made up of a mixed group of immigrants; the foremen were tough, and the contractors not too reliable. He suffered another setback at the end of the season when the contractor disappeared without paying any of his employees.

Jacob then went to work on the Erie Canal, and later secured a job as a porter in a warehouse in Cuylerville, Livingston County, owned by Hamilton Odell. Subsequently, he arrived in the thriving community of Syracuse, which by then had a population of about 18,000 and a considerable settlement of Germans, including a small group of German Jews. Jacob saw the possibility of many opportunities in this community. He began as a pack-peddler, did not do too well, and opened a fruit stand in the Granger Block. He was now twenty-six, and boarded with Mrs. Bondy on East Jefferson Street.

In 1853, two sisters, Zilli and Regina Straus, came to Syracuse from Württemberg, Germany. Not being able to speak a word of English, they took jobs as domestics with some of the leading German families. They were healthy, intelligent, and good-looking girls. The young Jewish men of Syracuse began taking notice—and perhaps our amateur matchmakers took a hand, as it was considered a good deed to bring a marriageable young man and a Jewish girl together. And so a marriage was arranged, and Zilli Straus and Jacob Marshall were married on September 1, 1855.

Now that he was married, Jacob looked around for some enterprise that would bring him a steady income. Someone told him that there was a good market for furs and hides. He secured a horse and wagon, called on the farmers in the surrounding country to buy the hides and skins, and from the trappers in swamp lands he bought pelts and furs. He did not get rich, but it was a living with prospects for improvement. After a while his business grew better, and he decided to rent a store at 22 James Street, in order to cut down the necessity of so much traveling. The farmers and trappers would bring the hides and furs with them when they came to the city.

The Marshalls' first house was on Mulberry Street, next to the Temple of Concord. They occupied the top floor, where Louis and two other children were born. Later, when the business was well established, they bought a house at 22 Cedar Street. This was the Marshall home for the rest of Zilli's and Jacob's lives. After they passed away, their oldest son, Louis, presented the house to the Jewish community to be used as a social center.[23]

THE LIGHTS. Abram Light was not just another penniless immigrant when he arrived from Semnitz, Hungary, in 1849. He brought with him his wife, Mindell, and several children, of whom the oldest, Solomon, was then thirteen years of age. Before Abram migrated, so it was told, he was in some manner connected with the Hungarian government, and it was said that Emperor Franz Joseph paid for his passage to this country. Light would have had more of the Old World's money when he arrived here if it were not for a slippery gentleman who made his acquaintance aboard ship. This person had been in America before, and he told Light there were great opportunities to make a lot of money in America if one knew the right people and made proper investments. Light entrusted him with a considerable part of his wealth. When they left the ship it was the last Abram saw of that very smooth gentleman.

Abram Light was well versed in Hebrew, took an active part in organizing Temple Adath Jeshurun, and often led the congregation in prayer services. He was engaged in the tobacco and cigar manufacturing business for many years. Most significantly, Abram and Mindell Light had eight children, three sons and five daughters. Two sons, Solomon and Lewis, enlisted in the Civil War in a company of young Jewish men who joined as a body in the 149th Regiment. Solomon was discharged because of illness. The third son, Samuel, later moved to Shreveport, Louisiana. His daughter, Betty, married Lyons Weisberg; Rebecca married Moses Weisman and went to Marshall, Texas. Sarah married Moses Oberdorfer; Lena married Jacob Brown and moved to Chicago; and Esther married James Shimberg, one of the brothers who successfully introduced trading stamps in England. She and her husband later moved to Paris and London.

Abram Light retired from business at a fairly early age. He was an avid reader—it was said that he read three papers every day, each in a different language. He lived to be ninety-three, and died on March 19, 1905.[24]

THE BRONNER FAMILY. Israel Bronner reached Syracuse in 1841. It is noteworthy that he was fifty-two years of age (considered to be past middle age in those days) when he arrived. He brought with him a wife and a grown-up family of four sons and two daughters. This was rather unusual, since most immigrants came early in life and single. Those who did come with a wife were usually recently married, with either very young children or none at all.

It was undoubtedly due to the Bronner children having had part or all of their education in Europe that they were proficient in Hebrew and classical subjects and were able to start immediately to make a mark for themselves in their new environment.

The Bronner sons and daughters soon married into the families of the other early Jewish settlers—the Marshalls, the Lights, the Oberdorfers—and so their roots remained in Syracuse.

The father, Israel, was a man of stature and well educated. He soon established himself in business with a dry goods store at 9 Franklin Street. He had been in this country only fourteen years when he passed away at the age of sixty-six. In this short time he made a name for himself. He was one of the founders of the Temple of Concord, and participated in many secular activities of the Syracuse community. The *Syracuse Standard* of November 13, 1855, printed the following tribute to him:

DEATH OF MR. ISRAEL BRONNER

Mr. Bronner, of whom we gave a brief notice yesterday, has been a resident of this city about fourteen years. He was born in Germany, was a man beloved in the land of his birth, received a good education and early training in his business, which with perseverance and industry made him well off as to the things of this world. Leaving his home, he settled in Syracuse and while among us had always attended to his own business, led an exemplary life, treated every man well, and made all his acquaintances love him. He was a good merchant, a loving husband, and a kind, indulgent father, and an excellent citizen. He died on Friday evening last, after an illness of about one hour, aged 66 years.

He was buried on the following Sunday and followed to his last resting place by a long procession of mourners—among whom we noticed many of the Christian faith mingling their tears and sympathy with their Jewish brethern.

As death is a great leveler of Kings, Empires and Nations, and as we all one day will return to dust—Gentile as well as Jew—we hope to see ere long, those uncharitable emotions that are too apt to rankle in the bosom of Christians removed.

Learn to love and respect a man for what he is, not for what he is worth, esteem him for his goodness, kindness and benevolence no matter what place on earth may so fortunate be as to give him birth.

It is of particular significance to note that, at this early stage in the history of the Jewish community in Syracuse, the death of a Jewish man is recorded in the press with such kindly feeling towards the deceased and a gentle plea for forbearance between Gentile and Jew.

The Bronners continued as one of the prominent Jewish families in Syracuse. Israel's sons operated the dry goods business of Bronner & Kraft. Isaac Henry, the oldest, was elected president of the Temple of Concord in 1848. He was an ardent advocate of Reform Judaism. In April of 1854, Isaac Bronner stood up in the pulpit and spoke to his fellow congregants as follows:

This Society, though small in numbers, but rapidly growing under the bright sun of progress, feels that steps must now be taken to create and inaugurate a new age of a prophetic Judaism. We must put into practice the advanced views of our times. There is no other way to vitalize Judaism, if we desire to promote the high ideal of monotheism and our spiritual and social life. Thirty-five hundred years ago our prophets visioned what we now call "Reform Judiasm." [25]

It was not until 1861, when Reform was fully accepted at the Temple of Concord, that the Orthodox-minded members, including Isaac's brother, Moses, walked out of the temple to form their own synagogue.

Isaac Henry Bronner was also a financier. In January of 1855 he was elected a director of the newly formed Albany Savings Bank. The following appeared in the *Syracuse Standard* of January 31, 1855:

OVERSIGHT—Our Albany correspondent, a day or two since, sent us the list of Directors of the new Savings Bank, to be established in this city, in which the name of Isaac H. Bronner was inadvertently omitted. The omission was entirely unintentional but we are informed some persons insinuate that it was intended as an insult to Mr. Bronner. Nothing can be farther from the truth.

On January 24, 1857, he was elected as second vice-president of the Onondaga County Savings Bank, which had been chartered two years previously. Isaac Bronner continued his interest in Jewish and civic affairs in Syracuse until 1873, when his health became impaired and he decided to go to Europe to seek rest and to recuperate. The following notice appeared in the *Syracuse Journal* of July 7, 1873:

AUCTION SALE OF HOUSEHOLD FURNITURE

Wednesday, July 9th at 9 A.M., at 23½ S. Clinton Street. Mr. I. H. Bronner, having resolved to remove with his family to Europe, has but four days to dispose of his entire household goods as above, consisting of a rosewood parlor set in satin damask, black walnut sitting room set in hair cloth, large size French plate gilt frame mirror, and several other mirrors, extension table, black walnut bedroom sets, Brussel and ingrain carpets, feather beds, hair matresses, pillows and bedding, Grover and Baker sewing machine, large size cook stove with copper boiler, crockery, glass, parlor stoves, and a general assortment of kitchen utensils. Sales positive. Terms cash.

B. A. Isaac, Auctioneer

The *Journal* of July 16, 1873, told of his departure:

Mr. I. H. Bronner, of the firm of Bronner Bros., left for New York yesterday, where he will sail on Thursday for Europe, in the steamer Silesia. Mr. Bronner will be absent five or six years, and goes for the benefit of his health, which has become much impaired from arduous labors. He is accompanied by Mr. Israel Bronner, of Louisville.

It is not known when or if Mr. Bronner returned from Europe to America.

Moses Bronner, brother of Isaac, and his family moved to Rochester in 1868 and established a dry goods business at 79 Main Street in that city. He had been in business in Rochester for only four years when he suddenly passed away on February 28, 1872, at the age of forty-one. He left a wife and six children.[26]

When another brother, Seckel, reached the age of seventy-six, the local newspaper took note of the occasion:

Mr. Seckel Bronner, who is a native of Wuertemberg, is still hale and active at the age of seventy-six years. He is a good Hebrew scholar, an omnivorous reader of books and a good public speaker. Fifty years ago he married Miss Julia Friedman, of New York, and there are four sons issue. He is president of the Bnai B'rith Lodge. Socially Mr. Bronner has always been very prominent.

His son, Mr. Henry Bronner, who is a trustee of the Society of Concord, was born in New York City in 1859. In 1890 he married Miss Clara Marshall, third daughter of Mr. and Mrs. Jacob Marshall. There are three children issue—two boys and one girl.

Mrs. Clara Marshall-Bronner, who is a sister of Mr. Louis Marshall, occupies the position of president of the Ladies Auxiliary, Society of Concord, which society is indebted to this charitable lady for its success and present flourishing condition.[27]

Benjamin, one of the original four brothers, who was called Bernhard at times, put a notice in the *Syracuse Journal* of October 16, 1863, stating that

His name was announced as a delegate to the Democratic Convention and that he did not want to be a delegate and his name was used without his consent.

Samuel Bronner was among the first to enlist in Company A of the 149th Regiment, composed of Jewish men from Syracuse. He was made a lieutenant on September 17, 1862. The *Syracuse Journal* of September 17, 1862, reported:

His friends presented him with a splendid sword and accoutrements. Mr. August Falker made the presentation speech and Lieut. Bronner replied happily.

Emanuel Bronner, son of Seckel Bronner, married Rena Oberdorfer. For a number of years he conducted a business in Auburn, New York. After he retired he returned to Syracuse and was active in the Temple of Concord. For many years he headed the Sunday school committee. His daughter, Marjorie Bronner Pierson, is a great-granddaughter of Israel Bronner, who arrived in Syracuse in 1841. She continues the family tradition of being active in the Temple of Concord.

MARCUS CONE. We do not know when this enterprising young man arrived in Syracuse. His name appears in the first Syracuse directory, published in 1851, as the owner of a dry goods store located at the corner of Genesee and Warren Streets.[28]

Marcus Cone was a bachelor and a man of substance. He undoubtedly was one of the earliest Jewish settlers. When the Merchants Bank was established in 1851, he made a cash deposit of $4,200 in a special account, and $420 in a regular account. This was the largest cash deposit made, and he was elected a director of the bank.[29]

In 1851, when the congregation of the Temple of Concord was about to move into its new edifice on the corner of State and Harrison Streets, Marcus Cone was elected treasurer of the congregation and was appointed to head the procession from the old temple to the new on the day of the dedication ceremonies.[30]

In 1852 an advertisement in the local papers stated that Marcus

Cone had formed a partnership with Charles Adler, and henceforth the name of his business would be known as Cone and Adler.[31] Three years later, he sold his share of the business to Anson P. Thayer, and the firm became known as Adler and Thayer.

Marcus Cone left shortly thereafter for a visit to Germany. While he was in his native town of Alberweder, he suddenly became seriously ill and passed away on November 17, 1856, at the age of thirty-four.[32] It was a terrible shock to his many friends and business associates in Syracuse.

When his will was probated, it was found that he did not forget the city where he had made his success. It stated that "I bequeath the sum of $2,000 for the purpose of establishing a society in the City of Syracuse, to be called 'Cone's German-Hebrew Benevolent Society' and that the proceeds of the funds shall be distributed among the indigent German Hebrews of Syracuse." [33]

In accordance with the will, this society was formed and recorded as such in Onondaga County on March 25, 1857. The trustees were Martin A. Mark, Jacob Leve, Joseph Weisman, Edward Manheimer, Jacob Stone, Moses Bronner, and Sigmund Manheimer.[34]

JACOB STONE. The name of Jacob Stone first appears in the annals of Syracuse on the occasion of the dedication of the Temple of Concord in 1846. Rabbi Isaac Mayer Wise recalled that Jacob Stone had introduced him to the people of the congregation, and Wise was impressed by his wit, intelligence, and understanding of human nature. The visiting rabbi greatly appreciated Stone's judicious evaluation of the local Jewish community.

The exact year of Stone's arrival in Syracuse is not known. However, early city directories reveal that in 1851 he was a partner with M. and J. Jacobs at 21 North Salina Street, and in 1857 he appears as a member of the firm of Stone and Manheimer, dealing in millinery and dry goods in the Bastable Block. His home was at 6 Mulberry Street.[35]

Jacob Stone's outstanding achievement in Jewish communal affairs was that he was president of the Society of Concord when the new temple on the corner of Harrison and Mulberry Streets was being built. The description of the building and the part Jacob Stone took therein are well covered by Isaac Leeser's report of the dedication ceremony of that building.[36] Stone resigned as president of the congregation soon after the dedication. When the Civil War started he helped to organize a Jewish company. During the recruiting activity he offered $200 to the first man who would volunteer.

He left Syracuse for New York after a great tragedy in his life, the death of his son, a talented young man of twenty-six who was regarded as a rising leader in business and social affairs and was beloved in the community.

The *Syracuse Journal* of February 11, 1893, carried this notice of Jacob Stone's death: "Jacob Stone died in New York on Sunday, February 9, 1893, aged 63 years. The funeral on Tuesday from his residence 153 W. 49th Street."

LEWIS B. NEWCITY. Louis Naistadt and his wife reached Syracuse in the eighteen-fifties. It can be said that he had several "firsts" to his credit. It appears that he was the first Jewish immigrant to come here from the city of Neustadt in Russian Poland. He very promptly anglicized his name to "Newcity." He was the first resident *hazzan* in Syracuse, and at different times served in all the local congregations, remaining longest at the Rosenbloom Shul. He was the first grocer in Syracuse who catered chiefly to the Jewish trade,[37] and his business was generally known as "The Jewish grocery store." The Newcitys raised a large family and were well regarded in the community, as is evident by the celebration of the Newcity's golden wedding anniversary, which was an outstanding social event in the Jewish community. The *Syracuse Standard* of April 8, 1895, gave the following report:

JEWISH CELEBRATIONS—GOLDEN WEDDING—
NEWCITY, LEWIS B.

THEIR GOLDEN WEDDING—

A large number of friends gathered together, yesterday at the home of Mr. and Mrs. Lewis B. Newcity at No. 1245 Mulberry Street, to congratulate them on the fiftieth anniversary of their wedding. Mr. and Mrs. Newcity are at the head of one of the oldest Jewish families here; having made this city their home over 40 years ago. They received many valuable presents from friends, and relatives all over the country, Rev. Adolph Guttman, D.D., of the Reformed Jewish Congregation made some very timely and appropriate remarks, and also said it was the first time that he ever had the pleasure of officiating at a golden wedding. The refreshments were served and it was a joyous occasion. . . .

THE HENOCHSBURGS. The first record of any Henochsburg in Syracuse is 1846. Rabbi Isaac Mayer Wise, in his memoirs, wrote that Aaron Henochsburg was on the welcoming committee when he arrived in Syracuse to dedicate the first Temple of Concord in 1846. Aaron's name is again noted as a member of the building committee when the next temple was built in 1851.[38] The Henochsburgs came here from Columbus, Ohio, the first known instance of a Jew coming to Syracuse from the west instead of the east. He arrived with a family. His son, Joseph, was six years old at the time. Aaron established a wholesale millinery business, and the 1874–75 directory lists Carrie, Frances, Joseph, Moses, Seymour, and William Henochburg as clerks, all but two being employed in the millinery establishment.

The Henochsburg family played a leading role in business and social circles in Syracuse. William served as president of the Temple of Concord in the 1890's. Over the years, however, the old generation died off and a number of the second generation moved away from the city, as did Moses Henochsburg, who went with Jacob Wiseman to Marshall, Texas, in 1879. Two brothers, both bachelors, Joseph and Seymour, continued the millinery business at 33 South Salina until 1917, when they sold the business and retired.

Ten years later, on January 1, 1927, friends of the Henochsburg brothers were greatly shocked to learn that Joseph had committed suicide the previous evening at his home on Forman Avenue. The *Syracuse Post Standard* carried a full account of the suicide, together with a fine tribute.[39] Among other things, it recalled that the deceased was noted for his many informal philanthropies which endeared him to all who knew him. His former employees in particular felt the blessing of his kindly spirit. It was said that "no one who ever worked for him was allowed to pay a medical bill if Mr. Henochsburg learned of their illness."

In earlier years Joseph was active in Masonic circles. He was at one time master of Salt Springs Lodge. Pallbearers were Isaac Rosenbloom, Benjamin Stolz, Sigmund Frensdorf, Isaac Myers, Aaron Marshall, and Max Thalheimer, all leaders in the Jewish community and sons of pioneer families.

THE BLOOMS. Joseph and Leah Bloom came to Syracuse in 1849, directly from Lodz, Poland. They brought with them their eight-year-old son. It was this little boy, Moses, who left a mark in the Jewish community.

The Bloom family was one of the early arrivals from Eastern Europe. They soon joined others who came from the same section and who had formed a *minyan* of their own called Beth Israel. Later, Joseph Bloom took an active part in organizing the New Beth Israel congregation (Grape Street Shul) in 1854, which has remained Orthodox over these many years. Moses followed his father's interest in Beth Israel and in 1871, at the age of thirty and single, was elected president. Soon thereafter he had the distinction of being married in the same synagogue of which he was the president. He had a reputation for being mild-mannered and conciliatory. He was re-elected time after time and remained president for a period of twenty-five years. At the end of his administration he was presented with a silver Kiddush cup engraved with his name and "For Honorable Service Rendered."

In business, Moses Bloom started as a clerk for the A. S. Yates Clothing Company. In 1861 he formed a partnership with Joseph Grossman in the clothing business. They were together for ten years. He then opened a store of his own on North Salina Street, a few doors from the Empire Hotel, which stood on the corner of West Genesee Street.

The Beth Israel congregation was not the only interest of Moses Bloom. He found time for other worthwhile Jewish and civic causes. He was active in fraternal organizations as a member of the Free Sons of Israel and the Sons of Benjamin. He was honored at the end of fifty years of continuous membership in the Salt Springs Masonic Lodge with the presentation of a silver trowel to mark the occasion. Moses also belonged to the Standard Club.

Mr. and Mrs. Bloom had two sons and four daughters. Stella Bloom Goldwater, the youngest of the daughters, still resides in Syracuse with her daughter, Mrs. David Brodsky. She recalls with nostalgia the Beaux Arts balls and dances of the old Fortnightly Club at Freeman's Hall, at one of which she met her husband-to-be.

Moses Bloom passed away on December 9, 1916, and was buried in Mount Sinai Cemetery.[40]

SOLOMON SHIMBERG came in the 1840's, among the earliest of many arrivals from Neustadt. He, like many others, started out as a pack peddler. He evidently worked hard and saved his money, for soon he opened a clothing store at 9 North Salina Street, but he is best remembered as part-owner of the peddlers supply store known as Shimberg and Silverman, located on Grape Street. For many years that store was an institution in the Jewish neighborhood. Solomon Shimberg was one of the founders, and for a number of years the president, of the Beth Israel synagogue, but in 1872 he joined his other townsmen from Neustadt to form the New Adath Yeshurun, which for many years was known as the Neustadter Shul. Solomon Shimberg died in 1902 at the age of seventy-one, and is buried in the Beth Israel cemetery.

MOSES L. LEITER and his wife, Bertha, came from Wurtemberg, Germany, in 1852, with four sons and four daughters. In due time, the girls married and moved away. Their brother, Henry, went to live in Rochester. Lazarus, Herman, and Louis remained with their parents. The boys were only eight, nine, and ten years old when they arrived, but they grew up fast, and all left a mark in the business and social life of Syracuse.

Louis was the first to make a success in business. He started out as an apprentice watchmaker, and soon opened a jewelry store of his own in the Wieting block. A business neighbor in the same block was Firman and Co., dealers in pianos and other musical instruments. When that company decided to dissolve, Louis Leiter and his brothers decided to buy them out. The following notices appeared in the *Syracuse Journal* on January 17, 1873:

Dissolution Syracuse, N.Y. Jan. 1, 1873

The firm of Firman and Co., No. 2 Wieting Opera House, Syracuse, N.Y. has this day dissolved by mutual consent. R. G. Firman is retiring from the late firm. All debts and accounts due will be paid to Leiter Brothers, who are our successors.

Signed Firman and Co.

Notice

The business of selling pianos, organs, sheet music and other miscellaneous goods will be continued at the old stand No. 2 Wieting Opera

House, under the firm name of Leiter Brothers, where at all times may be found the most complete assortment of goods in Central New York, to which the attention of buyers is most respectfully solicited.

Leiter Brothers

Thus Louis Leiter went from jewelry into the piano business, taking his brothers Herman and Lazarus with him. Leiter Brothers developed the piano and musical instrument business until they were leaders in that field in Central New York for a period of over fifty years.

Moses Leiter died in 1884. The first of the Leiter sons to pass away was Herman, in 1904. He left $42,000 to Syracuse charities; $16,500 went to the Temple of Concord for the express purpose of building a new temple. This money was the nucleus and the stimulant that resulted in the erection of the temple which is still standing at the corner of Madison and University Avenue.

It was said of the youngest brother, Lazarus, that he was one of the most amiable and cultured men in Syracuse.

Louis Leiter passed away at the ripe age of eighty-six. For most of his life he was active in the business and social life of Syracuse.

CHARLES ROSENTHAL, 1843–1926, was the first Jewish male child born in Syracuse. Little is now known of his parents. It is claimed that his father arrived in Syracuse at the age of fourteen via the Erie Canal. If that was so, he would be among the earliest Jewish settlers, having arrived about 1825 or 1826. His given name, where he came from, and whom he married are not recorded or remembered by his descendants.

Charles had two brothers, Milo and Isaac. Milo is named on the list with other young Jewish men who enlisted in Company A of the 149th (Fourth Onondaga) Regiment. Charles, while not on the list, also enlisted in the Civil War. When he returned, he claimed exemption from paying dues at the Temple of Concord, stating that the trustees of the Temple promised all those who enlisted would not have to pay dues for the rest of their lives.

Throughout his life, he was active in local fraternal organizations. He was one of the founders of Lessing Lodge I. O. O. F., a member of the Free Sons of Israel, B'nai B'rith, and others.

Charles was in the wholesale tobacco business, located on the corner of South Franklin and East Fayette Streets.

He and his wife, Mary, had three sons: Meyer, who married Mary

Port, and was for many years in the wholesale toy business; Abraham, of New York; and Samuel, who moved to Cleveland, Ohio.

DRY GOODS AND NOTIONS PEDDLERS

In the early days, the Jewish immigrants usually turned to peddling. Their choice of occupations was limited; very few had any skills needed in this country. As we have stated previously, the first immigrants were attracted to Syracuse because the Bernheimers, who had a peddler supply store in the village, would trust them for their first pack of dry goods, direct them where to go, and instruct them in their first few words of English.

Peddling in the country was not a job for a weakling. There were many difficulties and pitfalls to overcome, and many peddlers did not long endure. It must have been with much timidity and fear that they started out on their first trip.

Syracuse in the 1850's was the hub of a number of short railway lines that extended southward to Binghamton, northward to Oswego and Watertown, west to Auburn, and east to Utica. The trains would stop wherever there was a cluster of a few houses. Thus, on Monday morning the peddler would leave Syracuse with a pack of dry goods on his back and a basket of notions on his arm and get off at the first train stop. After he canvassed the few houses, he would start walking toward the next village, hoping to find some farmhouses on the way. The farther the houses were from the towns, the more likely he would find good customers.

For those who were strict about observing the dietary laws it was doubly hard. They would take along some bread and hard-boiled eggs, which had to last them until Friday when they took the train back home.

Many of the villagers and farmers were friendly and would welcome the peddler, buy something if they needed it, and perhaps even buy something out of compassion. Others were sometimes hard on the peddler; many of them had never seen a Jew before, and some would slam the door in his face. Often he had to sleep in barns or under haystacks, taking a chance on being molested or robbed. Such was the case with Nathan Adler.[41]

Nathan, a peddler and a familiar figure in southern Cayuga

County, was a brother of Charles Adler, a partner in Cone and Adler Dry Goods Store. An early account describes Nathan as "a slightly built agreeable young man in his early twenties. The country girls referred to him as the 'handsome peddler.'"

On the night of November 6, 1849, Nathan Adler stopped at the Baham's farm, just outside the village of Venice, Cayuga County, hoping to find a night's lodging. The Baham family in November of 1849 consisted of John Baham, Sr., his wife, and six children. The elder three boys were Albert, twenty-four, Alfred, twenty-two, and John Jr., about twenty. On that day Mrs. Baham had been injured by a collapsing corn crib, and the home was in confusion.

When Nathan arrived, Albert Baham suggested that he could sleep in the barn, and provided some buffalo skins to serve as bedding and covers. Nathan took his peddler's pack and a small trunk that he carried with him and went into the barn. That was the last time anyone saw Nathan Adler alive.

Charles Adler in Syracuse waited for his brother's return and, when he did not show up after two weeks, he went out looking for him. He knew the general direction where his brother peddled and traced him all the way from Syracuse until he came to the Baham farm, where he learned that Nathan had been there on November sixth. He could trace him no further and went back to Syracuse to seek aid and counsel.

The Jewish community of Syracuse was not very large in 1849, but its members were greatly distressed over the missing Nathan and feared that foul play had befallen him. Several of the merchants dropped everything else and went back with Charles Adler to Venice. They were diligent and skillful investigators, and they never rested until Nathan's body was found. The Syracuse Jews were also excellent witnesses at the inquest. One of them, Isaac Garson, a grocer of Syracuse, was with the posse that found the body. "How do you identify the body?" he was asked at the inquest. "I identify the deceased by his clothes, by his teeth, by the badge of his religion, he being a Jew. . . ."

Suspicion immediately rested upon the Baham brothers. It is likely that the crime was premeditated, since Nathan had been commissioned by Charles Adler to collect a note owed by Albert Baham. This note was never found. Further, after November sixth, the three boys had been extremely generous in giving rings and handkerchiefs to the neighborhood girls. Some of these gifts, as well as other articles found in the Baham house, were recognized as being from Nathan's pack. Also, a girl of the neighborhood testified that at about the same time Albert had been in possession of some eighty-five to ninety dollars.

The theory gradually emerged that Nathan Adler had been killed that night after the boys went out to the barn to sleep, and that the body was hastily buried in a shallow grave in the big Venice woods, about a mile from the Baham farm. The three Baham brothers were indicted and held for the grand jury on the charge of the murder of Nathan Adler.

After a number of adjournments, the trial was held on November 19, 1850, at which time Thomas A. Johnson, Justice of the Supreme Court, presided. Albert Baham did not testify in his own behalf. On December 5, 1850, he was convicted of murder and sentenced to be hanged on January 24, 1851.

John Baham, Jr. was tried before the same court on January 7, 1851, and he also did not testify on his own behalf. He was sentenced to be hanged on March 14, 1854. The third brother pleaded guilty to manslaughter, second degree, and was sentenced to five years and three months in Auburn prison.

Other authentic tales relate how peddlers were taken advantage of, molested, or ridiculed. Nevertheless, peddling was a way of getting started in a new land, and over the years immigrant Jews continued to peddle. Gradually the method of peddling changed. As soon as a peddler saved up enough money, he would take off his pack and buy a horse and wagon so that he would be able to cover more ground and carry a larger variety of merchandise. Some opened small dry goods stores in various towns that they had covered as peddlers. In time, practically every village and town surrounding Syracuse had a Jewish merchant. Other peddlers started to specialize in one kind of merchandise or other, such as jewelry, piece goods, spectacles, and the like. Teenage boys often peddled with such items as stationery and matches.

W. Lee Provol, a one-time Syracusan, in his autobiography, *The Pack Peddler,* written in 1937, tells how, as a small boy in Syracuse, he turned to peddling matches in order to augment the family income, and found that even this humble occupation was fraught with difficulties. Willie Provolsky (as he was then known) was peddling his matches in Jamesville, a small town just outside Syracuse, when he was arrested in a carpenter shop for stealing tools. He was kept overnight in jail, and the news spread rapidly in Syracuse, especially in the Jewish neighborhood. A Jew caught stealing was considered a blight on the whole community. The family engaged a young attorney, Joseph Bondy, who secured bail for the boy. He had the trial, which was set for Saturday—the Jewish Sabbath—postponed to the following Monday. Meanwhile, strong feelings were aroused among the residents of Jamesville, and virtually every unsolved crime of the previous year in the village was charged by rumor to the unfortunate young peddler. One observer remarked that only the appearance, arm in arm, of a local priest and a Syracuse rabbi prevented a riot on the day of the trial.

The testimony at the trial revealed the motives behind the accusation. A local merchant, also a witness to the arrest, was asked about the type of goods sold in his store. "I carry them [matches] in stock but have no chance to sell them because these 'sheeny' match peddlers have cut the price so low that I haven't sold a box for a long time." When the merchant was asked if he objected to peddlers, he replied, "I certainly do. They ought to be driven out of this country and sent back to the land they came from." Another witness testified that he had seen the lad put tools into his pack. For the defense, several witnesses testified to the good character of the young peddler.

The case was decided in favor of the defendant when one carpenter testified that he had seen the main prosecution witness insert the tools into the peddler's basket. It was shown that a local merchant had tried to have the boy framed, in order to encourage passage of a local law requiring peddlers to be licensed.

W. Lee Provol, the boy match peddler, and the son of a Syracuse pack peddler, dedicated his book to "The Memory of the Vast Army of Courageous Pack Peddlers by the Son of One of Them." They traversed a continent on foot, endured the hardships and dangers of pioneers, and ventured into businesses along the way. Their memories and monuments are still around in Syracuse and elsewhere in the country.[42]

CHAPTER II

Decade of 1850–1860

In October, 1851, the Reverend Isaac Leeser of *The Occident and American Jewish Advocate,* after a hurried trip in the area, reported his impressions of three Jewish communities in central New York. At Utica he found a congregation with a poorly kept place of worship and a Polish rabbi who served as *hazzan,* preacher, and *shohet.* Rochester had a congregation and a "minister," but no synagogoue building. The situation in Syracuse was more promising:

Syracuse, New York—In this city exist three benevolent Societies, the Society of Brotherly Love of which William Henochsberg is President, Israel Bronner Treasurer, and M. Henochsberg Secretary. It has lately laid the foundation of a widows' and orphans' fund. The other is called "The Mutual Assistance Society," under the Presidency of Isaac Garson; Solomon Lederer is Treasurer, and Mr. C. Marks Secretary. The members of both number about fifty each. The annual contribution is three dollars, and the weekly relief during sickness is the same amount. The last is a ladies' society, called "Gamilith Chessed" and has sixty-five members. The President is Mrs. Fanny Bamberger, and Mrs. Rosa Stone is Treasurer and Secretary. All three attend to the funeral rites of the respective members. The Synagogue costs about $10,000, of which a considerable sum is still unpaid. It has a clock under the western gallery, which performs its work in silence; wherever one is introduced or in existence in Synagogues, we hope that pains will be taken to obviate the peculiar annoying, and monotonous ticking which we have observed in some places, by which the worship is greatly interrupted.[1]

33

It is worth noting that Syracuse—with its three benevolent societies, a $10,000-temple, and a silent clock that did not disturb the worshippers—was apparently making greater progress than were its neighbors. It is obvious, in any case, that as Syracuse through the 1840's grew from a village to a city, the Jewish population kept pace in relative numbers. Moreover, these early immigrants who had moved out as peddlers from their supply base at Bernheimer and Block's notion store had rapidly become Americanized. Like their Yankee predecessors, they were industrious and thrifty, intending as soon as possible to give up peddling and make permanent homes in the city with their families. New immigrants assumed the peddler's pack, while the earlier settlers ventured into various forms of business, chiefly of a mercantile sort.

In 1854, according to the *Israelite*,[2] there were 180 Jewish families living in Syracuse. If we estimate the average family as consisting of four members, and take into consideration the single men, of whom there were a considerable number, a good guess would be that there were close to 1,000 Jewish souls. The general population of the city at this time was estimated to be 25,000, which suggests that the Jews represented about 4 percent of the population, a percentage which has been almost uniformly maintained to this day.[3]

Two city directories published between 1850 and 1860 give specific evidence concerning the diversity of businesses and occupations in which Jewish citizens were engaged.[4] In the following list of names, selected from the 1851 directory, most are known to be Jewish. The others, according to their names and the location of their homes, we believe to be Jewish.

General Merchandise and Clothing Stores

M & J Jacobs	21 North Salina St.
Isaacs & Barnett	1 West Genesee St.
Joshua Jacobs	13 East Water St.
H. G. & H. L. Lazarus	36 East Genesee St.
Nathaniel Marks	74 East Genesee St.

Dry Good Stores

Bronner & Kraft	9 Franklin St.
Cone, Adler & Co.	34 East Genesee St.

Grocery Stores

Moses Bronner	101 East Fayette St.
Lewis B. Newcity	120 East Genesee St.
Mier Weisman	Corner Mulberry & Jefferson Streets

Butchers

Jacob & Henry Garson	Canal Street North of Locks

Peddlers

Joseph Bloom	32 Harrison St.
Morris Einsteen	39 Mulberry St.
Lewis Ekstein	22 Cedar St.
Aaron Henocksberg	49 Madison St.
Simon Lavendall	122 E. Genesee St.
Henry Lavinson	126 Mulberry St.
Solomon Rosenbloom	53 Orange St.
Isaac Risendale	61 Cedar St.
Jacob Sugarman	47 Madison St.
Isaac Wolf	125 Mulberry St.

It is quite safe to assume that there were more Jewish peddlers than those listed. Peddlers were mostly away during the week; some were unmarried and without permanent addresses, so that the census takers undoubtedly missed many of them.

It is worth noting that most of the names were of German origin, because this decade was the era of the German Jewish immigration.

Names in this directory were probably inaccurate, and in many cases were misspelled—especially the Jewish names. The Jewish housewives were not adept in the English language so that many of the names, as they were pronounced by them, evidently were not understood by the census takers. As a consequence, some names were misspelled, and not all of the members of a household were listed. For example, it is probably safe to assume that the names "Mier Weisman" and "Meyer Weisman" referred to the same person.

Further evidence that the Syracuse Jewish community was growing rapidly can be seen in the files of depositors of the Syracuse Savings Bank. The bank was opened in 1848, and the ledgers of that year yield evidence of a substantial—if not affluent—Jewish community, well established and willing to be part and parcel of a young, vibrant, and progressive Syracuse.

The following persons, who we believe were Jewish, had accounts at the Syracuse Savings Bank between 1848 and 1859: [5]

Simon Zenner	Israel Guffin
Isaac Wolf	Sussman Oppenheimer
Israel Harrison	Jacob Suggarman
Seligman Googenheimer	John Eckstein
Louis Bronner	Getta Rosenback
Jacob Hyman & Bros.	Myer Weisman
Jacob Klein	Levi S. Jacoby
Myer Isaac	Levi Kahn
Solomon Goldberg	Leopold Ellsner
Gabriel Bondy	Moses Rosenback
Moses Wolf	Moses Goldberg
Levi Seiberman	Yetta Goldstein
Hyman Weinheimer	David Stolz
Regina Strauss	Lazarus Dreifus
Moses Sugarman	Philip Moses
Charles Moses	William Meier
Asher Schreiber	Jacob Stulz
Ester Hymen	Rebecca Cohen
Jacob Weiss	Leopold Schwartz
Abram Sugarman	Gates Weisman
Yetta Lochtenberg	

While the list of names included in the early ledgers of the bank give evidence of the growing Jewish population, it must be remembered that not all the Jews of Syracuse had either the funds to open a savings account or the willingness to trust their hard-earned savings to the hands of strangers.

In *Winsor's Syracuse City Directory for 1857–8*, we find a number of advertisements, of which four were by Jewish firms. One was Rosenfeld Brothers, the Red Coat clothing store at 29 North Salina Street. Another was M. & T. Thalheimer, dealers in groceries, flour, and provisions at the corner of Mulberry and Fayette Streets. There were also Isaac Kahn, dealer in hides, oil, and leather, and Adler-Thayer & Co., a wholesale dry goods business at 10 Franklin Street; Godfrey Lazarus and Company, with Harris Jalonack as a partner; Abraham Stern, jeweler; Stone and Manheimer, millinery and dry goods (Jacob Stone and Edward Manheimer); Seman (Simon?) Manheimer, grocer.

Among those listed as heads of families were ninety names which, according to name, occupation, and residence, we assume to be Jewish. Of these we find that twenty-seven were listed as peddlers, seventeen as owners of dry goods stores, eight as grocers, three as liquor dealers, eleven as clerks (possibly working for relatives). Others were listed as a cigar-maker, a jeweler, a leather goods dealer, and a secondhand furniture dealer. Leopold Elsner was registered as a physician and druggist. Isaac H. Bronner appears as second vice-president of the Onondaga Savings Bank.

CONCORD BUILDS A NEW TEMPLE

The first *minyan* of 1839 increased to a substantial Jewish community of 100 families by 1850. In this one decade, the Temple of Concord outgrew its quarters three times. The *minyan,* which was started in the back of the Bernheimer and Block store, was now ready to build a temple that would compare favorably with other houses of worship in the city—one that would add prestige to the Jewish community.

Under the leadership of Jacob Stone, a substantial Jewish merchant who was now president of the Temple of Concord, a campaign to raise funds was initiated. The congregation consisted of eighty members. Each member was assessed $23. Bonds were sold at $10 each, and were eagerly taken up by the wealthier members.

The preparation and the plans of the new temple aroused widespread interest in the community. A lot was purchased for $1,400 on the northeast corner of Mulberry and Harrison Streets.[6] A planning committee was appointed, and E. T. Hayden, a well-known architect who had much experience in planning and building churches, was retained. The contract for construction was given to Gabriel Blumer, a reputable builder, at a cost of approximately $10,000.[7]

A strong difference of opinion arose among the members of the congregation concerning the ritual of prayers that would be used when the temple was completed. This placed a heavy burden on the building committee and caused much confusion in regard to the construction of the interior of the temple. The older members and the founders of the congregation leaned toward Orthodoxy. The late-comers and the younger generation wanted to follow the Reform movement, as advocated by Rabbi Isaac Mayer Wise. For example, the location of the reader's desk (the *bimah*) which according to the Orthodox tradition usually stood on a platform in the center of the synagogue, was compromised in favor of the Reform element, and the reader's desk was placed on the platform together with the pulpit in front of the Ark. To please the Orthodox, balconies were erected around three sides of the temple, so the ladies could sit separated from the men, and a ritual bath (*mikvah*), with the convenience of hot and cold water, was built in the basement. When the building was finally completed in the fall of 1851 in time for the High Holiday services, both the interior and exterior far surpassed the highest expectations of the community.

The local papers praised the edifice and the spirit of the Jewish community for its accomplishment. One reporter stated, "The Temple is an ornament to the section of the city in which it is located." [8] Another wrote, "The Jewish population comprises some of the most industrious and frugal of our citizens, and their beautiful house of worship will doubtless be an inducement for others of the same creed to settle in this city." [9]

The members of the Temple of Concord were justly proud of their accomplishment. The consecration ceremony was to be held on Friday, September 19, and Saturday, September 20, 1851. Invitations were sent to the city officials, the clergy, and all other dignitaries of the city.

As a leader of the American rabbinate to officiate at the consecration ceremony, they invited the Reverend Isaac Leeser, who in 1851 was at the height of his career in America—an author, translator, editor and publisher, a pioneer of the Jewish pulpit in the United States, and founder of the Jewish press in America. He preached from the pulpit at the leading congregation, Mikveh Israel, in Philadelphia. Through some mishap, his letter of acceptance was so long delayed that the committee feared he would not arrive in time. They then also invited the well-known Reverend Dr. Morris Raphall, Rabbi of B'Nai Jeshurun Temple in New York, to officiate instead of Leeser. As the Reverend H. A. Henry, late of Cincinnati, happened to pass through Syracuse at the time, he was also invited to stay for the ceremony and act as *hazzan* on the occasion. Thus, there were three rabbinical dignitaries present. According to Isaac Leeser he arrived just in time for the occasion and "had nothing to do but to be a spectator of the solemn proceedings." [10] We are fortunate that the Reverend Leeser's letter of acceptance arrived too late for him to officiate, since he then had time to observe and describe the events of the two most glorious days for the Jewish community of Syracuse up to that time.

We were able to secure from the American Jewish Archives of Cincinnati the complete text of the article written by Leeser, as it appeared in his Anglo-Jewish periodical, *The Occident and American Jewish Advocate* of September 1851. It is a historical document of great worth to Syracuse because all other data regarding the building and dedication which might have been recorded in the annals of the Temple Society of Concord cannot be located.

In the preface to the article, Leeser tells of having visited Syracuse seven years previously and states that at the time (1844) ". . . No congregation [other than in Syracuse] existed nearer than Albany [from the east]; and in the entire region west [of Syracuse] that there was no public assembly for the worship of God, except at Cleveland, in Ohio."

He goes on to say that the Jews of Syracuse had increased rapidly and that "It must be taken into consideration that the far larger portion of the members, who now number eighty-six, mostly married men, are persons of very limited means; and but few among them, perhaps not above ten, can be styled comparatively rich. Still did this fact not deter them from devoting their money and their time,—this capital of the poor,—to the service of their God, and they resolved, as with one voice, in the spirit of *concord* and brotherly fellowship, to erect a more permanent and a much more spacious building than had hitherto served them."

We continue now with Leeser's account of the dedication ceremonies.

A Description of the New Synagogue, *Kenesseth Shalom* (Temple of Concord) by Rev. Dr. Leeser.

When we reached Syracuse, we were prepared to see a good building, from the reports which had reached us on our journey; but we confess to our astonishment, when we beheld a large, roomy, and lofty house, every way worthy to serve as a place for the dwelling of the

God of Jacob. It is, from the front to the rear wall, sixty-four feet in length, of which twelve feet are appropriated for the vestibule and stairways, leaving the entire length of the main Synagogue fifty-two feet. The width is forty-eight feet; but, as the gallery on the west extends over the entry, the ceiling covers the whole length, so that the breadth just named is in perfect harmony with the other dimensions. There is a gallery running along three sides, and an upper one for the choir, whenever they shall have it, and on the west, fronting the ark. The ceiling is vaulted over the side galleries, and from them springs another vault over the center, giving a beautiful finish to the whole. From the middle of this is suspended a beautiful glass chandelier, the metal work of which is of gilt lacquer, and it has forty-two gas burners, in three tiers. It was manufactured by the Messrs. Cornelius, of this city, at a cost of four hundred dollars, and from its loftiness and graceful proportions, it is a real ornament to the building. The seats are disposed off in two rows, with a broad walk between them, and a narrower margin on the sides, and are divided off in the centre, in the form of church pews, but without any doors. The portion near the ark is semicircular, as are also the steps leading thereto and the ark itself, over which is a handsome stained glass window, on which are inscribed the initial portions of the ten commandments. We regretted to observe the absence of a Reader's stand, in lieu of which there is a sloped reading table within the limits of a balustrade which surrounds the ark; within which are also two sofas for the President and Vice-President of the Congregation. There is also a movable pulpit, which can be placed when required within the opening of the balustrade just named, so that the preacher may face the audience. The wood work down stairs is painted in imitation of black walnut, whereas the columns and gallery are of a neutral color, the walls being plain white. There are five windows on each side of the house, four of which are in the main Synagogue and one in the entry. The material used is for the basement blue limestone, and brick for the superstructure. A flight of stone steps leads to the main entrance, where we saw a tablet bearing the names of the officers and of the persons who were instrumental in the erection of the house, to wit: Jacob Stone, President; I. H. Bronner, Vice President; Henry Eckstein, Treasurer; Isaac Garson and Morris Marks, Trustees; E. Ettenheimer, M. Cone, A. Henochsberg, I. Bronner, I. Oppenheimer, J. Silberman, R. Rosenbach, M. A. Marks, S. Bamberger, M. Goldstein, M. Wiseman, and S. Manheimer, Building Committee; E. T. Hayden, Architect, and G. Blumer, Builder. In the basement, which is lofty, there is a dwelling for the sexton, a meeting room for the congregation, and a school room, besides a *Mikveh*, supplied with both hot and cold water. The school and meeting-rooms are so arranged with folding doors that, upon an occasion requiring it, they can be transformed into a large hall, well lighted, running the entire length of the main building.

. . . .

Active preparations had been going on for some days to put everything in order; a pretty carpet had been placed in the center aisle, round the balustrade and within the same; a beautiful new curtain, the sides composed of heavy scarlet brocade, and the centre of red velvet, the whole the gift of Mr. M. Cone, as appears by a Hebrew inscription which it bears, had been suspended before the ark, and was only completed by the pious labours of various ladies, about two o'clock on the morning of the joyful day; the galleries had been ornamented with wreaths and festoons of flowers and evergreens, and the outside front been likewise ornamented in the same manner, whilst all around the building boughs of cedar, pine, and spruce had been placed, and a double row was set up in front for the expected procession to pass between: when, about one o'clock in the afternoon, the congregation assembled in the old Synagogue, which was crowded with worshippers, to perform the afternoon service, which was read by the Rev. Mr. Henry. This having been accomplished, Mr. Jacob Stone, the worthy president of the congregation, briefly and feelingly addressed the audience in the German language, reminding them that they all recollected how they had cheerfully dedicated the building in which they there met for the last time, only five years before, and how they had discovered that it had become unable to contain all those who desired to resort thither, and that now they were preparing to enter a new house of God, more capacious, more durable, more beautiful, and better calculated to be a dwelling of Jacob's God; and he dwelt then upon the motives of thankfulness which they thus had in having been permitted to accomplish so great a deed with such limited means as had been originally at their command. We observed many eyes wet with tears; for all *felt* the truth and force of the brief allocution of the President. The hour of two having at length arrived, the procession was put in motion, under the supervision of Mr. M. Cone, the Chief Marshal, aided by several other gentlemen. In front walked a good band of music, followed by the boys of the congregation, walking two and two, one bearing a banner, inscribed, on one side in Hebrew and the other in English, with "And I bore you on eagles' wings, and brought you to me," with the date of the consecration. Then came the girls, all dressed in white, also walking two and two, the foremost bearing wreaths, and one of them a cushion, on which was laid the key of the new Synagogue. Next came a canopy, carried by four young men, under which went the bearers of the Law books; then followed the ministers, accompanied by Dr. L. Elsner, a member of the congregation, who was to deliver a German address; after which came the officers, &c., the other members and strangers bringing up the rear. Arrived at the new building, the boys placed themselves in front in two rows, when the President stepped up and received the key from the builder. The doors were then opened, and the procession entered; when the usual ceremonies took place, the circuits were made with the *Sephardim*, as we have described before this on other occasions. Mr. Henry, his sons assisting him as a choir, read the prayers and chanted the psalms in a very agreeable manner, and, we doubt not, to the satisfaction of all present. When the Laws had been deposited for the first time in their new receptacle, Dr. Raphall ascended the pulpit, and spoke for near an hour in his customary emphatic and eloquent manner, on the text, "And they shall make me a sanctuary, and I will dwell amongst them." He spoke of the object and reasons for erecting places of worship, demonstrating that to us it was a duty enjoined by religion, and not a mere natural necessity, nor the desire to propitiate by a gift the divine favour; therefore existed a necessity of so conducting ourselves, in and out of the Synagogue, as to make our appearing there acceptable in the sight of God, who otherwise would demand of us, in the words of the prophet, "Who asks this at your hands to tread my courts?" The learned divine exhorted his audience to peace and concord, that the good work of that day accomplished might bring precious fruit, and conduce to their spiritual welfare . . . Mr. Henry next recited a prayer for the prosperity of the congregation, when a collection was taken up; after which Dr. Elsner delivered a German address on the text, "I rejoice when they say unto me, Let us go to the house of God," dwelling upon the last term in contradistinction to "the house of prayer," as we devote the house to God, and it is his precincts we enter by his gracious permission. The 150th Psalm was chanted when Dr. E. had finished; after which Mr. Henry read the evening service, assisted by his sons and the congregation, in a beautiful style; and at the conclusion of all, the numerous assembly, composed of Israelites and Christians, to such an extent as to fill the whole house without over-crowding it, left for their homes, highly gratified with what they had witnessed and heard, and rejoicing that they had been spared to see that day.

The Erie Canal where it crossed Salina Street, about 1910. (*Courtesy of Onondaga County Savings Bank*)

Harvesting salt from solar vats. (*Courtesy of Onondaga County Savings Bank*)

**Cohen's Big Store on the towpath of the
Erie Canal at Sprakers Basin.** (*Courtesy of
Onondaga Historical Society*)

Babette Doppelmayer Oberdorfer.
(*Courtesy of
Mrs. Theodore Pierson*)

David Oberdorfer.
(*Courtesy of
Mrs. Theodore Pierson*)

Regina (Straus) Stolz. Portrait of her husband, David Stolz, on wall. (*Courtesy of Max Stolz*)

Jacob and Yetta (Marshall) Stolz. (*Courtesy of Louis Stolz*)

Moses Bloom, son of pioneers Joseph and Leah Bloom, arrived in Syracuse in 1849. (*Courtesy of Mrs. David Brodsky*)

The Jacob Stolz Shop at Mulberry (now State) and Cedar Streets. Jacob and son Louis are standing at the extreme right, the assistant shoemakers at left. (*Courtesy of the Syracuse Herald*)

TOLZ, CUSTOM BOOT AND SHOE MAKER

The Bronners. Three generations of the descendants of Israel Bronner: Seckel, his son; Henry, his grandson; and Marvin, his great-grandson. (*Courtesy of Mrs. Theodore Pierson*)

Myers Block and Hall, where most congregations met before building a synagogue of their own, just before it was demolished. Adjoining is the Grand Opera House. (*Courtesy of Onondaga Historical Society*)

Solomon Rosenbloom, founder and benefactor of Adath Jeshurun, better known as the Rosenbloom Shul. (*Courtesy of the Rosenbloom family*)

Rothchild's Bath and Barber Shop on Harrison Street near Grape (now Townsend) Street. Standing, Isidore and Abraham Rothchild. Their father is leaning against the building. Their grandfather is sitting in the doorway.

Jacob Marshall with his sister, Yetta Marshall Stolz.
(*Courtesy of Louis Stolz*)

Mary Doppelmayer Weisman (Aunt Mary) surrounded by her seven
sons and daughters. Standing, left to right: Yetta Exstein, Moses
Weisman, Fanny Marcus, Jacob Weisman, Carrie Kariel. Seated
are Solomon and Joseph Weisman.   (*Courtesy of Mrs. Lillian Foster*)

The Reverend Isaac Leeser, of Philadelphia, recorded the dedicatory ceremonies at Temple of Concord in 1851. (*Courtesy of American Jewish Archives*)

The Reverend Dr. Morris Jacob Raphall, rabbi of B'nai Jeshurun Congregation in New York, who delivered the dedicatory sermon at Temple of Concord in 1851. (*Courtesy of American Jewish Archives*)

Temple of Concord, dedicated on September 20, 1851, on the corner of
Mulberry (now State) and Harrison Streets. This picture was
taken in 1856, after the cupola was toppled during a storm. The
cupola was never replaced. See front cover for the original design.
(Courtesy of American Jewish Archives)

The Reverend Dr. Adolph Guttman when he first arrived in
Syracuse in 1883 to serve as rabbi
of Temple of Concord   (*The Hebrew Standard*)

The Reverend Louis Glazier, assistant to Dr. Guttman
at Temple of Concord.   (*The Hebrew Standard*)

A Board of Trustees in Concord's history. Standing, left to right: August Falker, Lee Schoener, Gates Thal-heimer, David Danziger. Seated, left to right: Ben Bronner, William Henochsberg, Dr. Adolph Guttman. (*Courtesy Temple of Concord*)

Early next morning the people again met; and they displayed their liberality by offering nearly four hundred dollars towards the funds of the congregation; and there being then only Israelites present, we could judge more correctly of the extent of the Kahal, which consisted of upwards of one hundred adult males, besides the ladies and children. The service extended to about two o'clock, the various *Mi-Sheber-ach* occupying a great deal of time,—much more, we confess, than we thought proper; but if ever this method of collecting funds can be justified, it was excusable in this instance, in view of the peculiar position of the congregation.

Thus ended the consecration of the house of God at Syracuse, in which much was said and done which ought to have more than a mere envanescent effect; and we seldom, if ever, were present on an occasion so well calculated to arrest the attention of the wayfarer on the path of life, and bid him ponder not so much on his mortality as on the bright hopes of that life where an everlasting *saffath* [Sabbath] is the portion of those who have feared the Lord.

Leeser apologizes for having written such a "hasty sketch" and states further, "it is no doubt imperfect in many respects and silent on many persons that should have been mentioned." [11]

The dedication celebration carried over to Sunday, and a dinner was tendered to the officers and visiting dignitaries at the home of Isaac Garson. Gifts were presented to Raphall and Leeser. In responding speeches, much praise was extended to the president, Jacob Stone, for his accomplishment in managing the erection and dedication of the new temple. All the speeches were in German; everyone present understood that language, since to most of them it was their native tongue. Many expressed regret at the announcement by the president that, at the end of his term, he would not stand for re-election. The Reverend Leeser remarked on leaving, "For our part, we say freely that we are rejoiced that we were at Syracuse on that occasion, and hope to witness many similar ones in other places hereafter." [12]

THE BETH ISRAEL CONGREGATION

The *minyan* of 1839, which later was formed into the Society of Concord, was composed mostly of German immigrants. It should be borne in mind, however, that by 1844—only five years after the gathering of the first *minyan*—there were enough East European Jews in Syracuse to establish a second *minyan*. The East Europeans evidently did not feel comfortable in the predominantly German congregation, so they withdrew to form their own *minyan,* which they named Beth Israel. At first they held services in the home of Moses Hart on Adams Street. Later, they moved to Myers' Hall on the corner of Montgomery and Genesee Streets. For ten years this *minyan* met in different places and not always regularly. In some years they only prayed together at the High Holidays. On September 29, 1854, the following notice appeared in *The Israelite:*

Syracuse, N.Y.—The new congregation of this city to which we referred in a previous number, consists of Englishmen, Polanders, and Dutchmen, who severed from the old congregation, on account of the Hazan whom they thought was ill treated. They are well organized, elected a Hazan who is also teacher, Shochet, and Mohel, and are reported as a promising society. The beautiful Mayer's Saloon has been rented and furnished for a temporary synagogue.[13]

By 1854 the Beth Israel *minyan* had been augmented by a contingent of English Jews, who came to Syracuse in a group in the later 1840's. Among them were the Isaacs, Jacobs, and Lazarus families. There were others, but we are not certain who they were or how many. They had an initial advantage over other immigrants in that English was their native language. Moreover, they were proud of their origin, and it is still recalled by older residents that certain families wished to be distinguished from other Jews bearing similar names, by being referred to as "the English" Jacobses, Isaacses, Lazaruses, etc. Like the Germans, the English newcomers were mostly peddlers and business men. It is known, for example, that Godfrey Lazarus owned a dry goods store on North Salina Street, and Samuel Lazarus operated a clothing store in the Franklin block.

The English settlers, in general, took an active part in the religious and social life of the Jewish community. Thus we find "English" names prominent in the organization of the New Beth Israel congregation on August 7, 1854. This second local synagogue erected its own building on Grape Street near Harrison in 1856, and was known for over sixty years as the "Grape Street Shul." The first book of minutes of the congregation has been preserved in the archives of Beth Israel, now Temple Beth El. These records reveal the concerns and experiences of the early settlers in organizing and managing a Jewish house of worship.

The first secretary of the new congregation was Godfrey Lazarus, who interpreted for the Yiddish-speaking members and also possessed a fine penmanship, so that the minutes are written in a flourishing, legible hand. Their first president was Joshua Jacobs, who, like the secretary, was one of the English contingent.

The meetings were conducted in Yiddish and recorded in English. At a later meeting it was resolved that at least one-half of the trustees must be English-speaking.

The following paragraphs from the minutes of August 3, 1854, give a glimpse of the activities of the new congregation:

Meeting called to order, Mr. J. Jacobs in the chair. Report of the committee to find a place of worship was called for. The committee reports that they obtained a room in the Myers Block for $100 per year, gas and seats extra. Moved and seconded that the room be taken for nine months. Carried. The following gentlemen were appointed to serve on the Shule committee: Henry Moss, Moses Goldstein, Simon Sondilen. The following gentlemen were appointed to find a burial place: N. Marks, A. Issacs, S. Sondilen, M. Goldstein. A motion was made and accepted that the Messrs. Lazarus, Marks and Lyons be appointed as a committee to inform Mr. Lowenthal that he has been accepted as Chazan and teacher for the congregation. A Motion was made and seconded that we adjourn till three o'clock this afternoon. Carried.

Meeting called to order by Mr. J. Jacobs in chair. Motion made and seconded that every member of this congregation pay $12 per year, payable monthly. Carried. Moved and seconded that those members who wish to send their children to be educated should pay fifty cents per month and no member shall have the priviledge of sending more than two children to be educated for that sum. Motion made and seconded that a committee be appointed to wait on Mr. Myers and request him to allow the immediate use of the benches for the congregation. Carried. Motion made and seconded that any member being called to order by the chair and refusing to do so shall be liable to a fine of from twenty-five cents to five dollars. Moved and seconded that an advertisement be placed in the Asorian, to the effect that a new synagogue is being established in this city and any donations will be kindly received by the Pres., Vice-Pres. or Treasurer. Carried. Motion made and seconded that a vote of thanks be tendered to Mr. E. Moss for his services and kind offer. Carried. Motion made and seconded that a vote of thanks be given to Mr. L. Hart for the use of this room. Carried. Moved and seconded that we adjourn until next Sunday Aug. 21, 1854 at 3 o'clock in the afternoon. Carried.

(Signed) Godfrey Lazarus, Secretary[14]

It is to the credit of the organizers of the New Beth Israel synagogue that they knew what they wanted and went about it in a businesslike manner.

In looking through the rest of the book of minutes, one comes across some interesting items and names. The men who founded this new synagogue and others who joined them in its early years were *Ashkenazim* and held strictly to the Orthodox traditions. That is why they were much concerned about a *shohet,* a kosher butcher shop, and a *mikvah.* Following are excerpts from later meetings:

September 3, 1854—Mr. Abram Levy of Oswego was elected a member. Other names mentioned—A. Isaacs, Mr. Barnett, Mr. L. Harris.

September 17, 1854—Motion made and seconded that we obtain the cushions for the ladies and that the members are taxed 25 cents a month until they are paid. New members . . . Elias Moss, I. Isaacs, A. Harvey.

October 4, 1854—Report that the constitution was recorded in the county clerk's office. Rev. Lowenthal was notified that his services will no longer be required. New members . . . Van Norder, Dr. Elsner, Mr. Naistaat.

November 19, 1854—Moved and seconded that the V. P. be fined fifty cents. Mr. Bendetson presents a hammer [gavel] to the congregation.

January 7, 1855—General Meeting. Statement of income and expenditure from August 7, 1854 to January 1, 1855. Total income $576.74. Expenditures $564.49. Balance $12.25. The rest of the meeting was taken up with hiring and firing chazan [reader], shochet, and butcher. New officers and trustees: Joshua Marks, President, Henry L. Lazarus, Vice-President, Trustees, Alfred A. Isaacs, Mordicai Lyons, Nathaniel Marks. New Members, A. Portugueise and J. Bloom. Moved and seconded that a general meeting be called for January 14 at 6 o'clock and for the purpose of considering the building of a new synagogue. Mr. Marks and Mr. Isaacs having left the meeting before the business had been settled were fined one dollar by the President. New members, Frank L. Cohen, D. Ettelson, J. Bondy, J. Schriber, S. Sugarman, T. Overlander, N. Frank, W. Williams, H. Talener, H. Blumberg, Levy Bernstein.

September 30, 1855—New Officers: H. L. Lazarus, Pres., N. Marks, Vice-President, J. Bendetson, Treasurer, M. Jacob, E. Labishensky, J. Harrison and D. Ettelson, Trustees, Isaac Isaacs, Secretary.[15]

During the spring and summer of 1855 the New Beth Israel synagogue was built on Grape Street, near Harrison Street. A description and report of the dedication ceremony appeared in *The Israelite* of October 17, 1855.

LAYING OF CORNER STONE

Syracuse, N.Y.—On Wednesday October 17th 1855 cornerstone to a new Synagogue was laid before a great mass of spectators by Mr. Isaac Benjamin of this city; and under it, as it is customary, was placed some wheat, over which a chalice of oil was poured. A case containing a parchment was also enclosed by the stone, with the following inscription and list of officers:

In the year 5616, from the beginning of the world, in the month of Marsheschun [Marheshvan], on the 5th day, under the President of General Pierce of the United States of America, the first stone of this congregation was laid by Benjamin Isaacs, Esquire.

The following officers were present:

President—Henry L. Lazarus; V. Pres.—Nathaniel Marks; Ex-President—Joshua Coles; Treasurer—Jacob Bendetson; Hon. Secretary—Isaac Isaacs, Trustees—Moses Jacobs, Eliah Sabisrisky, Israel Harrison, Daniel Ettleson.

By the Grace of the Almighty God it is the hope of all present, that this House of Worship may stand until the sound of the last trumpet.

The following address was then read by Isaac Isaacs:

Brethren!—Allow me to express a few words on this eventful occasion, which I hope will not be out of place. We commence today the rising [raising?] of a second House of Prayer to the God of Israel in this young city, that but a few years ago was amongst the wilds of North America. This rapid progress ought to be a source of pride to us, and will, we doubt not, be hailed by our brethren in this country and in Europe as an omen of the success of their co-religionists in the West. The Hebrews rely not on converting others to their faith. We are as we were 5,000 years ago—the children of Israel worshipping God in our own manner, and in the melodious, eloquent and impressive languages of old. We are numerous, and thanks to the bounty of our kind Almighty, we are individually prosperous. Then let us be liberal in supporting our ancient ritual. If in these latter days we cannot offer burnt offerings, there may be other sacrifices we can make equally acceptable to the most High. I hope, that the structure we this day meet to celebrate the commencement of, will bring together numerous congregations of contrite hearts in our own days, and that when we shall pass away, this Synagogue may become the honored relic of the Jews here, much too small to hold the worshippers that shall assemble, and that our unborn progeny may be engaged in similar exercises to which we are this day engaged in. In the meantime, let us act in harmony, and by penitence, prayer and charity, honor the name we bear of Israelites.

The reader then read the following in Hebrew, translated by Mr. I. Isaacs.

Except the Lord build the House, the builders labor in vain; except the Lord keep the city, the sentinel watched in vain. It is in vain for us to rise up early, to sit up late, and to eat the bread of sorrow, whilst his beloved sleep in peace. Lo! Children are an heritage of the Lord; and the first of the womb is his reward. The children of youth are as powerful in aid as arrows in the hand of a mighty man; Happy is the man whose quiver is filled with such; they shall not be ashamed, but shall contend with the enemies in the gate.

After the ceremonies were concluded a numerous party sat down to a cold collation at Mr. Isaacs' residence. Thus pleasantly terminated an eventful day to the children of Israel in Syracuse.

N.B.—the reason why the wheat is put in, is because the Jews are dispersed, but as the wheat is split on one side, on the other it is whole; so it signifies that they will once more be a nation. The oil means that they consecrate the chief of their means to the Lord for the advancement of His glory.

The Synagogue Desecrated

When men entered the synagogue on Sunday, December 16, 1855, for morning prayers, they were astounded to find that vandals had entered during the night and had taken the *Sifrei Torah* (scrolls of the Law) out of the Ark, leaving them strewn over the floor.

At a meeting the following day, December seventeenth, it was proposed by E. Labishinsky and seconded by M. Jacobs that a meeting should be held in the synagogue for the purpose of fasting and prayers, because of the desecration of the *Sifrei Torah*.[16]

Up to this time there were no recorded acts of overt anti-Semitism in Syracuse. However, there was a strong feeling that latent anti-Semitism existed among certain groups. Occasionally one heard words of derision like "dirty Jew" or "sheeney." Jewish children were admonished not to go beyond Jackson Street into the Irish neighborhood.

New Arrivals Before the Civil War

The Jewish community grew rapidly in numbers. Three families who arrived in the 1850's and made notable contributions to the Jewish community and to the community at large in business, medicine, and finance were the Elsners, Stolzes, and Falkers; for over half a century they were among the leaders who were part of the history of the Jewish community.

Dr. Leopold Elsner. Dr. Elsner was a man of many qualifications and served the Jewish community well. He came to America from Presburg, Hungary, and claimed to have participated in the Hungarian Revolution. He was banned from that country at the same time as Ferenc Kossuth, the hero of that revolution.

In the history of the Utica Jewish community written by S. Joshua Kohn, it is stated that "Leopold Elsner arrived in Utica in the early 1840's and was the minister of the first Jewish congregation and served as cantor, ritual slaughterer and circumciser." Kohn further states that, "his name is found in the 1850 ledger of the Utica Savings Bank, where he is described as being 40 years of age and 5' 6" tall." [17]

In 1851 Leopold Elsner moved with his family to Syracuse. It is quite safe to say that he was not very happy in Utica. The Jewish settlement there was comprised mostly of Polish Jews. Having attended the University of Prague, he was well educated in German and therefore felt more at home in Syracuse with its sizable group of German Jews.

On arriving in Syracuse he immediately became active in the Temple of Concord, which was without a rabbi at the time, and he delivered a number of sermons in German.

In Syracuse he was referred to as Dr. Elsner, though we do not know that he ever earned a medical degree. It appears that he went around to other cities, for the history of the Jewish community in Rochester says that in the 1850's "There was no *mohel* in Rochester. Dr. L. Elsner, a Syracuse physician, was called to Rochester about once a week to perform some circumcisions." [18]

Dr. Elsner settled on the North Side, where most Germans resided, and built up a comfortable medical practice. During his career in Syracuse he gained a fine reputation as a man of integrity, sociability, and a fine sense of humor.

Dr. Leopold Elsner passed away on September 2, 1881. He left a widow and eight children.[19]

THE FALKERS. Shipwrecked on their voyage to America, Joseph Falker, his wife, four daughters, and one son arrived in 1854. In the disaster the family lost all their possessions. They came from Musbach, Rheinpfalz, Germany.

It did not take Joseph Falker long to establish a business in leather findings, hides, and wool, and he prospered exceedingly well. August, his son, was thirteen when the family arrived. He had acquired a good education in the school of his native town. He was fond of reading and he improved himself greatly through private study. He developed into a man of recognized culture and refinement. He became an excellent speaker and an authority on matters of finance.

The Falkers, father and son, were staunch advocates of Reform Judaism in those early days of religious controversy in the Temple of Concord. August became a trustee at the age of twenty-one, and a few years later he was elected president. It was under his staunch leadership that the temple turned from Orthodoxy to Reform.[20] This change almost wrecked the temple. When the great schism took place, many of the founders withdrew and organized a separate congregation. Skill was required to set matters right again, financially and organizationally.

For many years August Falker held the leadership in the temple as president and later as a trustee. His father, Joseph Falker, died in 1889 at the age of seventy-eight.

August Falker was also prominent in business and financial circles in Syracuse. He was a second vice-president of the Onondaga Savings Bank. He was active as a Mason and became master of Salt Springs Lodge. He was also a leader of B'nai B'rith, and held high office in other organizations.

August married Etta Elsner, daughter of Dr. Leopold Elsner, and their only son, Jesse, distinguished himself as a graduate of Harvard University in sociology and political science.

August Falker passed away on February 4, 1909, at the age of sixty-eight.[21]

Mrs. August (Etta Elsner) Falker occupied as high and important a social and official position as any Jewish woman in Syracuse. Her family was highly intellectual—her father was first a synagogue functionary and then an eminent medical practitioner. Three of her brothers were also in the medical profession. The oldest brother was the prominent Dr. Henry Elsner of Syracuse.

Mrs. Falker was educated at Syracuse High School as well as privately. She began, after her marriage, to make a study of philanthropy, and shortly was given the opportunity to engage in practical charitable activities. She was one of the managers of the Auxiliary of St. Joseph's Hospital, vice-president of the New York Trade School for Women, one of the directors of the Boy's Club, and one of the originators of the Ladies Auxiliary of the Society of Concord. She was the first president of this auxiliary and continued in that position for four years.

A great public honor was bestowed upon Mrs. Falker by President (then Governor) Theodore Roosevelt, when she was appointed manager of the Western House of Refuge at Albion, New York. The appointment was for six years, and Mrs. Falker was reappointed for a second term by Governor Frank W. Higgins.

Mrs. Falker held a high position in the social world. She was a prominent member of the Kanatenah Club and held office on the board for many years.[22]

THE BROTHERS STULTS. In 1845 two orphan boys barely in their teens set out on foot from Schuttenhofen in Bohemia to wander through Europe. Their parents, Joseph and Hannah Stults, had recently passed away, leaving no property, so that the two older sons had to fend for themselves. The youngest of the family, Samuel, was put in the care of relatives, while David and Jacob started out to learn trades and see the world. Jacob carried a pack containing the tools of a shoemaker, and David, the oldest of the brothers, took along a small supply of cloth, needles, thread, and scissors. They wanted to serve as apprentices, in order to reach the status of journeymen in shoemaking and tailoring.

Doing odd jobs for food and shelter, the boys walked through Bohemia and came finally to Vienna in Austria. There they readily found work as apprentices. For over a year they worked in Vienna; then they took to the road again. Being more aggressive, Jacob wanted to keep on walking until he had covered all of Europe. David, however, wished only to see the rest of Austria and Hungary before returning to Schuttenhofen. Thus they parted, Jacob pushing on through Germany, Demark, Sweden, and Poland, learning the language of each country he visited.

After a year of separation, as David was turning back toward Schuttenhofen, he came face to face with Jacob on the bridge over the Danube at Budapest. It was an accidental but a joyful meeting, and the brothers remained together for a time in Budapest. Then Jacob turned toward the east and Constantinople; David went home and set to work at tailoring and teaching his younger brother Samuel the trade. It was a hard way to make a living among the poor people of Schuttenhofen, but David stuck to it until 1856.

At about that time the exodus from western European countries to America was at its height, and glowing accounts of the great opportunities to be found there spread from mouth to mouth in Europe. It was told in Schuttenhofen that their town fool, who had emigrated (and whom no one at home would trust even to run an errand) had secured a well-paying job in America and was on his way to becoming a successful merchant. Deciding that they could not do worse, David and Samuel joined the stream of emigrants and, after a perilous crossing of sixty-three days on an unseaworthy vessel, reached New York in 1856.

The miserable conditions of sweatshop tailoring in New York led David to accept an invitation to visit a relative in Hamilton, Ontario. He was informed in advance that it would be a long, hard journey. He was instructed to take the Erie Railroad to Binghamton and to change at Binghamton to a train for Syracuse. In Syracuse he was to change again to a train for Oswego, and from there to take a boat to Hamilton. When he arrived in Binghamton David was confused and got back on the train he had just left. The conductor did not discover him until he arrived in Ashtabula, Ohio. David was then put on another train and returned to Binghamton. This time he found the right train, which brought him to Syracuse. At the depot, someone he met told him that there was a shortage of tailors in Syracuse, so he decided to stay, instead of going on to Canada. In this manner, the first of the Stults family became a settler in the Jewish community of Syracuse.

For some time David was employed by other tailors, but after a while he went into business for himself at 79 Grape Street. This move brought about an unplanned change of the family name. A painter who was preparing a sign for the new shop asked David how to spell his last name. David replied that in Germany it was spelled S-T-U-L-T-S, but that he did not know what the English spelling should be. When he later went out to inspect the sign he saw above the door "DAVID STOLZ, TAILOR," and that is how the family has been known since.

Brother Jacob, the shoemaker, decided to follow David and Samuel and emigrate to America. Samuel became a pack peddler and settled in Lyons, New York, where he operated a dry goods store. After working a year in New York, Jacob had saved $90 and came to Syracuse. He wasted no time but immediately set himself up as a custom boot and shoemaker. His excellent workmanship was soon recognized, and it brought him the wealthy residents of this growing city as customers.

At the outbreak of the Civil War, fearing that if the war continued there might be a shortage of leather, he went to the wholesale leather dealers, Ellis, Wicks & Company, and said he had $250 saved up. He wanted to invest that, and as much more as they would give him credit for, in leather. Ellis and Wicks had faith in the little Jewish shoemaker and extended him credit for $5,000. He took it all out in leather. Jacob guessed right. The price of leather quadrupled during the war, and he emerged a rich man. Although he was still a bachelor, he nevertheless invested in a house at 21 Cedar Street, directly across from the Jacob Marshall home.

As time went on, Jacob and David grew tired of living at boarding houses, and looked around for marriageable girls. Both found them in the Marshall family. David married Regina Strauss, a sister of Mrs. Marshall, and Jacob married Yetta Marshall, a sister of Jacob Marshall.[23]

PRELUDE TO THE CIVIL WAR

In the decade between 1850 and 1860 the slavery issue was uppermost in the minds of most Americans. The strife between the North and the South was growing in intensity, and many citizens of Syracuse were active in the abolitionist movement. Dr. Samuel J. May, a noted clergyman of the Unitarian Church, was the leader. When President Millard Fillmore signed the Fugitive Slave Act in 1850, the citizens of Syracuse were more determined than ever that they would assist escaped slaves on their way to Canada and freedom. Syracuse became a station on the "underground railroad."

Several escaped slaves were living and working in Syracuse, and a vigilance committee was formed to protect them. In case of danger, it was arranged to have the church bells toll. On October 1, 1851, the federal marshals arrested one Jerry McHenry, an escaped slave. As he was being arraigned, a group of twenty men broke into the courtroom and in the commotion pushed Jerry out of a window. Men were waiting ouside and quickly hustled him into a buggy, dressed him in woman's clothing, drove him to Oswego, and put him aboard a ship bound for Canada. The building where the hearing took place was marked for many years with a bronze plaque and was known as the "Jerry Rescue Building."

The American Anti-Slavery Convention was held in Syracuse May 7, 1851. Daniel Webster visited here and spoke for the Fugitive Slave Law, bitterly denouncing those who fought against it as traitors.

In 1852 the Women's Rights Movement held their national convention in Syracuse. Two thousand women attended, and Laurette Mott, a Syracusan, was elected president. Its many liberal-minded leaders had made of Syracuse a city with a social conscience.[24]

CHAPTER III

The Civil War Years

During the first years of the 1860's, all other events were overshadowed by the Civil War. Abraham Lincoln was elected President in November, 1860, and South Carolina seceded the following month. Fort Sumter was fired upon on January 9, 1861. By all accounts, the Civil War had begun, even before Abraham Lincoln was inaugurated on March 4, 1861.

Syracuse, a hotbed of the antislavery movement, was aflame with patriotism, ready and willing to do its share for the cause of the Union. On April 15, 1861, Lincoln called for 75,000 state militia to join the Union Army for three months' service. The next day, in Syracuse, Captain John Butler and his seventy men, who called themselves "The Zouaves"—dressed in their colorful uniforms of blue jackets, canary yellow vests, red baggy trousers, and tasseled fezzes—entrained for Albany, where they were joined by other militia units and sent off to the front. Though legally they could be called for only three months of service when out of the state, most of the Syracuse company remained on active duty and fought through the full length of the war.

Shortly after the departure of Captain Butler and his Zouaves, and in answer to a call from President Lincoln for more volunteers, the 12th Regiment was formed in Onondaga County. In May it was sent to Elmira for basic training, and in July it was engaged in battle with the enemy in Virginia.

In 1862 came the call for 300,000 more men. This was answered in Onondaga County by the formation of the 122nd Regiment, under Silas Titus as commanding officer. They were mustered into service in

August. That same year, still another regiment was mustered into service—the 149th, under Colonel Henry A. Barnum.

During all this, a draft for recruits was put in motion by orders from Washington. It was not very effective, because it had many loopholes. Married men and the heads of businesses were exempt, and anyone could buy his way out by paying $300 for a substitute. The campaign for volunteers was continued. There were parades and speeches, with much excitement and fervor in the streets, in fraternal organizations, and in the churches. Reports from the front indicated that the war was not going well for the Northern forces. More men were needed. As patriotism inspired the ethnic groups, the Germans from the North Side formed a company under Captain Nicholas Grumbach. The Irish had formed a company earlier.[1] The Jewish people, too, wanted to do their share, but there was a division among them over the question of Jewish group participation. Some claimed that Jews should participate as individual citizens; others held it was better to band together as a means of counteracting the various accusations and sly remarks that were being made. In that way, they would make known their patriotism, serve the Union, and show the Know-Nothing party and its followers that the Jews were not un-American aliens.

Contrary to the feelings that prevailed among Jews on the other side of the Atlantic, especially in Russia where the persecuted Jews were loath to go into the army, here in Syracuse many young Jewish men gladly volunteered.

During the week of August 24, 1862, a campaign for recruits was held. A recruiting office for Jewish volunteers was open during the day, and at night patriotic meetings were conducted. In the Temple of Concord, the Reverend Dr. Solomon Deutsch made an impassioned patriotic plea for volunteers, and the president of the congregation made an appeal for relief money. By the end of the week twenty men, enough to form a company, had been recruited, and nearly $3,000 had been raised for an army relief fund.

The following letter from a Syracusan to *The American Israelite* describes with perception and patriotic enthusiasm the happenings in the week of August 24, 1862, when the recruiting of Company A, 149th Regiment (The Jewish Company) took place.[2]

Syracuse, N.Y., Aug. 31, 1862
Editor of the Israelite:

I take great pleasure in informing you of the great patriotic movement of the Israelites of this city in the gallant and noble cause of the Union and Liberty.

The first meeting for this purpose was held on Sunday the 24th inst., 9 o'clock, A.M. in the Synagogoue of the Society of Concord. A large audience assembled. The following prominent citizens were chosen officers:

F. D. Manheimer, Esq. President;
Jacob Levy and Joseph Falker, Vice-Presidents;
Baruch Stern, Treasurer;
B. Bronner, Secretary.

The chairman stated the object of the meeting, when immediately a bounty subscription fund to aid volunteering was opened. Also an enrollment list for a military company to be formed with the following prominent young men as follows: S. Light, Captain; Samuel Bronner, 1st Lieutenant; W. Harris, 2d Lieutenant.

Mr. Jacob Stone said: I am too old to volunteer for my country but the first young man who will do so shall receive $200 as my substitute.

His request was complied with. Many other young men signed the roll. The sum of nearly three thousand dollars was received in cash. Stirring war speeches were made, and thus a noble work was commenced.

We continued our meetings from evening to evening—always with a crowded house—and the patriotism manifested in their meetings was never witnessed in Syracuse. The most prominent Citizens and eloquent speakers of Christian denominations addressed our meetings, and the great hall of the synagogue resounded with high and patriotic words.

It seems as if the spirit of Judah Maccabee had come down to arouse his people and when I sat in the synagogue listening to the remarks of some able speakers, I rejoiced, for here in this house of Jewish worship, I see the Jew and the Gentile sitting friendly together, listening to one great object—aiding one noble cause, pointing to one noble work—the maintaining of our glorious republic—whose unsurpassed institutions give to us all: "Liberty-Equality."

We had another rousing meeting last night. The Reverend Dr. Deutsch addressed the audience in English, and his patriotic words and eloquent language were very much applauded and when the Rev-

erend speaker sat down a storm of applause was raised and the cry of
"go on—go on", was cheeringly heard.

Monday we opened our recruiting office—began to work—some of our
merchants absented themselves entirely from their business, devoting
their time to military business, and when the sun on Saturday evening
went down on Onondaga's shore, the first company, Company A, of
the Onondaga Regiment, got up by the Israelites of Syracuse, was mustered into the service of the United States, to the delight of all citizens.

Night closed upon us, when headed by martial music and the flying
banner of the Stars and Stripes, we marched out on Mulberry Street—
cheers on cheers were given—it was Company A of the 4th
[149th Regiment] Regiment.

I rejoice in that movement; it shows the Israelite knows his duty to
his government and country.

And our ladies? were they idle? No, sir! They collected among
themselves the sum of $200 for a regimental flag to be made by them
to be presented to the 4th Onondaga Regiment.

The military committee has concluded that the Jewish Ladies of
this city shall have the honor to make and present the Regimental flag
—it will be done worthy of the daughters of Israel.

I know, dear sir, you delight in the honor and progress of our nation, and by letting this communication find a place in your valuable
journal, you will oblige,

Your friend,

(Signed)   Emeth

The first man to volunteer for active service was Solomon Light,
who was selected as captain. Samuel Bronner was next and was appointed lieutenant. The names of the Jewish volunteers who enlisted
on August 24, 1862, and the dates of discharge are as follows: [3]

Captain Solomon Light: Due to sickness in family, discharged January 17, 1863. Born March 28, 1835, in Semnitz, Hungary. Died October 3, 1874, in the 39th year of his age. Buried in Rose Hill Cemetery.

Lieutenant Samuel Bronner: On account of business, discharged
February 8, 1863.

Simon August: Age 28; 80 Harrison Street; honorably discharged
February 8, 1863, due to disability.

Harris Flato: Age 28; wounded November 24, 1863; hospitalized,
nothing more was heard. He did not return to Syracuse.

Jacob Hyms: Age 19; hospitalized January 18, 1863; honorably discharged due to disability, March 25, 1863.

Samuel [Schmerel] Harrison: Age 22; wounded May 25, 1864; in hospital at muster-out of regiment.

George C. Jacobs: Age 22; mustered out July 7, 1865.

Harris Lazarus: Age 28; transferred to 4th Artillery, October 15, 1862.

Moses Lehman: Age 29; 78 Almond Street; mustered out May 29, 1865.

Herman Levi: Age 42; honorably discharged for disability.

Herman Liebman: Age 36; wounded and captured, May 3, 1863; paroled. Wounded June 16, 1864; transferred to Veterans Reserve Corps, January 2, 1865.

Lewis Light: Age 21; wounded January 17, 1864; transferred to Veterans Reserve Corps, September 4, 1864.

Michael Lovich: Age 25; September 8, 1862, promoted to captain. Killed by accidental discharge of his own gun on May 4, 1863.

Lazarus Newman: Age 26; (1874 directory, 49 Madison Street); wounded July 20, 1864 (lost foot); in hospital at muster-out.

Isaac Rosenberg: Age 25; no record after December 10, 1862.

Milo Rosenthal: Age 18; wounded May—, 1864; mustered out June 12, 1865. Buried in Woodlawn Cemetery.

Moses Rothchild: Age 19; killed in action, November 24, 1863, at Lookout Mountain. Buried in Rose Hill Cemetery.

Charles Shalensky: Age 24; died of typhoid fever on March 10, 1863.

Jacob Simmons: Age 20; no record after December 9, 1862.

Nathan Wyman: Age 19; Sergeant, September 18, 1862. No record after February 14, 1863.

Frank Robicek: Did not enlist in the 149th Regiment with the Jewish Company. He is known to have been Jewish, enlisted in Syracuse, and there is proof of his honorable discharge.

Another interesting item from the *Syracuse Standard* of September 19, 1862, is the following:

PRESENT TO LIEUTENANT BRONNER

The friends of Lieutenant Bronner, Co. A, 149th Regiment, have presented him with a splendid sword and accoutrements. Mr. August Falker made a neat presentation speech, and Lieut. Bronner replied happily.

Patriotism among the Jewish womenfolk was also high, and it is known that in some cases mothers and sweethearts encouraged their young men to join. The following account testifies to their zeal and loyalty:

AN INTERESTING OCCASION

Presentation of a Regimental Flag to the 149th Regiment—Sword Presentation to Col. H. A. Barnum—Remarks by Rev. Dr. Deutsch, Colonel Barnum and others.

At an early hour last evening, the City Hall was densely crowded with people called together to witness the interesting presentation ceremonies which took place there. Hundreds were unable to gain admittance to the hall, and were obliged to go away disappointed at being unable to take part in the proceeding.

At eight o'clock Mr. Abram Levy called to order and on his motion Hon. Allen Menrur was made chairman.

Mrs. Abram Levy, Mrs. Edward Manheimer and Mrs. Abram Stern, the committee of the Jewish ladies, occupied seats on the platform.

Shortly after the organization, Col. Barnum of the 149th entered the hall and was greeted with applause as he made his way to the platform. The Light Guard, Co. D, 51st regiment—headed by Dresher's Brass Band and bearing the Regimental Flag, escorted the procession from the Jewish synagogue on Mulberry Street to the City Hall, and marched into the hall, and up to the platform where space had been reserved for them. The flag was placed in the care of the committee of ladies, and hung over the chairman's seat to be in full view of the assemblage.

The band then performed several National airs.[4]

The following excerpt from *Central New York, an Inland Empire,* was written by W. Freeman Galpin and gives an account of the action in which the Jewish men participated (Vol. II, 233).

The 149th (Fourth Onondaga) Regiment was mustered in September 17–18, 1862, to serve three years. The unit left Syracuse September 23 and had its first experience under fire near Occaquan Creek, Va. on December 28. After a brief stay at Harpers Ferry, the regiment was moved from one point to another, and it was not until the spring of 1863 that it was again under fire in Chancellorsville. Later it joined in following Lee's troops as they marched into Pennsylvania, participated in the defence of Culp's Hill at Gettysburg and then followed Lee as the southern troops withdrew. Following this campaign and under the command of General H. W. Slocum, it was transferred to the western theater of the war. The regiment suffered terribly at Wahautchie Valley and gallantly took part in the attack on Lookout Mountain. During the winter of 1863–4 it remained in camp, but in the spring joined with Sherman in his march to the sea. It saw active service at Peach Tree Creek and was at the siege of Savannah. In April, 1865, while at Raleigh it heard the news of Lee's surrender and with that its days of fighting were over. It was mustered out of service at Bladensburg, Md. in June, 1865.

Twelve thousand men from Syracuse and Onondaga County entered the war—a thousand over the required quota—many of whom did not return. Those who remained behind kept the mills and factories running, supplied the wares and the ammunition, and in this way responded to the call of duty for the cause of the Union. The greatest and most tragic civil war in history came to an end. However, that was not the end of sorrow for the citizens of Syracuse. On April 26, 1865, the people of Syracuse stood with bowed heads as the funeral train bearing the remains of the Great Emancipator, Abraham Lincoln, passed through the city.

New Arrivals during the Civil War

During and immediately after the Civil War there was a considerable number of new arrivals, many of whom distinguished themselves and left their mark on the community.

THE DANZIGER BROTHERS. In 1853 I. Henry, Isaac, and Jacob Danziger had settled in Cortland, New York (thirty miles south of Syracuse), where they had a clothing store, as well as a clothing factory in the adjoining town of Homer. Ten years later, when their manufacturing business outgrew the little town of Homer, they moved their plant to Syracuse.

The three brothers made an impact on the community, both socially and industrially. At the height of their industrial activity they employed over a thousand hands and gave work to many of the Jewish immigrants. With offices in Chicago and New York and many traveling salesmen, their business flourished. Among the key employees who traveled for them were William Wolf and A. Amdursky, both of whom made their homes in Syracuse and were active in the Jewish community. The Danziger brothers stood high in the social life of the city. I. Henry was appointed a commissioner of health and was also a director and later president of the Temple of Concord.[5]

LOUIS MANSON came to Syracuse in the middle sixties, a poor immigrant boy. He had a hard life at first, peddling in the country. Being Orthodox, he ate only kosher foods out of a bag he carried with him. He slept in barns and came home only on weekends to honor the Sabbath.

Out of his first earnings Louis sent for some of his relatives, among whom was his nephew Mark Gais. Turning his satchel of jewelry over to Mark, Louis established a wholesale jewelry business. He raised a family of three boys and three girls, all but one of whom received a college education. Mark Gais later married one of Louis' daughters, Carrie, and the families of Manson and Gais contributed much, particularly to the Orthodox group of the Jewish community.[6]

MOSES HEIMAN, aged twenty-two, arrived in Syracuse in 1868, directly from Schneiderwohl, Prussia. Shortly afterward he married Theresa Schloss, daughter of two of the earliest Jewish settlers, Joseph and Nanette Schloss. Theresa was a native-born Syracusan, and therefore had high social standing. Moses did well in business and for many years owned a popular peddlers supply store. Two children were born to Moses and Theresa—Fanny Heiman (Ferguson) and Dr. Mark Heiman, both of whom became very active members of the community in later years.[7]

THE REVEREND MARCUS RUBIN. Some of our early Jewish settlers will be remembered not only for their own achievements but also for the contributions made to the community by their sons and daughters. Such a man was the Reverend Marcus Rubin, who came to the United States in 1860 and settled in Oswego, thirty miles from Syracuse. Reverend Rubin served this small Jewish community as *hazzan*, teacher, *shohet*, and butcher. Some time prior to 1871 he moved to Syracuse. He was elected as *hazzan* and teacher for the Beth Israel Synagogue, and he also operated a butcher shop. Here he prospered, and with the help of his growing children was soon the owner of the building on the corner of Harrison and Grape Streets that was known as the Rubin Block. Rubin's Hall on the third floor of the building became the favorite place in town in which to hold Jewish weddings. The corner of

Harrison and Grape Streets was to the Syracuse Jewish neighborhood what Forty-second Street and Broadway is to the theatrical district of New York.

When her husband passed away in 1882, Reverend Rubin's widow, Fannie, with the help of her eldest son, Moses, age thirteen, took over the management of the butcher shop and Rubin's Block, and all older residents testify that she did so admirably.

The contribution of the Rubin family to the Syracuse community can be seen in the accomplishments of their five sons and three daughters.[8]

Moses Rubin, real estate broker and banker, was for seventeen years a member of the Onondaga County Board of Supervisors and chairman of the committee on county buildings.

William Rubin, an attorney, was a graduate of Syracuse University Law School, a prominent lawyer, and assistant corporation counsel of the city for five years. He was a large holder of business property.

Harry Rubin of Binghamton was the founder and half-owner of the largest furniture store in the Southern Tier of New York State. Together with his brother-in-law, Simon Rosenthal, he operated The Fair Store. Harry Rubin, a popular bachelor, was a leader in business and civic affairs of Binghamton for many years. It was common knowledge that Harry Rubin could have been elected mayor, or to any other office in Binghamton. Although he was interested in politics, he never chose to run.

J. Robert Rubin, the youngest of the family and a Syracuse University graduate, married out of his faith to Reba Hitchcock, his high school sweetheart and daughter of one of the socially prominent families in Syracuse. Marrying out of the faith was not looked upon lightly in the early years, especially by the Orthodox. Mrs. Rubin, the mother, grieved deeply over her son's marriage to a non-Jew, even though the girl came from high society. When someone asked her how her son Robert was getting on, she was heard to say, "I have no son Robert." Robert and Reba moved to New York, where he became a foremost attorney for several theatrical enterprises. He was a director of Loew's, Inc., counsel for Metro-Goldwyn-Mayer, vice-president of Paramount Theaters, and a trustee of Syracuse University.

The fifth brother, Isaac, died at the age of twenty-three on July 30, 1895.

Of the three daughters, Esther married Simon Rosenthal of Binghamton. Anna and Jane taught school for many years and neither married.

These are but a few of the important families added to the Jewish community in the 1860's.

SCHISM IN THE TEMPLE OF CONCORD

During the course of the Civil War, and even long before, dissension was brewing in the Temple of Concord. The earliest settlers, the founders of the original *minyan*, were, in the main, Orthodox. The old traditions and the rituals that they brought with them from the old country were inbred with their Jewishness. They resisted any changes in the form of worship, particularly those advocated by Rabbi Wise. However, some of the later arrivals from Germany and the new generation favored making changes towards Reform immediately.

It is evident that in 1851, when the new temple at the corner of Harrison and Mulberry Streets was being built, the traditionalists were still in control, for special balconies were built in which the women sat apart from the men, and even a *mikvah*—a ritual bath used by Orthodox women—was built in the basement.

After the temple was completed, bitter strife continued between the Orthodox and those who advocated Reform. This is manifest through the letters that were sent by both sides to the Anglo-Jewish press, setting forth their arguments and seeking assistance from other Jewish communities:

Syracuse, March 31, 1861
Editor of the Israelite:

At a general meeting of the Society of Concord held in their vestry room on Sunday the 31st of March, 10 o'clock A.M., the following officers were chosen for the coming year.

> Jos. Falker, President,
> Jos. Schwarz, Vice President,
> A. Stern, Treasurer,
> H. Ekstein, Thalheimer, E. Manheimer,
> Friedman, Trustees

The result of this election is greeted with great joy and enthusiasm by all friends of reform, who labored earnestly, faithfully and zealously to gain the victory. Never since the existence of the community was so much interest, so much zeal, so much anxiety felt and exhibited by either party at an officers' election. The ultra orthodox party, opposed to any Synagogue reform, contrived all possible means to defeat the reform party, caucuses were held, liberal inducements made to those whom they expected to vote their ticket; in short all batteries were set a playing through which a gain could be imagined. But slowly and surely and skillfully maneuvered the Reform Party, and when the day of election dawned, when the hour arrived, they in a body marched to the battle ground, the votes were cast, and the day gloriously won.

Vox populi—vox dei. The orthodoxy, seeing their candidate in the first fire defeated, got discouraged and only kept up a slacked fire by the balloting for v.p.—and finally retreated from the battlefield, beaten and disheartened.

Thus the community is redeemed from the iron grasp of orthodoxy —the men opposed to all reform—all progress demanded by time and circumstances—the lead of the society is once more in the hand of a wise and enlightened administration—and [it] is sincerely wished that the hope of the better classes will be realised. Let there be light!

The Rev. Dr. Deutsch, this highly learned Rabbi, this talented Scholar of Israel! he is with us; last Saturday again his voice resounded in the hall of the Synagogue, in a suitable and powerful sermon, taking Ezekiel, chap. 7, for his text.

His preaching created great enthusiasm among his friends and even the ultra orthodoxy, always opposed to the Dr.'s preaching, was stunned and seem to yield to the force of his arguments and the enthusiasm of his language.

It is hoped that the new administration will immediately take steps to secure the services of the learned Dr. or at least his permanent sojourn among us.

The Rev. Dr. Deutsch is the man for us; his influence and services are wanting for us, wanting for our children, wanting for the reform and welfare of the community; for his open, manly language in his Sermons; we deeply respect him; his sentiments and views of religion we heartily endorse, therefore all hail, all success to the noble champion of Israel.

Very respectfully, thy friend, dear Israelite.

Signed—Truth and Justice.

N.B. Tomorrow, great installation Preaching in the Synagogue.[9]

The following letter addressed to *The Israelite* portrays, in the language of the time and in the spirit of deep religious feeling, a true advocate for reform. It is regrettable that the author of this letter and others who wrote to the Jewish publications in those days used pseudonyms. How much more their letters would mean today if we could identify the writers by name!

Syracuse, N..Y, July 29, 1861

Dear Israelite:

Go forth and proclaim through the world the sublime and inspiring truth "The Lord our God is the only One."

Pardon me, my old friend, when again I'll trespass upon your time by informing you of some of the congregational affairs of the Society of Concord, and as it hails from "Reform Quarters." I'll beg admittance in your valuable paper—that paper which battles so heroically for Judaism and its interest—that paper which bears the sublime motto "Let there be light." Since the present administration has come to office, the great reform movement thus far succeeded. The synagogue service is undergoing a favorable change, so much different from what it was in those days when "blind orthodoxy" swayed its scepter over the community. If your learned and esteemed Editor would give us the pleasure of a visit, he, who knows the congregation from its earliest existence, would be delighted with this change wrought in so short a time. We have procured an organ, a well instructed choir, and peace and harmony and contentedness prevail in the society to such an extent as never known heretofore. And why not? The reform party consists of men who understand their mission, who are inspired by it, and who will not shrink from any sacrifice which its progress demands. True, there is a low grumbling heard by a few in some distant corners of the Society, about organ and choir, but, "nobody hurt."

Saturday morning, the 20th inst., I walked out on Mulberry Street. It was the Sabbath of Consolation—I entered the Synagogue. The organ was playing, the choir singing, the service was grand, and a solem dignity and devotion spoke from every face, my heart rejoiced in such worship and my soul exclaimed: How goodly are thy tents, O Jacob, thy dwellings O Israel.

The first part of morning prayers over the Rev. Dr. Deutsch mounted the pulpit and taking for his text, "Comfort ye, comfort ye, my people," preached a sound and eloquent Sermon. I will endeavor to give you a little sketch of it. The Rev. Preacher after giving an historical account of the rise and fall of the first and 2nd Temples, and the events connecting with it, thus continued: 1800 years have gone by since Jerusalem was taken, since the world-renowned Temple is burnt, Israel is dispersed to all corners of the globe, the stake and the sword wrote his history with a bloody pen, but all this suffering could not shake the sacred principle of his divine religion which he bore away from the burning temple. The Temple is burned! but from every grain of dust scattering from the rubbish of the consumed Temple into every wing on earth a new Temple rose—a Synagogue in which the eternal truth is proclaimed, "Hear O Israel, God is our Lord, God is one."

He then went on and explained the difference between "The Sabbath of Admonition" and "The Sabbath of Consolation." The former, like a time of a forthcoming storm, points to events from which we have not recovered yet to this day, a nation while looking on the records of history stands yet woe and sorrow stricken—once so mighty, once so great, so powerful, and now? going—going—lost—There comes the latter, and calls:

"Be consoled, my people, be consoled for know you, that day when the temple was burnt, the Messiah was born, as our sages remarked too—not an Individual—not a personal Messiah, but a grand and heavenly mission was born." The temple is burned—but be consoled, rejoice! for from its ruins the mighty truth of Divine religion, imprisoned so long on the mount of Zion, sallied forth, and that is the great misson born on the 9th day of Ab—and Israel, suffering Israel, chosen to be the same bearer of this mission, and this is the decree of Providence.

Go forth and proclaim to all nations the eternal principle of divine religion, "God is our Lord, God is One."

When the Dr. finished, the congregation was delighted with the historical truth and force of argument pointed out in his sermon, the impression was an inspiring one. Having recorded a little sketch of it only what I bore away on the wings of memory, I can not do justice to the sermon nor its able author. Some of our Christian brethren who happened to be at the synagogue were no less impressed with the grand ideas the Rev. Preacher unfolded.

We expect a grand and solemnizing service next holidays. Good bye, my dear Israelite. Wishing you many hundred new and paying subscribers, I am, respectfully,

Your old friend,

JUSTICIA

An indication of the strong feeling that this split engendered was the manner in which the traditionalists voiced their protest, principally against the high-handed methods of President Falker. They wrote a forceful statement of accusations against the officers of the temple, a justification of their own action, and an appeal for funds to be published in *The Occident and American Jewish Advocate* (a monthly that was inclined toward Orthodoxy and had a wide circulation among the Jewish communities of the Eastern seaboard), as follows:

A NOTE BY THE EDITORS OF THE ADVOCATE— NEW CONGREGATION IN SYRACUSE, NEW YORK

We lay before the public the subjoined appeal from a portion of the Israelites of Syracuse, who have been compelled by circumstances which they detail to separate from the mass of their brothers. We are not personally acquainted with the gentlemen who have signed the circular; but we have every confidence that their statement merits the serious consideration of all lovers of peace and religion, and we trust that they will be aided to come speedily in possession of the means to obtain a place for worship and a quiet field in which to inter their dead. We can heartily sympathize with men who are driven from the house they have reared for the worship of God, who wish to preserve the spirit of ancient Judaism only to find former friends, with whom they labored in adverse times, become enemies in the days of prosperity. It is painful to contemplate such a state of things, and to feel that the only remedy left is to quit old associates and to start a new society; for it is far better to worship God in the company of a few devoted spirits in peace and concord, than to belong to a numerous body whence the spirit of kindness has fled. We trust, therefore, that the appeal made through our pages in part will not be in vain, and that our friends will respond promptly to Messrs. Schwartz and Thalheimer, in the full assurance that any contribution forwarded to them will be duly appreciated and properly applied to the promotion of Judaism.

APPEAL AND JUSTIFICATION

As the doings of the Congregation Society of Concord have of late become quite well known abroad, we, the new congregation Adath Jeshurun, owe it to ourselves, resting our cause upon the sayings of the Law-giver, *Shemoa bein ache-chem,* to give, in as limited a space as possible and strictly according to the truth, the real state of affairs, that we may appear righteous before God and Israel.

Nearly twenty-three years ago, the majority of the present congregation Adath Jeshurun formed what is known as the Society of Concord, to whose prosperity we devoted our time, energies and means without stint. In time a Synagogue was built, costing nearly $10,000. Every thing went on satisfactorily until about three years ago, when impure elements forced their way into it, creating quarrels, enmity, law-suits, and finally separation, through the unlucky choice of a president, who, like a Bavarian petty official, agitated and through low intrigues, heaping wrong upon wrong, deprived members of their holiest right. Lawsuits without number were created between members and the obstacles were placed in the way of a moderate reform by us; it was only a frivolous and arbitrary play with that which the true Israelite considers as holy, that met our unqualified condemnation.

Of the many high-handed outrages to which we were subjected, we will only mention the following:

First. A mortgage of the Society's real estate of $2300, held by a then member of the Society of Concord, and now a member of the new congregation, who some years ago had taken an assignment of this mortgage from the original holder, the same having become due and foreclosure threatened, and the Society not being able to pay it, thereby preventing the forced sale of the Society's property, was, after mature deliberation, for the purpose of hindering and delaying this member to collect the same, declared null and void; and he only succeeded after factious opposition, and only then by means of the law, to obtain that which he had in all honesty advanced to save the Society's property from being sold away from them.

Second. Finding that by such means no success would follow, the said mortgage was paid up and a new one was created for the short space of six months, and shortly after becoming due, the parties who now hold this new mortgage, and who are also members of the Society of Concord, for a purpose of their own, threatened to foreclose and sell to the highest bidder, not only the Synagogue, but also the cemetery, and actually did foreclose. Previous to this foreclosure, a meeting was held by the members, in which nearly two-thirds of the whole Society participated, and signed a petition to the Board of Trustees, asking them to desist from their purpose of allowing the property to be sold, inasmuch as the member who had previously held the mortgage, and whom it was purposed to deprive of his pay, again stood ready to advance the money for five years, shame be it said, by its own members. We challenge any one of said Society of Concord to gainsay the truth of this humiliating fact.

Third. To still carry on their high-handed proceedings, and to perpetuate their power, recourse was had to stratagem. At the last annual election of a President and Trustees, our Constitution and By-Laws were set aside and trampled under foot for the purpose of creating new members, many of whom were not eligible, and the very man who for three years past had created so much mischief and discord, and who had time and again in public assembly declared that it was his purpose not to desist until the very shingles of the Synagogue were lawed away, was again chosen as President, and this time, in utter violation of our Constitution, which expressly provides that a President is only to hold the office for one term, for three years.

Thus there was no other alternative left us, as honorable men, than to resign from a congregation which we had built up and nursed, driven out, as it were, by the persistent and unrelenting abuses of a man who, but a few years ago, came among us as a stranger. Twenty-five members resigned at *once,* and some eight have done so since.

And now the new congregation Adath Jeshurun, consisting of about thirty-five members, and daily growing larger, is placed in a position without a house of worship, and should it please the Almighty to remove from among us any of its members, without a place of burial and devoid of all means to create either.

In view of the facts set forth in this circular, the congregation Adath Jeshurun believe they are justified in appealing to their sister congregations and other benevolent institutions and individuals throughout the United States, for a helping hand. The object is a laudable one, and your contributions will tend to replace, to a not unimportant number of Israelites, that which they were in such an inhuman manner deprived of.

Contributions will be thankfully received and duly acknowledged by either of the undersigned.

Leopold Schwartz, President

Morris Thalheimer, Secretary
Syracuse, July 1, 1864

It is difficult to convey the bitterness and the heated arguments which were engendered by the division among the members of Temple of Concord over the controversy whether the Society Temple of Concord should follow the *Ashkenazi* Orthodox form of worship, or proceed with the Reform method of worship, as advocated by Rabbi Isaac Mayer Wise.

President Joseph Falker strongly advocated the Reform. The new administration succeeded in introducing organ music, choir singing, English translation of Hebrew prayers, and family pews for men and women. But there was hard and active resistance on the part of the Orthodox minority. The next decree by the president, that all men must remove their hats during the divine service, brought the long and arduous dispute to a climax. The Orthodox group rose up in indignation. The Reform group kept adding decrees, including one to raise dues from $8 to $16 per year. This was aimed at the Orthodox, because among them were more of the poorer members.

Thus, the Temple Society of Concord, *Keneseth Sholom,* which has a name that stands for peace and harmony, was torn asunder. The Orthodox group, composed mainly of the original founders of the congregation, led by Joseph Wiseman and Samson Bamberger, walked out in a body.

Solomon Rosenbloom, Morris Thalheimer, Leopold Elsner, Jacob Marshall, and Hessel Rosenbach were among those who withdrew from the Society of Concord in 1861. The secessionists formed their own congregation and held divine services in temporary quarters.[10]

Thus we come to the end of the schism. Controversy so long and bitter was bound to leave scars. Friends became as strangers, and families were divided.

Morris Thalheimer left the Temple of Concord while his brother, Max, remained. Joseph Wiseman left; his brother, Meyer Weisman, stayed. Jacob Stolz and his brother, David, parted. Moses Bronner joined the new group, and the rest of the Bronners stayed. And so it was in many families; the schism took years to heal.

This sort of division was not unusual among the Jewish communities in America in the latter part of the nineteenth century, but whereas in most other communities the reformers left and the traditionalists remained, in Syracuse the situation was reversed. In other communities the German Jews usually left as a body; here the German Jews were divided, some leaving and others remaining. Those who left organized the congregation of Adath Jeshurun.

ADATH JESHURUN CONGREGATION

The Adath Jeshurun Congregation was the result of the schism from the Reform Temple of Concord. Its place of public worship became popularly known in Syracuse as "Rosenbloom's Shul." The congregation was organized on June 6, 1864, receiving the charter on March 3, 1866.[11] Joseph Schwartz was the first president; Joseph Wiseman, vice-president, and Moses Bronner, treasurer.

The first place of worship was a one-story building on Harrison Street. Then, in 1887, Solomon Rosenbloom purchased a lot on Orange Street. Through his efforts and with the cooperation of Morris Thalheimer, Daniel Rosenbloom, and K. Wolf, a beautiful Gothic-type edifice was erected. Solomon Rosenbloom, the mainstay of the congregation, occupied the position of president for twenty-five consecutive years. His son Daniel succeeded in the presidency, occupying the position for three years until his death on August 27, 1905. David Oberdorfer was the treasurer until his death. The first functionary was Lewis B. Newcity, who officiated till 1875. He was succeeded by Reverend Jacob Levi, who was followed by Reverend Isaac J. Blaustein.[12]

The dedication ceremonies were recorded in *The American Israelite:*

The handsome temple of the congregation of Adath Yeshurun [Jeshurun] in Orange Street, between Madison and Harrison, was dedicated on Friday, August 26th. The members justly felt proud over their achievement; they have struggled vigorously and often times despondently against adverse circumstances, and the beautiful little edifice is a fitting emblem of their ambition. Every pew was occupied long before the hour for beginning the services, and admiring glances and flattering remarks were made by both Jew and Gentile on the elegance of the surroundings. A procession of the pastor and officers of the congregation, headed by seven little girls dressed in white and carrying bouquets, entered the temple at 5:30 P.M. to the music of a quartet composed of Misses Levy and Goldstein and Messrs. Trautman and Bitter, Professor Fiske organist. Arriving at the pulpit, little Annie Berwin, in a clear and unfaltering voice, presented the key of the temple to the President, Mr. S. Rosembloom, who responded briefly and appropriately. The Rev. Jacob Levi, pastor, then offered a prayer, after which the Rev. Joseph Stolz, of Chicago, delivered the dedicatory sermon, which in point of eloquence and rhetoric, was an extraordinary effort. His large audience could but take pride in the brilliancy of this young son of Judaism, who but a short time ago left his native city of Syracuse and is now at the head of one of the largest and wealthiest congregations in the West. The regular Friday evening's services followed the sermon, and the addition of singing by the quartet and pastor with the benediction by the Rev. Mr. Stolz. The programme was carried out with precision, the singing being especially good. Special services were also held this morning.

The officers of the new temple are: President Solomon Rosenbloom; Vice-President, K. A. Wolfe; Treasurer, D. Oberdorfer; Secretary, M. J. Altman; Trustees, Jacob Liebman, David Stolz, Phillip Zenner, M. Lehman. The Bonding committee are Morris Thalheimer, S. Rosenbloom, Daniel Rosenbloom and K. A. Wolfe.[13]

The *Syracuse Daily Journal* of August 26, 1887, described the new temple as a handsome wooden structure, which had cost about $8,000 with its furnishings. The auditorium on the top floor seated 256 persons. School rooms were placed in the lower level of the building.[14]

Mainly through the guidance and munificence of the Solomon Rosenbloom family, the Adath Jeshurun Congregation on Orange Street survived for sixty-one years. In 1925, when it closed its doors, the remaining members of the Rosenbloom family rejoined the Temple of Concord.[15]

THE ROSENBLOOM FAMILY. From 1847, the year of Solomon Rosenbloom's arrival in Syracuse, until his last son, Isaac, passed away on March 18, 1954, the Rosenbloom family was a factor in the Syracuse Jewish community.

Solomon Rosenbloom, the pioneer, was born November 20, 1822, in Altenheim, Bavaria. In 1846 he came to America, remained in New York City for one year, then moved to Syracuse, where he began his career as a peddler. In 1848 he married Hannah Hermann, who lived in Syracuse at the time but with whom he had been acquainted in Bavaria.

Originally Solomon had learned the shoemaker's trade. When he was ready to go into business, he opened a shoe store in the old Bastable Block on East Genesee Street. In 1869 he took his elder sons into the business, and from then on the store was known as S. Rosenbloom & Sons. Solomon was now able to devote more of his time to the needs of the community and synagogue, leaving business matters to his sons. Both did well. The sons built up the business from the one little shoe store until, at the end of the century, they had one of the largest department stores in Syracuse (now occupied by E. W. Edwards & Son), with branch stores in Utica, Oswego, Auburn, Providence, Rhode Island, and Akron, Ohio, as well as large holdings in real estate.

In the meantime, Solomon was looking after the *shul* business and devoted most of his time to the building of Adath Jeshurun, which he served as president for twenty-five years. When he bought a plot of land on the corner of Colvin Street and Jamesville Road for a cemetery, it was called Rosenbloom's Cemetery. The *shul* was maintained by father and sons for more than sixty years, until the congregation merged with the Temple of Concord.

Solomon Rosenbloom died on November 20, 1896, and is buried in Rosenbloom's Cemetery. This cemetery continues to be maintained from bequests left by the sons. (See Appendix A.)

Each of the seven sons gave a good account of himself during his lifetime, in business, philanthropy, and politics. Daniel, the second-born, was the most prominent. He was connected officially with the Public Library, was elected a member of the Board of Education, and was offered the Democratic nomination for mayor, which he refused because of his health. He died at the age of fifty-four.

Of the seven sons, five remained bachelors. The two who married were Marcus, the eldest, and Isaac, who lived the longest. He died at the age of ninety-two on March 18, 1954.[16]

Moses Oberdorfer with his family. From top left: Jonas; Moses' wife, Sarah (Light) Oberdorfer; Minnie; Rena. Seated: Jesse and Moses Oberdorfer. (*Courtesy of Mrs. Minnie Goodman*)

Gates Thalheimer and his family. From left: Ethel (Thalheimer) Oberdorfer; her husband, Jonas Oberdorfer; H. Hiram Weisberg and his wife, Mabel (Thalheimer) Weisberg; Gates Thalheimer; and grandchildren, Jane and Babette Oberdorfer. (*Courtesy of H. Hiram Weisberg*)

Trustee Meeting Wed Eny nov 18 54.

I Jacobs. in the chair HL Lyons V.C.
Trustees present A Isaacs. N Marks.
M. Lyons: E Labushinsky. absent J Bendettson
absent. the last two Trustees were fined seven.
motion made and seconded that we adjourn till
Thursday Eny. Nov 24th 54.

Trustee Meeting nov 24th 54.

J Jacobs. in the chair. A Isaacs vice Chair.
Trustees present. A Isaacs. N Marks.
M. Lyons. E Labushinsky. J Bendettson.
HL Lazarus. absent. the last three Trustees
were fined 50 cents. Motion made and seconded
that we adjourn till Dec 3rd 1854. carried
for the purpose of Receiving monthly dues. and.
for the adoption of Constitution and Bye Laws.

Sunday. Dec 3rd 1854.
General Meeting

J Jacobs. President. in the chair
HL Lazarus. Vice President
Trustees present.
E Labushinsky.
J Bendettson
M. Lyons.
A Isaacs.
motion made and seconded that the minutes
be approved of. carried
all fines collected heretofore to be Refunded carried
moved and seconded that we read the laws —

Reproduction of an original page from the first book of Minutes of
Beth Israel Congregation, November 23, 1854.
(*Courtesy of Congregation Beth Israel*)

Beth Israel (Grape Street Shul) on Grape (now Townsend) Street, dedicated in 1855. (*The Hebrew Standard*)

Louis Marshall, national Jewish leader. (*The Hebrew Standard*)

Benjamin Stolz, noted attorney, president of Temple of Concord. (*Courtesy of Max Stolz*)

Gates Thalheimer, president of Temple of Concord, 1897-1928. (*The Hebrew Standard*)

George Freeman, owner of Freeman's Hall. (*Courtesy of Mrs. Benjamin Friedman*)

Dr. Nathan Jacobson, Professor of Surgery at Syracuse University Medical College.

Dr. Henry L. Elsner, Professor of Internal Medicine, Syracuse University Medical College.

Dr. Jacob J. Levy, Professor of Anatomy, Syracuse University Medical College

Dr. I. Harris Levy, noted physician and professor at Syracuse University Medical College.

Samuel Shubert, founder of Shubert Enterprises. (*Courtesy of the Shubert Office*)

Moses Rubin, Supervisor, Fifteenth Ward. (*The Hebrew Standard*)

Colonel Joseph Bondy, attorney and patriot. (*Courtesy of Arline Bondy Davis*)

William Rubin, Assistant Corporation Counsel. (*The Hebrew Standard*)

Temple Adath Jeshurun (The Rosenbloom Shul) on Orange (now McBride) Street. *(Courtesy of Onondaga Historical Society)*

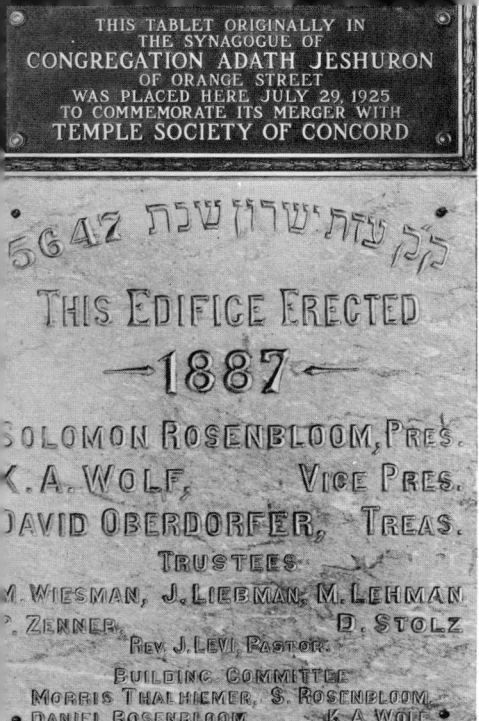

THIS TABLET ORIGINALLY IN
THE SYNAGOGUE OF
CONGREGATION ADATH JESHURON
OF ORANGE STREET
WAS PLACED HERE JULY 29, 1925
TO COMMEMORATE ITS MERGER WITH
TEMPLE SOCIETY OF CONCORD

בא עזת ישרון שנת 5647

THIS EDIFICE ERECTED
→1887←

SOLOMON ROSENBLOOM, PRES.
K. A. WOLF,   VICE PRES.
DAVID OBERDORFER,   TREAS.

TRUSTEES
M. WIESMAN, J. LIEBMAN, M. LEHMAN
P. ZENNER,   D. STOLZ
REV. J. LEVI, PASTOR.

BUILDING COMMITTEE
MORRIS THALHIEMER, S. ROSENBLOOM
DANIEL ROSENBLOOM,   K. A. WOLF
C. E. COLTON - ARCHITECT

Tablet of 1887, of Adath Jeshurun's
founding, together with Plaque of
1925 commemorating the reunion of
the two congregations.
(*Courtesy of Temple of Concord*)

The Reverend Max Wechsler and his Hebrew Class in 1899.
(*Courtesy of Mrs. Louis Nesbit*)

Temple Adath Yeshurun (Naistadter Shul), Mulberry (now State) Street, founded in 1870, erected in 1878. (*The Hebrew Standard*)

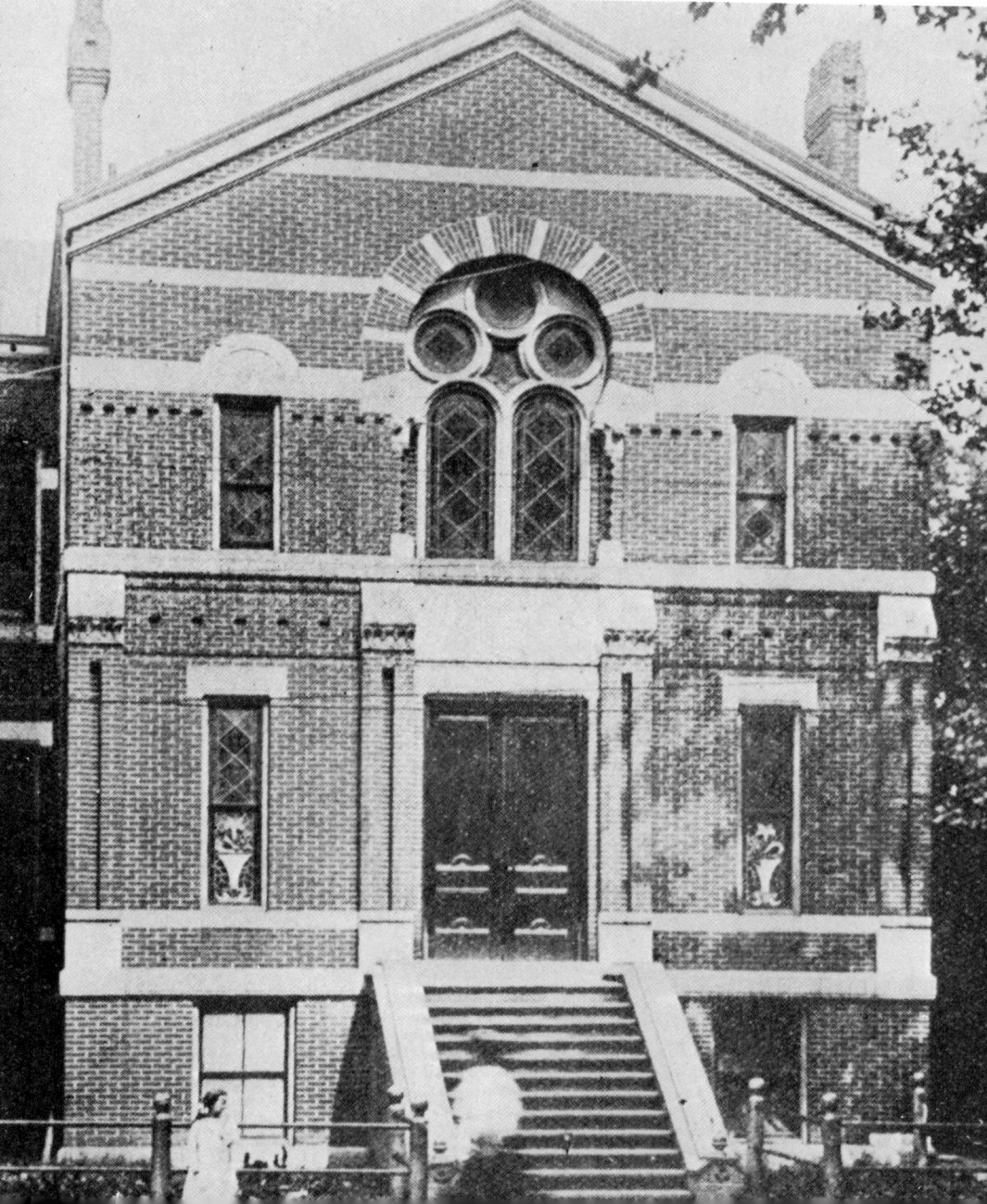

Poiley Tzedeck Synagogue, Almond Street near Adams, dedicated in
1896; demolished to make way for Interstate Route 81 in 1964.
(*The Hebrew Standard*)

Henrietta and Samuel D. Solomon, leaders and
workers for Judaism for over half a century.

T. Aaron Levy, the Reverend Max Wechsler, and Sol Marquisee looking at
a portrait of Joseph H. Hertz, the first rabbi of Temple Adath Yeshurun.
(*Syracuse Standard*)

Congregation Ahavath Achim (Beth Hamedrosh Hagodel), 905 South Orange (now McBride) Street, dedicated in 1909. Demolished to make way for Pioneer Homes. (*Courtesy Onondaga Historical Society*)

Congregation Ahavath Achim on Almond Street, dedicated in
September 1940, in use until 1968. Rabbi Samuel Yalow on left.
(*Courtesy of Syracuse Post-Standard*)

Anshe Sfard Synagogue, Orange (now McBride) Street, dedicated in 1917. (*Courtesy of Onondaga Historical Society*)

The present Anshe Sfard Synagogue on East Genesee Street, opposite Cambridge Street, dedicated in 1953.
(*Photo by Sherman Sable*)

The second edifice of Congregation Beth Israel, corner of Irving Avenue and Harrison Street, 1925-65. (*Photo by Bergan and Klineberg*)

CHAPTER IV

The Years of Adjustment
and Coalescence

Not all of the notable pioneers who were instrumental in establishing the Syracuse Jewish community remained here to live out the rest of their lives.

There were usually two reasons, diametrically opposite, why they were motivated to move away. One was that after years of living in Syracuse they had not done well and heard of other cities where there were better opportunities, usually farther west. The other reason was that they did *very* well, and Syracuse became too small for them. Then they would move east, looking to larger cities, where greater opportunities for cultural and social life were available, and also to places where they might hope to earn better returns on their investments.

A SYRACUSE COLONY IN TEXAS

ISAAC WOLF was one man, however, who left Syracuse for an altogether different reason—a matter of health—and thereby became the first of a contingent who established a Jewish community in Texas. Isaac married Sophia, one of the five Doppelmayer girls, and thereby became related through marriage to the Weismans, Heimans, Exsteins, and Doppelmayers.

In 1857 Isaac Wolf is listed in the city directory as a peddler, living at 148 Montgomery Street.[1] He suffered from a bad case of asthma. His doctor advised him that the only way he could find relief was to leave Syracuse and go west where it was high and dry. He got as far as Marshall, Texas (which is not exactly the Far West). There he entered the cotton brokerage business and sent for his family. With them came Daniel Doppelmayer, his wife's brother. Because of his asthma, Isaac Wolf was exempt from service in the Civil War, but Danny enlisted in the Confederate Army in Clark's Regiment, Sixth Brigade, on February 24, 1862.[2] As soon as the war was over, Danny came back to Marshall and opened a dry goods store.

Word was received in Syracuse about how well they were doing, and the trek of relatives of the Wolfs and Doppelmayers started. Thus a Syracuse colony in Texas was formed.

Joe Weisman, son of Meyer Weisman, left Syracuse for Texas in 1866 and joined Daniel Doppelmayer in the dry goods business.

Jacob Exstein (the name was earlier spelled "Ekstein"), a cousin of Isaac Wolf, followed the latter, as did Benjamin Exstein. Abraham, the husband of Yetta Weisman, was the only one of the five Exstein brothers who chose to remain in Syracuse. It is interesting to note that three first cousins (whose parents were all Doppelmayers) married three Exstein brothers. Yetta Weisman (daughter of Mary Doppelmayer Weisman) married Abraham Exstein, Eva Doppelmayer (daughter of Meyer Doppelmayer) married Isaac Exstein, and Bertha Wolf (daughter of Sophia Doppelmayer Wolf) married Jacob Exstein.

Joseph Grossman, who was married to Caroline Light, left Syracuse with his six daughters for Texas on February 27, 1867. Two sons were born in Marshall. Max A. Bernstein, who also went to Marshall from Syracuse, married one of the Grossman girls, Molly, in 1884.

Joe Weisman's dry goods business continued to prosper, and in 1879 he sent for his brother Jacob to join him. The following is a report that appeared in the *Syracuse Journal* of November 11, 1879:

A PLEASANT SURPRISE

The many friends of Mr. Jacob Wiseman will hereafter miss him at the post he has so long occupied and the duties of which he so faithfully discharged in the office of the W. U. [Western Union] Company. He leaves for Marshall, Texas, tonight, and the good wishes of his friends not alone go with him in imagination, but a substantial expression of the same in the form of a beautiful fifteen-volume edition of

Dickens was presented to him to cheer him in his new field of labor. The presentation was made at the residence of Dr. Nathan Jacobson and the surprise was very complete.

Quite a colony of Syracusans have settled in Texas and all are meeting with splendid success. The business of some of them has increased to such an extent that they have sought for employees in our own city and have offered splendid inducements for them to come there and reside.

Another item, in the *Syracuse Journal* of January 19, 1871, reported a tragedy that occurred among the men who had settled in Texas:

MURDERED—Last October, Frank Ferguson, with others, left this city to locate in Texas and carry on a jewelry business, taking with them Simon Goldstein, of Utica, to peddle goods for them. News has just reached Utica that Goldstein has been waylaid and murdered on the road. He was well known among the Hebrews of this city.

The Joe Weisman Department Store, the leading retail establishment in Marshall, Texas, recently celebrated its ninetieth anniversary. The store is operated by two grandsons of the original founder: Martin Hirsch is the president of the corporation, and Joseph Weisman Hirsch is vice-president.[3]

THE LAZARUS BROTHERS. Few descendants of the original English migration now live in Syracuse. One remaining member is Benjamin Ross, whose mother was an Isaacs, reportedly related to the family of Rufus Daniel Isaacs, the first Marquis of Reading, a British jurist and statesman (1860–1935).

One branch of the Lazarus family achieved fame beyond Syracuse. The census of 1855 listed Henry L. Lazarus as aged twenty-four and married to Anna Isaacs, aged nineteen. Henry is last recorded in the city directory of 1859, as the proprietor of a clothing store in the Franklin block. He died shortly thereafter, leaving his widow and two sons. Anna moved to New Orleans in 1868, taking with her fifteen-year-old Solomon (who adopted his father's given name, Henry Lawrence) and Samuel, two years younger.

The career of Henry Lawrence (Solomon) Lazarus, as recorded in the *National Cyclopaedia of American Biography*, illustrates both the opportunities for success and the threats of prejudice which confronted a Jew in nineteenth-century America. Young Henry returned from New Orleans to New York State to continue his education, and later completed his legal studies at Louisiana State University. Although he was under the statutory age for admission to the bar, he passed a special examination with distinction before the state supreme court and was granted permission to practice law in May, 1873. The next year he joined a legal firm in New Orleans, and in 1880 the governor of Louisiana appointed him a judge of the civil district court of the Parish of Orleans. The *National Cyclopaedia* asserts that "political and race persecution" led him to resign this position in 1887. Later, however, after years of success in private practice, he was appointed to the Louisiana state supreme court, on which he served for seven years.

Judge Lazarus was married in 1875 to Sallie Ella Solomon of South Carolina. They had three sons and three daughters. It was said of him that "his hospitality is unbounded and his charities extend to all creeds and all conditions." He came back to Syracuse in 1881 and on other occasions to visit his relatives.[4]

Samuel L. Lazarus, the other brother, who was born in Syracuse in 1855, went from New Orleans to Texas in 1875 and entered the cattle business. He became a vice-president of the American Live Stock Company in 1889, and in 1891 turned his attention to railroads. Over the next decade he was the receiver of the bankrupt Texas, Louisiana and Eastern Railroad, and president of the Red River, Texas and Southern Railroad. Moving to St. Louis, Missouri, in 1902, he became president of the Acme Cement Plaster Company and an influential leader of the local Democratic party. He served as president of the St. Louis City Council, 1913–15, the last incumbent of that office before a new form of city government was adopted. He died in New York City in 1926.[5]

EARLY JEWISH POLITICIANS

JACOB LEVI, SYNAGOGUE FUNCTIONARY AND POLITICIAN. What is a combination *hazzan-shohet-mohel* doing in politics? Jacob Levi was all that, and a good politician, too.

He arrived in Syracuse in the 1860's with his wife and family.

He had been in this country for fifteen years when he took a position with the Temple of Concord as a reader. He was actually a *hazzan,* and a very good one. But the temple had an organ and a mixed choir, and hence did not need a *hazzan* in his full capacity. Leaving the Temple of Concord, Jacob Levi went over to the Rosenbloom Shul on Orange Street, which was strictly Orthodox. Here a *hazzan* could chant the prayers, with the traditional melodies and incantations. However, even as a full-time *hazzan,* Jacob Levi had a hard time trying to make a living as a synagogue functionary, so he went to the Solomon Rosenbloom family for advice.

At this time, Jacob Levi lived at 706 East Jefferson Street, in back of the Rosenbloom home on East Genesee Street. The seven Rosenbloom sons were making a mark for themselves in business and politics. Marcus and Abe Rosenbloom had considerable influence in the Democratic party. Levi hoped that the Rosenblooms might be able to get him a political job. In a talk with the Democratic boss, the Rosenbloom brothers learned that the party was looking for a candidate to run for alderman in the Seventh Ward. Jacob Levi seemed an ideal person for the job. He was a very personable man; he wore a small, trimmed beard and talked with a slight German accent, which was not uncommon in those days. The Rosenblooms presented Jacob Levi as a possible candidate. The Seventh Ward was made up largely of Jewish and Irish families, and certainly he could count on the support and votes of the Jews. The Democratic boss could easily take care of the Irish.

Jacob Levi ran for alderman in the Seventh Ward in 1869 and was elected. He made an excellent alderman, and was liked by the other members and learned the ways of politics quickly. Three times he was re-elected, and once was proposed as president of the council.[6] He had the distinction of being on the committee which went to Elmira to select the first steam fire engine for Syracuse, an important assignment for those days.

For over twenty years Jacob Levi was highly influential as a politician in the Seventh Ward, popular among both Jews and non-Jews. He brought up a large family of sons and daughters. One of his sons, Aaron, became a copy writer and editorial consultant for the *Syracuse Herald.*

In his obituary, printed in the *Syracuse Standard* of July 21, 1892, it was stated that Jacob Levi was born in Tachan, Austria, in 1827, and died at his home on Jefferson Street in 1892.

GEORGE FREEMAN arrived in this country in 1866 at the age of eighteen. Like most other immigrants, he was absolutely penniless. Being an apprentice tailor, on the way over he repaired the ship captain's coat, for which he received sixpence, but someone relieved him of it before he arrived in New York.

From Castle Garden (a reception point for immigrants in Battery Park, New York City) the Hebrew Aid Society sent him to New London, Connecticut, where he found work as a tailor, remaining there until he learned that they needed tailors in Rochester. Not long thereafter we hear about him in Homer, New York, where the Danziger brothers had a clothing factory. While there he married Lena Cashman, aged fourteen. Two years later, in 1873, he arrived with his wife and a child in Syracuse, where they remained. He rose to be one of Syracuse's foremost citizens in business, real estate, and politics, and became known as a "man about town."

In the 1875 city directory he is listed as a tailor at 83 Madison Street. Later he was foreman at Woodhull, Goodale and Bull, large clothing manufacturers. He remained with them a number of years, until he opened his own factory on West Washington Street.

Next he built a large four-story brick building on the corner of Grape and Jefferson Streets, known as the Freeman Block and Hall. Freeman's Hall became a Jewish institution in Syracuse, where the Purim Balls, the town meetings, and the fancy weddings took place.

Those were the days when Jewish parents splurged to give their daughters a grand wedding. That was what the parents saved for, and if necessary went into debt for—a wedding to which most of the Jewish population was invited, and one that people would talk about for years. For that there was only one place, Freeman's Hall.

George Freeman went into politics, and for over a quarter of a century he, together with George Bedford, ruled politically over the Seventh (later the Fifteenth) Ward. The area was populated by the Irish and the Jews. It was said that George Bedford controlled the Irish vote and George Freeman the Jewish vote. Freeman was elected alderman of the Seventh Ward for the first time in 1893, and later represented the Fifteenth Ward. He served on the board of aldermen of Syracuse for fourteen years.[7] He was never defeated, and a good politician he was. If any Jew needed a favor at City Hall or a friend in court, he could depend on George Freeman.

To complete his reputation as a "man about town," he was a good sport as well. When Syracuse was about to lose its baseball franchise, George Freeman, in partnership with Sime Shimberg, bought the ball club and Star Park. In two years they lost $38,000 and dropped the venture.

We are able to look in at the wedding of one of his daughters in Freeman's Hall, as described by a reporter in the *Syracuse Standard* on March 22, 1898:

At Freeman's Hall last evening Miss Harriet May Freeman, daughter of Alderman and Mrs. George Freeman of this city, was married to Simon J. Silverman of New York City, Rev. Adolph Guttman D.D. officiating.

There have been many brilliant weddings in Jewish society in Syracuse, but none approximated this with its profusion of flowers and furnishing which made Freeman Hall look like fairyland. It was a magnificent display, to entertain and provide for two hundred and fifty guests, was no small undertaking.

Standing under a canopy, Dr. Guttman awaited the arrival of the young people whose lives he was to unite. The groom, Mr. Silverman, was attended by the brother of the bride, Samuel G. Freeman. Following were the ushers:

David Freeman, Charles Mullin, Samuel Mason and Charles Freeman.

The groom's parents, Mr. and Mrs. L. Silverman of New York, came next, and the bride's little sister, Henrietta Freeman, was close behind.

Before and after the ceremony countless carriages dashed up in front of Freeman Hall, to the canopy, in a long procession. A chart of the dining room made it easy for head waiter, Tom Clark, of the Yates, to seat the guests, and no confusion resulted, though two hundred and fifty guests sat down at the tables.

The stage was heavily banked with greens and smilax. Glowing amid the greens, with all their brilliancy reflected various colored incandescent lights stood out with startling brightness. Roses and tulips were the prevailing flowers. Each table was plentifully supplied with them.

Apart from the banquet hall was a reception parlor. This had also been prettily decorated. A cozy oriental booth with handsome draperies and rich Persian rugs occupied one side of the wall and it was evidence of lavish taste. Even the window casings were shut from view by the use of rich rugs and draperies. The lavish hospitality of Alderman and Mrs. Freeman was apparent everywhere.

We cannot say that the Freemans were the preeminent Jewish family in Syracuse, but we can safely say they were one of the most popular. The Freemans married while very young; he was about twenty and she was fourteen. They had eleven children. Later, their children, Charles and Jesse Freeman and Mrs. Sime Silverman, were connected with the theatrical profession. George and Mrs. Freeman became acquainted with many leading actors and actresses of the stage, and this enhanced their social standing in the community. Mrs. Freeman was one of the first ladies to take up contract bridge in Syracuse and was considered an expert player. Their home was the center of Jewish and social affairs for many years.[8]

Lena Cashman Freeman was born March 27, 1856, in Sweden, came to the United States as a young girl, and met George Freeman while she was living with her parents in Homer, New York. She died in Syracuse at the age of seventy-six.[9]

THE MOSS FAMILY ARRIVES. Isaac Moss, his pregnant wife, Sarah, and their daughter, Rebecca, arrived at Castle Garden (with the help of a Baron De Hirsch grant) in 1884.

The Immigrant Aid Society of New York tried to be helpful to the Moss family, and learned that Isaac Moss was an experienced harness maker. The harness and leather trade was centered in Newark, New Jersey. When the agent tied a tag to Mr. Moss's coat marked "Newark" he forgot to insert the name of the state, and so Isaac Moss and his family were placed on a train bound for Newark, New York. They arrived at the little village of Newark at midnight. They awoke the station master, who luckily could speak German. He informed them that there were no harness makers there, and that the nearest cities were Rochester, to the west, or Syracuse, fifty-five miles east, and that there would be a train going either way during the day. They chose to go to Syracuse.

The stationmaster telegraphed ahead that a Jewish immigrant family would be getting off in Syracuse. The railroad agent in Syracuse contacted the Jewish Immigrant Committee.

The Moss family arrived in Syracuse and was met by Daniel Rosenbloom and Jacob Alderman. They were put up over night in a home called "Tammany Hall," which was used for the temporary housing of newly arrived immigrants. The next day they were settled in a house on Mulberry Street, and Isaac Moss was taken to Frazer and Jones, who manufactured harnesses.

Sitting on the same bench at Frazer and Jones with Moss was Herbert Greenleaf, who became his best friend. Herbert taught him English and helped him to become an American citizen. Greenleaf went on to establish the Greenleaf Funeral Parlors, and Moss became a politician. He was elected Republican committeeman of the Eighteenth Ward, and held that post for many years. He was also appointed a court interpreter, since he could speak several European languages.

Isaac and Sarah Moss brought up a fine family and were respected by Jew and Gentile alike. They said "hard work was a joy—just living in America is enough." They passed away within a year of one another.[10]

The New Adath Yeshurun—Another Synagogue

In 1870, thirty-five young men, seat-holders of Beth Israel (the Grape Street Shul), left to form a new congregation. They named it the New Adath Yeshurun, to distinguish it from the original Adath Jeshurun (popularly called the Rosenbloom Shul), which had seceded from the Temple of Concord in 1864. Another mark of difference was that the original Adath spelled Jeshurun with a "J" in the old German style, while the New Adath decided to transliterate more closely to the English pronunciation of the Hebrew and spelled it with a "Y."

Why the thirty-five young men left Beth Israel to form a new congregation is not clear. It is assumed that because most of the men were "townsmen" from the city of Neustadt in Poland, just across the border from Germany, they were more oriented towards Germany than towards Poland. Their synagogue became known as the Neustadter Shul. During their first years of existence they worshipped in Kaufman's Hall, but in 1872 they obtained a state charter and a year later bought a lot at 75 Mulberry Street on which to build a temple.[11]

The *Syracuse Journal* of June 29, 1878, announced the laying of the cornerstone as follows:

On Monday afternoon, July 1st, at two o'clock, the corner stone of the new brick Synagogue to be erected by the congregation of Adas Jeshurun [Adath Yeshurun] will be laid with appropriate ceremonies. The new church edifice is located on Mulberry Street, between Madison and Harrison Streets. The foundation walls have been completed and the corner stone is to be laid with ceremonies peculiar to the Jewish religion. Riano's brass band will furnish the instrumental music, and the scholars of the Sunday school the vocal. In addition to the corner stone laying exercises, addresses will be delivered by Rev. H. Birkenthal, of the Congregation of Concord, Rev. Jacob Levi, Rev. S. R. Calthrop, Rev. E. W. Mundy and others. The public is cordially invited to attend the ceremonies.

The new edifice was completed in 1878, a modest but adequate house of worship. The entrance to the main sanctuary was up high steps. The lower floor contained classrooms, a *mikvah,* and a small apartment for the *shamas* (sexton). The main sanctuary had balconies for the ladies, which later became useless when the ladies moved down and shared the pews with the men.

For many years the New Adath Yeshurun Synagogue struggled along without a rabbi; they had only a *hazzan* and a *shamas,* the latter also doubling as a teacher of the youth.

Beginning in the 1890's there was agitation among the members to have a rabbi, not so much for the usual duties of an Orthodox rabbi (as guardian and interpreter of Jewish law), but to have a lecturer, a preacher of sermons in English.

The Board of Trustees advertised in 1893 for an Orthodox lecturer and teacher. Joseph Hertz, who was then a student rabbi at the Jewish Theological Seminary in New York, was the candidate selected from the number that applied. An agreement was reached that he would conduct services on the holidays while still a student and, after his graduation, take full charge of the congregation as their rabbi.

After graduating with high honors, Joseph Hertz was installed as rabbi of Temple Adath Yeshurun on June 5, 1894. Accompanying him to his installation were distinguished men of religion—Dr. Joseph Blumenthal, president of the Jewish Theological Seminary of America;

Reverend Dr. H. Pereira Mendes; Reverend Dr. Bernard Drachman; and Max Cohen, editor of the *American Hebrew*.[12]

The *Syracuse Journal* of June 17, 1894, reported on his installation:

The Synagogue was appropriately decorated with smilax, ferns and cut flowers. A large portion of the time was occupied by the reading of the scriptures. The Cantor was Mr. Dlugow of Chicago, and Mr. Blumenthal read the scriptures. Doctor Mendes preached the installation sermon. Doctor Hertz was born in Hungary twenty-two years ago. In 1887, he entered the Jewish Theological Seminary in its first class and, while pursuing an eight year's course there, he entered a school of philosophy in Columbia College, where he received his degree this week. His graduation thesis was: "The Ethical System of James Martineau."

This afternoon a public reception will be held at Freeman's Hall, at which short addresses will be delivered by Reverend Doctors Mendes and Drachman of New York, and Reverend Doctor A. H. Guttman and I. H. Danziger of this city will also speak.

Temple Adath Yeshurun has been fortunate that, from the time of Rabbi Joseph Hertz (1894–1896), many rabbis of distinction have occupied the pulpit. Some left when they were called to larger communities, and practically all distinguished themselves in the cause of Judaism. After Rabbi Hertz came Rabbi Henry Morais, followed by Abraham Hershman, Max Drob, Jacob Kohn, Adolph Coblenz, Jesse Bienenfeld, and the present rabbi, Irwin I. Hyman, who has filled the pulpit of Adath Yeshurun since 1935 with dignity and notable achievements for the congregation and the community at large.

The rabbis of Temple Adath Yeshurun have all, with the exception of Coblenz, been graduates of the Jewish Theological Seminary of America. It was the original aim of that seminary to train rabbis oriented to the ways of life in America, as well as educated in Jewish tradition. In Temple Adath Yeshurun today, the sermons are preached in English at Sabbath and holiday services. The principal prayers are translated and recited in English. The cantor is accompanied by an organ and choir, and the seating is mixed. American Jews have been quick to accept this form of worship because it is not as strict as Orthodoxy nor as liberal as Reform. Adath Yeshurun, the Conservative temple, has the largest membership among the synagogues and temples in Syracuse.

THE REBBE AND HIS HEDER

The titles *rabbi* and *rebbe* both mean "teacher." The former usually refers to one who is a graduate of a yeshiva or a rabbinical college; the latter is a teacher (*melammed*) who may not have a formal education. In the days before Sunday schools, Sabbath schools, and Hebrew day schools there was only a *melammed*, or *rebbe* to teach Jewish children.

Up to and including the first quarter of the present century, it was customary for Jewish boys to be taught by a *rebbe* who came to his home to instruct him in Hebrew, or students would go to the *rebbe's* house, called a *heder*.

Inasmuch as there were no prescribed qualifications or standards for a *rebbe*, any Jew who could read Hebrew (and had little aptitude for earning a living otherwise) could become a *rebbe*. There were exceptions; occasionally there was a *rebbe* who was a learned man, and who had the ability to teach. Such a man was Rebbe Levy of Syracuse.

HARRIS LEVY came to Syracuse from Poland in 1872. His family name was "Heute," but, as with many other immigrants, when he arrived at the immigration office and pronounced his name, the authorities suggested that he choose a more Americanized name. He therefore chose "Levy."

Harris Levy was a student of the Talmud and well informed in many cultural subjects. He learned to speak English readily and could read and write both English and German. All his alumni are in accord that his *heder* was different from most others.

He not only taught his students Hebrew and Jewish history; he also taught them how to live like a Jew. A strict disciplinarian, he required his students to come to his home at 7:30 A.M. to attend morning prayers and to report immediately after regular school and stay until 5:30 P.M. Any student who violated the Sabbath was expelled from his *heder*. He was equally strict with his own family of boys and girls. An example of his rigid adherence to tradition can be seen in the fact that his children's bicycle would stand idle in the back room on the Sabbath for all the boys to see that his family did not violate the holy day.

Among Rebbe Levy's friends was a Catholic priest with whom he visited and discussed the Bible. His students were boys from the leading Jewish families, and many men in Syracuse today who possess a good Jewish background came from Rebbe Levy's *heder*.[13]

LOUIS D. GLAZIER AND REVEREND MAX L. WECHSLER

Two learned men with parallel aims and duties served the Syracuse Jewish community with distinction. Both contributed greatly to instilling Jewish consciousness and Jewish values in the youth of our community.

LOUIS D. GLAZIER came to Syracuse as a young married man well grounded in Jewish learning. He was an authority in Hebrew, Chaldean, and other Semitic languages, a writer of poetry, a translator from the German into Hebrew, and an all-around scholar.

The intellectuals in Syracuse quickly recognized his attributes, and soon he was appointed assistant to Rabbi Guttman in the Temple of Concord. Syacuse University also acknowledged his scholarship, and called on him frequently for translations of ancient languages.

At Concord he acted as secretary of the congregation, collector of dues, and, above all, as teacher of the Bar Mitzvah boys. His Hebrew class was referred to as the "German Hebrew Heder," and the boys referred to him lovingly as "The Professor." [14]

The following appeared in the *Hebrew Standard*, New York, November 15, 1907:

MR. LOUIS GLAZIER

Unassuming in manner and simple in his habits, Mr. Louis Glazier is not only one of the best Hebraists in Western New York but also an excellent English and German scholar. He is, moreover, a poet, his Hebrew verse being beyond cavil. When fifteen years of age, he translated Schiller's *Robbers* into classic Hebrew and was praised for his work by no less an Hebraist than Kalman Schulman, his fellow townsman.

Mr. Glazier was born at Vilna, Russia, in 1859. After studying Hebrew and the Talmud at various schools and famous "Yeshiboth," including that of Walozin, he graduated from the "Rabbiner Schule" and was appointed by the Russian Government to a position in Su-

walki where he had charge of the public school. The same year he
married Helena Davidson, a daughter of a prominent Jewish citizen of
Suwalki.

After conducting the Jewish school for six years, Mr. Glazier became noted as a vigorous writer on the social question of the Jews in
Russia, but drew upon himself the enmity of the government, which
led to his expatriation. He left his family in 1884 and came to America. He studied, under great difficulties, at Cornell College, Ithaca,
and taught at Syracuse until under the guidance of Dr. Adolph Guttman, he became assistant at the temple. Mr. and Mrs. Glazier have a
family of five thoroughly educated daughters. Their hospitality is
proverbial in Syracuse.

Mr. Glazier keeps his hand well in journalism. He is an ardent Republican and a close associate of Senator Horace White.

REVEREND MAX L. WECHSLER arrived in Syracuse in 1887 directly
from his little "shtetl" (village) of Kreitzberg at the age of eighteen, a
bright young man, well versed in Talmudic studies. His first position
was as a teacher at the Hebrew Free School on Orange Street. Later,
he opened a candy store and sold religious articles as well at 707
South State Street.

He then became affiliated with Temple Adath Yeshurun as assistant cantor, reader of the weekly portion of the Torah, and *Baal Tek-
iah* (blower of the *shofar* on the High Holidays) but, above all else,
he was given charge of preparing boys for Bar Mitzvah. This preparation played a far more important part in the religious tradition at
Adath Yeshurun than in the Temple of Concord. At Adath it was un-
thinkable that a boy reaching the age of thirteen should not perform
this ceremony. For a period of almost fifty years, Reverend Wechsler
taught hundreds of boys the Bar Mitzvah lessons consisting of the
prayers when one approaches the Torah, the reading of the Haftorah
(the lesson from the prophets) in the original Hebrew with the proper *niggun* (melody), and of course, the speech that follows, addressed to the congregation but intended for the edification of the parents and relatives.[15]

He was an ardent Zionist and attended a number of national conventions of that organization. When he passed away,[16] Reverend
Wechsler left a partial list of the boys who had been in his Bar Mitzvah classes. Among them are some of the leading business and professional men in our city today. (See list in Appendix B.)

THE JEWISH ORPHAN ASYLUM

By 1870 the Jewish community had four places of worship and a number of charitable and social organizations. Some leaders of the community, mostly members of Temple Concord, felt that there was also a need for a Jewish orphan asylum. An association with that objective was incorporated as follows:

The undersigned, Gates Barnet, Jacob Weisman, Louis Marshall, Morris Thalheimer and Isaac Shevelson desire to associate together for benevolent and charitable purposes. I. The name of the society shall be "The Jewish Orphan Asylum Society." II. The officers shall be Gates Barnet, President, Isaac Shevelson, Vice-President, Morris Thalheimer, Secretary. Trustees: Louis Marshall, Dr. H. Birksen, Seckel Bronner, Marcus Rubin, Aaron Lesser, Sigmund Levy.

Recorded July 10, 1878, Thos. S. Scott, Clerk. Nicholas Peters, Notary. James Noxon, Justice residing in the 5th district of the State of New York

After the Syracuse Jewish Orphan Asylum was incorporated, word reached Syracuse that Rochester and Buffalo, cities immediately west of Syracuse with growing Jewish Communities, were also about to take steps to establish orphan asylums.

The Jewish leaders of Syracuse decided to delay their project until they could learn more about the plans of the other cities. Arrangements were made for a meeting of representatives from each of the three communities. This is the first record of a regional Jewish assembly of Western New York cities.

In February, 1879, the meeting of representatives from the three cities took place in Rochester in the vestry room of Temple B'rith Kodesh for the purpose of discussing and, if possible, consolidating the aims of the three different societies into one organization.[17]

Syracuse was represented by Isaac Danziger and Louis Marshall.[18] All present had the same objective in mind, and the meeting was harmonious. It was decided that a combined orphan asylum, to be known as "The Jewish Orphan Asylum of Western New York," to fulfill the needs of the three communities was feasible and desirable. However, before this could be incorporated, a number of questions had to be resolved. First, where should the establishment be located? Second, how were the necessary funds to be raised, and how much should each city contribute? These and other problems were left for a later time.

At a subsequent meeting and at the invitation of the Syracuse contingent, it was agreed that a grand fair and bazaar should be held in Syracuse during the week of November 23, 1880, in order to raise the necessary funds and to get the organization under way. All three cities were to participate and to arrange for booths filled with merchandise to be sold. It was suggested that the city which raised the most money would be considered as the first choice for the location of the orphanage.

This was by far the finest effort in fund raising ever attempted in Syracuse. The interest generated in the community was intense. Although the project was organized by the members of the Temple of Concord, every individual Jew and Jewish organization was expected to participate and to patronize the fair.

The bazaar was well publicized, and interest was aroused in the entire community of both Jews and Gentiles. The local press featured it prominently. A reporter of the *Syracuse Courier* described in great detail the preparations and the daily events at the fair.

GRAND JEWISH FAIR

THREE CITIES TO UNITE IN THE FINEST
FESTIVAL EVER HELD IN SYRACUSE
SHALL SYRACUSE HAVE A JEWISH ORPHAN ASYLUM?

During the week, commencing November 22nd and closing the 29th, a grand Jewish fair and festival will be held in Shakespeare Hall, in this city, for the purpose of raising funds to build a Jewish Orphan Asylum. . . .

. . . It is expected that inasmuch as the Hebrews of our city have at all times and occasions been ready and liberal in their responses to all charities, irrespective of purpose, creed or sect, they will, through their subscription committee, consisting of Messrs. Gates Barnet, I. H. Danziger, August Falker, Louis Marshall and Aaron Lesser, meet with a liberal response from all whom they may visit, and receive such encouragement at the fair as will be commensurate with the nobility of the undertaking and the enterprise of the instigators, and which will insure beyond question the erection in our own city of the Jewish Orphan for Central and Western New York.[19]

For the first time the Jewish community invited others to join with them in raising funds for a charitable institution. Following the event, the *Courier* gave a glowing account of the wonders of the occasion. We are including the full text of the description of the fair, first because of the style of reporting, and second, because it mentions the names of the men and women who participated and undoubtedly included the leading Jews in the city of that period.

THE JEWISH FAIR
SHAKESPEARE HALL TRANSFORMED INTO A BOWER OF BEWILDERING AND DAZZLING BEAUTY

A MAGNIFICIENT DISPLAY OF RICH, RARE, CURIOUS, AND USEFUL ARTICLES— BEAUTIFUL MAIDENS SERVING AS GANYMEDES— THE CHIEF ATTRACTION OF THE FAIR

The visitor at Shakespeare Hall last evening could not but be amazed at the grand transformation scene that had taken place since the hall was last thrown open to the public. Under the direction of our Jewish citizens the hall has been transformed into a veritable bower of beauty. When it was determined to hold the Jewish fair in Syracuse, the local committee resolved that nothing which could contribute to its success should be left undone. The result of the superior taste and artistic skill of the committee is evidenced in the unique and original decorations of the Hall which are on a scale of elegance and magnificence never before attempted in Syracuse. Not even the decorations which served to add to the attractions of the original grand charity ball [which were the talk of the town for years afterwards] are to be compared with them. To attempt to describe them would be like an attempt to paint the lily or gild the sunshine. The fair was opened to the public last night and as our citizens poured into the hall the exclamations of wonderment and delight were universal and unequivocal. The ceiling of the hall has been entirely covered, or transformed into a canopy of brilliant colored hues, giving the hall the appearance of a colossal tent. From the center depends a brilliant crystal chandelier, and the light which is reflected upon the contents of the gorgeous booths and the floor below makes the scene a brilliant and a dazzling one.

At eight o'clock last evening the formal opening of the fair took place.

Mr. Gates Barnet introduced His Honor Mayor Hendricks, who stated that this assemblage has gathered together in the cause of charity. The fair which was opened tonight would have the encouragement of our citizens, and would be a grand success. Mayor Hendricks extended a cordial welcome to the citizens of other cities who were present, and introduced the Hon. Irving G. Vann.

Mr. Vann gave a history of the formation of the orphan asylum, and stated that the projected asylum would welcome all creeds within its walls, and extend its care to citizens of all nationalities. The Hebrew residents of Syracuse, Rochester and Buffalo had united their efforts to increase the fund for building an orphan asylum. All friendly rivalry for the location of the asylum had been laid aside for the present, and the only strife was a contest to see which city could raise most money for the building. The citizens of Syracuse and her merchants had responded nobly, and the citizens of Rochester and Buffalo had been busy for months in preparing elegant articles for the fair. The result is the magnificent booths which are seen here tonight. The Hebrews of Syracuse have never appealed to the general public of Syracuse for charity. They do so now for the first time. They ask you to aid them in building a home for the friendless and the orphans. Let us all see to it that the fair is successful. In the future Rochester and Buffalo will be on our track and will strive to have the building located elsewhere than Syracuse. The city that does the best will secure the location of the building. Every citizen of Syracuse should be interested in securing the Asylum for Syracuse. It can be secured for our city despite the superior numbers in Rochester and Buffalo if our citizens will but do their duty.

Mayor Hendricks then announced that the Jewish Fair was formally opened to the public.

To attempt a detailed description of the fair and the thousand and one contents of the various booths would be a work beyond the power of the reporter. It can safely be said that the fair far exceeds any ever gotten up in Syracuse and may be described as a brilliant bazaar containing articles of the most artistic design and rare texture. The like of which have never been gotten together under one roof in Syracuse, on any occasion for under any auspices. Around the sides of the spacious hall are arranged the various booths, which are presided over by beautiful maidens. On entering the hall the reporter's attention was first called to the

GYPSY TENT

which is presided over by Miss Fannie Falck of Buffalo and Mr. Ben Marshall [brother of Louis Marshall] of Syracuse. This tent represents the future—The fair Sybil, Miss Falck, attired in the garb of a prophetess will for a few pence, cast the horoscope of the future for the visitors and unveil the hidden mysteries, that beset his path. Into the boiling cauldron she pours her mysterious compounds, and thence, evokes the toil and trouble, joy and happiness of the person who desires to know his fate. Next to this tent is the

AMERICAN TENT

and representing "The Present" and presided over by ladies and gentlemen from Buffalo. The following ladies and gentlemen have charge of this booth: Mrs. Leopold Marcus, Mrs. Solomon Rosenau, Miss Pauline Falk, Miss Addie Cohn, Miss Carrie Hershel, Miss Tillie Falck, Miss Becky Leman, Miss Ada Brown, Miss Denia Warner, Miss Fanny Levyn. Mr. Max Schwartz is supervisor of the booth, and the representatives present from Buffalo, are Rev. Dr. S. Falk, Siegmund Levyn, General Treasurer of the Orphan Asylum Association, Mr. Leopold Warner and Mr. H. Oppenheimer.

The Buffalo booth is a magnificient emporium filled with rare and costly articles. The display of embroideries is novel and elegant, and in fact every article in the booth, both ornamental and useful, is of the most elaborate and elegant description.

Buffalo has sent her fairest maidens to preside as the genii of this palace of beauty. Next to this booth is the

ART GALLERY AND POST OFFICE

both contained in an old log cabin, representing the past. The mysteries of the art gallery we are not permitted to reveal, but one can only say that paintings and statuary of the most unique and novel design are to be seen for a mere pittance. The gallery is in charge of citizens of Buffalo. Mr. Nat Rosenau presides, assisted by Miss Carrie Henschel. The post office is under the charge of Miss Minnie Schwartz and Miss Addie Cohn. Miss Fannie Levyn is the letter carrier, and we can only say that if Uncle Sam was served by such accomplished and fair attendants, the business of the post office department would increase in a marvelous degree. The citizens of Buffalo may well feel proud of the attractive and beautiful display made by their representatives.

THE SYRACUSE BOOTH

next attracts our attention. It is the largest in the hall and is as attractive as the art of intelligent and artistic attendants could possibly make it. It is filled to repletion with useful, rare, rich, artistic and costly articles. It is divided into departments representing a country store, cigar stand, candy table and the wheel of fortune. This booth is in charge of the United Orthodox society, President, Mrs. E. S. Silverstein; Vice-President, Mrs. H. Harrison. It is presided over by twenty ladies comprising Mrs. S. Shimberg, Hattie Wolf, Sophie Falk, Mrs. Shimberg, Kate Jalonack, Mrs. A. Abrahams, Susie Goldsmith, Mrs. L. Freeman, Fannie Lesser, Mrs. H. Halonack, Mrs. Kapelowich, Clara Henocksburg, Carrie Shevelson, Ray Labeskinsky, Rebecca Harrison, Kate Isaacs and Ida Goldman. It would be impossible to describe in detail the many useful and ornamental articles in this booth. Here may be seen magnificent sets of furniture, embroideries, and, in fine a bewildering array of elegant articles, a baby in a beautiful crib is one of the attractions of the booth. The ladies in attendance upon this booth will leave nothing undone to make the visit of our citizens agreeable and profitable.

Next to the Syracuse booth is the

ICE CREAM PARLOR

which is presided over by fair maidens and the delicious cream will prove doubly enjoyable when served up by their dainty hands.

Next to this booth is the

ORIENTAL BOOTH

which is presided over by Syracusans. Mrs. J. H. Danziger is president, Mrs. Jacob Hammel, vice-president, Mrs. S. H. Zenner, treasurer, and Miss Hannah Lowenthal, secretary. These ladies are assisted by Mrs. L. Leiter, Mrs. M. Rosenbloom, Mrs. Gates Barnett, Mrs. D. J. Hamburger, Mrs. H. Leiter, Mrs. Gates Thalheimer, Miss Frank Henocksburg, Miss M. Goldstein, Miss Bessie Lowe, Miss Mollie Bronner, and Miss Sarah Bamburger. It needs but a glance at this magnificent booth to see that Syracuse was determined that her sister cities of Rochester and Buffalo should not outrival or outdo our own citizens in their magnificent display. This booth indeed beggars description. It is magnificent beyond anticipation, and the articles it contains can only be appreciated by being seen. We particularly noticed a superb black satin apron, beautifully ornamented with paintings of flowers, the donation of Mrs. S. H. Zenner. The display of rare furniture, superb embroideries, costly silver ware and a thousand and one elegant articles, will prove an attraction to our citizens which cannot be resisted. We must not forget a $200 government bond which is to be given away to the person who holds the lucky number. The last booth is the

FLOUR CITY BOOTH

under the charge of citizens of Rochester. It is a marvel of elegance and beauty and is presided over by representative citizens of Rochester.

The Rochester booth is at once one of the most elegant and attractive in the fair. It contains elegant sets of furniture, superb embroideries, rare and costly articles of virtue and many articles of elaborate and unique design which are beyond the power of description. Rochester's most beautiful and attractive young ladies are in attendance, and our citizens will receive a cordial welcome at their hands. Beyond the Rochester booth is the

REFRESHMENT STAND

where refreshments may be obtained at all hours. This department is presided over by Mrs. William Henocksburg, Mrs. Jacob Hammill, Mrs. J. Marshall, Miss Julia Goldstein, Mrs. S. Bronner, Miss Phebe Hirsch, Miss Sarah Bamburger and Miss Mary Mayer.

THE FLORAL BOOTH

which is located in front of the stage, is presided over by Miss Lauferty, of Fort Wayne, Ind., Miss Mollie Bronner, of Syracuse, and Miss Dora Stern of Toledo, Ohio.

The stage has been transformed into a bower of flowers and rare exotics and is completely hidden by ferns and living flowers of the choices varieties.

We cannot attempt an adequate description of

THE MANY ATTRACTIONS OF THIS FAIR

It is a fact conceded by all, that our Jewish citizens are among the most enterprising and energetic in the community. Whatever they undertake, they accomplish, and always with distinguished success. It is not to be wondered therefore, that their fair, to raise funds for building an orphan asylum, is a success in every respect. The cities of Rochester and Buffalo have united with our own citizens and the result is a bazaar which exceeds in elegance and magnificence anything of the kind every before attempted in our city. It has been the aim of the committees having the fair in charge to place on sale articles of a useful as well as an ornamental nature, and they have well succeeded in a manner that is simply surprising. There are no trashy articles in the fair and our citizens may rely upon seeing such a display, as taken for all in all, they have never seen before at a fair. As a verification of this statement we need only state that Messrs. Leiter Brothers have donated a superb Weber upright piano which is to be put up at lottery, with the chances at one dollar each. The piano is worth a thousand dollars and whoever draws it will be lucky indeed. There are sets of furniture to be drawn, which are valued at hundreds of dollars, and innumerable articles possessing a solid value.

After reading the foregoing description of the booths and the portrayal of the beautiful maidens in the *Syracuse Courier* of November 23, 1880, it is unnecessary to speculate—the fair was exceedingly successful, and the Western New York Jewish Orphan Asylum was now an assured fact. It was not, however, until 1883 that, after many meetings and much debate, Rochester, because of its central location, was chosen as the place in which to establish the orphan asylum.

Looking over the names of the organizers, it can be seen that this was predominantly a German Jewish undertaking, and it soon became the focus of interest of the Reform movement in each of the three cities. It was considered a prestige organization and never lacked candidates for the board or willing hands for raising funds.

In the Syracuse branch of the organization there was much controversy about the choice of a director to serve on the board. The office was eagerly sought because, as a director, one could travel to Rochester for meetings, be able to socialize with the leading German Jews from other cities, and come back to Syracuse to talk about it.

The Western New York Orphan Asylum in Operation

The children in the new orphanage received a fine upbringing and as good an education as could be had in any institution. They attended the public schools nearby, while at the home there were classes in drama, art, and French. Children with ability were sent to

Hochstein's School of Music, and to Temple B'rith Kodesh for religious instruction.

For twenty-five years the orphan asylum was located on St. Paul Street. The organization then felt it was necessary to erect a new building, which was constructed at a cost of more than $100,000 on four acres of ground on Genesee Street. The Jews of Western New York pointed with pride to this well-organized, beautiful, and efficiently managed institution. In 1925 the orphanage cared for twenty-one children from Buffalo, six from Rochester, and three from Syracuse. There were never more than thirty-five or forty children at any one time in this institution.

Earlier, in 1914, an Orthodox Jewish Orphan Asylum had been established in Rochester, and the number of children in the Reform Orphan Asylum began to dwindle. The movement to send orphaned children and children from broken homes to foster homes was soon recognized as a better way to care for children than in institutions. In 1928, after a history of fifty years, The Western New York Orphan Asylum closed its doors.[20]

ANGLO-JEWISH PERIODICALS

We are indebted to the Anglo-Jewish and German-Jewish periodicals of the early days for much of the history of Jews in America. To disseminate the news and to comment thereon appears to have been considered a duty to the Jewish people. The two earliest weekly papers that found their way to the smallest communities where Jews had settled were founded by rabbis.

The Reverend Isaac Leeser founded *The Occident and American Jewish Advocate* in Philadelphia in 1843. The Reverend Leeser, author, translator and ardent defender of Judaism, started a publishing company in order to publish his own works, of which he wrote a large number. Rabbi Isaac Mayer Wise founded *The Israelite* in 1854 in Cincinnati, Ohio. His great aim was to advocate Reform Judaism.

There were other Anglo-Jewish periodicals in the early days, such as *The Asmonean,* 1849–58, and *The Jewish Messenger,* 1857–1903. By means of these periodicals, much of the news from the smaller and inland Jewish communities was spread to larger cities.

In order to secure subscribers in the smaller communities, the publisher would send agents to what in the big cities was called "the country." When an agent arrived in a community he would go to the temple or synagogue where he would find the more literate and learned members of the congregation, and there he would inquire for the news of the day. He would send back to his paper the subscriptions he had secured and also report on the Jewish congregations, societies, and whatever else of interest he thought worthy of reporting.

While he was in the community he would select someone whom he believed to be capable as a reporter for his paper and would give him a free subscription for his labors. Many of the "letters to the editor" and other reports of the Syracuse Jewish community were discovered (thanks to the American Jewish Archives in Cincinnati) in these periodicals, often signed Emeth or Justice, or some other pseudonym.

At different times there were Anglo-Jewish papers published in Syracuse. *The Jewish Advocate,* 1870, published by Schwartz Brothers; *The Hebrew Globe,* 1894, by Aaron Levy; *The Syracuse News,* published by Abe Levy; *The Hebrew Times,* 1936, by Louis Gassell; and *The Jewish Chronicle* by the Kay Brothers as late as 1947–48.

The first in Syracuse, and among the very early Jewish publications in America was a periodical, *Rebecka,* published in Syracuse, printed in German in 1864, by Dr. Ferdinand Leopold Sarner and Jacob Levi. Dr. Sarner was a rabbi who had occupied the pulpit of B'rith Kodesh in Rochester, New York in 1859 and 1860. When he left he was highly recommended by the congregation and the Board of Trustees. What he did from 1860 to 1863 is not known; it is surmised that he traveled around the country, lecturing. He could speak five languages.

In 1863 he enlisted as the first Jewish chaplain in the Union Army, was assigned to the 54th Infantry, and had an active combat career. He was wounded at Gettysburg; the wound did not heal readily, and he was ultimately discharged for physical disability on October 3, 1864.[21]

What induced Dr. Sarner to come to Syracuse and venture with Jacob Levi into the editing of the German-Jewish newspaper, *Rebecka,* is not known. The first issue appeared on November 9, 1864, with the following statement addressed to the public:

To the public

Office of "Rebecka", 88 Jefferson St.
Syracuse, N.Y.
November 9, 1864

Dear Ladies and Gentlemen!

While we, the undersigned redactors and editors of the Jewish newspaper "Rebecka", which is impartial with respect to political opinions and which you will receive today for the first time, have reason to think that we remove with it a requirement of the American-Israelite world, we greet you in the name of the all-merciful God, father of all human beings, and ask you to support our daring enterprise under the present circumstance. Our "Rebecka", which appears once a week, on Tuesday, 5 p.m., in Syracuse, N.Y., is, as already mentioned above, an objective organ of all Jewish interests and therefore it has nothing to do with any political organisation or with any articles of injuring character. Because of the fact that our reporters work in most of the European and non-European capitals we are able to give you every week the newest information and the most interesting. We accept correpondences and advertisements in Hebrew, English, French, Italian, Spanish, and Dutch. Price for the annual: $3.00, for 6 months: $1.50. The circumstances under which we begin this serious work may excuse us when we kindly ask our dear friends and subscribers to submit the first 6-month subscription, $1.50, soon after having received the first newspaper to the President of your congregation who, we do hope so, will be so kind as to send the collected amount of money to us either by express or by registered letter. If the President of the congregation should as the servant of the synagogue or school to collect the amount for 6 months, $1.50, we would ask the servant to keep 5% for his work. Because we, the undersigned redactors and editors of the Jewish newspaper "Rebecka", do not intend to cheat anybody out of the advance payment amounting to $1.50, we guarantee to send you 24 issues of our newspaper regularly. Today you only receive a specimen copy. We ask you for clearly written names, streets, housenumbers or mail boxes, places, etc. Please enclose with your advertisements, for which we kindly ask you, the approximate amount. The surplus we shall return to you or credit for you. Please, distribute our present specimen number.

The clergy of all denominations only pay half the price, $1.50 per year. Now begin your journey, dear "Rebecka"! Bring kind and hearty greetings to our friends, teach and edify our readers, ask our critics for indulgence, and say "many thanks" to those who pay promptly and do not blush before the faultfinders.

Yours faithfully,

Dr. Sarner & Levi, redactors and editors

Another article in the same edition contained the local news as follows:

Local news

The *ca.* 350 Israelites living in this town form four separate congregations. The [Keneseth Sholom Temple of Concord] congregation which is very close to Reform Judaism is a true example not only because of its very dignified, solemn and soul-refreshing service with organ and an excellent choir but also because of peace and good administration. The President, Mr. Joseph Falker, a high esteemed person who is very active in the reform movement, is supported by the Vice-President Mr. S. Lewenthal and the other Trustees: Henry Eckstein, S. Manheimer, J. H. Bronner, sen., Jacob Garson, E. Rosenthal, F. Hirsch, and Israel Jacobson. The school which is headed by Jacob Levi, the minister of the congregation, is in a flourishing situation and we can say—the author of this article had the opportunity to convince himself—that it belongs among the best schools in America. The Rabbi, Dr. Deutsch, who is responsible for the reformed character of the congregation, is very much recognized here, and all regret that he is moving to Baltimore. And we mention the beloved old Mr. Ettinger, too, who has already worked for ten years in the congregation, and we do hope that he will remain healthy. In the next edition of "Rebecka" we shall speak about the other three congregations, which we heartily greet. Unfortunately we cannot mention them here because of lack of space.

The rest of the paper was filled with articles more literary than religious, as well as part of a play that Dr. Sarner had written previously.

The second issue did not appear until December 20, 1864, with an apology for the delay, explaining that Dr. Sarner had been on the road visiting different cities seeking subscribers, advertisers, and news. In this second issue Jacob Stolz, the custom shoemaker, placed the following advertisement which, translated from German, reads as follows:

The Shoe and Boot Factory of Jakob Stolz
is at the corner of Grape and Cedar Street

If you are ill it is your own fault; for where can you get a pair of warm and well fitted shoes or boots? The shoes or boots you buy in the store become damp soon and this causes toothache, headache and other troubles. You do not have to pay just for looking. Come to my shop on the corner of Grape and Cedar Street and decide yourself what pair of shoes or boots I shall make for you—for a cheap price.

Jacob Stolz, manufacturer of all kinds of boots, shoes, etc., at the corner of Grape and Cedar Street. Professor Alberto Meyro will not leave Syracuse before having asked Jacob Stolz, at the corner of Grape and Cedar Street, Syracuse, N.Y., to make a pair of shoes for him.

Under local news, this notice appeared:

The report about Adath Jeshurun congregation which could not be put in this number, will appear in the next "Rebecka."

Dr. Sarner, redactor of Rebecka

There never was a next number, since *Rebecka* went out of business with this, its second issue. It is unfortunate, in modern times, that people have not saved copies of these periodicals. The Syracuse Anglo-Jewish papers would have been a fountain of important Historical Jewish events if we had the copies in front of us today. Advertisements in the local daily newspapers and through the Jewish Community Center bulletins did not unearth a single copy.

CHAPTER V

The Second Generation

In the 1870's and 1880's the sons and daughters of the pioneers began to take their place as leaders of the Jewish community. In these two decades the city of Syracuse made rapid strides in industry and education. At the same time, it more than doubled its population from 43,-000 in 1870 to 88,000 in 1890.[1] While we do not have exact figures on the Jewish population, it is estimated that in this period it grew from 2,000 to 4,000.

The first generation of the Jewish community laid a solid foundation; they built four places of worship, acquired two cemeteries, and organized a number of charitable organizations. The second generation was now ready to take an active part in the Establishment. They also organized literary and social clubs of their own. Some of the young Jewish men entered into their fathers' businesses. The Rosenbloom sons took their father's small shoe store and built it into a large department store, with branches in the surrounding cities. Young Gates Thalheimer went from his father's grocery store into the wholesale grocery business. The Oberdorfers purchased a going foundry establishment. There were some young men and women who went into the professions. Louis Marshall and Joseph Bondy became the first well-known Jewish lawyers in Syracuse, and Henry Elsner and Nathan Jacobson the first prominent Jewish doctors.

Following are biographical sketches of a few of the outstanding leaders of the second generation.

LOUIS MARSHALL

Many talented and ambitious young Jewish men left Syracuse looking for greener pastures, some going as far away as the Pacific coast, Texas, Chicago, Kansas City, Philadelphia, New York, and other cities. Quite a number were very successful; some became multimillionaires, some owned chains of theaters, others a chain of moving picture houses. But not one who went away brought more credit, honor, and distinction to his native city than did Louis Marshall, the gifted son of immigrant parents who settled in Syracuse in 1849.

Louis Marshall, son of Zilli and Jacob Marshall, was born in Syracuse on December 12, 1856. As a growing boy, he was healthy and sturdy. His mother was the guiding influence in his youth. Zilli Marshall was an intelligent person, and among the women of those days she was considered well educated. She spoke to the children in German, although they would answer her in English. She often read to Louis from Schiller, Scott, Hugo, and other literature that was popular in the mid-1800's.

Louis liked to play outdoors, and his favorite game was baseball. However, he found time to help his mother, but in a most unusual manner. She was a lover of poetry, particularly of Schiller's works. Often, as she busied herself with household tasks, her young son trailed her from room to room, reading aloud from Schiller's poems and gradually learning them so well that he was able to recite them by heart. This was good training, for he developed a retentive mind which later was one of his strongest assets in his legal practice.

As early as at the age of eight, he would go down to his father's place of business and help him with his bookkeeping. In his boyhood, debating clubs were in vogue. In 1868, as a precocious youngster of twelve, he joined one of these clubs, and was considered a leading debater. People wondered at his thorough knowledge of early American history, and in debates he would always be the passionate defender of the Constitution.

As a youth he resolved to become a lawyer. After high school he studied law for two years in the office of Nathaniel B. Smith, then

went to Columbia Law School in New York, where he completed a
two-year course in one year.

On his return to Syracuse in 1878, he entered the firm of Ruger,
Jenny, Brook, and French and later became a partner. He did most of
the case work for the firm, and once defended a Catholic priest before
a religious tribunal. In this case, he was called upon to argue orally in
Latin. Recognized as one of the leading attorneys in Syracuse, he was
often called upon to try cases before the New York State Court of Appeals.

In 1890, at the age of thirty-four, Louis Marshall was appointed by
Governor David H. Hill to a special commission to revise the judiciary
articles of the state constitution. He worked hard at the task, and
many of his recommendations were subsequently adopted.

Four years later he was elected to the state constitutional convention, and played an important part in the deliberations of that body.
Through activities in the constitutional convention he became acquainted with some of the leading members of his profession, particularly Elihu Root and Charles Evans Hughes.

He was interested in conservation of our forests, and urged the
state to dispose of the Onondaga Salt Reservation and to use the proceeds to acquire land in the Adirondacks.

All this while, he continued to live in the home of his parents at 22
Cedar Street. His parents were Orthodox, and he loved the many ritual observances, especially the ushering in of the Sabbath, the blessing of the candles, the *Kiddush,* and the special Friday evening din-
ners. So long as his mother and father were alive, Louis never missed
the annual Passover *seder* at home, even when he lived away from the
city.

His reputation as a gifted attorney spread rapidly while he was
still young. As early as 1880 he was called to New York to appear before the New York Court of Appeals, in a case of a contested legacy in
which a Mr. Sampson Simpson left $50,000 in trust for a nephew, and
at his death the trust fund was to go to Jerusalem. Louis did not win
this case, but the incident indicates that anything Jewish was not foreign to him, and that he would give freely of his time and energy for
a Jewish cause.

In 1894 he received a call from Samuel Untermeyer, who had been
a fellow student at Columbia Law School, to come to New York City

and join the law firm of Guggenheimer and Untermeyer. Thereafter, the focal point of his activities became New York City. He was accepted at once into the leading circles of his profession there and moved socially among the leaders of the German Jewish group.

Due to the earlier arrival of this group in America, and because of its leadership in commercial and banking affairs, the large population of Jews in New York City—particularly the Russian and Polish immigrants on the East Side—looked to the German-Americans for protection and leadership. Among the leaders were Jacob H. Schiff, a powerful financier; Adolph S. Ochs of the *New York Times;* Oscar S. Straus and his brothers, Isidor and Nathan; Joseph Seligman; and the Guggenheims.

The move to New York helped him to establish his political affiliations. Thereafter he consistently was a Republican. He had no political ambitions for himself; only one public office ever attracted him. In 1911 he was seriously mentioned for a possible appointment to the bench of the United States Supreme Court. However, he was passed over and never sought political office or appointment again.

In New York, Marshall became a member of the Temple Emanu-El and subsequently became its president. It was during his administration that Stephen S. Wise, then a young rabbi in Portland, Oregon, was called to the rabbinate of Temple Emanu-El, considered the most influential congregation in America. Unhappily, Louis Marshall and Rabbi Wise could not agree on the freedom of the pulpit. Wise insisted upon absolute freedom of utterance, whereas Marshall believed that on controversial matters only the trustees should speak for the congregation.

The differences between the trustees and the rabbi came out into the open through statements made by Rabbi Wise to the press. This Temple Emanu-El could not tolerate, so the rabbi and the temple parted company. The incident left a strained feeling between Marshall and Wise. Although they worked together for many Jewish causes, their friendship was rather formal.

Marshall purchased some land around lower Saranac Lake in the Adirondacks and built a home. Throughout the rest of his life he spent as much of the summer season as possible in "Knollwood."

Louis Marshall began taking greater and greater interest in civic affairs in New York City, especially in the problems of the masses of

Jewish working people on the East Side—their working conditions and their education in Americanism and Judaism.

He watched over the interests of all minorities, especially the Jews. He was the founder and leader of many organizations—local, national, and worldwide—for the relief and protection of Jews. He was later characterized as the "Attorney-General for the Jewish race" and the "watchdog of the household of Israel."

We can mention only a partial list of the projects and institutions in which he labored during his lifetime. He favored the abrogation of the Russia-United States Treaty of 1832, for the reason that Russia discriminated against Jews by refusing to issue visas to them, as they did for other American-Russian citizens. He carried the cause to the President of the United States and to the United States Senate until the treaty was abrogated.

He took a great interest in the Educational Alliance on East Broadway and Jefferson Street on the lower East Side of New York, and was a member of its board of trustees from three years after it was organized until his death. With the help of Jacob H. Schiff, he re-established the Jewish Theological Seminary of America and placed Dr. Solomon Schechter at its head.

He was active in the formation of the Federation of Jewish Philanthropies of New York. In 1905, together with others, he took the leadership in establishing the American Jewish Committee.

He was a consulting counsel in behalf of Leo Frank, a Jew who was convicted on a trumped-up charge of murder in Atlanta, Georgia, and he carried the case to the Supreme Court of the United States. The prisoner was later lynched with the connivance of the keepers of the prison.

He felt keenly the plight of the Negro in America, and took an active part in helping them, and was a director of the National Association for the Advancement of Colored People.

Marshall secured a public retraction and an apology from Henry Ford, in terms dictated by him, on the fraudulent "Protocols of the Elders of Zion," which Ford publicized through the columns of the *Dearborn Independent*.

During World War I, he helped to form the American Jewish Relief Committee, later called the Joint Distribution Committee. At the close of the war he spent four months in Paris presenting the Jewish viewpoint before the statesmen devising the peace treaty. He labored to secure the inclusion in the treaties of the international guarantees of the fair treatment of minorities.

Though not an active Zionist, he was interested in Israel as a refuge for the oppressed Jews in Russia, Poland, Hungary, and Romania. He helped to support the Hebrew University in Jerusalem, and invested in the Palestine Economic Corporation.

After he attained national and worldwide fame, Louis Marshall never forgot the city where he was born. As long as his parents were alive, he came back to Syracuse several times a year to see them and to visit with relatives and friends. After his parents passed away he still had connections that brought him to Syracuse—he was a trustee of Syracuse University, a founder of the New York State College of Forestry, and chairman of its Board of Trustees.

His son once remarked that his father, as a member of one of the busiest law firms in New York, "could not possibly have the time to see all the people who called for him, but when someone from Syracuse came to his office, he would see him at once and let others wait."

His last effort in behalf of the Jewish people was to secure the interest of the non-Zionists in Palestine, by helping to revise the Jewish Agency so that non-Zionists would be included as well as Zionists. It was during these sessions in Zurich, Switzerland, that he became ill and passed away on September 11, 1929.

Louis Marshall received many tributes toward the end of his career, at his death, and on the anniversaries of his death for many years after. On Marshall's seventieth birthday Elihu Root had this to say: [2]

His whole distinguished career has been a contribution to the administration of justice and the example of his life may be usefully insisted upon as an evidence that, by the possession of such qualities as his, great success may be attained.

On his death, Governor Herbert H. Lehman, speaking in Syracuse, said of him:

I know no one who was more generous with his time and money, more self-effacing and industrious in communal affairs. Even after he moved to New York and became a great lawyer Louis Marshall had an unending devotion to Syracuse where he got his start. He never ceased his deep regard and loyalty for his friends here and for this city.

I was a close and loving friend of our friend, Louis Marshall, and worked in close contact with him, especially at the outbreak of the war in 1914 when the American Jewish Joint Distribution Committee was formed to aid those abroad.

One of its great by-products was Jewish unity for there are always two things which will draw together conflicting elements—relief of misery and suffering and the combatting of prejudice and misunderstanding.

Louis Marshall was head of that committee at the time of his death. I remember his move at the close of the war to turn over $5,000,000 of its funds to Herbert Hoover for war relief in Russia and the money was spent there without regard to race.[3]

In 1934, on the fifth anniversary of Marshall's death, Felix M. Warburg gave this tribute to his memory:

Nobody has filled his place and probably never will. Others may try to emulate his noble intentions and have shown courage in attacking problems, but decisive as his views were at all times, even he was willing to consult his colleagues and to abide by their decisions most loyally, so that he became the voice of the combined wisdom of his friends in all walks of life. Through that he reflected more than anybody else the wishes of the people.[4]

And so Louis Marshall, born and brought up in the period of the early settlers of the Syracuse Jewish community, was an outstanding servant to mankind in general, and to world Jewry in particular.[5]

COLONEL JOSEPH BONDY. Joseph Bondy, the son of Gabriel and Miriam Bondy, was born on September 13, 1862. He attended Syracuse schools and graduated from the high school on West Genesee Street with high honors and as secretary of his class. Throughout his life he retained fond memories of this school, and later was instrumental in forming an alumni association, of which he was the first president.

Working his way through Columbia University, he graduated from the liberal arts college and law school in the same year. On his return to Syracuse he clerked in the law office of Costello and Ides for a year; then, together with Frank Hopkins, opened a law office under the name of Hopkins and Bondy.

As mentioned earlier, one of his first court cases attracted public attention, that of Willie Provolsky, a young Jewish match peddler, who was arrested for theft in the town of Jamesville just outside Syracuse. A Jew caught stealing was taken by other Jews as an offense against the entire community. Joe Bondy undertook the defense. After much sparring between the prosecution and defense, Bondy proved that it all was a frame-up, tinged with anti-Semitism. The young match peddler was declared innocent and set free.[6]

In addition to his career as a lawyer, Joseph Bondy had many other interests. A lifelong Republican, he was elected to the New York State Assembly in 1895, and was twice re-elected. While in the Assembly, he introduced some important legislation and in his last term was chairman of several important committees.

He enlisted in the Spanish-American War but did not see active service, being involved in his duties in the state legislature.

During the First World War, Bondy enlisted in the United States Army as a major in the Quartermaster Corps and was stationed in Washington, D.C. He subsequently was named a colonel in the Auxiliary Reserve, and served as director of Citizens Training and instructor in Constitutional History in the Citizens Military Training Corps.

He received renewals of his colonel's commission in 1929 and 1934. At the time of his second renewal he was issued a certificate by President Franklin D. Roosevelt citing his patriotism, valor, fidelity, and ability in the service of his country.

Over the years Colonel Bondy became widely known as an authority on constitutional law and was frequently consulted by members of the faculty of Syracuse University, who declared that his collection of papers on the Constitution was one of the best in the country. His interest in gathering a library of this consequence began in 1921, when he was appointed director of citizens training and teacher of constitutional history at military training camps. In a short time he had become one of the outstanding collectors of constitutional history and had acquired a library which consisted of more than five thousand volumes. More than two thousand of these had been published before 1800, and many were so rare as to be hardly attainable at any price.

Before his death, Bondy gave some of his books to Syracuse University and the Temple of Concord. The remainder were auctioned to book collectors in New York City after his death. It is reported that

Father Charles E. Coughlin, of Royal Oak, Michigan, purchased a considerable portion of Bondy's valuable collection.

Colonel Bondy was successful both as an attorney and as a business man. At one time, together with a partner, William Rubin, he owned considerable property, much of which was lost during the crash of 1929. Although he did not advocate organized charity, he made independent contributions wherever and whenever he saw the need. One such philanthropic deed was his offer of a portion of his estate at Star Lake, New York, to the United States government for use as a home for convalescent soldiers.

Few people now remember that Colonel Bondy was one of the first Jews to champion Zionism in Syracuse, at a time when that cause was scorned by many German Jews. He was frequently in disfavor because of his views, but he remained an independent thinker. He possessed great initiative and strength of purpose, and the term "rugged individualist" is very appropriate to the career of Colonel Joseph Bondy. He died on December 21, 1945, at the age of eighty-two, and is buried in Arlington National Cemetery.[7]

Frances Elias Bondy, wife of Colonel Bondy, was born in Los Angeles, California, on October 12, 1864. Her ancestry in America dates back to the earliest Revolutionary days. Mrs. Bondy's mother, Cecelia Simpson, married Jacob Elias in New York and moved to Los Angeles when that city was still a village surrounded by Indians. Mrs. Elias was most unhappy in Los Angeles, and prevailed upon her husband to move back East. They settled in Buffalo, and Jacob founded a lumber business which was carried on by his two sons for many years thereafter. Frances was a stately woman with an aristocratic bearing. Jewish friends and some who were not so friendly referred to her as "The Duchess." She lived to be ninety-seven and died in Syracuse on February 12, 1961, in the home of her daughter, Arline Davis.[8]

Moses Oberdorfer. Moses Oberdorfer, the son of one of the earliest settlers, had a talent for scenting success. After first trying his hand as a watchmaker, he became a liquor dealer in partnership with Joseph Wiseman on the corner of Washington and Mulberry Streets. Later he became acquainted with John W. Balch, who owned a brass foundry further down on Washington Street. Balch had been operating the foundry for forty years. He was getting on in years and needed help, both financially and physically. In 1881 Moses Oberdorfer bought a half-interest in the business, and the firm name was changed to Oberdorfer and Balch. At that time the foundry employed only ten men.

Later in that year the firm moved into new and larger quarters on Water Street, where it continued to operate successfully. In 1921 a new plant was erected in the Eastwood section of the city to meet the growth of the concern. This consisted of a plot of ground comprising twenty acres, with three acres of floor space in the various shops. The Oberdorfer Foundries, Inc. now employed over five hundred men, and the Oberdorfer fortune was well on the way.

GATES THALHEIMER was another native son who attained remarkable success. He was brought up in the grocery business and often delivered groceries after school in a wheelbarrow. In 1875, at the age of twenty-three, he gave up working for his father and opened his own grocery and produce store on the corner of Washington and Warren Streets, where the First Trust and Deposit Company now stands.

How well he succeeded is indicated by the fact that when an opportunity arose twelve years later to purchase the old and well-established wholesale grocery of John Crouse & Company, Gates was in a position to take advantage of the opportunity. Gates Thalheimer knew the grocery business from the ground up, and over the years developed this establishment until it became the largest individually owned wholesale grocery business in the country.

The Gates Thalheimer and Moses Oberdorfer families were united when Moses' son, Jonah, married Gates' daughter, Ethel, and the two houses continued to prosper.[9]

DR. HENRY L. ELSNER AND DR. NATHAN JACOBSON were cousins, born in Syracuse within two months of each other in 1857. Their careers ran parallel and were almost identical. As children they attended the same elementary schools and graduated from the same high school.

Dr. Henry L. Elsner was the son of Leopold Elsner, who first came to Utica, New York, in the early 1840's. When Leopold came to Syracuse, he settled on the North Side in the German neighborhood, where he operated a drug store and was known as "Dr. Elsner, the Herb Doctor."

Dr. Nathan Jacobson was the son of Israel Jacobson, who arrived in this country in 1850 and settled in Potsdam, New York, later coming to Syracuse with his family. In the early directories he was listed as a peddler, and in the 1875 directory as a grocer at 123 Mulberry Street.

The cousins, Henry Elsner and Nathan Jacobson, returned from their medical studies in Europe, as reported in the *Syracuse Journal* of August 14, 1878:

Dr. Nathan Jacobson and Dr. Henry L. Elsner arrived in New York Monday noon on the steamer "Austrada" and are expected home today. These gentlemen have been pursuing a thorough course of study in Vienna, Austria, and have visited the large hospitals of Berlin, Paris, and London. At London they met a large number of Syracusans who are abroad, and left them in good spirits. They will be gladly welcomed home by a large circle of friends. Both of the gentlemen intend practicing medicine in this city.

Immediately after their return, both young men set up offices for the practice of medicine. It was just the beginning of the era of specialization, and Elsner chose to become an internist and diagnostician. He was soon acknowledged among the foremost in his field, and was frequently called upon as a consultant by fellow doctors in and out of Syracuse.

In 1881 Dr. Elsner became associated with the faculty of the College of Medicine of Syracuse University, and filled a chair in medicine for thirty-five years until his death. Few professors in the college ever became more popular than Dr. Elsner. His teaching duties seemed to serve as a form of relaxation from his very heavy medical practice. His students adored him, and later formed "The Henry L. Elsner Alumni Association." The Henry L. Elsner Club is still in existence.

In addition to these duties, Dr. Elsner was consulting physician to the State Hospital for Crippled Children, the Syracuse Hospital for Women and Children (later the Memorial Hospital), and the Syracuse State Institution for the Feeble-minded, and served on the staff of St. Joseph's Hospital. At various times he also served as president of the Medical Society of the State of New York, president of the Onondaga Medical Society, president of the Syracuse Academy of Medicine, and as a member of a number of honorary medical fraternities.

A thorough student all his life, Dr. Elsner read fluently in several languages. Over the years he acquired one of the largest and most valuable medical libraries in the country. In addition to his library of ten thousand volumes, Dr. Elsner preserved the detailed history of thousands of medical cases. A great part of the material in his book, *Prognosis*,[10] was gathered from the studies of these histories.

When Dr. Elsner died on February 17, 1916, his character and work were commended in two eulogies, one by Dr. Adolph Guttman and the other by Louis Marshall. The friendship of Dr. Elsner and Louis Marshall dated from boyhood.

Dr. Guttman's eulogy centered about the favorite maxims of Dr. Elsner, such as the inscription above the fireplace in the living room of his home—"The Ornament of a House is the Friends Who Frequent It." In his private library hung a German saying, freely translated as "Work is Prayer."

Dr. Elsner was married January 5, 1881, to Pauline Rosenberg of Rochester, daughter of David and Amelia Rosenberg. Their home in Syracuse was known as one of the most hospitable in the city. Mrs. Elsner was in deepest sympathy with her husband's work and allowed nothing to stand in the way of its fullest development. She was an ideal physician's wife, always ready to subordinate social engagements or other activities to her husband's comfort and convenience. Mrs. Elsner was the first president of the Syracuse Council of Jewish Women, a member of Morning Musicals, and of the Onondaga Golf and Country Club. Dr. and Mrs. Elsner were the parents of one son, Henry Elsner, Jr., born February 24, 1893. Mrs. Elsner died February 22, 1916, five days after her husband's death.[11]

Dr. Jacobson's postgraduate studies in Europe were directed towards surgery, and immediately upon opening his office, he specialized in that field. His fame as a surgeon was not confined to Syracuse and vicinity. During his career he was an active member of various surgical societies and was chosen for positions of responsibility in their organizations. In 1886 he was appointed Instructor of Surgery at Syracuse University, and later was named Professor of Clinical Surgery. He also served as an officer of the Alumni Association and was elected a trustee of the University.

Shortly before his death, his deep interest in local hospitals occupied a great deal of his time. He was chief surgeon of both St. Joseph's and the Women's and Children's Hospitals. In the Medical College he was an inspiring teacher, and many of the best surgeons of Central New York received instruction and inspiration from him.

Dr. Nathan Jacobson published several books and wrote a large number of papers on the subject of surgery.

He was married January 3, 1883, to Minnie Schwartz of Buffalo. They had two children, Emma May, who married Dr. Joseph Wiseman, and a son, Gerald Nathan.[12]

When Dr. Jacobson died in 1913, the funeral service was conducted by Dr. Adolph Guttman at the Temple of Concord, and the eulogy was delivered by Dr. Roscoe C. Day, Chancellor of Syracuse University. This eulogy could very well have been spoken of both Dr. Jacobson and Dr. Elsner—collaborators in their profession, and of kindred lives and spirits:

"My thoughts take me back," the Chancellor said, "to a city of half a century ago, a small city, struggling on upward greatness. There played about the streets a little Jewish boy, born of a noble home, happily guided and directed.

"My thought runs over fifty years. His death summons a great city to stop and listen and drop a tear along the way of his funeral. And I wondered how it could be that this thing was so.

"What has thronged this temple and the streets about it with men and women from all walks of life to do him honor? He was not a statesman like that man of his race, the premier of a great nation, who shone with unusual brilliancy, nor that other Jew of world-wide philanthropy, nor the other who financed nations. He was a plain, unpretentious medical doctor.

"To be sure, he entered a profession that gave him an area of sacred usefulness. But he carried a sacred devotion into his sacred calling. It was service, and that peculiar quality of service that commanded the esteem and confidence of our city.

"The Catholics sought the professional services of this Jewish doctor. Their bishops, priests and sisters of charity, respected him, gave him their confidence and loved him. The Methodists made him a member of the faculty of the University they had founded. The alumni, combining all religions and faiths and representing a score of foreign lands, chose him to represent them on the University Board of Trustees.

"The citizens, without regard to creed, who founded one of our most tender and delicate hospitals, made him consulting surgeon. The city appointed him to investigate conditions of sanitation, while many organizations were honored by honoring him with election to their membership.

"This loyal Jew was not limited and restricted by such bounds as circumscribe religious denominations—he belonged to us all.[13]

SAMUEL D. SOLOMON. Samuel David Solomon was of the second generation. His father arrived in America at the age of fourteen and settled in the little town of Mohawk, a few miles east of Utica. Samuel was born on March 22, 1863. He attended the village school until the age of nine, when his father decided to move to Syracuse, in order that his children might have better opportunities and receive a higher education. Samuel finished high school and went on to Syracuse University from which he graduated with the B.A. degree in 1886. He studied law at Columbia University and entered legal practice in Syracuse in 1888.

What is memorable about Samuel Solomon was that from early youth until his last days he lived a life devoted to Judaism and Masonry. As a college graduate with a successful law practice, early in his career he became secretary of Temple Adath Yeshurun, and joined Rabbi Hertz in forming the first Zionist society in 1896. In 1897 he was one of the founders of the Hebrew Free School. He later became its president and for almost the entire history of that school he watched over its destiny. He was a founder of the United Jewish Charities, and at one time or another served on the board of almost every Jewish organization in the city.

As a Zionist, he, and practically he alone, kept the movement alive in Syracuse during its early years. He represented Syracuse at virtually every national Zionist convention. It was while attending one of these conventions that he met his wife, Henrietta Shapinsky.

He joined the Salt Springs Lodge of Free and Accepted Masons just before the turn of the century and immediately started going through the chairs. When he reached the senior warden's position he was passed over, and a non-Jew was elected master. This led to the organization of the Mt. Sinai Lodge in 1906, which has been composed mostly of Jewish members. Samuel Solomon was elected its first master. He was secretary of the Masonic Board of Relief for over thirty years and a member of the Grand Lodge of the State of New York Committee on Charity.

Sam Solomon was one of the earliest Jews to be elected to the Board of Education in Syracuse. Always interested in fostering art and music, he was a founder of the old Syracuse Musical Festival Association and drew up the by-laws for that organization. He died on February 11, 1948.[14]

T. AARON LEVY AND THE AMERICANIZATION LEAGUE

T. Aaron Levy contributed much to the city of Syracuse and as a result raised the stature of the Jewish people in this community. His influence in the field of culture and education in Syracuse lasted for a period of almost fifty years. T. Aaron Levy served on the Board of Education and was elected as its president in 1909. He was instrumental in establishing the first vocational high school in this city. For seventeen years he served as president of the Onondaga Health Association. He was chairman of the Onondaga Committee on Education and Culture. In 1938 he was elected to the state constitutional convention and was a member of the Committee on Character and Fitness of the Fourth Appellate Division, on which he served for nearly twenty years.

In 1935 the city established the Syracuse Housing Authority and named T. Aaron Levy as its first chairman. This committee, composed of public officials, served without compensation, and during its first two years devoted itself to the study of housing and living conditions. Its findings were summarized in the *General Report of 1937* and included detailed procedures and plans for setting up public housing projects. Requests for this report, with its new ideas, came from cities all over the United States and from as far away as South America, Africa, and India.

In 1937, during President Franklin D. Roosevelt's administration, the United States Housing Act was passed, which provided funds for clearing blighted areas and the erection of housing for low-income families. Syracuse was among the first five cities which received funds for this project.

When the Housing Act became effective, a site in Syracuse had to be selected and plans were developed. The site chosen was an area in the heart of what was known as "the Jewish neighborhood." Eight city blocks of old and dilapidated houses that the Jews of Syracuse were abandoning for better sections of the city were cleared away. This area was bounded by East Adams, Grape and Jackson Streets, and Renwick Avenue. Here the new housing development known as Pioneer Homes was constructed. These garden-type homes and apartments comprise 678 dwelling units, and after thirty years still remain as the finest of the low-rent dwellings established in Syracuse. They stand as a memorial to T. Aaron Levy, the first chairman of the Syracuse Housing Authority, and to the worthy volunteers on this committee.

During all this activity for the general community, T. Aaron Levy did not forget his traditional Jewish upbringing, but took an active part in the Jewish community from the time he was a teenager. He was among the first Zionists in Syracuse. As a youth he acted as secretary for Temple Adath Yeshurun, and was a leader in revitalizing the Young Men's Hebrew Association, now the Jewish Community Center. He also served as chairman of the committee which drew up the constitution for the Syracuse Jewish Welfare Federation. An example of his deep-down Jewishness is shown by the fact that when the Federation was about to cancel the support of the *mikvah*, Levy, a bachelor, spoke up in favor of continuing its support. He was also a director and president of the first men's club of the Temple of Concord—there was nothing of any consequence in Jewish life in which he did not participate.

The organization in which Levy served the longest and on which he bestowed the greatest devotion was the Americanization League. Up to the period of the First World War there had been a large influx of European immigrants, and the Syracuse Chamber of Commerce took notice of the situation. There was no denying that discrimination and prejudice against the new immigrants existed. The Chamber initiated and organized the Americanization League in April, 1916, and appointed T. Aaron Levy to establish it, with the purpose of bringing about a better understanding between the native-born and the newcomers.

The stated objectives of the Americanization League were "to abolish racial prejudices, barriers and discrimination . . . to maintain an American standard of living through the proper use of American foods, care of children and new world homes, to discontinue discrimination in the housing, care, protection and treatment of aliens; to create an understanding and love for America . . . to do all the above without interference in the religious life of any people." [15]

These objectives were made to order for T. Aaron Levy. He approached the leaders of all the foreign groups of the city—Italian, Polish, Jewish, Greek, Ukranian, Syrian, Armenian, Albanian, Indian, and Slovak. A committee and chairman were appointed for each group. He secured the help of native Americans interested in civic affairs and organized a bureau which arranged for prominent persons to speak at churches, lodges, and civic organizations. Speakers were sent to the larger industrial plants of the city to talk to the foreign workers at lunch time. Americanization classes were set up for adults in night schools. An auxiliary of women workers went into the homes of immigrants to teach mothers who could not attend classes how to read and write English.

The Jewish immigrant group took to their classes with vigor. The leaders encouraged the young aliens to go further in their education, and a number of young Jewish men and women who had been in America only a few short years were assisted in their desire to enter Syracuse University.

T. Aaron Levy suffered from a physical handicap, which required him to use two canes and sometimes crutches. However, this handicap was no deterrent to his activities. At the same time that he was engaged in civic affairs he maintained a law office and served as professor of jurisprudence at the College of Law, Syracuse University. He was a great admirer and student of Abraham Lincoln and wrote a book about him, *Lincoln, the Politician*.[16]

In 1941, at the twenty-fifth annual dinner of the Americanization League, T. Aaron Levy was presented with the Good Citizen's Medal by the Sons of the American Revolution, and in 1946 he was awarded the Arents Medal by Syracuse University for excellence in public service. In 1953, the Board of Education, desiring to honor and memorialize the name of T. Aaron Levy, changed the name of Nottingham High School on Fellows Avenue to the T. Aaron Levy Junior High School and gave the Nottingham name to the new high school that was being erected on East Genesee Street. T. Aaron Levy's life stands as the finest example of a Syracuse citizen, an American, and a Jew.[17]

BENJAMIN STOLZ, the youngest of three children, was born on October 13, 1867. David and Regina, the parents, were then well established in their own home on Grape Street. Benjamin was a healthy youngster who enjoyed the outdoors. He liked school and was a good student, but during school vacation he always found something useful to do. When he grew older and entered high school he secured a steady job working for his uncle Jacob Marshall as a bookkeeper. After school he would go directly to his uncle's hide and leather store at 22 James Street and stay until closing.

In high school he was a brilliant student. At graduation, Ben Stolz was the valedictorian. The subject of his speech was "On the Development of Mind and Character." This was an early indication of his serious approach towards life.

When he had finished high school, he mastered stenography, self-taught. His cousin Louis Marshall, who was a partner in the law firm of Jenney, Brooks, Ruger, and Marshall, gave him a job as his personal secretary. From then on there was no further question as to what profession he would follow. He regarded his cousin Louis with admiration and esteem and only wanted to follow in his footsteps. He earned enough money so that in 1887 he could enter Columbia Law School, graduating two years later with the degree of bachelor of laws, *cum laude.*

Returning to Syracuse, he entered the same law firm in which he had started as a clerk. But by this time his cousin Louis Marshall had left for New York, and the head of the firm, Mr. Ruger, had been appointed to the New York State Court of Appeals. Thus, the firm's name was changed to Jenney, Jenney and Stolz.

He later left that firm to form a partnership with George McGowan. They opened offices in the new Onondaga County Savings Bank building. This partnership lasted throughout their lives. When George McGowan passed away, the name was retained. It is still lettered on the office door on the ninth floor of the Onondaga Saving Bank building, where Max L. Stolz, the son of Benjamin, maintains the office of McGowan and Stolz.

On December 26, 1898, Benjamin married Rose Landsberg, daughter of the Rev. Dr. Max Landsberg of Rochester. They lived at 718 East Jefferson Street, in back of the Thalheimer homestead which faced East Genessee Street.

In 1926, he was nominated for attorney-general of the State of New York on the Democratic ticket. He had been a Democrat all of his life and was active in the higher councils of the party. He was particularly friendly with William Kelly, the Democratic boss of Onondaga County. When he was nominated for the attorney-generalship he was in Europe for his health, but did not hurry back to take an active part in the campaign. If he had, in the opinion of those that know, he could easily have defeated his Republican opponent, Albert Ottinger. As it happened, the rest of the Democratic ticket won, and Stolz was defeated by less than ten thousand votes.

Benjamin Stolz's record in philanthropic and charitable organizations is lengthy. He started his activities early in life. For many years he was a director of the Jewish Orphan Asylum of Western New York; president of the Marshall Memorial Society; treasurer of the Hebrew Loan Fund; director and honorary president of the Jewish Communal Home; and one of the founders and first president of the Federation of Jewish Charities. In 1912, he was elected vice-president of the Temple of Concord and in 1927, at the death of Gates Thalheimer, he was elected president, and served in that capacity until his death. He helped to form the Community Chest and the LaFayette Country Club.

He died on May 29, 1937, and was survived by his wife, Mrs. Rose Landsberg Stolz; his son, Max Stolz, who was associated with him in his law practice; and a daughter, Mrs. Milton Heyman, of Washington, D.C.[18]

Louis AND DAVID STOLZ were the sons of Jacob, the custom shoemaker, and his wife, the former Yetta Marshall. Louis, the older, dutifully went to Putman School, and to Rebbe Levy's *heder*. After school he was his father's errand boy. It was his job to deliver the custom-made shoes for his father. It did not do the boy any good to ask for a nickel for car fare, since he never got it. It made no difference how far the boy had to walk, the father said, "I walked all over Europe; the boy can walk in Syracuse."

After Louis started to go to high school, he let his younger brother David deliver the shoes, and he took a job with P. L. Ryan's Drug Store. For two years he worked after school without pay, for the privilege of learning the drug business. When he finished high school he worked full time at $3 per week. It was while working at Ryan's Drug Store that he made up his mind that he wanted to be a pharmacist. He left Syracuse at the age of nineteen for the Philadelphia College of Pharmacy, graduating two years later.

David was two and a half years younger than Louis. His boyhood followed the same pattern as that of his brother, and he entered the Philadelphia College of Pharmacy just as Louis was graduating.

Louis had a strong leaning towards chemistry. After graduating from college, he went to work at the Solvay Process Company in the chemical department. He could have continued work there, but he changed his mind and wanted to continue his studies to become a doctor of medicine. With that in mind, he went to New York and took the position as head pharmacist at Roosevelt Hospital, planning to save enough money to enter a medical school.

David, in the meantime having graduated from Philadelphia College of Pharmacy, returned to Syracuse and took a job as pharmacist with the George Thorpe Drug Store in the Yates Hotel Building. The two boys were happy in their work, but their father, Jacob, kept after the boys to open a drug store of their own. Not long thereafter, Louis, while in New York, received a telegram from David saying, "Father bought out Coogan's drug store in the Bastable Block. Come home at once." This was the beginning of the long history of Stolz Brothers' Drug Store in Syracuse.

For fifty-three years Louis and David Stolz operated their pharmacy, first in the Bastable Block and later in the State Tower building which replaced the Bastable Block, destroyed by fire. They established the type of drug store which is fast disappearing, for it was built on service and friendship. People would come from across the city to have a prescription filled by Louis or David, who had their own special preparations for a hand lotion and a cough syrup that people had confidence in.

They were held in the highest esteem by their fellow pharmacists. On their fiftieth anniversary in business, the Onondaga Pharmaceutical Association held a dinner in their honor. More than 200 persons were present and presented them with a plaque. The award praised them for their outstanding service in the field of pharmacy, good citizenship, spirit of real Americanism, and for service to their community.

Operating a drug store was not an easy job; it required twelve to fifteen hours a day, seven days a week. More than once Louis said he was sorry that he did not stick to chemistry as a profession, and David thought that he would have been better off if he had followed through with his original intention of studying medicine. Nevertheless, although the brothers worked hard, they still found time for home life and hobbies. Louis, from early boyhood, collected stamps, and later in life became an important amateur philatelist. He left one of the finest collections of United States stamps in the country. Another one of his outside activities was to sound the *shofar* at the Temple of Concord for the High Holidays. Starting as a young man, he sounded the *shofar*, never missing a single year, until he reached the age of eighty.

Going to see fires was David's hobby from the start of his career, and he had a deep interest in the welfare of firemen. Mayor Walter R. Stone appointed him to the Civil Service Commission, on which he served for four years.

The wives of the Stolz brothers did their bit to help the business along. They both assisted at the soda fountain and lunch counters when there was a shortage of help, acted as cashiers, and clerked behind the cosmetic counter.

In 1911 Louis married Evelyn Belloff, daughter of the clothing manufacturer, and one of the prettiest Jewish girls in town.

David married Helen Jacoby of New York City, whom he met through his friendship with Dr. Jacob Levy. David died on June 2, 1958, and his wife passed away on June 15, 1961. Louis Stolz passed away on January 16, 1969, at the age of ninety.[19]

SIMON S. SHIMBERG, only son of Solomon Shimberg, a Syracuse pioneer, was a remarkable person.

Blind for the last twenty-eight years of his life, he carried on a successful insurance business. A familiar figure on the business streets of Syracuse, one would see him with a companion to show him the way, or later with his son, Irving. A blind man usually elicits great sympathy, but not so with Sime Shimberg. When he started to talk to you, you would forget that he couldn't see you. He was up on the topics of the day and seemed to know what was going on around him. In talking insurance he hardly ever had to turn to his companion to look things up in the book. He was a good insurance salesman and was able to quote figures and premiums from memory. Considering the many kinds of insurance, you would just wonder at his retentive memory. Then you would realize that it was no doubt sharpened by his inability to see. He died March 30, 1931, at the age of sixty-two. Surviving were his wife, Clara; a daughter, Madeline; and his son, Irving.

IRVING SHIMBERG not only carried on where his father left off, but he built the firm of Shimberg and Gerber into one of the largest insurance agencies in Syracuse. Throughout his busy career in insurance, he found time to be a leader in all worthwhile Jewish projects and has contributed liberally of his time and money.

SCHOOLS AND SCHOOLTEACHERS

When you ask an oldtimer, "What do you remember of your early years?" his mind immediately goes back to his school days. Usually he can recall in great detail his school and teachers.

Children of the early Jewish immigrants and those Jewish children who were born here attended the schools in the Jewish neighborhood. The schools were usually known by the streets they were on. Those that were in existence in the 1880's and 1890's were the Adams Street School, Irving School, and Madison School. The largest of these, not called by the name of the street it was on, was the Putnam School, on the corner of Montgomery and Jefferson Streets, which had a large number of Jewish children. During the Jewish High Holidays, when Jewish children stayed out of school, this school might just as well have been closed, for even some of the non-Jewish children took advantage of the occasion.

Simon Strause appears to have been the first Jewish school teacher in Syracuse. He taught at the Townsend and Montgomery Street School from 1861 to 1864. The young Jewish ladies of the second generation started out as school teachers very early in the history of the community. Mary Silberman was teacher and principal of Adams Street School from 1869 to 1876. Sophia Strause, Marilla Goldstein, Bessie Lowe, and Yetta R. Loomis all started to teach school in the 1870's.[20] A list of the early teachers can be found in Appendix C.

LEADERSHIP

Who were the Jewish leaders in 1890? Hiram Danziger, who wrote to the *Rochester Jewish Tidings* on March 27, 1890, named the following with accompanying comments:

Having been requested by a reader of The Tidings to furnish a list of names of our leading representative Jews, I would suggest the following, although many names could well be added:

Louis Marshall	Daniel Rosenbloom
Dr. Nathan Jacobson	I. Henry Danziger
Dr. Henry L. Elsner	Joseph Bondy
Manuel R. Stern	Rev. Dr. Adolph Guttman
David J. Hamburger	Gates Thalheimer
August Falker	Herman Leiter
James Harrison	David Danziger
Lazarus Leiter	Jacob Hammell
Jacob Marshall	Isaac Danziger
Jacob Levi	Seckel Bronner

A careful perusal of the above list will easily convince one of the prominence of the Jewish gentlemen in Syracuse.

In public office we have Supervisor Joseph Bondy, Health Commissioner Danziger, and City Hall Commissioner Falker. Louis Marshall stands foremost in his profession, while such men as Gates Thalheimer, Messrs. Danziger, D. J. Hamburger, the Leiter brothers, and Rosenbloom brothers are considered leading men in their representative branches of business. With pride we point to Drs. Jacobson and Elsner, who are not only leading physicians, but eminent professors in Syracuse medical college.

When the list appeared in the paper it created a stormy controversy. Danziger was accused of prejudice and nepotism, inasmuch as he placed his father and two uncles on the list. The following week an angry subscriber sent in his comments on the list of proposed leaders.

Syracuse, April 3 . . . Allow a subscriber of your paper to express his opinion on the letter penned by the Syracuse correspondent containing the list of prominent (?) Jews. With due respect to the gentlemen who have been selected to fill the list, I think an injustice has been done to several of our really prominent Jewish citizens.

If the Syracuse correspondent would rake his brain a little he would find it hard to come to the conclusion that the old saying "first come first served" should be used in this case. Such old Jewish residents as S. Rosenbloom, M. Thalheimer and W. Henocksburg were the first men to bring into prominence the Jewish people in this city. They came first and when the question of popularity is submitted they should be placed at the head of the list. Old timers should not be forced out to make room for younger representatives.

It appears, that in making out the list, the correspondent did not define the word "popularity" properly. All the city respect these old residents and I am astonished that the President of the Society of Concord was not included. There are other men who should have been placed in preference to those already on the list. Take George Freeman. There is a self-made man, a man respected and honored by everyone. He is a business man from the word go. Another man whom I desire to call attention to is M. Oberdorfer, the only Jewish resident who is a manufacturer. He is a prominent business man and his popularity is not to be questioned.

This article may be criticized for its attack on the list, but when a house is built the carpenter gets the credit for his neat work, but it is just the opposite in this case, for now the Jewish people of Syracuse are built up to meet the times and the builders do not get the credit.[21]

Having in mind that Hiram Danziger was a member of one of the leading German Jewish families, it was quite natural for him to name other German Jews, and it appears that his criterion was that they must be members of the leading social club (the Standard Club) and belong to the Temple of Concord. East European Jews were almost completely left out.

THE TRANSITION PERIOD

The controversy over who were the Jewish leaders in 1890 occurred at a time when the German dominance over their East European brothers reached its climax. From about that time on, the Germans began to be rapidly outnumbered. They were the first to start moving out of the old Jewish neighborhood and, while they tried to be helpful to the newly arrived immigrants, they held themselves aloof.

Beginning with the 1900's, the Russian and Polish Jews began to make their presence felt. They were industrious and frugal; they built their own synagogues and charitable societies. Grape Street, between Madison and Adams Street, was completely filled with Jewish shops and stores. More traditionally religious than the German Jews, their businesses were all closed on the Sabbath. On Saturday morning they could be seen dressed in their best, going to or from the synagogues. In the afternoon they would be promenading or visiting their relatives and friends.

The children, many American-born, were growing up. They were going into business and entering the professions. The German Jews started taking notice of those Easterners who attained a standing in the community or had accumulated some wealth. A few were taken into the Standard Club and some joined the Temple of Concord.

The big change came with the beginning of the First World War. When the United States entered the war on the side of the Allies against Germany and Austria, the pride of the German Jews in their fatherland crumbled. The end of the war brought greater changes. East Europeans were taking over the leadership. In 1919, Temple of Concord elected Benjamin Friedman, a non-German, as their rabbi. In 1918, Hiram Weisberg, a non-German, married Mabel Thalheimer, daughter of the leader of the German Jewish families. David Holstein, not a German, was elected president of Temple of Concord, and Sam Shopiro and Louis Hurwitz, with Eastern European backgrounds, were accepted among the lay leaders of the Temple of Concord.

Today, to the second- and third-generation Jews there is no apparent difference between German and East Europeans, and the fourth and fifth generation do not know that there ever was a difference. Syracuse is now a united Jewish community.

❦ CHAPTER VI ❧

Charitable Organizations

IMMIGRATION AND CHARITY

The history of the Jews in America proves that it was not at all necessary for Peter Stuyvesant, governor of New Amsterdam, to enjoin, in 1654 the twenty-three Israelites who arrived in a vessel from Brazil, ". . . the Jews may enter, live, travel, and trade in the New Netherlands, provided that the poor among them shall not become a burden to the company or the community, but be supported by their own nation." [1]

Charity in the Jewish tradition is an act of duty. It is incumbent upon those who *have* to provide for those who *need*. The founders of the Jewish community in Syracuse, as well as elsewhere in America, provided for their own charitable needs. At first, individuals took it upon themselves as a personal obligation. As the community expanded, it was found necessary to organize charitable societies and benevolent associations for self-help and for assistance to others. The new arrivals—who usually came almost penniless—often had large families, and some who were stranded had to be helped on their way to other communities. Some of these societies came into being in the early 1840's, when Syracuse was still a village.

In 1851 an agent for *The Occident*, published in New York, came through Syracuse soliciting subscriptions and sent back the following report to his paper:

Syracuse, New York—In this city exist three benevolent Societies, the Society of Brotherly Love of which Wm. Henochsberg is President, Israel Bronner Treasurer, and Mr. Henochsberg, Secretary. It has lately laid the foundation of a widow's and orphan's fund. The other is called "The Mutual Assistance Society," under the Presidency of Isaac Garson; Solomon Lederer is Treasurer, and M. A. Marks Secretary. The members of both about fifty each. The annual contribution is three dollars, and the weekly relief during sickness is the same amount. The last is a ladies' society, called "Gemiles Hesset" and has sixty-five members. The President is Mrs. Fanny Bamberger, and Mrs. Rose Stone is Treasurer and Secretary. All three attend to the funeral rites of the respective members.[2]

Beginning with 1857, we have accounts of Syracuse Jewish charitable organizations as they were recorded in the County Clerk's office. We include the full text of these incorporated societies so that we may bring to mind the names of the men and women of long ago who organized these societies, some of which are still functioning. The first one so recorded was Cone's German Hebrew Society on March 27, 1857. Mention of this Society has been made previously with reference to Marcus Cone.

This was followed by a more general society which, according to its name, included the Russian and Polish Jews as well.

The Society Bikur Cholem—Gemilus Chasoden

Organized and incorporated: April 28, 1865
Purpose: To relieve the sick, bury the dead
    and to assist those in distress.
Trustees: Jacob Levi, Jacob Garson, Meyer
    Exstein, Moses Lester, Solomon Lederer,
    Lazarus Kraft, Leopold Swartz.
Harry Gifford, Justice of the Peace
I. LeRoy Morgan, Justice of the Supreme Court
Recorded June 12, 1865   Carroll E. Smith, Clerk [3]

In 1869, The Hesset Shel Emes Society was incorporated. According to the charter, it appears to have been better organized than earlier societies. Its purposes were spelled out more clearly.

Hesset Shel Emes Society

This is to certify that the persons undersigned together with such other persons as may hereafter join them have associated together to form a benevolent and charitable society for the purpose of assisting each other in times of sickness and distress.

I. The name of the society shall be "Hesset Shel Emes."

II. The object and business of said society shall be to furnish aid and assistance to the sick, poor and distressed members of said society and their families. III. The Trustees shall be seven in number. IV. The following persons shall be Trustees: Philip Stern, Hyman Bernstein, Mark Myers, Jacob Tumin, Maurice Roden, Isaac Solomon, Levi Bernstein. V. Said Society shall be located in the city of Syracuse. Signed, Philip Stern, Heiman Bernstein, Max Mairs, Jacob Tumin, Marcus Roden, Isaac Solomon, Levi Pakelinski, Abram Strasburg, Hersh Stelstone, A. Cohen, and Z. Midelstein.

J. S. Aiken, Notary: I hereby approve of the objects of said society, January 14, 1869. Le Roy Morgan, Justice of the Supreme Court, 5th Judicial District of New York. Recorded January 15, 1869. Theo S. Poole, Clerk.[4]

The two decades following 1880 saw the beginning of a mass migration of Jews to this country. These were the years when Czarist Russia bore down hardest on the Jews. Pogroms were breaking out in various parts of Russia; restriction upon restriction was placed on Jews. They could live only in certain cities; they were mostly excluded from agriculture, and very few could attend universities; they were dispossessed of their real estate; they were expelled from Moscow and other principal cities. It is no wonder that hundreds of thousands of Jews left Russia and Poland to come to America during those troubled years.

Both here and in Europe, societies were organized to aid and regulate this overwhelming immigration. The French, English, and German Jews formed the *Alliance Israélite Universelle,* a society to help immigrants who passed through their countries on their way to America. In America, the Hebrew Immigrant Aid Society was organized to help the immigrants as they landed in the ports of New York, Boston, and Philadelphia, and also to disperse them throughout the country. As it was, too many had already remained in these Eastern port cities.

Thousands of immigrants—as fast as they were taken off the boats —were put on trains and sent west to Chicago, Cleveland, and Milwaukee. Some were sent to parts even farther west in Montana, Wyoming, and Texas, with the understanding that they would be given free land on which to settle. The cities closer by were not neglected. In Syracuse, Rochester, and Buffalo the Eastern European immigrants were benevolently received, but were not actually wanted.

The German Jewish residents who had come to America in the

1840's and 1850's looked on their Russian and Polish co-religionists as if they were intruding on their domain. The antipathy of the German Jews toward the new immigrants grew in intensity as the Polish and Russian Jews kept growing in numbers.

In 1889 the Mansion House Committee in London sent a questionnaire to various cities in America, inquiring if they had room for more Jewish immigrants, and what skills were needed. Milwaukee answered that if more Jews were sent to that city they would be returned to England forthwith. Rochester replied that Russian and Polish immigrants were a bane to the country and a curse to the Jews of America. Syracuse's response was that the new immigrants were lazy and shiftless and relied largely on charitable institutions for relief.[5]

However, the German Jews of Syracuse did not have long to worry. The natural desire for self-betterment was strong among the Russian and Polish immigrants. They did not rely on charitable institutions very long, and soon organized their own societies for self-help.

Further evidence that the new immigrants accepted their responsibility to care for their own needs is indicated by an article that appeared in the *Syracuse Standard* of December 14, 1891:

JEWISH CHARITY—YOUNG MEN'S HEBREW AID SOCIETY

A PRACTICAL CHARITY. AN ORGANIZATION OF YOUNG HEBREWS TO AID RUSSIAN REFUGEES.

It is not generally known that there is in this city an organization that donates all its energies toward bettering the condition of Russian Refugees, but such an organization exists, and its name is the Young Men's Hebrew Aid Society. It was organized on August 13, last, and this evening it will give its first annual ball in Greyhound hall.

Its officers are: President, S. Holstein; Vice-President, M. Kaletzky; Treasurer, L. Jacobs; Recording Secretary, S. Gutstadt; Financial Secretary, S. Silverman, Jr. Since the society was organized, it has had an average of three calls a week upon its charity. The Russian Jew, who does not leave the land of his birth until forced to do so by the Czar, does not bring very much of the world's goods to this country.

About all he has when he lands are the clothes upon his back, his wife and a large family of children. The first thing he needs is money to tide over the interval of idleness that must ensue until he is provided with employment by which he can earn a living. In New York the exiles are cared for by a committee appointed for that purpose and are given money to pay their railroad fare to Utica, Syracuse, Rochester, Buffalo or further west if they desire to travel in that direction. The Syracuse society has settled comfortably, in this city, ten of these exiles besides assisting many others as far as Rochester, where a similar society either finds employment for them or sends them on to Buffalo, Cleveland, or Chicago, where they are cared for in the same manner. In the course of time every exile, if he be honest and determined to take the most of any opportunity that may be thrown in his way, finds himself engaged in some occupation, which, if not very remunerative at first, at least yields an income sufficient to keep the exile from the knowledge of the pangs of hunger. An officer of the Syracuse Society told a Standard reporter last evening that the Syracuse colony of the exiles was doing remarkably well. He told of the success of two of the members of the colony. These two men are unmarried and when they arrived here they had no money. The society took them in charge and gave to one of them two dollars with which to buy matches to peddle in the street, also paying his board for two weeks. This man proved to be a very industrious fellow, and in a very short time he had made enough money to buy a hand cart. He bought the cart and forthwith became a merchant, that is, he abandoned the match business and the Standard's informant thus describes the exile's success. "He is now making more money every week than I am." The officer of the society is a salesman in a leading business house and commands a good salary. So it can be seen that the rag and iron merchant has in him the qualities that enable men to scale nimbly fortune's ladder.

In the case of the other successful exile, it was learned upon his arrival in Syracuse that he was a fairly good tailor. He was offered employment in a tailor shop on Pearl Street, and he accepted the offer. He is now earning ten dollars a week. The Young Men's Hebrew Aid Society appears to be engaged in a charity that is practical.

UNITED JEWISH CHARITIES

It is not fair to say that all German Jews held themselves aloof from the needs of the new immigrants. Some were mindful of those who were here, and participated in the many charitable activities. As we have seen, Syracuse was well provided with Jewish charitable organizations. Some dated back to the 1840's and 1850's, when the community was predominantly German; some were initiated by the early Russian and Polish settlers; and still others developed when the East European Jews began converging on Syracuse in large numbers. Every time a new need was discovered another society was formed, until there was much duplication and overlapping.

In addition to all this, there were many requests for financial help from national organizations and *yeshibot* in Europe and Palestine. Messengers from these organizations came to the city and made door-to-door collections. The substantial citizens were beginning to be annoyed with the many small societies and with being repeatedly approached to join new ones.

As a consequence, the United Jewish Charities of Syracuse was founded in 1891. The Reverend Dr. Adolph Guttman was elected the first president. The stated purposes of the organization were to try to combine as many of the small societies as possible, and "to assist the Jewish immigrant to find his place in America." [6] Their aim was not only to help the new immigrants get settled, but also to teach them the English language and to educate them in the American way of living. This was the very beginning of social service work among Jewish families in Syracuse. The Jewish Family Service Bureau of today is a continuation of that movement started in 1891.

The United Jewish Charities was only partially successful in its attempt to bring all the small charitable societies into one organization. Many of the societies' presidents refused to give up their cherished positions as heads of the various societies.

Moreover, many small societies came into existence because most of the new immigrants were Orthodox Jews who strictly observed the dietary laws and traditions and wished to form their own societies for burial, ritual baths, and other purposes.

The United Jewish Charities carried on for a number of years as a volunteer workers' organization with social welfare being accomplished mostly by women. The membership and organization work was under the care of the men.

The next big change in the United Jewish Charities came with the start of the First World War. Urgent requests for help began to come from Europe and Palestine. In order to arouse the Jews of Syracuse to their obligation to the local and overseas needs of their brethren, the Seventeenth Annual Report of 1914 was printed in the form of a pamphlet and mailed to the residences of the entire Jewish community.

This pamphlet contains very interesting material and provides a good description of the trials and difficulties encountered by those who formed the organization. It begins with a message of greeting from the President, Dr. Adolph Guttman:

TO THE SUPPORTERS OF THE UNITED JEWISH CHARITIES:

The year 1914 has been one of the most trying years in the history of the United Jewish Charities. The demands have increased, while the regular contributions have decreased. This condition is a reproach upon those who persistently refuse to recognize their obligations to the needs of the Jewish Community. If all those who are able to give, would be doing their duty, we would have sufficient means to do the work as thoroughly and effectively as it should be done.

We are having a hard winter, owing to the fact that so many people are out of employment, and while we must help the sufferers at our doors.

Answer this appeal PROMPTLY and you will feel the better for having done your duty.

Sincerely,

ADOLPH GUTTMAN.[7]

In that year, after Dr. Guttman exhorted the members to greater giving, the recepts totaled $3,717.21.

The annual report of 1914 contained the names of each contributor and the amount each gave. The largest contributors were S. Rosenbloom and Sons and Gates Thalheimer, who gave $200 each. There were three $100-contributors—Sigmund Frensdorf, Marcus Rosenbloom, and Samuel Shopiro. The remaining contributors are listed as giving from $50 down to fifty cents.[8] At the end of that year, the name was changed to The Federation for the Support of Jewish Philanthropic Societies. Later, it was again changed to The Syracuse Jewish Welfare Federation.

THE SYRACUSE JEWISH WELFARE FEDERATION

There is no finer page in the history of Syracuse Jewry than the story of the Syracuse Jewish Welfare Federation.[9] Unlike the building of the temples and synagogues, the educational institutions, and the charitable organizations which were undertaken by groups who nourished different ideologies, the Federation has acted as a leveling device. It brought together the Jews of German origin and the Jews from Eastern Europe, the Jews who adhered to Reform and the ultra-Orthodox, the professional and the day laborer. It brought out the finest of the men and women of each calling. Many people gave of their time and their means in behalf of the Federation with a devotion and fervor unmatched by any other institution in Jewish life. It brought to the fore men who otherwise might not have been noticed by the community.

The First Fund Raising Campaign

In 1917 the United States entered the First World War. The Jewish leaders immediately recognized that their obligations to organized Jewish charity should consist of more than social work for poor Jewish immigrants—that there were national and overseas agencies which would require their aid.

Benjamin Stolz was the president of the Federation. Jacob X. Cohen, an enterprising young engineering student at Syracuse University, was able and willing to participate in Jewish activities and was appointed as a part-time secretary to the Federation. The campaign chairman was H. Hiram Weisberg, a young man who was making a rapid rise in the business and social life of the community and a fine representative of the up-and-coming generation of native-born Jewish Syracusans. This was the first campaign organized on a systematic basis. The workers were divided into groups of ten; each group selected a captain and met daily for lunch at the Communal Center on Cedar Street to report on their progress. The campaign was to last for one week, and on the last Sunday a novel arrangement was put into effect—Hiram and his vice-chairman, David Holstein, hired a horse and buggy and, like the medicine men of not long ago, stopped at the busy corners of the Jewish neighborhood. They had with them two young attorneys, Gerson Rubenstein and William Gerber, who acted as spellbinders; as soon as a crowd gathered, they started selling the idea that every Jew must be a member of the Federation and contribute to the cause. Over $3,000 was raised through this effort. At the end of the campaign, Mr. Weisberg gave the following report:

The campaign for members of the organization was inaugurated with a goal of 1500 members and subscriptions of $25,000. Our efforts met with such hearty support from the community that when the campaign was closed at the end of one week, the new Federation had 1731 members with a subscription totaling $32,771.

The Federation Joins the Community Chest

The next big change in charitable fund raising in Syracuse came in 1922, when the Federation joined the Syracuse Community Chest. At a special meeting of the board the following resolution was presented:

Whereas there has been organized in the city of Syracuse, a "Civic Chest" for the purpose of co-ordinating the collection and proper distribution of funds to support the various philanthropic organizations of this city and *whereas* the purposes of the Civic Chest are in direct harmony with the aims of the Federation for the Support of Jewish Philanthropic Societies, now therefore it is resolved that the Federation endorses the establishment of the Civic Chest and pledges its earnest support and willingness as a body to join therein.

The question was thoroughly discussed and unanimously passed.

J. X. Cohen, Sec't.

By cooperating with the Chest the Federation was relieved of further independent campaigning for funds, but it continued as a membership organization through which the Syracuse Chest was to distribute the funds from the Chest to the Jewish agencies. Those who had been the leaders in the fund raising for the Federation began vigorously to help the Chest. Moses Winkelstein was the Federation representative on the Chest board. The following table indicates the amounts requested and received by the Federation for the combined Jewish agencies:

	Budget Submitted	Funds Received
1924	$42,000	$39,000
1925	49,000	43,000
1926	53,000	46,000
1927	46,000	46,000
1928	52,000	46,000
1929	58,000	46,000

By 1930 the economic depression had begun. The Chest did not reach its quota, and the agencies were requested to tighten their belts. Our Jewish leaders who were active in the Chest were soliciting from the Jewish Community on the basis that the Jews were contributing less than their agencies were receiving. Many contributors resented and challenged this statement, which was never proven.

The Federation Reappraises Its Needs

At a meeting of the Federation on March 9, 1932, it was decided that the Friendly Inn, a society which helped itinerant Jews, the Hebrew Free Loan Association, which made small loans, and the Hebrew Free Bath (the *mikvah*), were to be taken out of future budgets submitted to the Chest. The budget request for the year was reduced to $36,000, and the Federation received $33,000.

On January 4, 1933, Rabbi and Mrs. Samuel Yalow appeared before the board of the Federation on behalf of the *mikvah* ritual bath, requesting that this agency be reinstated in the Federation. Rabbi Yalow maintained that if there was only one woman mindful of the religious concept of a *mikvah* and desired its use, then according to Jewish tradition it was mandatory on the part of the Jewish community to supply it.

It was stated that the original contributing membership had been lost when the bath first became part of the Federation, and that it was impossible now to arouse interest and collect money enough to maintain this institution. Though the *mikvah* was classified as a religious organization and thus ineligible for Chest funds, the assistance of the Jewish community was needed for its support. This request for financial help was not granted.

With the rise of Hitler in Germany in 1933, the demand for overseas help became more urgent, and Syracuse Jews increased their efforts to raise funds for national organizations and the needs of Jews in Europe. A special campaign was organized to raise money for overseas relief. H. Hiram Weisberg was again called upon in the emergency to be chairman of the campaign committee.

A New Constitution for the Federation

In 1935 a new constitution was formulated, one that better expressed the needs and aims of the time. The cumbersome name of "The Federation for the Support of Jewish Philanthropic Societies of Syracuse" was changed to "The Syracuse Jewish Welfare Federation," and it was agreed to engage a full-time executive director. On February 9, 1936, Max Stern, very knowledgeable about Jewish organizations and national and overseas Jewish needs, was selected as the director.

By 1938 Jewish refugees began to arrive in Syracuse in greater numbers. They required housing, employment, and rehabilitation. The Federation through the 1940's continued to increase the amount raised each year. In 1943, for the first time, Syracuse raised over $100,000 in a regular campaign. In 1944 it raised $137,000, and in 1945, $190,000.

The Federation Keeps Pace with Its Needs

Alexander Holstein took over the presidency from Rabbi Benjamin Friedman in 1945. The executive director, Max Stern, resigned, and Milton Fromer was selected to fill his place.

In 1946 Paul Flah became chairman of the campaign, and under the guidance of the new director the contributions amounted, for the first time, to more than $500,000, which was thought of as the peak of Jewish community giving. The goal for 1947 was set at $860,000, and the amount raised was $750,000.

The following year B. G. Rudolph was elected president. That was the year that David Ben-Gurion declared that the mandated territory of Palestine was now the State of Israel. Jews in Syracuse, as well as elsewhere in the world, were exhilarated and, in an overwhelming gesture of generosity, in 1948 raised the sum of $1,040,000—the largest amount ever raised in a single campaign. H. Hiram Weisberg was the campaign chairman, and was assisted in raising that amount by a dynamic young man, Morris Berinstein.

Berinstein came to Syracuse from Albany in 1941, immediately joined in Jewish activities, and was an effective member of The Federation for a number of years. He attracted national attention and later became a leading fund raiser for the United Jewish Appeal all over the country. Later he was elected president of the National United Jewish Appeal fund-raising campaign. The amount raised in Syracuse for the Federation in 1949 was $718,000.

Borrowing for the United Jewish Appeal

In the 1950's the Federation resorted to borrowing money from the local banks in order to advance funds to the United Jewish Appeal in anticipation of money that would be raised in future campaigns.

Tracy Ferguson was elected president of the Federation in 1951. He stated that this was a critical year. At one time the Federation had a million-dollar business, but it was now down to less than half that amount. He further proposed, in order that the Jewish community might be better informed, that the Federation publish a weekly or bi-weekly periodical which would help it in publicizing its campaigns. An effort was made to induce the *Syracuse Jewish Chronicle,* an Anglo-Jewish weekly published by the two Kay brothers, to merge their periodical with the plans of the Federation. This was tried for one campaign but was not satisfactory.

During the early 1950's the campaigns raised less and less each year. As a result, there was dissatisfaction and criticism. Self-study committees were appointed and program investigation committees were assigned to various agencies.

Moses Winkelstein, the chairman of the study committee, reported that the committee had found that there was considerable dissatisfaction with the operation of the Federation, and that the present board did not really represent all of the community; that the Federation had fallen down in the field of public relations; and that there was a division between the Federation and the Community Center. It was also the opinion of the committee that one of the problems was that of sheer physical fatigue. They pointed out that the campaigns of the previous few years had extended over six and seven months, and recommended that each campaign should be completed in one month, even if that meant raising less money. Following this report, the executive director, Milton Fromer, resigned.

Samuel Greene was elected president in 1954. Gerald Soroker was elected executive director. On June third of the same year an urgent request from the United Jewish Appeal was received that the Federation borrow $350,000 from local banks, to be repaid from future campaigns. The money was borrowed and forwarded to the United Jewish Appeal in New York as requested.

During 1956 the executive director, Gerald Soroker, resigned to go to Cleveland and was replaced by Norman Edell. The same year, on July first, the very energetic Lewis Goldner was elected president of the Federation.

Retrospection

With the advent of the 1960's, a change in the outlook of the Federation was noticeable. The strong emotional pull toward Israel and the pressure of the United Jewish Appeal were subsiding. Some of the old-timers who had been the leaders during the period of the Nazi atrocities and the birth of the State of Israel were fast giving way to a new generation of Jewish leaders in the community. Joseph Roth, for example, stepped into the shoes of his uncle, Philip Roth; Tracy Ferguson and Ted Pierson partly took over for their uncle, Hiram Weisberg; Melvin Rudolph and Jay B. Rudolph filled in for M. H. and B. G. Rudolph; Leonard Goldberg for his forebears, and Alex Holstein, Jr. for his father. The elder statesmen, so to speak, were there to advise and contribute, but the torch was passed to next of kin, the younger men and women.

The pace quickened with men like Lewis Goldner, Louis Yaffee, Hy Poltenson, Abe Altman, Sidney Grossman, Gerald Levy, Dr. Kenneth Gale, Saul North, and Herman Dubnoff, who took over the leadership of the Federation.

The new executive director, Norman Edell, guided many of the young leaders in this transitional period when he started a leadership training program which proved successful. It revealed that young people were willing to accept leadership, responsibility, and community service. The board recorded its approval and commended Gerald Levy and the executive director for instituting and supervising this project.

Louis Yaffee was elected president in 1962. During the year the

Community Center building fund was short $125,000, due to the construction costs running over the original estimates, and the Federation agreed to supply the funds as a loan, to be repaid over a period of years.

The *mikvah* organization requested a loan of $1,000 for repairs, to be repaid when Urban Renewal took over their site, and this request was granted.

On May 28, 1963, President Louis Yaffee reported that the various congregational schools had greatly improved, and that scholarships were being provided by the Federation where necessary. He therefore recommended that the community Hebrew School, since it had only twenty-two pupils, be discontinued. It was so voted, and thus the original Hebrew Free School, an institution begun more than seventy years earlier, ceased to exist.

It should be noted that the Federation board was now more alert to the fact that it represented the entire Jewish community and, as such, it began to pass resolutions and to make its voice heard on national and international affairs. A resolution was addressed to President Lyndon B. Johnson, in the name of the Federation, stating that it approved of the march from Selma, Alabama, in behalf of civil rights. Another resolution on the integration of Syracuse public schools was addressed to the Superintendent of Schools and to the Board of Education. A delegation of members of the Federation Board went to Washington, D.C., to be present at the "Eternal Light Vigil" protesting the treatment of Jews in the Soviet Union. In February, 1967, it was decided that Syracuse Jews devote a weekend in March in behalf of Jews in the Soviet Union, with special services to be conducted in all temples and synagogues, and a mass community rally at Nottingham High School auditorium.

In 1967 a committee was appointed to study community planning, with emphasis on Jewish education, the Hillel Foundation at Syracuse University, and the Jewish Family Service Bureau.

The presidents, the campaign chairmen, and all who took time away from their businesses and families over the years to serve the Syracuse Jewish Welfare Federation, and through it Judaism and humanity, deserve a place of honor in the annals of the Jewish history of Syracuse. (See Appendix D.)

THE JEWISH FAMILY SERVICE BUREAU
AND AID TO REFUGEES

In the very early years, Jewish charity in Syracuse was on a personal basis. When one learned of a family in need or distress, it was considered a personal obligation and duty to go to their aid, taking food, clothing, or coal directly to them. If an individual needed help, one usually took him directly into his own home, giving him shelter or whatever was necessary.

If financial help was needed, and one was not in a position to supply it, someone would go to friends or neighbors and collect funds in small amounts. It was not uncommon, before the turn of the century, to have two or three persons go from door to door, especially on a Sunday (when people would be at home), to collect funds for a poor Jewish family, without mentioning any names.

When a certain kind of need was found to be more constant, a few people would get together and form a charitable society. The officers and members all worked on a voluntary basis. This method may not have been as scientific or efficient as social service is now, but there was personal satisfaction and a human glow in participating in direct help to the unfortunate few.

Since 1936, however, the local charitable aid and service for Jewish people has been administered by the Jewish Family Service Bureau,[10] which in turn is an agency of the Syracuse Jewish Welfare Federation. It has its own officers and board of directors and a suite of offices in the business section of the city. The Jewish Family Service Bureau is operated by a professional executive director and two trained case workers, and is financially supported by the Syracuse Jewish Welfare Federation and the Community Chest.

The Jewish Family Service Bureau has taken on additional duties. "Meals on Wheels" was introduced in 1959 to aid those elderly and sick people unable to go out for meals, or who find it difficult to shop and prepare hot meals for themselves. The kosher meals are prepared by the Jewish Home of Central New York. Nine months after this project was started, the Family Service Bureau reported that fifteen individuals were being served two meals a day, one hot and one cold. On February 15, 1967, the president, Judge Morris Garber, reported that the functions of the Bureau included counseling service to parents and children, refugee settlement, "Meals on Wheels," and preparation and review of applications for the Jewish Home of Central New York and Camp Bradley Brook.

German and Other Refugees

Syracuse was fortunate to have the Family Service Bureau in existence when the Nazis came to power in Germany. When refugee families began coming to America, Syracuse welcomed a good number of them. It was the Family Service Bureau that received them and found homes and jobs for them.

As early as 1930, before the advent of Hitler, it became apparent that the Jews of Germany were being made the scapegoats for the loss of the First World War. Revenge and bitterness were in the hearts and minds of the Germans. What could be easier than to take it out on the Jews? Those among the German Jews who were wise and had the wherewithal began to transfer some of their funds to other countries, and some began to leave the country. Among the first to depart were the professional people—the teachers and scientists who were losing their positions merely because they were Jews, the doctors and lawyers who were losing their patients and clients for the same reason. In 1934 Syracuse became host to Dr. and Mrs. Julius Voehl, who aroused considerable interest since they were the first of the Jewish professional families to arrive in Syracuse from Germany. The Voehls were followed rapidly by others between 1934 and 1938. About thirty German families came to Syracuse, mostly professionals and merchants. Those who left before the war started usually had financial resources of their own. They were well received and were assisted in getting settled.

By 1938 Hitler had gained complete control of Germany and Austria, and life became unbearable for the Jewish population. Only those who could secure visas from some other country were permitted to leave, and even they were forced to abandon all their possessions. Jews were in a panic. Requests for visas from distant relatives and strangers began to come to individuals and Jewish agencies in the

United States. A visa could be obtained if an American citizen of means signed an affidavit stating that he would be responsible for the refugee, that the family would not become a public charge, and that he would agree to maintain the applicants until they could become self-supporting. For practically every request a visa was granted. During the years 1938 and 1939 about fifty more families arrived. The majority had relatives here, and others received help through the Jewish Family Service Bureau.

In 1939 Hitler's armies marched into Poland, and the Jews from Poland, Germany, and Austria began to be sent to concentration camps. In some instances, Jewish families received visas even after they had been placed in concentration camps, and they were permitted to leave for other countries.

The Joint Distribution Committee and HIAS (Hebrew Immigrant Aid Society), with representatives in European countries, were finding many Jewish families wandering through Europe. These were termed "Stateless Jews." As fast as passenger space was available and visas were secured, they were sent off to the United States, Canada, or South America.

In 1939 word was recieved from these rescue agencies that Syracuse would be sent one family per month. The Federation appointed Ira Silverstein as chairman of a committee to receive and resettle the refugees as they arrived. Considerably more than one family a month, often as many as four a month, came in during 1940. On March 31, 1941, the Family Service Bureau reported that, to that time, Syracuse had received 104 refugee families, and that during the year the Bureau had an average of six refugee families on relief.

The emigration of East European Jews, which had been hindered by the First World War, was almost completely stopped by the enactment of the quota system in this country in 1924. Those immigrants who were already here had formed their own charitable and benevolent societies and among them were the new Zionist groups, the Labor Zionists (Poale Zion), and the religious and traditional group, Mizrachi.

CHAPTER VII

The Community Expands

ZIONISM IN SYRACUSE

Even before Theodor Herzl convened the first Zionist Congress in Basle, Switzerland, on August 27, 1897,[1] Syracuse had a Zionist society.

Joseph H. Hertz, who came to Syracuse in 1894 as rabbi of Temple Adath Yeshurun, should be credited with bringing organized Zionism to Syracuse. The Jewish youth of Syracuse were attracted to him, and he was particularly influential in arousing the interest of two young men in Zionism—Samuel D. Solomon and T. Aaron Levy, both native Americans and dedicated Jews. Together, they organized the Zion Society of Syracuse in 1896.

In 1898, Dr. Richard Gottheil, a professor at Columbia University and president of the Federated Zionist Organization of Greater New York, was invited to come to Syracuse. Arrangements were made for him to deliver a lecture on Zionism at the Grand Opera House. Following is a report of the lecture as it appeared in the *Syracuse Daily Journal* on March 28, 1898:

THE ZIONIST MOVEMENT

Dr. Richard Gottheil, professor of Semitic languages in Columbia University, delivered a lecture in Grand Opera House last evening before the Syracuse Zion Society of this city, in which he discussed the Zionist movement which was formulated by the convention at Basle, Switzerland last August. Dr. Gottheil is the president of the federated Zionist societies of greater New York and vicinity.

The Syracuse society has grown rapidly since its organization and

Syracuse, N. Y.
April 20th 1923.

Honorable William M. Calder
United States Senate
Washington
D. C.

Dear Sir:-

    The undersigned respectfully urge you to support
and vote for the so-called Lodge Resolution now before the
Congress favoring the establishment of a National Homeland
in Palestine for the Jewish people, in accordance with the
provisions contained in the so-called Belfour Declaration
of the British Government of date November 3, 1917.

Frederick W. Betts, First Universalist Church

A. C. Flick, Syracuse University, Syracuse N.Y.

E. E. Sperry,   "   "   "   "

H. A. Eaton   "   "   "   "

G. A. Wilson   "   "   "   "

W. H. Metzler   "   "   "   "

James R. Day   "   "   "   "

William Yerington "   "   "   "

Albert C. Fulton   First Presbyterian Church

John H. Applebee May Memorial Church (Unitarian

William Rubenstein   40 x Gurney Bldg.

John B. Howe,   Syracuse Herald

Reproduction of petition circulated by Rabbi Samuel Yalow and signed by
the Reverend Frederick W. Betts and Chancellor James R. Day of Syracuse
University, and members of the faculty (all non-Jews), and sent to members of the United States Senate.

last evening the Opera house was crowded. Rabbi J. H. Hertz is president of the Syracuse society.

Another Zionist organization was started, called the Young Hebrew Zionist Society. William Gerber was the first president. It apparently did not last long, since nothing further is recorded about it.

In 1900 the New York State Zionist Federation held its convention in Syracuse. Rabbi Stephen S. Wise, a young Reform rabbi of New York and son of a rabbi who was a leader in Zionism, was the principal speaker.

Rabbi Hertz did not remain in Syracuse long. He soon left for South Africa, and later was called to become the Chief Rabbi of The United Hebrew Congregations of the British Empire.

When Rabbi Hertz left Syracuse, organized Zionism began to wane. Samuel D. Solomon almost single-handedly kept a semblance of a Zionist Club going. For a number of years, he acted as president, secretary, and delegate to the national conventions.

On November 13, 1917, a year before the end of the First World War, England announced the Balfour Declaration, which stated that "His Majesty's Government views with favor the establishing of a National Homeland for Jews in Palestine." The Jews in Syracuse, as elsewhere, were elated. Sermons on Zionism were preached from the pulpits, but again no great interest was manifested in a local Zionist organization.

It was not until the early 1930's that the national Zionist Organization of America began to take notice of Syracuse. The national office sent Abraham Goldberg, an author, lecturer, and pioneer Zionist, to call on the local rabbis. He secured names of people whom they thought would be interested, and arranged for a luncheon meeting at Ginsberg's Restaurant. As a result a committee was appointed, consisting of Dr. Aaron Burman, Sam Weinstein, and B. G. Rudolph, to revitalize the Zionist movement in Syracuse.

The New York office sent a regional director, Mr. Neurenberg, to help the committee get organized. Invitations and good publicity brought together a representative group. The meeting was held at the Syracuse Hotel, and Neurenberg and one of the rabbis spoke. B. G. Rudolph was elected president, Dr. Aaron Burman, secretary, and Sam Weinstein, treasurer.[2]

Rabbi Benjamin Friedman, the young Reform rabbi at the Temple of Concord, was sympathetic toward Zionism. He had grown up with Abba Hillel Silver and Barnet Brickner, both Reform rabbis, and all had belonged to the Herzl Club together as boys in New York City. The strong opposition to Zionism at Concord was disappearing. Since dues were only $5 per year, many Jews joined the Syracuse Zionists, even though they were not completely in sympathy with the movement.

Rudolph, Burman, and Weinstein rotated as president, the membership grew, and meetings were held regularly. A Zionist luncheon club met weekly at Ginsberg's Restaurant.

Rabbi Irving Hyman arrived in Syracuse in 1935 to serve at Temple Adath Yeshurun. He was a strong Zionist and immediately became active in the local movement. The membership of the local district of Z.O.A. at that time was the largest Jewish men's group in Syracuse, reaching over a thousand in the 1940's.

In 1937 Rabbi Hyman was elected by the Syracuse district, and endorsed by the national office, to be a delegate to the 20th World Zionist Congress in Zurich, Switzerland. Hitler and the Nazis were then at the height of their power in Germany. Jews who had connections and the means were escaping from Germany and Austria. England, trying to placate the Arabs, placed a quota on the number of Jews who could enter Palestine. The *Haganah* (an underground resistance group against England) was being helped secretly by the Zionists.

The Second World War was imminent. The Syracuse Jewish Welfare Federation had big quotas to meet, and the Zionists took an active part in the raising of necessary funds during the campaign.

In 1941 the Zionist organization planned a gala affair for their annual meeting on December seventh. At the business meeting in the afternoon Bernard S. Cohen was elected president. A banquet was to take place that evening on the Onondaga Hotel Roof Garden. Judge Bernard A. Rosenblatt, an eminent Zionist, came from New York for the occasion. As the afternoon meeting was about to adjourn, it was learned that an announcement had just come in over the radio that Japan had attacked the United States fleet at Pearl Harbor. President Franklin D. Roosevelt was to address Congress in the morning and request a declaration of war. The question arose whether to proceed with the banquet. It was decided that, inasmuch as all preparations had been made for the occasion, the program should proceed as planned.

Rabbi Friedman and his wife Mary were present at the banquet, and on his advice the program was curtailed. With the United States about to enter the Second World War, there was no gaiety in what was to have been a gala event.

During the war the Zionist District of Syracuse continued its activity, more determined than ever that Palestine should become the homeland for the Jews, particularly the remnants that survived the concentration camps after the holocaust and the death of six million Jews.

Germany surrendered in the spring of 1945, and Japan followed a few months later. In 1948 Israel was established as a state. However, the surrounding Arab countries refused to recognize Israel's independence and attacked the new nation. Those were exciting days, especially for the Zionists. Sam Abramson was elected president on October 21, 1948. The Syracuse Zionist organization sponsored a drive, "Food for Israel," and was determined to fill a railroad freight car with canned goods for Israel. Active in the food campaign were A. Solomon Menter, Sam Yellin, Nathan Share, Earl Hart, Aaron Burman, Sam Weinstein, B. G. Rudolph, Max H. Rudolph, Chester Sagenkahn, Rabbi Earl Stone, Joseph Byer, and Philip Roth. The Regent and the Wescott Theaters put on kiddie shows on Saturday afternoon, requiring one can of food for admission. Hadassah and other Jewish organizations assisted. On Sunday, December 19, 1948, volunteers with borrowed trucks loaded the freight car, and the canned food was on its way to Israel.

On October 19, 1949, Melvin Rudolph was elected president. His leadership brought about a greater participation in the Federation, and the Zionists undertook to collect the delinquent pledges. A resolution was passed to oppose the internationalization of Jerusalem and forwarded to President Harry S Truman.

Joseph Byer become active in 1950 and formed a Young Judea Group. The Zionists and Hadassah provided the funds for children to go to Hebrew summer camps.

B. G. Rudolph was elected president of the Western New York Zionist region in 1950. A regional office was opened in the Keith Building under the direction of Milton Parsons. Among the new men elected to the administrative committee were Sanford Engel, Irving Solomon, Max Gardner, William Schwartz, Ben Besdin, Mayer Kaplovitz, Meyer Branse, Jay Rudolph, and Lou Yaffee. Sol Kay was elected president in 1951. The Israeli Symphony was brought to Syracuse at a cost of $60,000. The receipts were just about enough to cover expenses, but the event provided good public relations for Israel.

A. Solomon Menter was elected president in 1952. Shashani Damari, a Yenenite singer, was brought to Syracuse to help in the sale of bonds for Israel.

Sanford Engel was elected president in 1953. When President Harry S Truman passed through Syracuse, Rabbi Hyman and B. G. Rudolph presented him with a scroll in appreciation of his recognition of Israel as a sovereign state on the day it was so declared. The national office raised the dues to $15, and the membership started to decline.

In 1954, Earl Hart was elected president, and in 1955, Rabbi Hyman assumed that office.

The Syracuse district of the Zionist organization now has a hard core of dedicated members. Although greatly reduced in numbers, they still carry on an active organization.[3]

Labor Zionism, the Folk Shule, and Ben Zion Miller

Labor Zionism, the Folk Shule, and Ben Zion Miller—when you thought of one, it immediately brought to mind all three.

In the early 1900's, the immigrants coming from Poland and Russia were more sophisticated than the earlier Jewish settlers from those countries. They had definite leanings toward socialism and, while they were pronounced Jews, they lacked the strong religious feelings which inspired the earlier Jewish immigrants. As soon as there were enough of them in the community, they formed the Arbeiter Ring (the Workmen's Circle). The group in Syracuse rented rooms on Adams Street and collected a library of Yiddish literature in order to promote Yiddish culture.

In 1915 they opened a cooperative bakery on Harrison Street. The object was to lower the price of bread for the working man and also to realize a small profit for their cultural activities. While Zionism was growing among the middle-class Jews, in this socialist group Zionism was not important.

However, in the large cities like New York, Philadelphia, and Chicago, the working-class group had formed the Poale Zion movement (Labor Zionists). It was with this movement that Ben Zion Miller became involved and organized a Labor Zionist group in Syracuse.

In 1902, at the age of eighteen, Ben Zion Miller had arrived in New York from his native city of Kovno, Lithuania. Socialistically inclined but with a strong Zionist background, he participated in the founding of the Poale Zion movement. At one of the meetings of this group he met Lillian Orland who later became his wife. They were married in 1909 and, at the urging of a cousin, came to Syracuse in 1913.[4]

Among the leaders of the Workmen's Circle there were men who realized the value of inculcating their ideology in the youth. Isidor Shapiro, assisted by Harry Aaron Pine and Ben Zimmerman, organized a branch of the Nazionaler Radicole, later known as the Folk Shule. They opened a classroom over Nathan Teckler's secondhand furniture store on the corner of Grape and Monroe Streets.

In the meantime, Ben Zion Miller organized a branch of Poale Zion. This group, too, was interested in education and joined the Folk Shule, but as Zionists they wanted Hebrew to be added to the Yiddish curriculum. A controversy then ensued between the Workmen's Circle and the Poale Zion society. It was finally settled by forming a parents' organization with representation on the board of directors, and thereafter they controlled the Folk Shule.

The Folk Shule carried on with no more than fifty pupils at any one time, under the capable direction of Sigmund Shapiro. Later, when he left, the Folk Shule was forced to close for lack of a teacher.

Poale Zion, under the leadership of Ben Zion Miller, built a center for their activities on Monroe Street. The Folk Shule was reorganized at this location and with a new teacher, H. Rosenberg, made considerable progress. When it later became necessary to obtain an assistant teacher, they secured a university student, Judah Shapiro. This young man was an excellent teacher, and later became a noted author and lecturer in Jewry. He was an organizer and the first executive director of the National Foundation for Jewish Culture, organized in 1960.

Herschel Rosenberg, the principal teacher of the Folk Shule, left to make his home in Palestine. Judah Shapiro graduated from Syracuse University and also left the city, so that the Folk Shule again started to go downhill.

At this point Ben Zion Miller began to take an active interest in the general Jewish Community. Those were the years in the middle 1930's when Hitler came to power, and the need for help for the Jews of Europe and Palestine was urgent. When the Syracuse Jewish Welfare Federation had to increase the pace of fund raising, Ben Zion Miller took a responsible part in the Federation. He was looked upon as the leader and the representative of Poale Zion and the Workmen's Circle, as well as of that group of Jews who were not as a rule affiliated with synagogues or temples. He made a fine appearance at meetings, spoke softly with a slight accent, and occasionally lapsed into Yiddish. Ordinarily, the business and professional men who headed the Federation looked askance on a man who represented a group of socialists, but Ben Zion Miller was looked up to. He worked hard for the Federation, and when allocation time came around, the organizations that he represented were usually well taken care of.

Ben Zion Miller was elected campaign chairman for the 1954 Federation campaign. At the end of the campaign he was tendered a testimonial dinner at the LaFayette Country Club. Most of the leaders of the Jewish community participated in the occasion, and appropriate and well-deserved plaudits were given him that evening. Through the efforts of Ben Zion Miller, the Poale Zion and the Folk Shule were accepted as integral parts of the Syracuse Jewish community. Their members, on their part, began to join the temples and synagogues. The second generation of this group—men like Sidney Greenberg, an eminent attorney, and Dr. Irvin M. Franklin—while still imbued with the ideology of their fathers, are far from the socialists that their forebears were when they first landed in America.

When Dr. Theodor Herzl organized the First World Zionist Congress in 1897, political Zionism was oriented more toward the West. Dr. Herzl, himself an Austrian and an assimilated Jew, appealed more to Western European and American Jews. Political Zionism stirred the Jews of Austria, Germany, France, England, and America.

At the Second and Third World Congresses, the Eastern European Jews joined in large numbers and brought new ideologies into the movement. The Jewish workers introduced the ideas of Poale Zion; they combined Zionism with Socialism and desired to establish Israel as a socialist state. Then came the ultra-religious group, Mizrachi, which formed the right wing of Zionism. It was their ideology to establish Israel according to biblical and Talmudic tradition, so that it should be governed by the laws contained therein.

We have already covered the general Zionist and the Labor Zionist groups. The third group, the Mizrachi, also had an organization in Syracuse, but it was never very strong numerically. At different times it was led by the Reverend Moses J. Braude and Rabbi Samuel Yalow.

At present there are no Poale Zion or men's Mizrachi chapters in Syracuse, and the general Zionists, which at one time had over a thousand members, are down to a small group. But what did happen in Syracuse, as elsewhere throughout the country, is that the women's counterparts of these organizations, Hadassah and Pioneer Women, have taken over.

The men feel that when they contribute to the local Jewish welfare organization they are doing their duty to Zionism and Israel, and they do not feel it necessary to belong to a separate Zionist organization.

Women's organizations like Hadassah, with three chapters in Syracuse, are doing a remarkable job in organizing and contributing to health and education in Israel. The Pioneer Women are active in support of agricultural schools in Israel, and Mizrachi women have two chapters in Syracuse, the Mizrachi Seniors and Rannana, the young women's branch. Their aim is not only to assist the original men's organization in support of religious law and tradition in the State of Israel, but also to foster and support trade organizations for youth.

THE REVEREND MOSES J. BRAUDE AND THE
JEWISH HOME OF CENTRAL NEW YORK

From the day he arrived in Syracuse, just before the turn of the century, until his death on March 26, 1957, Reverend Moses J. Braude was in the center of the momentum that moved the Syracuse Orthodox Jewish Community.[5]

As the spiritual head of the oldest Orthodox synagogue, Beth Israel (Grape Street Shul), he had the respect of the community. Young and energetic, he entered into the activities of every existing Jewish organization, and whenever an unfulfilled need was apparent he immediately set about to form a new society.

On August 14, 1900, he married Esther Pearlman, daughter of the Reverend Moses M. Pearlman. His father-in-law was cantor of Poiley Tzedeck Synagogue for fifty-five years and was a respected dignitary in the Orthodox community.

In 1903 Moses Braude organized the Hebrew Aid Society, an organization to help persons in need of small sums to tide them over periods of strain. This society, which existed over thirty years during the period when the immigration of Jews was at its highest, did a great deal of good for the new settlers. The recipients could repay the money in weekly installments. Assistance of this kind, in the old Jewish tradition, is considered the most virtuous of all charities.

While a number of other charitable organizations also owe their beginning to the Reverend Moses Braude, the one with which his name will always be remembered is the Jewish Home for the Aged. If it ever can be said that any organization owes its existence to one person that can truly be said of the establishment of the Jewish Home of Central New York. Reverend Braude started to agitate for what was commonly called an "Old Age Home" in 1910. However, it was not until 1912, when an elderly man, sick and helpless, was found lying in the basement of one of the Orthodox synagogues, that the Jewish community was aroused to action.

Reverend Braude gathered around him such stalwarts of the Orthodox community as Marx Rashkower, Harry Serling, Mark Gais, Abraham and Isaac Markson, Louis Manson, Jacob Cooper, H. Falkowitz, and Marx Goldman. He also understood that the ladies, usually more sentimental than the men, could be of great help. He therefore formed a Ladies' Auxiliary of the Home for the Aged. The organizers, and for many years the leaders, were Mrs. M. Tumin, Mrs. M. Silver, Mrs. Louis Manson, Mrs. H. Serling, Mrs. Elman, and Mrs. Weinstein.

On November 13, 1912, the Jewish Home for the Aged was duly organized. Two societies banded together to give the organization the impetus and the financial help it needed to get under way. They were The Friendly Inn (*Hochnoses Orchim*) and *Linas Hatzedeck*. The following were elected as the first officers: Marx Rashkower, president; Marx Goldman, vice-president; and Reverend Moses Braude, secretary.

This was strictly an Orthodox undertaking, as evidenced by the fact that no one from the Reform Jewish group came foward to help. This information was found in a letter from Dr. Nathan Jacobson, a distinguished representative of the Temple of Concord:

November 27, 1912

Rev. Moses Braude
City

Dear Sir:

I do not know whether you are the proper person to receive this communication, but not knowing of any one else to whom to send it, I am addressing it to you.

I saw in a Syracuse paper recently that I had been selected as one of the directors of the proposed Jewish home for the aged in this city. This selection has been made entirely without any consultation with me and is therefore without authority. Please notify those who took such action that I will not serve in this position and that I know of no good reason why such a home should be established in Syracuse. We have now more Jewish charities than we are able to take care of, and to add to the number means to make those already existing weaker and less capable of doing good for which they were created. Under no circumstances would I therefore serve as a director in the new organization and I must express my great surprise that any one saw fit to select me for any such position without first asking my consent. I am,

> Very truly yours,
> Nathan Jacobson (Signed) [6]

On November 26, 1912, the first meeting of the board of directors took place in the Beth Israel Synagogue. The location committee, composed of the officers of the Home and the leaders of the two supporting organizations, reported that they had purchased the Thomas Dunn estate on Irving Avenue. This consisted of two houses facing Irving Avenue and the Dunn homestead, an old but imposing house with seventeen rooms and several acres of ground extending to Renwick Avenue. The cost was $19,000, and the house was immediately available.

Entrance to The Jewish Home for the Aged on Irving Avenue, in 1914, where Memorial Hospital now stands. (*Courtesy of The Jewish Home for the Aged*)

The Jewish Home for the Aged on Irving Avenue in 1914.
(*Courtesy of The Jewish Home for the Aged*)

The Jewish Home of Central New York on East Genesee Street.
(*Courtesy of the institution*)

Entrance to The Jewish Home of Central
New York on East Genesee Street.   (*Courtesy
of the institution*)

Y.M.H.A. debating team and members, 1908, at Freeman's Hall. Gerson Rubenstein, president is seated in the center. (*Courtesy of Myron Small*)

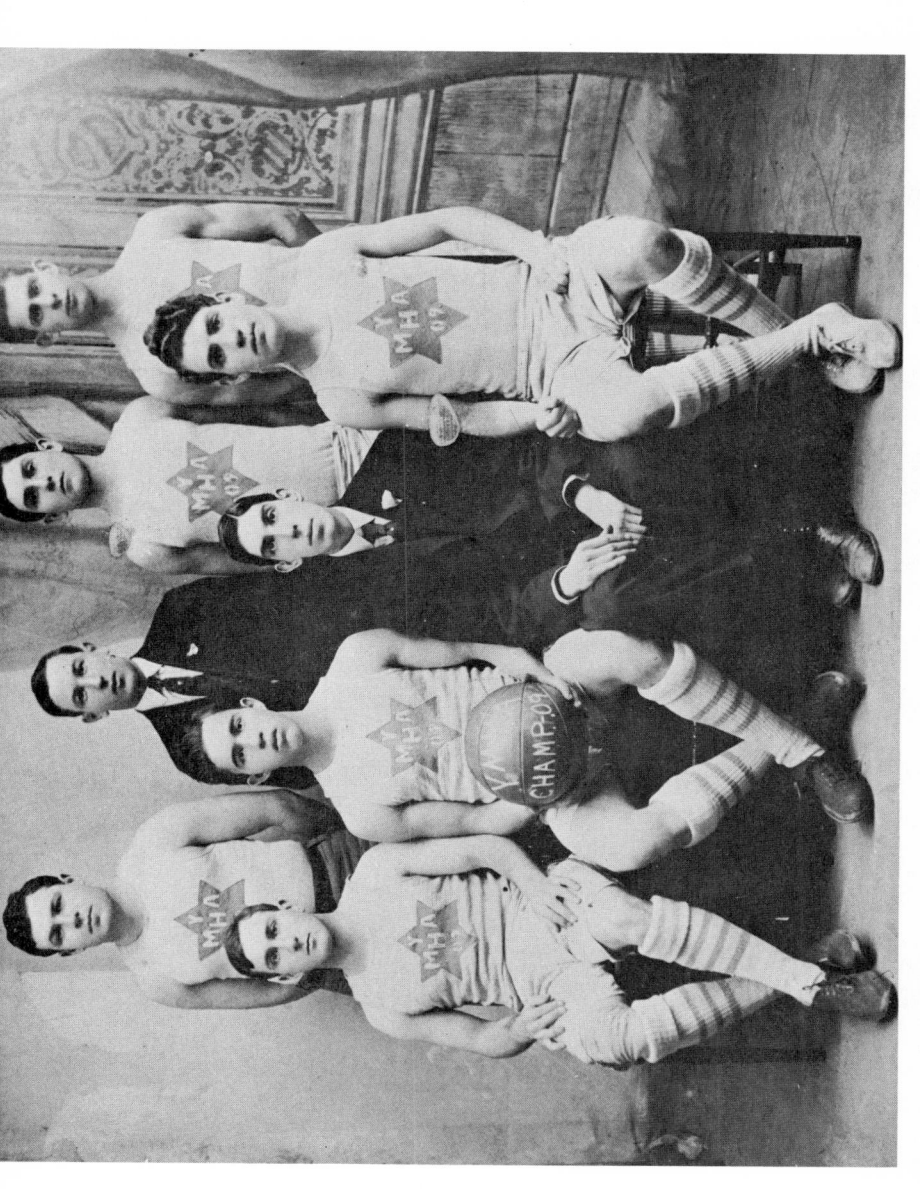

Y.M.H.A. basketball team, champions of the city league in 1909. Left to right, standing: Felix Jacobs, Max Rosenbloom (coach), Morris Schicofsky, Abe Rosenbloom. Seated: Isidor Rubenstein, Louis Pearlman, Irving Lewis (manager), Max Volinsky. (*Courtesy of Myron Small*)

Y.M.H.A. (left), and the Marshall Home (right) on Cedar Street, 1910.
(*Courtesy of Onondaga Historical Society*)

Architect's drawing of the Jewish Community Center on East Genesee Street, facing Fellows Avenue. (*Courtesy of the institution*)

Convention of the New York State Folk Shule teachers at The Folk Shule on Monroe Street. *(Courtesy of family of Ben Zion Miller)*

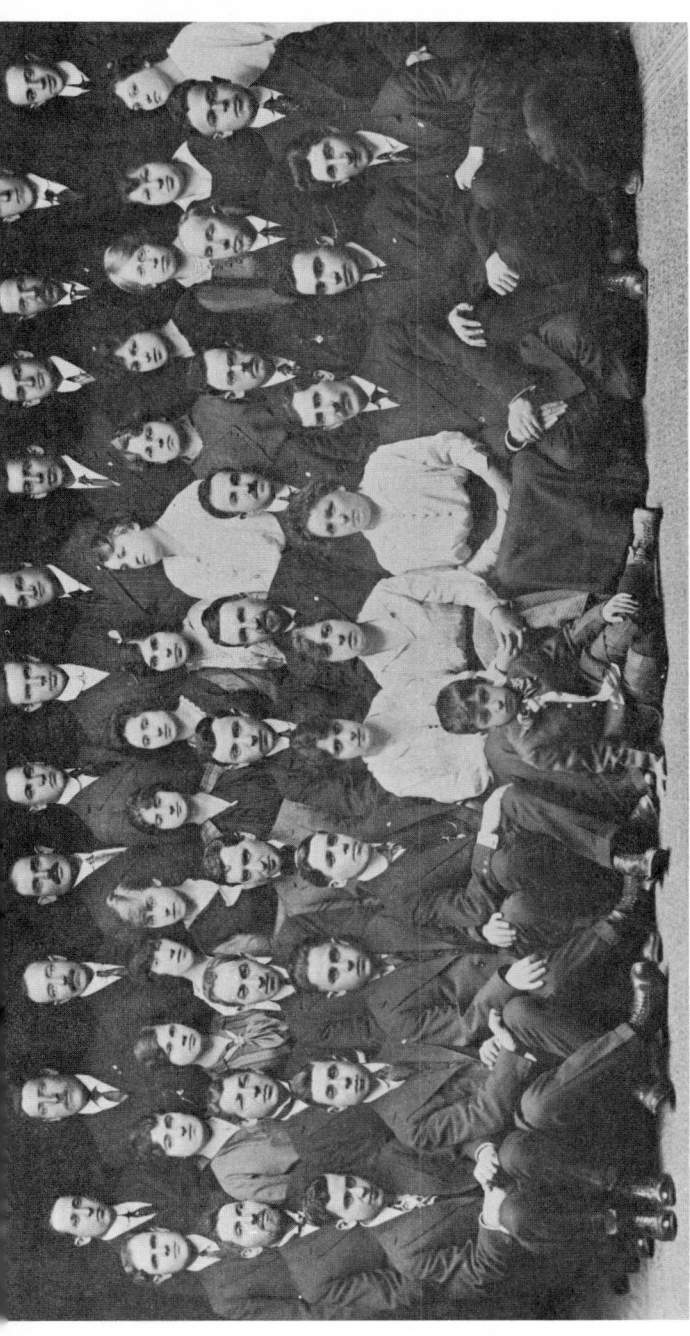

Syracuse Relief Committee

for

Jewish War Sufferers

FIRST ROW, LEFT TO RIGHT

1. Abraham Hurwitz.
2. Joe Friedlander.
3. Carl Hurwitz.
4. Michael Gruskin
5. Tillie Seldin
6. Philip Zimmerman
7. Rose Meadow
8. Fannie Shapiro
9. Gabriel Begleman
10. Hyman Herman
11. Bernard Chadwick

SECOND ROW, LEFT TO RIGHT

1. Morris Sklare
2. Harris Swidler
3. Harry Serling
4. Lazar Weltman
5. Solomon Feinstone
6. Robin B. Pelitz
7. Louis Shapiro
8. Max Zimmerman
9. Abraham S. Wolovelsky
10. Nathan Adler

THIRD ROW, LEFT TO RIGHT

1. Sam Kaner
2. Mollie Denemark
3. Rose Marble
4. Lillian Marble
5. Sadie LaVine
6. Etta Miller
7. Dora Miller
8. Sarah Miller
9. Goldie Weltman
10. Anna Grimm
11. Gussie Swidler
12. Sarah Freeman
13. Frieda Serby
14. Ida Zolmanoff

FOURTH ROW, LEFT TO RIGHT

1. Morris Killian
2. Solomon Katz
3. Oshar Rubinstein
4. Abraham Silver
5. Harry Trinin
6. Sam Port
7. John Shapiro
8. Benjamin Weiner
9. Mamie Karmen
10. Ezekiel Krilin
11. Abraham Elkin
12. Morris Zangwill

Syracuse Relief Committee for Jewish War Sufferers, World War I.

(Courtesy of family of Ben Zion Miller)

The Hebrew Free School, 1065 Orange (now McBride) Street, dedicated July 29, 1897. (*The Hebrew Standard*)

The Oberdorfer Brass Foundry on Water Street, about 1910. Oberdorfer's made many parts for the Franklin automobile. (*Courtesy of Mrs. Minnie Goodman*)

Temple of Concord, corner of
Madison Street and University
Avenue, dedicated
September 22, 1911.
(*Courtesy of Temple of Concord*)

Interior of Temple of Concord, before the new organ was installed in 1966. (*Courtesy of Temple of Concord*)

Temple Adath Yeshurun, corner of Harrison Street and Crouse Avenue, dedicated in 1922. (*Courtesy of Temple Adath Yeshurun*)

Architectural model of the new Temple Adath Yeshurun to be erected on Kimber Road. The ground-breaking ceremony was held on October 6, 1968. (*Photo by H. M. Zalmanoff*)

Temple Beth El on East Genesee Street, combining the congregations of Beth Israel and Poiley Tzedeck, dedicated September 11, 1965. (Photo by Rowan and Klineboer)

A committee was appointed to hire a caretaker for the home, and Marx Rashkower, Marx Goldman, and Jacob Gais were named as a building committee.

The founding of the Jewish Home for the Aged in Syracuse is a good example of the caliber of the leaders of the Orthodox groups in the early years of the twentieth century. Led by the Reverend Moses J. Braude and inspired by the traditional Jewish spirit of devotion to charity, this small group of men, without funds and lacking the support of the wealthier element in the Jewish community, were able to establish an imposing institution. But this most worthwhile institution, rendering a service to all of Central New York, did not grow by itself. It took many years of hard labor by dedicated people. Moses Braude and Mark Gais traveled to the surrounding cities—Utica, Binghamton, Watertown, and all towns in between—making speeches and soliciting pledges for annual contributions. The Home had to be furnished, the aged had to be cared for. Since the founders knew little about custodial care, they made mistakes, but they learned with experience. When the Home was renovated, and the old folks arrived and were looked after, the leaders were justly proud of their achievement. In the meantime their zeal and effort had attracted others, and many important names were added to their board of directors.

In 1924, after ten years of operation, it became known that Syracuse University was about to build a medical school on Irving Avenue, and that the Women's and Children's Hospital (now the Memorial Hospital) would like to move from West Genesee Street to Irving Avenue in order to be adjacent to the Medical College. The only place with large enough grounds was the site occupied by the Home. The directors were thrown into a dilemma—how could they give up the Home?

It was very difficult for the founders, who had labored so hard and had invested so much of their time and money, to think of selling their cherished institution. Some members of the board who seldom before attended meetings came to the special meetings called for the purpose of considering the sale. There was much pressure from outside sources. After all, the most prominent people in the city were on the boards of the University and the hospital. The founders held out. The University appealed to Louis Marshall of New York City, who was on the board of the University and a native of Syracuse. A letter arrived from him recommending that the Home be sold for $50,000. Mark Gais asked "How can we sell it for $50,000 when on the questionnaire from the Community Chest we have placed a value of $75,000 on the Home?" This was communicated to Louis Marshall, who suggested a compromise of $60,000.

After many special meetings and much discussion, it was decided to sell the site on Irving Avenue and to buy the property of Walter D. Stone on East Genesee Street just outside the city limits.

The people in the Jewish neighborhood were very much disturbed over this decision. They said that for ten years the Home for the Aged had been in their midst, and whenever they wished to visit with the old folks they could do so. Now, how could one desecrate the Sabbath by riding on a trolley to the Home? After all, they had a share in the Home. Did they not throw their nickels and dimes in the *tzedakah* box when they visited the Home? Why were they not consulted before the sale was made? The Reverend Moses Braude had much explaining to do when he walked to the *shul* on Grape Street.

When the new Home was dedicated in the spring of 1925, everyone admitted that the change had been for the best. The Walter Stone property consisted of a large country-estate type of home, much larger than the one on Irving Avenue. There were also a large cattle barn and two smaller barns. Louis Hurwitz presented the Home with a cow, so that the old folks could have fresh milk. Someone else presented a horse and two hundred chickens. More old folks were accepted, and in a short time the Home had more guests than there were rooms. The need for additional space became apparent.

In 1929 a large modern addition was constructed. In 1930 more land was purchased, and in 1935 still another addition to the Home was completed. In 1959 the original Walter Stone house was demolished, and a large building connecting the two wings was constructed. In 1965 apartments for elderly couples were added, through the munificence of Jessie and Harry Kaplan.[7]

As this is written, fifty-five years after its founding, The Jewish Home of Central New York is housed in a group of buildings covering more than twenty acres of high ground in a pastoral setting just outside the city of Syracuse. It is estimated that it has a value of several million dollars.

Besides housing more than one hundred of the sick and elderly, it has separate apartments for old and retired couples who desire and need the kind of service extended to people of their age. The Home is accredited as having all the necessary qualifications of a well-operated and efficient institution, and receives financial aid from state and local agencies.

There is something about an institution for the aged and homeless that evokes the concern of many people whom other spheres of philanthropy do not touch. As a result, the Home has never lacked efficient leadership and dedicated volunteer workers.

SYRACUSE—A GOOD "THEATER CITY"

Syracuse had the reputation of being a good theatrical city. From the day the old Wieting Hall burned down, and John M. Wieting rebuilt it into a theater called "The Wieting Opera House," Syracuse enjoyed good theaters.

In the early days the elite of Syracuse looked down on the theater. Show business was thought to be for the common people. But when the Wieting was rebuilt for the third time in 1872, and such stars as Mary Anderson, Edwin Booth, Sarah Bernhardt, Joseph Jefferson, and others of this caliber were brought to Syracuse, the theater was accepted by all of the people.

Other theaters then came along. The Barton Block, which at one time housed Thalheimer's grocery store, was rebuilt as the Grand Opera House and was commonly called "The Grand." The Bastable Theater was built where Bernheimer and Block had their notions store, and Richard Mansfield dedicated the house. There were now three theaters—the Wieting, which accommodated the stars and the road shows; the Grand, which was turned into a vaudeville house; and the Bastable, which featured the stock companies and was called the house of the "10-20-30 shows" (Orchestra, 30¢; balcony, 20¢; and gallery seats, 10¢). Those were the days of matinee idols, of whom the most popular for many years in Syracuse was Frank Wilcox.

Syracuse also produced stars of the stage, the best known of whom was Edna May, a letter carrier's daughter who "made good." She was recognized on both sides of the Atlantic and made her biggest hit in

"The Belle of New York" as the Salvation Army lassie. Edna May later married the multi-millionaire, Oscar Lewisohn.

Another well-known star from this city was "Mme. Pauline L'Allemand," born Pauline Ellsasser on the North Side. About 1900 two Jewish brothers, Jack and Phil Kaufman, joined the "Avon Comedy Four," and were "top-liners" on the vaudeville circuit. Irving Kaufman, a younger brother, did well as a blackface comedian and as a monologist in the early days of radio.[8]

Simon Silverman, who married Harriet Freeman of Syracuse, also played an important part in American theater. He entered the theatrical news reporting business by starting the periodical, *Variety*, with the $500 his father-in-law, George Freeman, gave him as a wedding present. His wife helped him by writing a woman's column under the heading "The Skirt." *Variety* is still the leading theatrical paper in the United States.[9]

The Boys from Syracuse

THE SHUBERTS. David and Carrie Shubert arrived in Syracuse about 1880. They came from Poland and had five children: Sarah, Lee, Samuel, Jacob, and Dora. The three oldest were probably born in Poland, while the two youngest claimed to have been born in Syracuse.

David started out as a peddler, but was not an outstanding success. Until the boys were old enough to augment the family income, they were very poor and lived in a small wooden house behind another house on Grape Street. Later they moved to Orange Street, and before long their situation improved.

As the children grew, each became an asset to the family. Sammy started to pass out handbills for the Grand Opera House when he was eight. Later he became a program boy at the Wieting. Lee peddled newspapers, and Jake sold candy. As soon as Sam moved up to be assistant treasurer of the Wieting, the wheel of fortune turned in their direction. The family moved into a better home on Adams Street near the old Adams Street school. Lee was at first a clerk and later, with a partner, opened a "Gent's Furnishing Store" in the University Block.

Jake obtained a job at the Grand Opera House, and Sam became acquainted with many of the theatrical people who came to play at the Wieting. A visiting producer promised Sam that, if he should some day want to take a show on the road, Sam should come to see him in New York City. Sam took him at his word, went to New York City, and the producer made good on his promise, giving him a show with the title of "The Texas Steer." Sam took the show to many cities in the West, and it was a hit. For the first time in his life Sam made some real money, and came back to Syracuse determined to lease a theater in his home town. With the help of some friends, he induced the owners to lease him the Bastable Theater.

Sam turned the Bastable from a vaudeville into a stock company theater, and it was an immediate success. When the theater began to prosper, Sam put Lee and Jake in charge and went back to New York to take another show on the road—but what he really wanted was to lease more theaters like the Bastable. He kept working at it and soon took over the Majestic in Utica, a theater in Rochester, and others in Buffalo and Troy.

Sam now had the beginning of a circuit of theaters in upper New York State. However, he was not satisfied until he had a theater in New York City. He took Jesse Oberdorfer in as a partner, and together they leased the Herald Square Theater on Thirty-Fourth Street. That brought Sam recognition in the theatrical center of the world, and from there it went on and on. Samuel Shubert was the proverbial dynamo; he was also the spark plug and the builder. His untimely death at twenty-nine in a train accident in 1905, while he was on his way to sign a lease for another theater in Pittsburgh, was a deep tragedy in the house of Shubert.

Sam's two brothers, Lee and Jake, carried on until they owned or controlled nine hundred theaters throughout the country. Of the forty legitimate theaters in New York, twenty were owned or leased by the Shubert brothers.

Both Jake and Lee Shubert are gone now. Before Jake died, Lionel O. Grossman, a relative in Syracuse, solicited contributions for charitable institutions from him. During the last eight or ten years of his life he gave each year $4,500 to the Syracuse Cerebral Palsy Fund (a favorite agency of Lionel Grossman), $4,000 to Temple Adath Yeshurun, and $2,500 to the Jewish Home of Central New York, with a request that the gifts be anonymous. The large Shubert Enterprises are now headed by Larry Shubert Lawrence, a grand-nephew of Sam, Lee, and Jake Shubert.[10]

MARCUS HEIMAN. Another Syracusan, the son of Isaac and Celia Heiman, also became a leader in theatrical enterprises. Marcus got his start with the Shuberts. While still in his teens he was treasurer of the Grand Opera House, later becoming treasurer and manager of the Bastable Theater.

From there he went on to Boston and Chicago and the Fuller Theater in Madison, Wisconsin. He founded the chain of Finn and Heiman Theaters, with show houses throughout the Middle West. He also owned and operated theaters in Baltimore, Washington, Boston, Pittsburgh, Chicago, and Los Angeles. At one time he headed the Radio-Keith-Orpheum vaudeville circuit. He died in New York at the age of seventy-three and is buried in Syracuse. Throughout his life he was a contributor to theatrical and charitable organizations, and was a member of the Lambs' Club and the Athletic Club of New York City.[11]

The Movies

With the advent of moving pictures, the three legitimate theaters in Syracuse were slowly phased out. The nickelodeons and cinemas took over the entertainment field. Where the Wieting Theater once stood now stands the Lincoln Bank garage; the State Tower building now stands on the site of the Bastable Theater; and the Merchants' Bank drive-in branch on East Genesee Street occupies the site of the former Grand Opera House.[12]

Mitchell Fitzer and his brother Ben were among the first to bring moving picture theaters to Syracuse. The early movie theater was primitive, usually being nothing more than a vacant store with ordinary folding chairs and a bed sheet for a screen. The patrons were mostly children, admission was five cents, and if a little brother and sister came together they could get in at the rate of two for five cents. However, the growth of moving picture houses was rapid, and each time a new one opened it was an improvement over the last. The Fitzer theaters, which lasted for years, were the Dreamland on West Onondaga Street near Salina, the Rivoli on West Fayette Street, and the Happy Hour on North Salina Street.

The Cahill Brothers, Ed and Bill, who owned three or four saloons, closed down some of their barrooms and opened movie houses. The first of the theaters built especially for moving pictures was the Crescent, put up by the Cahills in 1910 in the 400 block of South Salina Street where the Addis Company specialty store stands today. The shows were continuous, with vaudeville acts interspersed between the movies. The Crescent was also the first theater to have "talkies," or sound pictures. Later the Cahills built the Temple Theater across Salina Street from the Crescent. After many years it was leased to the Schine Enterprises, and the name was changed to the Paramount.[13]

The Schine Enterprises also were started in Syracuse. Meyer Schine came to Syracuse as a young man. His first venture was to lease a ten-cent movie house on West Fayette Street, the Idle Hour; later he leased the Crescent from the Cahills. It was a small beginning, but before long he and his brother Louis operated one of the largest chains of theaters and hotels in the country.

The Shubert brothers' success was instrumental in establishing the theatrical careers of several Syracuse Jewish men. Myron Kallet, starting out as an usher in the Grand Opera House when it was owned by the Shuberts, became assistant treasurer while still a mere lad. Early in his life he went to Oneida, New York, where he opened his first moving picture theater in the Madison Block, calling it the Madison. It has been remodeled and brought up to date a number of times, but the Madison is still coupled with the name Kallet when one thinks of going to the movies in Oneida. Mike and his brother Sidney have prospered. At one time they owned forty theaters, the television station in Utica, and radio stations in Rome and Oneida.[14]

Another rags-to-riches story is that of Samuel P. Slotnick, who started with a small ten-cent movie house in 1918. He struggled along until the open-air theaters became popular. He opened several around Syracuse; all were successful. His son Herbert now operates a chain of eight theaters and nine popular restaurants in Syracuse. He also has interests in another chain of restaurants that cover the country from coast to coast.[15]

THE SYRACUSE IMPRESARIO. Murray Bernthal is to Syracuse what Sol Hurok is to America, the impresario of Syracuse. A musical artist in his own right, he came to Syracuse in 1928 as a freshman at Syracuse University. After graduation he busied himself with odd jobs in the musical field, and in 1941 originated a symphonette orchestra in which he participated as a musician and leader.

In 1947, Bernthal became the musical director of WSYR, a radio and television station. While there he became acquainted with E. R. Vadeboncoeur, the director and business manager of WSYR. Together they formed and produced the Famous Artists Series of concerts, bringing to Syracuse such artists as Mischa Elman, and famous orchestras such as the Boston Symphony. In 1948 they developed the Country Playhouse project in Fayetteville, a suburb of Syracuse. This has brought to Syracuse audiences some of the best stage shows on the road. It was a success from the start, and the summer theater in Fayetteville was in operation for sixteen years until the city of Syracuse offered the use of the auditorium in the new Henninger High School, where Murray Bernthal continues to bring outstanding theatrical groups to Syracuse. In his academic career, Murray Bernthal is associate professor of music at Syracuse University.[16]

JEWS IN POLITICS

The Jews of Syracuse entered into the stream of Syracuse politics early in the history of the community. Some were nominated for municipal offices by both the Democratic and Republican parties. A number of outstanding men and women were appointed to positions of trust.

One of the earliest Jews elected to office was Jacob Levi, a functionary in the Rosenbloom Shul. He was elected in 1869 as an alderman from the Seventh Ward and was re-elected twice. Joseph Bondy was chosen county supervisor from the Seventh Ward in 1889, and was returned to office in 1890 and 1891. In 1896 Bondy won the nomination and election to the New York State Assembly, where he made an enviable record. George Freeman, a very colorful person, served eight successive terms as alderman from the Seventh Ward between 1893 and 1906.[17]

For the past seventy years we have had men and women of the Jewish faith on the Syracuse Board of Education almost continuously. In 1898 Daniel Rosenbloom, one of the seven Rosenbloom brothers, was the first to be elected to the board. He was chosen as president and served for four years. In 1907 the scholarly attorney, T. Aaron Levy, was elected to the board and served as president between 1909 and 1911. He was followed in 1926 by the congenial N. Wesley Markson, who served three terms. In 1936 one of the leading Jewish women in Syracuse, Dora Mason, began a term of office which continued for twenty-four consecutive years. After her came the popular man-about-town, Harry Marley, who was on the board for eight years and was chosen as president during his last term. Dr. Kenneth E. Gale was a very able member of the board from 1960 until he resigned in 1967, and in 1968 the up-and-coming business leader, Norman M. Pinsky, became the latest Jewish member of that body.[18]

Following the Reverend Jacob Levi and George Freeman as aldermen, Emanuel Goldstein was elected in 1914 to represent the Sixteenth Ward and served one term. Max Rosenbloom, the hardware merchant was alderman of the Eighteenth Ward from 1930 to 1938, and Irving ("Sonny") Simon represented the Fifteenth Ward from 1934 to 1938.

In 1938 the city charter was revised and, instead of an alderman representing each ward, the city was divided into five council districts; one councilman is elected from each district, while four other councilmen and the president are elected from the city at large. After the charter was changed, Jacob Rosenberg represented the Fourth District from 1942 to 1945, and Albert Orenstein represented the Fifth District for eight years, from 1958 to 1965, during the last four years of which he was the Republican majority leader. In 1966 Robert Leverton was elected councilman from the Fifth District and is now serving as the Republican majority leader.

Supervisors

Since Joseph Bondy was elected supervisor of the Seventh Ward (the Jewish neighborhood) in 1889, there has been a Jewish man on the board almost continuously for over seventy-five years. Moses Rubin took Bondy's place on the Board of Supervisors in 1893 and served with distinction for four terms. Harry Cohn was elected supervisor in 1905; his tavern on Grape Street near Jefferson was a mecca for politicians from all over the city. They could always count on a good plate of cold roast duck and hot baked beans (the specialty of the house). He represented the Fifteenth Ward, which included most of the old Seventh Ward, for fifteen years. Levi L. Silverman was the supervisor of the Sixteenth Ward for one term. Nathan Abelson took his place and served until 1920, when he was named as Municipal Court judge.[19] From then on we have had the following Jewish men serve on the Board of Supervisors: Joseph Stolusky, Eli Gingold, Bernard Cohen, Albert Orenstein, Leonard Shapero, and Ephraim Shapero, who is the 1968 chairman of the County of Onondaga Legislature, which supplanted the Board of Supervisors in 1967. Bernard Cohen has the distinction of being the only Democrat ever elected as supervisor from the Seventeenth Ward.

The following have served, or are serving as judges: Nathan Abelson began his term as judge of the Municipal Court on March 4, 1931; Jesse Cantor, County Court judge, on January 1, 1954; Jacob L. Serling, City Court judge, on January 1, 1959; Richard Aronson, Supreme Court judge, in August, 1961; Albert Orenstein, County Court judge, on January 1, 1966; Morris Garber, City Court judge, on January 1, 1965; and Benjamin Gingold, Family Court judge on January 1, 1969.[20]

Appointments to various commissions have been accorded to Jewish citizens who have merited recognition by their deeds and interest in the Jewish and civic community. We go back to the 1890's and find that I. Henry Danziger was Commissioner of Health, Mrs. August (Etta) Falker was appointed by Governor Theodore Roosevelt to be a director of the Western House of Refuge at Albion, New York, while her husband, August Falker, was a commissioner at City Hall. Daniel Rosenbloom, who was offered the nomination for mayor and declined, was a member of the Library Board. Louis Marshall, while still living in Syracuse, was a member of the Commission for the Revision of the State Constitution. T. Aaron Levy was the first chairman of the Community Housing Authority;[21] later Philip Holstein became the chairman, and now Bernard Cohen is chairman. Hiram Weisberg was appointed as a member of the city Charter Revision Commission in 1935, and acted as the vice-chairman of that body until the new charter was put into effect in 1938.

In the early days, the men and women who were elected or appointed to public office did not forget that they also had an obligation to the Jewish community. Daniel Rosenbloom, T. Aaron Levy, Samuel D. Solomon, Moses Rubin, George Freeman, are just a few names which come to mind of men who devoted themselves ardently to all Jewish community activities.

CHAPTER VIII

The Evolution of Jewish Education

The gradual evolution of Jewish education in the Syracuse Jewish community traverses the whole range of its history, beginning with the days when a *melammed* (teacher) would visit the children in their homes, through the time of the rebbe's *heder*, followed by the Hebrew Free School, until we arrive at today's congregational schools. It was a long, slow ascent, and on the way one or two generations were missed and received hardly any Jewish education at all.

The *melammed* was not a teacher in the full sense of the word; he usually was a Jew who could read some Hebrew. The Hebrew *heder* consisted of a room in the rebbe's home filled with ten to twenty healthy boys between the ages of five and thirteen, who came at three-thirty or four o'clock after being in public school for six or seven hours. Under such circumstances it was difficult for the Rebbe to hold the attention of the students; all a boy would usually learn was the Hebrew alphabet and the reading of a few Hebrew prayers by rote. Perhaps Rebbe Levy's *heder*, which we mentioned earlier, was the exception.

There were many poor Jewish families who found it a financial hardship to send their children to the *heder*. It was then that the more substantial Jewish citizens set about to form a Talmud Torah, or Hebrew free school.

On December 18, 1885, the following item appeared in *The American Israelite:*

166

The latest event in which every member of the congregation is interested, is the opening up of a Hebrew Free School for our poor Jewish children. Through the effort of Dr. Guttman the school was opened where the poor boys and girls receive instruction once a week in Hebrew history and morals and the girls in all kinds of needle work. A staff of 20 ladies assist the doctor in this noble work. May this noble undertaking be crowned with success and may God bless superintendent and teachers.

The same paper on July 10, 1890, carried this item:

Hebrew Free School

On Sunday June 20th the Hebrew Free School held a picnic at 3 Rivers Point. It was in every way a success. The Principal of the school is Prof. Glazier who is admirably qualified to act in that capacity. The membership of the school is 82 and is daily increasing.

This was a beginning, but not yet a Talmud Torah or Hebrew free school in the full sense of the word. It was not until July 30, 1897, that a fully organized Hebrew school was opened at 1065 Orange Street.

THE HEBREW FREE SCHOOL

The following notice appeared in *The American Israelite* on August 5, 1897:

HEBREW FREE SCHOOL DEDICATED
Syracuse, New York—July 30, 1897

The new Hebrew Free school at 1065 Orange Street was dedicated last evening. The committee in charge was as follows. Arrangements, Daniel Rosenbloom, M. D. Rubin, Samuel Manson, August Falker, George Freeman, and S. D. Solomon. Building Committee, L. Harris, M. Joel, R. Gais, L. Cohen, L. Glazier, and L. Manson.

The program for the services: prayer, the Reverend Dr. Hertz; opening address, L. Manson; presentation of keys, L. Harris; address, Daniel Rosenbloom; selection by orchestra; address, I. H. Danzinger; selection by orchestra; closing address, I. K. McGuire, Mayor.

The name "Hebrew Free School" did not mean that all children could attend free. Those parents who could afford it were expected to pay in accordance with their means and the number of their children who were attending. Still, there were numerous children whose parents could not pay anything, among whom were often the children of recently arrived immigrants.

Almost from its very beginning, the Hebrew Free School had to struggle to raise funds. The temples and synagogues which were trying to maintain Sunday schools and Hebrew schools of their own gave little help. It was, therefore, left to a few dedicated individuals and the Jewish lodges to support the Hebrew Free School, which continued to struggle to survive.

Thus we come to the twenty-fifth annual meeting, which was held on April 23, 1916.[1] Samuel D. Solomon, who was one of the original organizers at the dedication ceremony and was now the president, announced that there was "a deficit in the funds of the treasury due to the tuition falling off, and which was caused by poor supervision." A. Wolonelsky then announced that "David Lodge resigns from membership," and the secretary read a communication from the Yehuda Davis Lodge that it, too, "wishes to resign from membership." There were, however, representatives of other lodges present who announced that their lodges would remain and help to support the school. S. D. Frey, representing the Queen Esther Lodge; Morris Hurwitz, representing the Samuel Lodge; E. Goldstein, representing the Central City Lodge; and W. Cohen of the Brith Sholem Lodge were elected directors by acclamation. A committee was appointed—consisting of L. Shapiro, S. D. Frey, and B. Simon—to visit various other lodges and solicit their support. It was this hard core of dedicated men, such as S. D. Solomon, L. J. Davis, H. Serling, Henry Joseph, S. D. Frey, B. Simon, and L. Shapiro, who stood by the Hebrew Free School through those trying days and held the school together.

In the main, it was the Orthodox element in the city that furnished the students and supported the school. There was not always full agreement on the curriculum, as can be seen from the following report of the head teacher to the board of directors:

Syracuse, New York
September 15, 1904

To the Board of Directors of the Hebrew Free School:

Having been requested to present a course of study as a fixed standard to follow, I have made haste to comply with your wishes with the express understanding that if my personal course, which I have decided upon only after careful deliberation, be approved and ratified by the Board of Directors of this school or by a committee appointed for this purpose, [it] shall be deemed inviolable and not subject to any whimsical notions of any person unless it be changed by due authority. The Hebrew Free School, speaking in general terms, undertakes to educate the Jewish youth of this community from 7 to 13 years of age. . . .[2]

The Hebrew Free School summer picnics became a tradition. These were planned for the pupils and their families, and were open to the entire Jewish community. Committees were appointed to make arrangments, and the picnics were usually held at Long Branch or Three Rivers. Tickets were on sale weeks in advance and provided a source of income for the school.

At a picnic held on July 1, 1906, at Three Rivers, a tragedy occurred that saddened the entire Jewish community. Two young people were drowned. The *Syracuse Journal* gave the following account the next day:

TWO MEET DEATH AND THREE NARROWLY ESCAPE WATERY GRAVE

They were to have been married in a few weeks. The girl was drowned at Three Rivers, while her fiance came near losing his life.

Four homes are in mourning because of a sad accident that happened yesterday afternoon at the Hebrew Free School picnic at Three Rivers. It was a merry throng of nearly 1,000 who started out to enjoy a day's outing. Sorrow, however, soon filled many hearts when it was learned that a party of five young people, out for a row, had capsized and two were drowned and the rest had a narrow escape.

The boat contained Miss Anna Voit, her fiance, Joseph Weinstein, Morris Rubenstein and his sister, Anna, and Miss Esther Isaacs.

Miss Voit and Mr. Rubenstein were drowned.

Because of this tragedy picnics were not held for several years, and when they were resumed they were never popular again.

In 1938, during Franklin D. Roosevelt's administration, Syracuse had been selected as one of the first cities in which to build Federal low-cost housing. The site selected for this project was part of the old Jewish neighborhood. The Hebrew Free School was in that section, and was thus forced to look for another location. Among the various places considered was a home at 1120 East Genesee Street near Wal-

nut Avenue. Originally, it was presented to the Jewish community by
Mr. J. Cooper to be used as a Jewish orphan asylum, the one in Rochester being considered not kosher enough to satisfy the Orthodox element in Syracuse. However, this venture was not successful; evidently
there were not enough orphans in Syracuse whose guardians wanted
to take advantage of a strictly kosher home.

The home was now available,[3] and the Hebrew Free School trustees made arrangements to take it over, going to considerable expense
to remodel it into classrooms. The Hebrew Free School was now back
in operation, but attendance began to dwindle. The new location was
not the most desirable, for it was neither in the old Jewish neighborhood, which still contained some children, nor in the new Jewish
neighborhood which was forming east of Westcott Street.

Those were the years when the Community Chest was supporting
all the Jewish agencies, even the Hebrew Free School and the *mikvah*.
In 1941 when the Federation took over from the Chest the support of
the strictly religious agencies, the Hebrew Free School appealed to
the Federation for financial assistance. Max H. Rudolph, the president, stated at a Federation meeting that "they have 125 children and
two teachers in attendance." The request was for $2,600, or for permis-
sion to hold a fund-raising campaign of their own. The school was
promised continued support for operation, but no funds for capital improvements or plant alterations.

In 1945, rumors reached the Federation that the Hebrew Free
School was not being operated efficiently and that the attendance had
dropped considerably. The Federation thereupon appointed a committee, with Harold C. Greenstein as chairman, to call upon the American Association for Jewish Education to conduct a survey in Syracuse,
including the schools at the temples and synagogues.[4]

The survey was duly made by Dr. Judah Pilch, a competent Jewish
educator. A report of the survey was presented to the Federation by
Harold C. Greenstein on April 17, 1945. The report stated that "modern Jewish Education is now a highly technical subject and none of
the recommendations made in this report could be carried out without
the employment of a professional educational director whose first duty
would be to form a Bureau of Jewish Education." The Federation accepted the report and Hayyim Margalit was hired as the first director.
The Hebrew Free School was moved to one of the two buildings pur-

chased by the Federation at 2305 East Genesee Street, a site adjacent to the new Jewish neighborhood which was spreading out from Westcott Street to the eastern boundary of the city (where the Jewish Home and Temple Beth El now are located.)

With the improvement and increase in attendance of the religious schools in the temples and synagogues, in contrast to the decreasing enrollment in the Hebrew Free School, it was evident that there was no further need for a separate Talmud Torah. Thus, in 1965, this institution, which had its beginning in 1897, came to an end.

Congregational Schools

We now go back a number of years to record what the temples and synogogues were accomplishing for Jewish education in their congregations.

In the early days of the Temple of Concord, various attempts were made to establish a Sunday school, but due to frequent changes of rabbis there was no defined program or continuity of performance. It was not until the advent of Rabbi Guttman in 1883 that Sabbath and Sunday schools were firmly established. The Sabbath school was for the children of the members, where they were taught Bible history in German and English. The Sunday and daily school was called a mission school, or "Hebrew Free School," for poor children; it attracted mostly girls who were taught plain sewing.

Dr. Guttman also emphasized confirmation. What the requirements were at that time we do not know. A description of one of these early confirmation classes is contained in a letter from Syracuse to *The American Israelite,* dated May 30, 1883. It said in part:

. . . After the usual Hebrew readings, and singing by the choir, at the opening of the doors of the sanctuary, the confirments with President Marks at their head, walked up the aisle and chapel steps to the altar. The boys arranged themselves on the right of the minister and the girls on the left. . . . each of the boys and girls delivered an essay, some in German. . . . Then followed the most impressive part of the whole service, the blessing of the children by their parents. This was very affecting. Tears dimmed the eyes of the spectators as the father's trembling hand was placed upon the child's head, while the sobs of the children, as well as the parents could be heard. . . .

The ceremony of confirmation has now become a tradition and is carried on at all Reform and Conservative temples that maintain their own congregational schools.

The Congregation Adath Yeshurun was founded forty years after the Temple of Concord. From the very beginning it placed stress on the education of youth. They had Hebrew school three to five afternoons a week. The emphasis was on the preparation of boys for Bar Mitzvah, which was the culmination of the endeavor.

When Rabbi Hertz became the rabbi of Temple Adath Yeshurun in 1894, the Hebrew and Sunday school was further developed, and larger attendance was the result. At the turn of the century, the Reverend Max Wechsler joined the teaching staff. His department was the Bar Mitzvah class, in which were taught the blessing over the Torah, the Haftorah, and the Bar Mitzvah speech.

In 1921 the congregation moved into its new temple on Harrison and Crouse Avenue, and with it came new and modern classrooms and a new rabbi, Jesse Bienenfeld, and his wife. It was the rabbi's wife, Emma, who took charge of the Sunday school. Those who worked with her claimed that she was the most capable principal the school had had up to that time. Confirmation also became part of the educational system.[5]

Rabbi Irwin I. Hyman came to Temple Adath Yeshurun in 1935 and brought with him many innovations in teaching and curriculum. The most significant of these was the "junior congregation" concept. The objective was to hold the interest and continue the education of teenagers after the Bar Mitzvah. Rabbi Hyman had the full support of the president, Isaac Markson, and the program was successful from its very beginning. The members of the junior congregation elect their own officers and conduct their own services, under the guidance of a counselor. For many years the counselor was the Reverend Isaac Simon, who was also the teacher of the Bar Mitzvah class. The junior congregation has been in operation for over thirty years and still holds the interest of the youth of the temple.[6]

In 1919, when Rabbi Friedman assumed the leadership of the Temple of Concord, there were about sixty students attending classes. Sessions were conducted in the Herman Leiter Social Hall, where improvised classrooms were partitioned off by sliding doors.

As the enrollment of students increased during Rabbi Friedman's ministry, he was assisted by the following religious school principals: Dr. Mandell Shimberg, Jacob X. Cohen, Mrs. Rae Bragman, Mrs. Bessie Shriro, and Rabbi Jesse Ross. In 1960, Jewish education in the Temple of Concord was greatly enhanced by the addition of the $350,000 Hiram and Mabel Weisberg Religious School Annex.

The election of Rabbi Theodore Levy in 1962 as associate rabbi with Rabbi Benjamin Friedman brought about a number of changes. Rabbi Levy assumed supervision of the Sunday and Hebrew schools. He introduced a revised curriculum, more traditional practices, and closer supervision of the teachers. Whereas not too long ago the Temple of Concord administration looked askance at the Bar Mitzvah ceremony, now there is hardly a Sabbath without the celebration of a Bar Mitzvah or a Bas Mitzvah (a similar ceremony for girls).[7]

When Beth Israel was located on the corner of Harrison and Irving Avenue, from 1926 to 1965, the congregation and the rabbis tried hard to maintain Sunday and Hebrew schools, but the location was against them. Families with young children had moved away, and mothers would not send children to what they considered a slum area.

Since Beth El opened its new synagogue on East Genesee Street, with a modern school, they have had no difficulty attracting children to their Sunday and Hebrew schools. Greater stress is placed on the Hebrew classes. They have an enrollment of 230 children in their combined school, and they take pride in their junior congregation of forty to fifty children.

THE BUREAU OF JEWISH EDUCATION

The growth of the congregational schools can be attributed in a large measure to the Bureau of Jewish Education, established in 1945. Jewish education in Syracuse at that time was at a low ebb. The Hebrew Free School, the Folk Shule, and the Arbeiter Ring School were fast losing ground. Although it was only in existence for fifteen years, the Bureau of Jewish Education under the leadership of Judge Albert Orenstein, Donald J. Ball, and Louis Yaffee, and with the guidance of the American Association for Jewish Education, brought about a realization that Jewish education was a community responsibility and should no longer be controlled by different ideological groups. It brought in professional help, men such as Hayyim Margalit, Dr. Isaac Levitats, and Melvin Schein to supervise the Bureau at different times.

The Bureau recommended a standard curriculum for modern Jewish education and the employment of qualified teachers instead of volunteers. It also set rules for Bar Mitzvahs and confirmations, and proposed that after-school Hebrew classes be held three to five afternoons each week. It established Hebrew classes for high school students and secured from the Syracuse Board of Education recognition of the Hebrew language for credit on Regent examinations.

While the congregational schools at first resisted external direction, they at last recognized that parents joined a congregation as much to secure a Jewish education for their children as for their own religious fulfillment. The congregations accepted the recommendations of the Bureau and, as a result, their schools have greatly improved. This has brought about an extended Jewish educational system with more children participating than ever before in the history of Syracuse.[8]

The Jewish population of Syracuse and nearby suburbs is estimated to be 11,000, consisting of about 3,000 families. In 1968 there were about 1,300 children, ages five to sixteen, receiving a Jewish education.

The Hebrew Day School

We now come to a new form of Jewish education in Syracuse. The concept of a Hebrew day school as envisioned by Leo Feigenbaum and the organizers of the Hebrew Academy did not last, but in 1960, Samuel Eber, Richard Wilkins, and Sidney Cohen, members of Young Israel, with the assistance and blessing of Rabbis Jacob Epstein and Stanley Wexler, organized the Hebrew Day School.[9] Samuel Eber secured a house at 3528 East Genesee Street as a home for the school. Although it was far out on the eastern border of the city, it was a good location for a private school. The building was situated on an acre of ground and had a large play yard.

In its first year the school operated with one Hebrew teacher and one English teacher. The second year (1961), Mrs. Gladys Wexler, wife of the rabbi of Young Israel, took charge, and under her direction the school reached an enrollment of ninety, including the nursery school.

The Hebrew Day School was never fully accepted by the Jewish community and, since income from tuition was not sufficient to meet payments on the mortgage and pay the teachers, it was soon in financial difficulties.

At the end of the 1963 school year, the school was forced to give up the house at 3528 East Genesee Street and was granted permission to use the building at 2305 East Genesee Street, owned by the Syracuse Jewish Welfare Federation.

Further difficulties arose over the curriculum, since not all the children were from Orthodox homes. Some of the children came from "secular" homes, in which the parents were professional and University people who wanted their children to have some Hebrew education but cared little about religious traditions. The school, being a member of the National Association of Hebrew Day Schools, wanted to keep its program traditional, and there was much discord at the board meetings. On top of all this, the city condemned the building at 2305 East Genesee Street as being unsafe for a school.

In 1965 the Hebrew Day School moved to the classrooms of Temple Adath Yeshurun and secured a new principal, Rabbi Moshe Alon, a native Israeli who had been in this country fifteen years. For the previous five years he had been principal of a Hebrew school in Hamilton, Ontario, Canada. Rabbi Alon made a fine appearance and spoke English fluently with a slight British accent. He was well regarded here and was successful in persuading some people to help the school financially. A man of vision, he tried to raise enough funds to build a home for the school. A pledge of $25,000 was obtained from Max Gilbert for that purpose, with the understanding that the school would be known as the Max Gilbert Academy. Unfortunately, Mr. Gilbert passed away during the year and had only paid $2,000 on his pledge.

The difficulties on the board continued, and at the end of 1967 Samuel Eber and Rabbi Alon resigned. The school is now back at its original location at 3528 East Genesee Street, with quarters in the new Beth El synagogue, which was built on the grounds originally owned by the Day School.

In 1967 William L. Shimansky was secured as the principal. He is a graduate of the Teacher's Institute of the Yeshiva University, an ordained rabbi, and a very personable young man with experience as a pedagogue. The school continues to teach from kindergarten to the sixth grade in English and Hebrew, and has a student body of between forty and fifty children. Rabbi Shimansky is also director of the Institute for Advanced Hebrew Studies, which has a small class of six students who seek advanced Jewish learning.

FROM THE YOUNG MEN'S HEBREW ASSOCIATION TO THE JEWISH COMMUNITY CENTER

The Jewish Community Center in Syracuse is an outgrowth of the earlier Young Men's Hebrew Association, whose history goes back to 1861. The first record of the Association's existence is found in a notice that appeared in *The Israelite* of April 5, 1861:

Syracuse, N.Y. There is a society just started here—it is comprised of 48 members and is called "Y.M.H.A." and is gotten up for the purpose of learning to debate and to form a singing club. We raised $100 at the second meeting.

Here is the first evidence that the young Jewish men of Syracuse were seeking social and cultural contacts outside the temples and synagogues. The name "Y.M.H.A." was a counterpart of the Young Men's Christian Association, which was just becoming a popular place for young Christian men. The purpose of having a singing club followed the idea of the German singing and beer-drinking societies, which were already popular in Syracuse. Debating was the cultural part of the activities, and had more appeal to the Jewish youth.

However, it was not until January 15, 1886, that the next notice of the Y.M.H.A. appeared in *The American Israelite:*

The Y.M.H.A. recently started in this city will have a literary and musical entertainment on Wednesday Feb. 24th. The proceeds will be given to the Hebrew Free School. It is certainly a good purpose to assist an institution which opens its doors to the poor and uncared for children—giving them the bread of life.

On March 28, 1886, another notice appeared in *The American Israelite:*

Y.M.H.A.

On Monday night February 22nd, the entertainment of the Y.M.H.A. took place at Greyhound Hall. The Society deserves special mention on account of its practical workings and beneficial influence over our rising young men. The essays and debates have commenced, and they now started to form a library. They deserved the fullest support of every better-thinking Israelite in our city. Dr. Guttman who takes a lively interest in this Society and frequently attends their meetings was appointed honorary member.

The entertainment on February 22nd was for the benefit of "The Hebrew Free School," "Ladies' Aid Society," and the association itself. Each of these societies received $50. After the performance of a neat little farce in two acts in which Mess'rs H. Danzigger, Hiram Danzigger and B. Bronner excelled, proving to be very acceptable amateur actors, dancing was enjoyed until morning. The whole affair proved to be an enjoyable one.

(Signed) Emeth

It is unfortunate that the only records we have of the early days of the Syracuse Y.M.H.A. were the few letters which were sent to *The American Israelite*. We assume that the young men went on singing and debating and having an occasional dance or entertainment to which the young ladies were invited.

The next notice about the Y.M.H.A. appeared in the *Syracuse Standard* of February 8, 1891:

JEWISH SOCIETY Y.M.H.A.

Saturday evening at the residence of Mr. and Mrs. R. J. Rich, No. 405 Irving Street, a banquet was tendered the Y.M.H.A. by David Rich. The house was handsomely decorated for the occasion. The Toastmaster called on the following for toasts; Marx Holstein, S. Pakalinsky, Wm. Rubin, O. Oppenheimer, S. Morrison, O. A. Blumenfeld, M. E. Morresh, S. J. Ferguson, H. Brill, Wm. Lesser, David B. Rich.

The Y.M.H.A. continued in existence, but apparently there were not enough young people with cultural interests to maintain its popularity. Meanwhile, a new generation was emerging—young men who came to America as small children, as well as the American-born sons of the earlier immigrants. Many of these boys went to work at an early age, selling newspapers on the streets, peddling matches, and helping in the family business. Like all boys, however, they also longed for a few hours of vigorous recreation each week and a convenient place in which to play their games throughout the year. Wher-

ever there was an open lot one could find a group of Jewish children
playing baseball or football. Some of our Jewish boys developed into
good athletes. They formed baseball clubs and football teams and arranged games against the Irish boys, of whom there were a great
number living on the periphery of the Jewish neighborhood. Jackson
Flats was the meeting ground where many a good baseball and football game took place, often ending in a fight.

As fine as these outdoor games were, there still was no place for
Jewish boys and young men to participate in indoor athletic activities
such as basketball, volleyball, swimming, boxing, wrestling, and the
like. Fortunately, some philanthropic citizens established a boys' club,
intended as a place for the poor boys in the neighborhood to play and
as a means of keeping them off the streets. Many Jewish boys took advantage of this fine opportunity and joined the Boys' Club.

However, there was still no place where the older Jewish boys and
young men could go, with the exception of the Y.M.C.A., which by its
very name indicated that it was primarily intended for the use of
Christian youth. There were no objections to young Jewish men and
boys belonging, and many did join and made good use of the fine facilities available in the heart of the business district of the city.

The Boys' Club and the Y.M.C.A. served the Jewish boys and
young men well. However, ethnic groups from the same backgrounds
usually prefer to socialize among their own. This group attachment is
particularly strong among Jews. At times it is forced on them because
they are not always fully accepted in some social organizations and
country clubs. In Syracuse there are still social groups which let it be
known that Jews are not desired as members.

The ethnic feeling was so strong among the boys and young men
who longed for a place of their own that in 1906,[10] led by Myron
Small and Max Rosenbloom, they converted a large barn in back of
the Small residence on State Street into an athletic club. Other teenage boys were attracted to the new club. Among the early members
were Phil Harris, Jessie Tumposky, Abe Rosenbloom, Sime Glick, Sam
Bauman, and Meyer and Louis Prowda. Paying only small weekly
dues and doing most of the work themselves, the boys turned the old
barn into an athletic arena.

The barn soon began to be noticed by a group of young men who
had some standing in the community—Gerson Rubenstein, a young

lawyer, Morris Ferguson, a well-known athlete and sign painter, Manuel Goldstein, Simon Cohen, Sam Kaletsky, T. Aaron Levy, and Clarence Miller. All of these were rising young men, sons of the East European settlers, who felt the need of a young men's group but did not care to meet in a barn. In 1908 this group of young men called a meeting at Freeman's Hall to revitalize the Y.M.H.A. Gerson Rubenstein acted as temporary chairman and was elected the first president. The old Y.M.H.A. was back in business. Subsequently, the third floor of the Freeman Hall Building—the large room that formerly was the George Freeman clothing factory—was rented and made over into a basketball court. Other adjoining space was used for club rooms. Soon afterward they invited a group of young ladies to organize an auxiliary, and the Y.M.H.A. was again well on the way up.

The program for the first grand dance of the Y.M.H.A., held on Monday evening, October 11, 1908, lists the following officers: Gerson Rubenstein, president; Myron Small, vice-president; Frank Goldstein, secretary; Isador Jacobs, financial secretary; T. Aaron Levy, treasurer; D. B. Sugarman, W. W. Gerber, and G. Silverman, trustees.[11]

This social affair was followed by another dance held on October 31, 1909, given by the Ladies Auxiliary. The program lists the following as the officers of the Ladies Auxiliary: Miss Etta Kaplan, president; Miss Lena Glick, vice-president; Miss Jennie Kelson, treasurer; and Miss Freda Arkin, secretary. The following young women served on the reception committee:

Fannie Harrison	Tillie Markson
Jennie Belloff	Clara Fitzer
Bertha Cohen	Blanch Kutz
Tillie Marquisee	Dina Cooper
Sara Greenberg	Corina Jalonack
Jennie Shavalinsky	Anna Weisberg

The organization grew in membership, and all the affairs were well attended. However, it was decided that Freeman's Hall was no longer adequate for all the activities. The problem was solved when, shortly after the death of Jacob Marshall in 1910, the family donated the old Marshall homestead at 22 Cedar Street jointly to the Y.M.H.A. and the Council of Jewish Women. This was the home in which Zilli and Jacob Marshall had lived for over forty years, and where their children were born and raised. Besides providing an immediate home for the Y.M.H.A., the house had a sentimental value to the Jewish community.

With funds donated by the Council of Jewish Women, the old homestead was remodeled. It then provided an assembly room for about one hundred people, an administrative office, and club rooms on the second floor, which were also used for a Sunday school conducted by the Council of Jewish Women.

The following item appeared in the *Syracuse Herald* of March 30, 1913:

SYRACUSE JEWISH CITIZENS—TWO IMPORTANT ORGANIZATIONS

The Council of Jewish Women is one of the most important and effective organizations of women in Syracuse. Mrs. M. Gais is President. This and the Y.M.H.A. are at present housed at the Marshall Memorial Home, but arrangements are being made to build a separate home. The Council has about 120 members and the Y.M.H.A. 150 members. Simon Cohen is President of the latter. The Council conducts Sunday School classes, both for boys and girls.

Boys and young men continued to use the third floor of Freeman's Hall as a basketball court and for other athletic sports, and some fine basketball teams were developed. Those were the days when amateur basketball was popular. The Y.M.H.A. teams were the "Submarines," the "Pets," and the "Midgets," who were champions of the city in their division for a number of years.

When the newness of using the Marshall home wore off, it became apparent that it, too, was inadequate. It served a purpose as a gathering place for young men and women, but it had no facilities for large assemblies or dances. Above all, there was no room within the house for athletic games. The need for more space for the Y.M.H.A. was pressing. Therefore in 1913 it was decided to construct a building with modern facilities on a lot adjoining the Marshall home.

The Y.M.H.A. during the War Years

Before the plans for the new Y.M.H.A. building were completed, war broke out in Europe, and the United States found it necessary to enter the war on April 6, 1917. After that, all thoughts of building an addition to the Marshall home had to be abandoned for the duration of the war.

The United States Army requisitioned the New York State Fair Grounds, just outside Syracuse, for an embarkation camp, and many thousands of soldiers were encamped adjacent to the city. When soldiers were given leave, they filled the streets of Syracuse. The city opened recreation centers for the men, and the Y.M.H.A. Marshall Memorial Home hung up a big "Welcome" sign. The Ladies Auxiliary arranged dances and other forms of entertainment. Primarily it attracted Jewish soldiers, and young Jewish girls acted as hostesses. Before the war was over a number of marriages resulted from these contacts.[12]

When the war ended in 1918, talk of building a suitable addition to the center was revived. A building committee, consisting of T. Aaron Levy, Louis Hurwitz, and Morris Ferguson, was appointed. Plans were drawn up, and a campaign for a building fund was put in operation. The new structure was to cost $100,000. The plans called for a two-story concrete block construction, a swimming pool and locker rooms in the basement, an assembly hall on the first floor, and club and classrooms on the second floor.

After the building was completed, the name was changed to "The Jewish Community Center." This building, together with the Marshall home, served as the gathering place and center of social activity for the Jewish youth of Syracuse for thirty years.[13] During these years most of the Jewish population moved away from the Fifteenth Ward, and the old Jewish neighborhood became the Negro ghetto.

After many years of concern, a study of the situation was made by the Jewish Welfare Board of New York, which advised that a new location was imperative if the Community Center was to be of any service to Jewish youth. A building committee and a program study committee were appointed. Like the first attempt to build a center, these plans, too, were thwarted by war, for the committees had just begun their work when the Second World War broke out.

The Jewish Community Center after World War II

Nineteen forty-five—The Second World War was over; Germany surrendered in May, Japan in August. In 1943 the Jewish Federation had given permission to hold a limited fund-raising campaign for the purpose of erecting a new Community Center in a location nearer to the center of Jewish population.[14] However, this project had to wait until the end of 1948 before the leaders could begin again to stimulate the community in regard to its needs.

During the war the neighborhood around Cedar Street, where the Commnity Center was located, had deteriorated further. Some of its activities were transferred to the social hall adjacent to Poiley Tzedeck Shul on Almond Street.

The survey of the Jewish Welfare Board, made in 1944, recommended the Dann Estate on East Genesee Street, opposite Fellows Avenue, as the most suitable location. In 1947 this property was purchased. It consisted of two beautiful homes of the 1900 period, built of stone with red tile roofs, and a large lot running through to Lexington Avenue.

An application was made for a change of zoning to permit the erection of a building to be used as a community center. Much to the surprise of the planning committee, they encountered considerable opposition in the neighborhood. They were even more astonished when the loudest and most pressing opposition came from the Jewish neighbors—not only from those who lived on Genesee Street adjacent to the property, but from Jewish residents on Fellows Avenue and Allen Street, several blocks away from the location. As a result, the Zoning Commission turned down the application. It was learned, however, that no change of zone was required to use the property as a school.

One of the homes was immediately remodeled into a nursery school and an educational center. The other, in which Dr. and Mrs. Sydney Stringer still lived, was acquired a year later. The lower floor in the remodeled home was used as a lounge for teenagers and offices for the director of the Community Center. The upper floor was given over to the Jewish Family Service for temporary use by refugee families.

Subsequent investigation of the zoning regulations convinced the planning committee that rezoning was not necessary in order to build a center for a community program.

In 1948 a new program and planning committee was appointed to carry through an extensive and thorough assessment of program needs and desires of the Jewish community. Some 150 persons, leaders of all

the Jewish civic and cultural organizations, were involved in this survey, which took almost a year to complete. When the master plan was
finished, which included all the facilities deemed necessary, a rough
estimate from the Jewish Welfare Board Building Bureau indicated
that the cost would be a million dollars or more. From practical considerations, it was decided that no such money was available in Syracuse, and plans were therefore made to build in units, the first unit to
include those facilities designated by the program committee as having the highest priority. The estimated cost of the first unit was set between $550,000 and $600,000.

During 1949, 1950, and 1951 the Community Center was in improvised quarters, using one of the Dann homes and the garage, for a
limited program. In 1952 a campaign for funds was added to the regular Federation campaign, and $150,000 was raised. Thus, with the
money on hand from the 1943 campaign, more than $400,000 was
available for building purposes. The Federation provided an interest
free loan of $175,000 to make the total sum close to $600,000. The plan
was to leave the Dann property intact and build the first unit in back
of one of the homes. Ground was broken the same year. James Marshall, son of Louis Marshall, came from New York for the laying of
the cornerstone. The new Center building was completed and opened
in 1955. It immediately attracted hundreds of families from the Jewish
community.

In 1959 the original house, that had been left standing in front of
the new building, was demolished. In the same year discussions and
preliminary planning took place to complete the second unit of what
was envisioned to be a "whole Center for a whole family."

Another fund-raising campaign was begun in the fall of 1961 for
the sum of $500,000. When final plans were completed, it was found
that the actual cost would be $600,000. The Welfare Federation again
came to the assistance of the project and made a grant of $125,000. By
1963, the "whole Center for the whole family" was completed and in
use. In addition, the Center now owns Camp Fren-Le, used as a day
camp, and operates Camp Bradley Brook as an overnight camp.

Thus, beginning in 1861 as a literary, singing, and debating club,
the Y.M.H.A. in a century has evolved into the Syracuse Jewish Community Center, a facility that serves more than 1,300 family memberships. With additional club memberships, it caters to approximately

5,000 individuals and serves the entire community. Its budget in 1967 amounted to $290,000.

LODGES AND FRATERNAL ORGANIZATIONS

During the last half of the nineteenth century and into the early decades of the twentieth, lodges and fraternal organizations were popular, especially so among the Jewish people. There was a definite need for them in those days, since there were few places where men could meet and socialize except in saloons. Another good reason for joining was that few people carried life insurance. Several of the lodges offered some form of insurance, and practically all guaranteed a decent burial, as well as the brothers' pledge to care for the widows and orphans.

Not all lodges were open to Jews, and so they formed their own. One of the first lodges in the city, organized in 1851, was Jacob Lodge #91, Independent Order of Odd Fellows. The charter was granted to Isaac Garson, Samuel Rosenbach, Jacob Stone, Henry Garson, Moses Henochsburg, and David Obersdorfer, all of whom had been among the pioneer Jewish settlers. The name was later changed to Lessing Lodge #163, which is still in existence.[15]

Jacob Stolz, in 1858, was one of the first Jews in Syracuse to join the non-Jewish Onondaga Odd Fellows Lodge. He chose the Onondaga Lodge since it was composed of German-speaking members with whom he felt perfectly at home. At the age of ninety-five, just before he passed away, he was honored as the oldest living Odd Fellow in Syracuse and probably in the country.[16]

In the 1870's there were three Masonic lodges in the city: the Central City, the Syracuse, and the Salt Springs. The latter was the only one which accepted a few Jewish members. August Falker went through the chairs and was elected Worshipful Master of Salt Springs Lodge four times, in 1869, 1870, 1873, and 1874.[17]

By 1900 there were perhaps a dozen Jews in this organization of about 350 members. Among them was a young lawyer, Samuel D. Solomon. He started going through the chairs, but when he got as far as the Senior Warden (the next office below Worshipful Master) he was passed over, and the Junior Warden was elected in his stead. It was quite obvious that what motivated and brought about this action was the fact that Sam Solomon was a Jew. This was not only a personal affront but an offense against all the Jewish members. It was clear that the few Jewish members were being tolerated but not fully accepted. However, a small group of non-Jews felt this action to be not only an injustice to an individual but also a bad precedent for the lodge. Further, they felt that it was against the high moral teachings of brotherly love which are so exaltingly glorified by the Order of Free and Accepted Masons. This small group of twelve to fifteen men, together with the few Jewish members, petitioned the Grand Lodge for a charter to start another lodge in Syracuse. The charter was granted, and Mt. Sinai Lodge #864 was organized in 1908.[18] Samuel D. Solomon was elected the first Worshipful Master. This lodge has a history of more than sixty years, and is still composed almost entirely of Jews. The Jewish Masons of Mt. Sinai were also selective, and when, as it happened, a few prominent Jews were rejected for personal reasons, another Jewish lodge was chartered in 1920, the Philo Lodge. Isidor Rothschild was the first Worshipful Master. Today there are two so-called "Jewish" Masonic lodges in Syracuse.

In 1867 B'nai B'rith organized a chapter in Syracuse. Solomon Lederer and Charles Rosenthal were elected president and vice-president, respectively.[19] B'nai B'rith, however, has had a checkered career in this city. At different times it lost ground and disappeared. With the advent of such national leaders as Henry Monsky, Philip Klutznick, and Label Katz, interest in B'nai B'rith reawakened. In 1936 a new lodge was activated, the Louis Marshall Memorial Lodge.[20] Judge Jesse Cantor was elected president. Although it was started under fine auspices, it did not last. In 1940 the lodge was reinstated, with A. Solomon Menter as president. It has since prospered. In 1952 the Thomas Jefferson Lodge was formed, with Earl Hart as its first president. There are now two lodges of B'nai B'rith in the city.

Other Jewish lodges in Syracuse flourished for a time and then disappeared. Examples of such transient groups are Free Sons of Israel (organized in 1873), B'rith Sholom Lodge, Queen Esther Lodge, and Moses Montefiore Lodge #19 of Kesher Shel Barsel. Jews now often complain that they are over-organized, but evidently they always were.[21]

SOCIAL CLUBS AND CULTURAL SOCIETIES

Early in the history of the Jewish community of Syracuse, social clubs and cultural societies were formed. Young men, in particular, felt the need of companionship and congenial surroundings in which to spend their evenings and leisure days in enjoyable pursuits. The first clubs included primarily the German Jews, who constituted an elite in the Jewish population. Later, prosperous Polish and Russian Jews were accepted into membership in these clubs. Such groups developed, not only because Jews were seldom invited to join social organizations of the non-Jewish community, but also because Jews—like most immigrant minorities—felt more "at home" among their own people.

Among the foremost of the early social clubs was the Standard Club, organized in 1882.[22] The officers were August Falker, president; Sol Tumin, vice-president; Moses Heiman, secretary; Gates Rosenthal, treasurer; and David Danziger, A. Z. Heiman, and Philip Gates, trustees. These young men established club rooms on the corner of Grape and Jefferson Streets. The rooms were elegantly furnished; there were card rooms, a pool and billiard room, a kitchen, and a dining room. The meals, they claimed, were "as good or better than anywhere in town." For a lady to be invited to dinner at the Standard Club was something to talk about. The annual Standard Club full-dress ball became the Jewish social event of the year.[23]

Later a competing Jewish social club was formed, the Genesee Club, and in 1899 the two clubs consolidated. After long discussions as to whether it should take the name of the Standard Club or the Genesee Club, a compromise was reached, and it was called the Fayette Club.

The Progress Club was organized in 1875 [24] as a literary and social club, with emphasis on literary activities. The elected officials were Samuel Stern, president; A. H. Lowenthal, vice-president; H. L. Elsner, secretary; and M. Ettinger, treasurer.

Three years later, the *Syracuse Journal* of July 29, 1878, reported an outing held by this club:

The picnic of the "Progress Club" to Cazenovia, yesterday, was very successful in every respect. About 400 people left the city at 9 A.M., returning about 8:30 P.M., and a pleasanter day could not have been wished for. Although the good people of the vicinity were averse to the letting of boats and steamers on Sunday, a generous offer on the part of Mr. D. K. McCarthy obviated what might have been unpleasant for those who desired to go upon the beautiful lake. Mr. McCarthy, with his characteristic liberality in this regard, placed his steam yacht *Percy* at the disposal of the excursionists, and there were few who did not take advantage of the offer. Everybody returned pleased with the day's sport and all agreed that the German and French idea of spending the "Sabbath" was indeed beneficial for the proposed Jewish Orphan Asylum, for the benefit of which the picnic was given.

A young ladies' club, named the Children of Israel, a strictly "Misses" club for cultural and social entertainment, was formed in 1878, and among their stated aims was to "lend a helping hand toward the promotion of interest in the Hebrew Orphan Asylum of Western New York and for their own improvement in literary works." The officers were Miss Anna Barnett, president; Miss A. Cohen, vice-president; Miss M. Harrison, recording secretary; Miss D. Isaacs, treasurer; and Miss A. Isaacs, conductor.

Over the years other clubs were formed, mostly among the young adults and teenagers. One was called the Concord Library Circle, another the Jewish Culture Society, and—surprising for those days—one was called the Radical Club.

Another popular social and charitable organization was the Fortnightly Club, formed in 1905 with David Holstein as its first president. The club dances and annual charity balls at Freeman's Hall were always looked forward to and well attended.

Samuel Shopiro and Sigmund Frensdorf bought the old Dunfee home at 515 East Genesee Street in 1912. It was a very imposing structure and well located. Since at this time there were no men's social clubs, a number of Jewish business men decided to form such a club and house it in that building. They called it the Eureka Club, but unfortunately it lasted only a short time.[25]

Golf and Country Clubs

A new era was ushered in when golf became the fashionable sport of the affluent society. The Onondaga Golf and Country Club, organized in 1898, was among the first in this part of the state. It was only for the elite, and it was costly. Only two Jews were accepted as members, and these not so much for their wealth as for their standing in the community—Dr. Henry Elsner, foremost diagnostician in the city, and Dr. Nathan Jacobson, the leading surgeon.

The Bellevue Country Club was established in 1915. If a Jew had a friend who belonged, or if his broker or banker introduced him, he had a chance of getting in. It is known that Sam Shopiro, H. Hiram Weisberg, Philip Holstein, and Dr. I. Harris Levy belonged.

After the First World War, times were more prosperous, and in the early 1920's some Jews began thinking of forming a country club of their own. Sam Shopiro, a member of the Bellevue Country Club, and by this time an experienced golfer, was the one above all others who spearheaded the interest among wealthier Jews. The first founders' meeting was held on the porch of his home at 309 Euclid Avenue during the summer of 1920. Among those who attended were Hiram Weisberg, David Holstein, B. B. Given, William Gerber, Ralph Shulman, Dr. I. Harris Levy, and Morris and Louis Hurwitz. A committee was appointed to look for a location. The following week the committee brought in their report, and among the locations suggested was the Warner farm on LaFayette Road. It was about five miles from the center of the city in a southeasterly direction, only a short distance from the residential section in the eastern part of the city where most Jewish people had their homes. The Warner farmhouse was set well back from the main road and was large enough to be turned into a clubhouse. There was also a nearby carriage house that could be turned into a "pro" shop and locker room.

The Warner family was anxious to sell and offered the 106 acres, buildings and all, for $30,000. The founders, the men who met on Sam Shopiro's porch, decided to buy it. The club was organized, named the LaFayette Country Club, and opened for membership in 1921. David Holstein was elected president. During the spring and summer of 1922 one hundred members were signed up, and six holes were made ready for play. By today's standards the six holes were not much of a golf course. The tees were patches of bare earth, and, since it was before the advent of wooden tees, two pails were furnished, one filled with sand and the other with water, from which a golfer made his own tee out of wet sand. The greens were cow-pasture grass, cut down with an ordinary lawnmower.

In the spring of 1923, just as the golf season opened, the pro shop and locker room burned down. There was considerable inconvenience for a few months, but those eager for golf kept on playing. A new pro shop and locker room were built, both of which were a vast improvement over those which had burned down. Then, during the winter of 1923, the main clubhouse was completely destroyed by fire. It was a strange coincidence that both caddy shop and clubhouse should burn down, one shortly after the other. Once again the members endured a period of inconvenience, but this time a fine and greatly enlarged clubhouse was built on the same location where the former clubhouse had stood.

The club was quite deeply in debt, and the Depression of the 1930's made it touch and go for a few years. Many members dropped out, and the few who remained were forced to buy more bonds to keep the club going. Since then, the LaFayette Country Club has grown and prospered. Now there are eighteen holes, a swimming pool, an enlarged clubhouse, and about 350 regular members, as well as house members, junior members, and pool members. Besides providing recreational and social activities, it has been a great asset to the Jewish Community for banquets, weddings, and Federation functions.[26]

The Luncheonaires

The nucleus for the Luncheonaires, a Jewish luncheon club, emerged from a teenagers' group, the Uneek Club. The sponsor and advisor to this club was Colonel Joseph Bondy. He permitted the members to use his offices in the old Bastable Block as a meeting place. When they grew in numbers, they moved to the building on the corner of East Genesee and Orange Streets. However, as the teenagers became old enough to go to college or to marry, a number of them left the city, and soon the Uneek Club was no more.

Schrafft's restaurant was an institution in Syracuse for over fifty years. When Schrafft's moved from South Salina Street, where Woolworth's now stands, to a much enlarged restaurant on South Warren Street, some of the Uneek boys, who were now in business or professions, began to meet there for lunch. Among them were Mannie Manheim, Asher Markson, Sam Bragman, Leke Harris, Bill Aberson, Paul Flah, Joe Brooks, Harold Weisenberg, Chuck Goldstein, Al Saul, and Jack Simmons.

At first only six or eight would gather at a large table in the back of the restaurant, but when they grew in numbers and were getting a bit noisy, Frank Shattuck, son of the founder of the Schrafft chain, suggested that they move to the second-floor restaurant. Just as Mannie Manheim (by then a successful real estate operator) had been a leader of the Uneek Club, he became the self-appointed president of the new luncheon group. Mannie was dubbed "The Führer" who "ruled the club with an iron head" for fourteen years. Jewish men in business and the professions, either by invitation or their association with members, gravitated into this group. Among them were Phil and Alex Holstein, Ben Arnold, Ben Rudolph, Saul Alderman, Harold Greenstein, Johnny Wilson and his son Jerry, Bill Smith, Louis Young and Hecky Marley. Soon there were fifteen or twenty at every lunch.

With all the kibitzing and horseplay that went on, Frank Shattuck suggested that he would give up his office on the second floor and let it be used as a private dining room. This room became an establishment, and for three decades it served as the home of the Luncheonaires. The membership included many leaders of the Jewish and civic institutions of Syracuse.

Phil Holstein brought a meaningful purpose to the club. His family was instrumental in founding the Fresh Air Camp for Boys on Cazenovia Lake. When this camp was moved to Eaton, New York, and greatly enlarged for the use of both boys and girls, the suggestion was made that here was a worthwhile project which the club could aid and foster. It was agreed to sponsor an annual charity ball, the proceeds to be contributed to Bradley Brook Camp, its new name.

Now, the club had a purpose. The Luncheonaires' charity ball has been, for the past twenty years, the social highlight of the year in the Jewish community, and the proceeds are now distributed to many more children's camps in the area.

In 1964 Schrafft's restaurant closed its doors. Sorrowfully, the Luncheonaires were forced to give up the room where they had lunched for over thirty years and they moved to a private dining room at the Hotel Syracuse. Many of the original members have passed on; others have moved away, but, with a new member added now and then, the Luncheonaires still carry on. (A list of members is given in Appendix E.) Their charity ball continues to be held each year and grows in popularity.[27]

The Temples and Synagogues Follow the People

Beginning with the 1900's, the early Jewish settlers began moving eastward and upward, beyond Irving Avenue which for years had been the eastern boundary of the Jewish neighborhood.

In nearly all cities there are, or were, "uptown" and "downtown" sections. In Syracuse, the business section, in which the large department stores are located and where the City Hall and the Court House stand, is still referred to as "downtown." The Jewish neighborhood adjacent to the business district was also referred to as "downtown." As soon as some of the earlier arrivals acquired sufficient money (having lived in the neighborhood twenty or thirty years), they bought homes in the "uptown" area. Some moved up East Genesee Street; others went on, past the University, to Euclid Avenue and adjoining streets. This gradual exodus not only provided a show of status and a better residential area for the more prosperous families, but also made room for the new immigrants who moved into the homes that were vacated.

The Temple of Concord

The temple was built in 1850 on the corner of Mulberry and Harrison Streets. When it was erected, Mulberry Street was a wide residential street, lined with elm trees, and the temple was considered one of the finest houses of worship in the city. Five or six years after it was built, a big windstorm blew down the steeple. It fell on the house next door where Jacob Marshall's family lived. The newspapers said it was a miracle that no one was killed. The steeple was never replaced, and for the rest of its existence the temple looked like a hen minus its head.

By the turn of the century the street had become commercial, and the structure itself was beginning to show its age. The ladies of the Auxiliary, in particular, were beginning to be ashamed of the appearance of the temple and the neighborhood. They began to agitate for a new building and were willing to do something about it. They held rummage sales, bake sales, and charity balls. The *Syracuse Herald* of February 16, 1898, had this to say about one of their activities:

The charity ball given under the auspices of the Ladies auxiliary of the congregation, Society of Concord, at Freeman's Hall last evening was the leading social event of the season in Jewish circles.

The ball was held with the intention of raising money to add to a fund, which is already in existence, for the purpose of building a new Temple.

The hall was magnificently decorated for the event in an entirely Oriental fashion, and upon entering the reception room, one might think that he was surely in a Turkish palace, so thoroughly was the idea of decoration, in this line carried out.

Gates Thalheimer was elected president of the congregation in 1897. He, too, would have liked to see a new temple built but, as a hardheaded businessman, he wanted to know where the money was coming from.

In 1901, at the annual meeting, a resolution was passed that "the time was ripe for a new temple building." Jacob Stolz, the custom shoemaker, was the first to contribute $50, followed by Henry Bronner, who pledged $100. After this flurry, there was much talk but little action.

In 1904, Herman Leiter, a devoted member of Concord, died. When his bequests became known, there was an unexpected windfall, for he left $16,500 expressly for the purpose of building a new temple. With this bequest and the nest egg that the Ladies Auxiliary had saved, the men began to bestir themselves. Gates Thalheimer at last saw the possibilities and became an ardent advocate for a new building.

The president appointed a committee to look for a site. The committee reported that there was a good location available at the corner of Madison Street and University Avenue, but they felt that the price was too high. This brought further delay.

At a meeting on April 15, 1906, Gates Thalheimer, the president, said, "There is every possibility and means to build this Temple. I guarantee that the members will not be called upon to increase their dues. Furthermore, should there be a deficiency in the current expenses for the maintenance of the Temple, I shall fill such deficiency myself." [1] This was quite a statement the president made, and everyone knew that he had the means to back it up. By late October of the same year, $15,000 more was added by the members to the building fund. Still the committee thought that there was not enough money to begin construction, and two more years passed without anything further being done. By this time Gates Thalheimer was so keenly disappointed that he refused to stand for re-election, but a week later he yielded to the demands of the other leaders and returned to the office of president, on the condition that the money on hand be used to start building a new temple.

The lot on the corner of Madison Street and University Avenue was purchased for $11,400. Henry Danziger was appointed chairman of the building committee. Alfred E. Taylor of Syracuse and Arnold W. Brunner of New York were retained as architects.

Ground was broken on May 25, 1910, the cornerstone was laid on September 18, 1910, and the temple was completed and dedicated on September 22, 1911. On the following Friday evening, services were held for the first time in the new temple. The Reverend Dr. Guttman delivered the dedicatory sermon, and with great solemnity and thankfulness the sanctuary was opened. George K. Van Deusen, the organist, arranged a special musical program.

For many years the temple was referred to as "The New Temple of Concord." The building committee, the architects, and the builders deserve the greatest approbation and esteem for the esthetic design of this temple.

The temple sits on a terrace high above the street. It is Grecian in style, with four large Ionic columns in the facade. The exterior is of light gray limestone, symmetrical in form, and more graceful in style than the box-like designs of modern public buildings.

The interior is exquisite in its simplicity. The recessed area behind the high proscenium arch contains the Ark and the pulpit. Above the Ark is the choir loft. Originally, the majestic organ pipes, almost reaching the ceiling, gave a sense of structural harmony with the choral and organ music.

This temple, built in 1911, was the first of the synagogues to move out of what was then known as the Jewish neighborhood. It can stand for many more years and still blend harmoniously with the atmosphere of the university campus which is close by.

George K. Van Deusen, an Episcopalian, who arranged the music for the dedication services, once said, "Rabbi, when I die and am to be buried, promise me that you will recite the Kaddish at my funeral service. It is a beautiful prayer and has come to mean so much to me." [2] George Van Deusen was organist at the Temple of Concord for thirty years, and when he died Rabbi Friedman recited the memorial prayer in St. Paul's Episcopal Church as the organist had requested.

Not long after the Temple of Concord was completed, the University Methodist Church, on the corner of East Genesee Street and University Avenue, was destroyed by fire. Concord tendered to them the use of its auditorium and all its facilities. When the church was restored seven months later, the officers presented Concord with a bronze plaque commemorating its generosity.

In 1915 the Ladies Auxiliary, always on the alert to raise money for the temple, published the *Concord Cook Book*,[3] compiled by Mrs. Adolph Guttman and Mrs. Levi Oppenheimer. Fifteen pages of solicited advertisements added to the income from the sale of the book. The book was a success and brought several thousand dollars to the Ladies Auxiliary.

The unassigned pew system at the Temple of Concord was introduced in 1921. From time immemorial, to sit up front, close to the Ark, was considered a badge of honor and a status symbol in the community. At the annual congregational dinner in 1921 the change was brought about. It was not easy for the families who had held the same assigned pews for generations to give up this cherished privilege.

Rabbi Samuel Goldenson came from Albany to explain the unassigned pew system. This system provided for members to pay dues according to their ability, and people could sit wherever space was available.[4]

On the following pages is a diagram of the seating arrangement, as it was around 1900.[5] In spite of the non-assigned pew system, members of some of the old-line families still gravitate to the same seats in the temple where their forebears sat.

The One Hundredth Anniversary

On December 1 and 2, 1939, the one hundredth anniversary of the founding of the Society of Concord was celebrated. It was a most important historical occasion for the Jewish community, and was fittingly commemorated at religious services in the temple and at a celebration at the Onondaga Hotel.

The ceremonies started on Friday evening. Dr. Benjamin Friedman, rabbi of the temple, conducted the services. The guest preacher was Dr. Jonah B. Wise of the Central Synagogue of New York. Participating in the services were the Reverend Dr. W. Waldemar Argow of the May Memorial Church and Rabbi Irwin I. Hyman of Temple Adath Yeshurun of Syracuse.

At the Saturday morning services the speaker was Dr. James G. Heller of the Isaac M. Wise Temple of Cincinnati, Ohio. Participating in the service were Bishop Malcolm C. Peabody, Episcopal Diocese of Central New York; Rabbi Jacob X. Cohen, Associate Rabbi, Free Synagogue of New York (mentioned earlier as secretary of the local Jewish Welfare Federation); Rabbi Earl Stone, Jewish Institute of Religion, New York; and Rabbi Jesse Ross of the Temple of Concord staff.

On Saturday evening, the hundredth anniversary banquet and pageant were held in the Grand Ballroom of the Onondaga Hotel. Taking part in the program were Rolland B. Marvin, mayor of Syracuse; Dr. William Pratt Graham, chancellor of Syracuse University; Reverend Dr. Lynn J. Radcliffe, president of the Syracuse Council of Churches; Rabbi Philip S. Bernstein of Temple B'rith Kodesh, Rochester; Reverend Dr. Ray Freeman Jenney, of the Park Central Presbyterian Church, Syracuse; Reverend Gannon F. Ryan, Catholic counselor at Syracuse University; Rabbi Benjamin Friedman; the president of the Temple, David M. Holstein; and Hiram Weisberg, vice-president and toastmaster.

The entertainment of the evening was offered by the younger element of the congregation—many of them descendants of the founders.

Seating arrangement at the old Temple of Concord on State and Harrison Streets at about the turn of the century, as recalled by the late Louis Stolz when the assigned pew system was still in effect.

The Abraham Abrahams family Louis Mann	Abraham, Max, and Gates Thalheimer and families	Joseph and August Falker and families	Mrs. Burgony Gates Hamburger and family
The David Jacobs family	The Benjamin Marshall family	The Henry Bronner family Samuel and Edna Weil	The Danziger brothers and family
George Freeman and family	The Milton Marshall family Abraham Rosenberg and family	Mr. and Mrs. Max Leopold The Herman Leiter family	Mr. and Mrs. Isaac Danziger Mr. and Mrs. Gerson Brown Benjamin Shire
The Aaron Marshall family	Stella Klopfer The Henochsburg family Mr. and Mrs. Moses Edinger	Jacob and Moses Hammel The Louis Leiter family The Levi sisters	The Isidore Kutz family

Marcus Joel Moses Bloom and family	Dr. and Mrs. Henry Elsner and family	Dr. and Mrs. Nathan Jacobson and family Mr. and Mrs. Israel Jacobson	Bertha and Hattie Rosenberg Martin Finkelstein and family
The Gabriel Mitchell family	Moses Heiman and family The Sabolovitz family	Jacob and Yetta Stolz and sons, Louis, David, and Joseph	Jane and Anna Rubin Moses and William Rubin
The Gates Wiseman family Fannie Friendly Mr. and Mrs. Levi Oppenhiemer	Charles Rosenthal and family Milo Rosenthal and family	Mr. and Mrs. Leopold Schoener Adolph Holstein and family	Mr. and Mrs. William Newcity The Raphael Gates family
The David Wolf family	Jack and George Ferguson and families The Zenner family	The Lowe sisters The Simon Lowenthal family Dr. Oliver Blumenthal	Emanuel Lewis and family The Joseph Bondy family
The Moses Levi family	Morris and Myron Kopelowitz Bertha and Sigmund Frensdorf Mr. and Mrs. Marcus Amdursky	The Brill family Sigmund, Joseph, and Rose Levy	Dr. and Mrs. I. Harris Levy T. Aaron Levy Dr. and Mrs. Jacob Levy
The Saul Bergheimer family Elias Volinsky and family	David and Adeline Levey The Jacob Strauss family	Pearl, Jack, and Clara Levy	Joseph and Seymour Henochsburg Moses Henochsburg Hannah Newcity
Solomon Tuch and family Monroe and Minnie Goldinger	Moses Goldstein and family Jacob Alderman and family Louis Glazier and family	Mr. and Mrs. Simon Shimberg William Solomon and family	The William Wolf family Mrs. Rachel Goldman

They presented a pageant depicting the arrival of the early settlers and the founding of the Temple Society of Concord in 1839.

Rabbis of the Temple of Concord

In the early days, the Jewish spiritual leaders were all Europeans. The congregations which were springing up in America did not so much need ordained rabbis (of which few were available) as they did religious functionaries who could serve as *hazzans*, *shohets*, *mohels*, and teachers. While many people respectfully referred to the latter as "Rabbi" (and some assumed that title), of the seven dignitaries who served the Temple of Concord from 1841 to 1883, most went by the title of "Reverend." The first of these was Abraham Gunzenhauser, who served from 1841 to 1846. He was followed by Reverends Joseph Goodman, Jacob Levi, Bernhard Illowy, Herman Birkenthal, Solomon Deutsch, Isaac Cohen, and David Burgenheimer.[6]

THE REVEREND DR. ADOLPH GUTTMAN arrived in 1883. By that time the Temple of Concord was firmly established as a Reform congregation. Dr. Guttman came well recommended, directly from the town of Leipnik in Moravia. Leipnik was renowned as a center of Jewish studies, and Adolph Guttman belonged to one of the learned families of that town.

At first Dr. Guttman preached in German, and even after he had learned to speak the English language, he refused to preach in it until he acquired a proper pronunciation. In this he followed the advice given him by Dr. Gustave Gottheil who said, "Practice before a mirror and pronounce words with the 'th.' When you have mastered the pronunciation, the message to your congregation will be impressive, but it cannot be so when your mispronunciation of English words raises a titter or laughter." Not until he was fully satisfied that he had mastered speaking without an accent did Dr. Guttman preach in English.[7] He frequently said that he benefited greatly from his association with Syracuse University, where he taught Hebrew and German. After a time Dr. Guttman became an accomplished orator in English and was invited to speak at many public gatherings.

In 1887 Rabbi Guttman married the principal of his Sunday School, Marilla Goldstein, a native Syracusan.[8] The congregation gave them a wedding present of $400. Dr. Guttman's long tenure as rabbi of Temple of Concord afforded him the opportunity to become widely known in the general community and respected by the clergy of other faiths. He brought credit to the Temple of Concord and enlarged its influence in the community.[9]

Dr. Guttman instituted many organizations within the Temple. He founded the Men's Club, which later became the Brotherhood. He also started the Collegiate Society of Students at Syracuse University and other social and cultural groups.

Toward the end of the First World War Dr. Guttman was getting along in years and let it be known that he wanted to retire. The congregation started to look for a young American rabbi. The war was over, and many young rabbis who had served as chaplains were ready to accept pulpits. Ordained as a rabbi on August 22, 1919, at Hebrew Union College, Chaplain-Lieutenant Benjamin Friedman was recommended by Louis Marshall. The Temple of Concord had great respect for Louis Marshall's opinion, and when he recommended Benjamin Friedman as a candidate for rabbi he was as good as elected. Rabbi Friedman was twenty-five years of age when he arrived in Syracuse, and he preached his first sermon in his chaplain's uniform.

RABBI BENJAMIN FRIEDMAN served the Temple of Concord for fifty years.[10] When he retired at the age of seventy-five he was as vigorous as many men of younger years. As the membership grew larger, an associate rabbi was secured in 1962, Rabbi Theodore Levy. Dr. Friedman shared the pulpit on an equal basis with his associate, who is thirty years his junior. Rabbi Friedman retains his vigor; from his early youth he has exercised to keep in physical condition. Bicycling, handball, and golf have been his favorite means of keeping fit.

In the city at large he is looked up to as a leading representative of the Jewish community. As a clergyman and citizen, he has participated in and provided leadership in many worthwhile endeavors.

Rabbi Benjamin Friedman has received the degrees of Bachelor of Hebrew Letters, Doctor of Divinity, Doctor of Sacred Theology, and many other honors. In February of 1950, he was presented with the gold medal award of the Freedom Foundation of Valley Forge for his sermon on "Freedom of Speech," given in the Temple of Concord on March 25, 1949.

He is beloved by his congregation—they never fail to honor him on special birthdays and important anniversaries. To be with one congregation a lifetime is, in itself, a sign of a rabbi's consecration and dedication to his congregation. In his retirement he continues as rabbi-emeritus of the temple.

RABBI THEODORE S. LEVY. Rabbi Levy came to the Temple of Concord in 1962 as associate rabbi.[11] He was a natural complement to Rabbi Friedman, young and liberal-minded in a broad sense.

Born on April 16, 1926, in Pittsburgh, Pennsylvania, he is the recipient of a Bachelor of Arts degree from the University of Pittsburgh, a Bachelor of Hebrew Letters from the Hebrew Union College, and a Master of Sacred Theology from Temple University. He was ordained at Hebrew Union College in 1951.

Before coming to Syracuse he occupied pulpits at Huntington, West Virginia, and Waterbury, Connecticut. With his wide and deep education in theology and classical studies, he took over the administration of the religious school, with more than five hundred students and thirty teachers. He became active in all phases of temple organizations. He shared with Rabbi Friedman in conducting the services and in ministering to the congregation.

In Syracuse he serves on the Mayor's Commission on Youth, is a member of the board of the University Hill Corporation, and of the Syracuse Interfaith Commission on Religion and Race, and on the board of the Jewish Family Service Bureau. He is also teaching the first course in Jewish history and culture at LeMoyne College, a Jesuit institution. On Rabbi Friedman's retirement, Theodore Levy took over the full responsibility as spiritual leader of Temple of Concord.

The Temple of Concord Presidents

In the long history of the Temple of Concord many notable men have served as presidents. The first president was Max Thalheimer, and the name Thalheimer has been prominent in the temple ever since. Isaac H. Bronner was the second president, followed by Joseph Falker, the president who served during the most trying period of the congregation, marked by the controversy which split the temple in two between the Reform and Orthodox groups. After Falker came the two Lowenthals, Simon and Isaac, followed by Lazarus Leiter, Henry

Danziger, and Moritz Marks, who served for twenty years to 1890. From 1890 to 1897 there were two presidents, William Henocksburg and August Falker, son of Joseph.[12]

Gates Thalheimer was elected president in 1897, which marked the beginning of a new era. He was a proud and dignified person. When he became president he was at the height of a successful business career. He loved Concord and was looked upon as the leading Jew in Syracuse. He paired well with Rabbi Guttman, each having respect for the other's ability. It was mainly through Gates Thalheimer's efforts that the temple was moved from State and Harrison Streets to the corner of University Avenue and Harrison Street. It was no easy task to persuade the ultra-conservative members of the congregation to raise close to $100,000 for a new edifice. Gates Thalheimer served the Temple of Concord with devotion and dignity until the day of his death on December 21, 1928.

After Thalheimer died, Benjamin Stolz, the vice-president, was elected president. He served the temple well in the German-Jewish tradition for ten years until he passed away in 1937.[13]

The new temple, together with a new, young rabbi, Benjamin Friedman, attracted many new members to the congregation, and they were not all Germans. The wave of German-Jewish immigration to America had ceased years ago. The up-and-coming new generation of Jews were of Polish and Russian descent, and they were taking a more active part in the administration of the Temple of Concord.

After Benjamin Stolz, Vice-President David M. Holstein was elected president in 1937, and the solid line of German-Jewish presidents, which had endured from the very beginning of Temple of Concord, came to an end. David M. Holstein served as president for five years, until ill health forced him to move away from the city. H. Hiram Weisberg, the vice-president, was married to Gates Thalheimer's daughter, Mabel. When David Holstein left Syracuse, H. Hiram Weisberg was elected president on October 4, 1942, and the mantle of leadership passed to one related to the Thalheimers by marriage. He served the temple with great zeal and distinction until 1966. During his long tenure, great strides were made and many improvements were introduced.

In 1960, the Hiram and Mabel Weisberg Religious School was donated by President Weisberg in memory of his wife. The entire cost of construction was defrayed by Mr. Weisberg. This was the largest single gift donated to the Temple of Concord, $350,000.

On June 2, 1963, Syracuse University conferred the degree of Doctor of Laws on H. Hiram Weisberg. A well-deserved and fitting tribute was paid to Mr. Weisberg by the chancellor of the University, Dr. William Pearson Tolley:

H. Hiram Weisberg, great human being, wise, effective, self-made businessman, exemplar of the responsible citizen, devoted religious leader, warmhearted and generous friend—you have earned an enduring place of respect and affection among the citizens of Syracuse and the State of New York. . . .

As a responsible citizen you have generously set aside time and energy for your community far beyond the call of duty. Twice President of the Syracuse Chamber of Commerce; twice President of the Community Chest and its Campaign Chairman. . . .

For a life rare in quality and influence and for your inspirational leadership and loyalty, we are proud to declare you an alumnus of Syracuse University. . . . and I confer on you the degree of Doctor of Laws, *honoris causa*. . . .

After twenty-four years of continuous service to the Temple as president, Hiram Weisberg voluntarily retired. On January 9, 1966, Tracy Ferguson, a nephew by marriage of Mr. Weisberg, was then elected president. Tracy Ferguson and his wife, the former Babette Oberdorfer, are descendants of the early Jewish settlers and founders of Temple of Concord.

TEMPLE ADATH YESHURUN FROM 1910

That little *shul* on Mulberry Street, popularly referred to as the *Neustadter Shul* (to signify where the founders and most of the early members came from), was becoming too small. The notable rabbis teaching and preaching there were drawing large attendance at Friday evening services, and it was impossible to make room for all those who wanted seats for the High Holidays. Many old members had moved uptown, and when the neighboring Temple of Concord moved away, the Ladies Auxiliary insisted that the *shul* also be moved out of the old neighborhood. Much talk of a new temple started in 1912, but there was no action. Then the First World War broke out in 1914, and all of Western Europe was immediately involved. America, too, was greatly affected, and when the United States entered the war in 1917 all thought of building a new temple was abandoned.

After the war a new temple was deemed a necessity, and a site was purchased on the corner of Crouse Avenue and Harrison Street. Adath Yeshurun was fortunate in having Israel Kaplan as president, Morris Hurwitz as vice-president, and many other members over the years who had gained in financial worth and social status. These were some of the men who raised the money and built the new temple: David Grody, Meyer Winkelstein, Louis Maxon, Moses Silverman, Isaac Markson, Jacob Bennet, Joseph Burdick, Joseph Kurzwell, Sigmund Sugarman, and Sam Wiseman.

During the building of the temple, the congregation was without a rabbi, but before it was completed Jesse Bienenfeld was elected. Rabbi Bienenfeld was a very capable administrator, and with his guidance the temple was completed in 1922.

When Morris Hurwitz was chairman of the building committee, he planned well indeed. The result was an imposing edifice, able to seat 1,100 people, more than double the seating capacity of any other synagogue in the city of that time. It had also a separate chapel for daily services, a spacious social hall with a fully equipped stage, classrooms, a library, and a gymnasium.

In 1924 Isaac Markson was elected president, and the Markson era of Temple Adath Yeshurun began. For twenty-five years Isaac Markson devoted every hour of his spare time and much of his worldly goods to the temple, with the exception of one year when he was ill, in which Jacob Bennet took over as president.[14]

During most of the years Isaac Markson was president his wife, Ella, was president of the auxiliary and matched her husband in devotion to the temple. When Isaac Markson retired as president, his son Asher succeeded in that position, and for eighteen years he carried the Markson banner as president of Temple Adath Yeshurun. Leopold Goldberg, Isaac Markson's son-in-law, was also imbued with the spirit of service to the temple from the time he joined the family, serving as treasurer for over thirty-five years. Sidney Grossman was elected president and served until 1967, when Melvin R. Rudolph became the president.

Temple Adath Yeshurun has been fortunate in its selection of rabbis, beginning with their first rabbi, Dr. Joseph H. Hertz. It has had some of the leading rabbis in the Conservative wing of Judaism. Rabbi Irwin I. Hyman came to Temple Adath Yeshurun in 1935 as a young man just out of the Jewish Theological Seminary of America. Almost immediately upon his arrival in Syracuse he took a special interest in the Jewish students attending Syracuse University, many of them in their teens and perhaps away from their homes for the first time. He offered his services voluntarily to Dr. William H. Powers, dean of Hendricks Chapel, and later he worked with Dean Charles C. Noble. He has participated in practically every worthwhile organization in Syracuse. Rabbi Hyman served as president of the Syracuse Jewish Welfare Federation, president of Syracuse District Zionist Organization of America, member of the boards of the Community Chest, the American Red Cross, the Jewish Family Service Bureau, and many others.

In 1943, during the Second World War, he enlisted as a chaplain in the United States Army and served for three years. He was adviser to the Chief Chaplain on Jewish Affairs on the European front. For his duty in the service he received the Bronze Star and the Army Commendation Medal, and left the service with the rank of Major.[15]

In 1964 Rabbi Hyman was appointed chairman of the Mayor's Commission on Human Rights. His leadership and understanding of the civil rights involved in this most complex problem of the Negro and other minority groups was of tremendous importance in enabling the Syracuse community to tide over a rough period.

He was acclaimed "Man of the Year" by the Jewish War Veterans and presented with a plaque on that occasion. On December 18, 1966, on the occasion of the eightieth anniversary of the Jewish Theological Seminary (his Alma Mater), he was presented the honorary degree of Doctor of Divinity.

It is not by the plaudits of his peers alone that Rabbi Hyman is best known in Syracuse, but rather by the deeds in his day-to-day service to his congregation, the community, and to humanity at large.

Rabbi Hyman and his wife, Rachel, enjoy very unusual vacations. For many years they have taken sea voyages on freighters and tramp steamers and, over the years, have covered all the oceans and principal ports. The rabbi claims that only on these small steamers, with no more than ten to twenty passengers, can he find the time to relax, study, and meditate. In 1966 he visited Russia and brought back a report on the Jewish situation in the U.S.S.R. A few weeks after the Arab-Israeli six-day war in June of 1967, he visited Israel and returned with a glowing report of the Israeli victory.[16]

The Cantors of Temple Adath Yeshurun

The reading and chanting of the services in Orthodox or Conservative synagogues is conducted by a *hazzan,* especially on the Sabbath and holidays. Temple Adath Yeshurun has had a number of notable cantors. One who was with Adath the longest and was the most revered was Rev. Moses Fineberg.

MOSES FINEBERG was what is better described as a *Baal Tefillah* (the leader of worship), who would read the prayers with a melodious chant. Many of the old-timers still long for the intoning of the prayers with the supplication and pleading in the voice of a *Baal Tefillah.*

Cantor Fineberg served as cantor and teacher for forty-two years. He was a tall man of dignified appearance. In his later years he had a white, neatly trimmed beard. When he would rise in the pulpit wrapped in a full-length prayer shawl and a tall cantor's hat, he indeed looked the part of a saintly man. Cantor Fineberg retired when the temple on the corner of Harrison and Crouse Avenue was being built in 1921. He had come to America at the age of twenty and lived in Syracuse most of his life. He died on September 23, 1924, at the age of seventy-seven.[17]

SAMUEL ARLUCH was another of the notable cantors of Temple Adath Yeshurun. Samuel Arluch came to the temple in 1932, as a cantor of renown with a thorough knowledge of rendering the prayers with all the intricacies of the cantorial profession. He had a magnificent tenor voice, and would quite often change into a falsetto tone.

During his years in Syracuse his son, Harold, reached fame as a composer of popular music. His son's outstanding success was the ever-popular "Stormy Weather." He composed many more song hits under the name of Harold Arlen, and Cantor Arluch was often accused of inserting some of his son's compositions into the liturgical music of the services. He remained with Temple Adath Yeshurun for fifteen years.[18]

HAROLD LERNER. Since 1953 Harold Lerner has been the cantor and musical director of Temple Adath Yeshurun. He came to the cantorial profession quite naturally, as a descendant of a long line of illustrious European cantors.

His love of music and a good singing voice led him to become a choirboy at an early age. Later he entered the Julliard School of Music in New York, and at the same time attended the Jewish Theological Seminary. With his traditional Jewish background and musical ability, he decided to study for the cantorial profession.

His first position as a cantor was in Boston: four years later he came to Syracuse. Young, personable, and possessing an excellent tenor voice, he was well accepted by the congregation.

Cantor Lerner immediately became active in the musical circles of the city. He continued his study of music at Syracuse University and made many appearances on the concert stage in central New York. His appearances with the Syracuse Symphony Orchestra have been praised by local music critics.

He recently demonstrated further his versatility in the field of music by composing two musical narratives, "Back From the Fair," and "A Tale of Two Cities," based on the stories of Sholom Aleichem.[19]

After Harold Lerner's concert celebrating his tenth year in Syracuse, Earl George, music critic of the *Syracuse Herald-Journal*, wrote the following: "Harold Lerner marked his tenth year in Syracuse with a concert at Lincoln Auditorium last night that showed his audience . . . and in effect, the whole musical community . . . how fortunate we have been to have had an artist of such accomplishment in our midst for the past decade." [20]

Itinerant Cantor

Every fair-sized Jewish community is in need of a qualified person who can take the place of a regular cantor, or teach a Sunday school class, or prepare a boy for his Bar Mitzvah. His regular vocation might be that of a merchant or a professional person, but on the High Holidays he becomes a cantor. In Syracuse such a man is David Altfield, cantor and singer of sweet Jewish melodies.

DAVID ALTFIELD came in 1919, married a Syracuse girl, and entered upon a business career. He has officiated at almost every congregation in Syracuse and the surrounding communities. He has acted as the cantor in the Watertown synagogue and at Temple B'nai Israel in Auburn. When the Suburban Jewish Center was organized in North Syracuse, David Altfield was called upon to serve as their cantor and also to assist in their Sunday school. Congregation Anshe Sfard has also called on David Altfield to act as their cantor on the High Holidays in recent years.

But Altfield's forte is as a dramatist in Jewish theater and as an organizer of Jewish musicals. Dr. Bernard Carp, field secretary of the National Jewish Welfare Board, with a regional office in Syracuse, collaborated with David Altfield to hold the first Jewish Music Festival in Syracuse in 1947. This has become an annual event and has been followed by many other communities. The sweet, sad Jewish melodies have a great magnetism, especially for the foreign-born. The children who have been rocked to sleep by their immigrant mothers with the familiar Jewish lullaby *Rosenkes mit Mandlin* (Raisins and Almonds) cannot easily forget it. It still lingers in their memory.

David Altfield has dedicated many years to the preservation of Yiddish song and theater.[21]

CONGREGATION NEW BETH ISRAEL
(THE GRAPE STREET SHUL)

This pioneer Orthodox synagogue was built in 1856. We have covered the early history of this congregation in a previous chapter. Now we come to the years of 1924–1925. By this time the Temples of Concord and Adath Yeshurun had moved away from the old Jewish neighborhood and were growing in membership, but Beth Israel was still on Grape Street and losing ground rapidly. In membership it was down to a few of the old-timers who still lived in the neighborhood and some of the descendants of the founders, who belonged out of sentiment for their forebears. Much talk had been going on that someday soon they would have to build a new synagogue in a different location.

During the High Holidays of 1924, the Rev. Moses Braude, their beloved *hazzan* and preacher, made a strong plea to raise funds for a new synagogue. Ten thousand dollars was raised on Yom Kippur. With that amount as a nucleus, a building committee was appointed, consisting of Marx Rashkower, Abraham Fredman, Mark Gais, and Reuben Manson. They selected a site on the corner of Irving Avenue and Harrison Street, only three blocks away from where the old synagogue stood for over seventy years. The principal reason for not moving further uptown was stated "as out of consideration for the old members." Some of them still lived in the neighborhood, and they would not have been able to walk to the *shul* on the Sabbath.

The new edifice was completed and dedicated in 1926. It was built of tapestry brick in a Byzantine style of architecture. Although Rev. Braude was their *hazzan* and spiritual leader, they found it necessary to engage an English-speaking rabbi who could preach the sermons and supervise the Sunday and Hebrew schools.

Rabbi Shepherd Z. Baum was called to the pulpit of the Temple of Beth Israel. He stayed a few years, and was succeeded by Rabbi Mordecai Hirshsprung. It was not, however, until 1948, when Rabbi Jacob Epstein came to Beth Israel, that they found a rabbi who suited their type of Orthodox congregation.[22]

Rabbi Jacob H. Epstein received his secular education at the University of Chicago and his religious training at the Hebrew Theological College (Beth Medrash Latorah) in Chicago. He was ordained a rabbi in 1944. Before coming to Syracuse he served as the rabbi of Congregation Beth Hamedrash Hagodel in Rochester, New York.

In 1954 Beth Israel celebrated its one hundredth anniversary. Much preparation went into organizing for this historic occasion, but when the celebration was over and the trustees took a realistic look at their situation, they discovered that the builders of the synagogue, with all good intentions, had made a mistake. By building on the corner of Irving Avenue and Harrison Street the synagogue remained on the periphery of the former neighborhood. During the two previous decades, practically all the members had moved out of this part of the city. As the Jews left, Negro families looking for cheap housing moved in, and soon the new Beth Israel was surrounded by a Negro neighborhood. Children playing on the streets would break windows, and other acts of damage occurred. In the fall of 1958 they had a bomb scare. Someone called while the early morning prayers were in progress, saying that there was a bomb planted in the synagogue, timed to explode at 8:30 A.M. The police were called, and the occupants were told to evacuate the premises at once. No bomb was found; evidently the alarm was the work of a crank.[23] Later that year, fourteen of the stained glass windows were found broken. Rabbi Epstein and the younger group of members advocated building a new temple elsewhere in the city.

The other Orthodox synagogues in the neighborhood were also having their troubles. The old folks were dying off, and the younger people were moving away. Temple Beth Israel sent an invitation to the other Orthodox congregations to merge with them and to build one large edifice far enough out in the eastern section of the city that adequate parking space would be available. Beth Israel then discovered that one of the hardest things to accomplish in Jewish life is to convince an Orthodox congregation to give up its separate existence.

Negotiations were started with the Young Israel Congregation, because its synagogue was in a good location on the corner of East Genesee and Allen Streets. But negotiations broke off after Young Israel insisted that the merged congregation should continue to be affiliated with the National Association of Young Israel.

Poiley Tzedeck, another Orthodox congregation, lost its home in 1960 when the New York State Highway Department demolished their synagogue to make way for Interstate Route 81. Some of the older members had already started to attend services at Beth Israel, since the traditions and ritual of the two were about the same. Poiley Tzedeck had $240,000 which it had received from the state for its property, and would thus make a very desirable partner. It took two years to consumate the merger. At the time of the merger Abe Gordon was president of Beth Israel, and Hyman Brenner was president of Poiley Tzedeck.

In 1963 the Beth Israel building on Irving Avenue was sold to the Bethany Baptist Church, a Negro congregation, for $100,000. The church wanted immediate possession, so the combined congregations were forced to worship in the Community Center while their new synagogue was being constructed.

Poiley Tzedeck

The Poiley Tzedeck Congregation on Almond Street was organized in 1888. Unable to build a synagogue at once, the members worshipped at different homes and halls until 1896, when they built a synagogue at 817 Almond Street. It became known as the "Rushishe (Russian) Shul." In 1914 an additional building to be used as an educational and social center was erected beside the original *shul*. This institution served the strictly Orthodox community in Syracuse for almost seventy years. Poiley Tzedeck was more like a *beth hamidrash,* where people gather to study Torah. They had the distinction of having a number of very learned rabbis of the old school, who continued to study the Talmud with a group of elderly men and any others who wanted to continue their learning of Jewish lore.[24] The mainstay of the synagogue was Reverend Moses N. Pearlman, who served the congregation over forty years as *hazzan, shohet,* and *mohel.*

Like the other Orthodox synagogues in the old Jewish neighborhood, along in the 1940's Poiley Tzedeck began losing ground. The old-timers were dying out and the new generation was moving elsewhere in the city. Just as they were about to close the synagogue for lack of support, along came New York State with plans to build Interstate Route 81 through the middle of Almond Street. This necessitated confiscating the Poiley Tzedeck property. The appraisal committee placed a value of $240,000 on both buildings. What was left of the Poiley Tzedeck congregation now had a nest egg of $240,000 but no synagogue. Beth Israel had a synagogue on the corner of Irving and Harrison Streets and no money. Talk of a merger was soon started, but it took several years to conclude an agreement.

The Merger of Congregation Beth Israel and Congregation Poiley Tzedeck

The merger was consumated in 1963. A committee was appointed to look for a location to build a new synagogue. A suitable site became available when the Hebrew Day School was forced to give up a house and an acre of ground in the 3500 block of East Genesee Street which they had occupied for two years and could no longer support. This location, on the edge of the city, would have been out of the question for a synagogue only a few years before, but the trek eastward out of the old Jewish neighborhood had been so rapid and complete that this site was now considered suitable for a temple.

In 1964 Morris B. Swartz, an eminent young attorney, was elected president of the combined congregations. He immediately surrounded himself with a group of younger men from both organizations and set to work to build the new temple. Preliminary plans indicated that the cost would be approximately $750,000. Even with $450,000 of the combined resources, they were still short $300,00. The enthusiasm for the building of a new temple in a new location was such that on the Yom Kippur evening of 1964—under the leadership of Herman Dubnoff and with a strong plea from Rabbi Epstein—the full amount of $300,000 was raised. It is interesting to note that the new ecumenical spirit prevailing in Syracuse was demonstrated by a gift of $1,000 from Bishop Walter Foery of the Roman Catholic Diocese and another contribution of $1,500 from a leader of the Italian community, Joseph Pietrafesa.

The building was dedicated on September 10, 1965, a very fine modern edifice, complete with classrooms, social halls, kitchen, an air-conditioned auditorium that seats 600 and can be expanded to seat 1,500, a chapel (or *minyan* room) for daily worship, a library which is also used as a board room, administrative offices, a recreation center for the youth groups, and a rabbi's study, large and decorous.

When one views this temple, one realises that Temple Beth El has gone a long way. Although it holds to the same traditional prayers and form of worship, it has kept pace with the times. Although the prayers are traditional, they are conducted with great decorum. No longer are the prayers recited aloud by individuals, but in unison and with greater participation of the congregation. Men and women are seated together in the main auditorium, and ample parking space is provided for those who live too far away to walk to services.

The facilities of the building have become a popular center for weddings and social functions. Nicholas Goffredo was the architect and Celi Budder, Inc., the general contractor.[25]

Ahavath Achim

This congregation was organized in 1896. They worshiped in homes and rented halls until 1913, when they found it possible to erect a synagogue on Orange Street. After the structure was completed and dedicated, they were so proud of the new building that they added the words *Beth Hamedrash Hagodel* (The Great Synagogue) to the original name of the congregation.[26]

Yudel Rabinowitz, the kosher butcher, was president. It was said that he ruled the congregation with an iron hand, and under his leadership it grew in membership and influence among the Orthodox people. In 1919 Rabbi Samuel Yalow was invited to come here from Ansonia, Connecticut. He was only twenty-six years of age and had received a thorough education in both European and American *yeshibot*.[27] Since he was very blond, the short, light hair on his face was inconspicuous, and he appeared for many years to be beardless. Many people wondered why such a strict Orthodox congregation would have a rabbi without a beard.

In 1921 Rabbi Yalow applied for entrance to Syracuse University and was granted a Methodist scholarship. He graduated with a Bachelor of Arts degree in 1925. Rabbi Yalow is the author of a number of books in Hebrew, the latest of which is *Shalmei Shmuel* [Gift of Samuel] (Israel, n.d.), a discourse on the Talmud. He has served as the Rabbi of Ahavath Achim for over forty years. In 1969 the synagogue building was torn down to make way for the construction of Interstate Route 81. After faithfully serving the Orthodox community of Syracuse for fifty years, Rabbi Yalow is now left without a pulpit.[28]

Esther Yalow, his wife, was a notable person in her own right. The daughter of Rabbi Isaiah Marcus, she was born in Kovno, Lithuania, and came to America when she was six. After graduating from a state teacher's college, she taught school in Richmond, Virginia. She was very active in women's organizations, especially in the Council of Jewish Women, the Jewish Family Service Bureau, the Board of the Jewish Federation, the Women's Mikvah Association, and many other worthwhile institutions.

Rabbi and Mrs. Yalow had two children. Their son Aaron is a graduate of Syracuse University, holds a Doctor of Philosophy degree from the University of Illinois, and is a medical physicist at Montefiore Hospital in New York and a professor of physics at Cooper Union School of Engineering. He is an Associate Fellow in the American College of Radiology, member of Phi Beta Kappa, and a contributor to scientific and medical publications.

Mrs. Esther Yalow passed away on October 18, 1968,[29] and was buried in Israel. A memorial service was held in Syracuse on November 24, 1968.

Anshe Sfard in Syracuse

The Anshe Sfard Synagogue in Syracuse was started by a small group of Eastern European Hasidic Jews who followed the *Nusah Sfard* (Sephardic ritual) and who came from around Odessa and Kishinev. The Sephardic Jews are very proud of their heritage. They are descendants of the Jews who lived in Spain and Portugal up to the time of their expulsion by the Spanish Inquisition in 1492. They were particularly interested in having a synagogue of their own because they differed from the *Ashkenazim* in their ritual of worship and their pronunciation of Hebrew. Their first place of worship in Syracuse was a hall on State Street over a harness shop. In 1907 the congregation elected Solomon Bonfield as their president.

In 1917 they raised enough funds to build a synagogue at 815 South Orange Street, and also acquired a two-acre plot for a cemetery. Among their spiritual leaders they had Rabbi Simon and, for many years, Rabbi Moses Jacobson. Their cantor was Reverend Weitzman. Among their lay leaders and presidents have been Messrs. Rensin, Resnick, Tauber, Stuckmeister, Katz, Usher Greenberg, and William Schwartz. Not all their rabbis and leaders were Hasidic Jews, but they were all devoted to their congregation, Anshe Sfard.

In 1950 the congregation sold the synagogue on Orange Street and bought a house at 2013 East Genesee Street, which they remodeled extensively into a very presentable synagogue. Their present leaders are Maurice Agronin, president; Samuel Spivak, chairman of the board; Eva Agronin (wife of the president), secretary and president of the Ladies Auxiliary.[30]

A new Sephardic congregation was formed in Syracuse in time to observe the High Holidays of 1968. This congregation is composed of Jews who were compelled to leave Moslem countries during and after the Arab-Israeli war. They were brought to America by the United

Hebrew Service Association and, on arrival, were sent to Syracuse since it is a city with diversified industries. The Syracuse Jewish Family Service Bureau found homes and assisted them in securing jobs or other means of earning a livelihood.

These Jews say that the present Anshe Sfard synagogue in Syracuse is not Sephardic enough for them; that their prayer ritual differs; and that their prayer modes and melodies are nearer to the Biblical motif than are those used by European and American Jews. They therefore formed their own congregation. Temple Beth El has given them the use of its recreation hall for their High Holiday services. Together with those Jews who came from Salonica, Greece, there are at present about thirty families of true Sephardic Jews in Syracuse. The leaders and organizers of this Sephardic congregation are Joseph Peppi, Isaac Azreia, Isaac Horasi, and Jules Merrill.[31]

LEO FEIGENBAUM AND YOUNG ISRAEL

J. LEO FEIGENBAUM came to Syracuse in 1933 to manage the General Material and Wrecking Company, which his father-in-law had established. He was twenty-five years old and had just married. He was a native American, a college graduate, and a strict Orthodox Jew. He had obtained his elementary and high school education in a *yeshiva* in Cleveland, Ohio. Almost immediately on his arrival he became active in Jewish organizations. His particular interest was Jewish education. Very much concerned by the lack of a Hebrew day school, he started to agitate for one but was unable to arouse any enthusiasm among the leaders of the community. On several occasions he made a strong appeal to the Welfare Federation for funds for a day school on the same basis on which they were supporting the Hebrew Free School and the Folk Shule. Each time, however, help was not forthcoming.

J. Leo Feigenbaum was not one to give up easily. He found support from a small group of Orthodox Jews who were interested primarily in establishing a synagogue on East Genesee Street, in the section into which Jews were moving. At one time they obtained options for the purchase of property on each of the corners of Genesee and Allen, and Genesee and Fellows Avenue, and also the Dann property directly across from Fellows Avenue where the Community Center now stands. When the Federation committee members were looking for a location for the Jewish Community Center in the same neighborhood, they had to ask Leo Feigenbaum to release his option on the Dann property in order that they might buy it.

Young Israel of Syracuse was duly incorporated in 1945, in accordance with the Religious Corporation Law of the State of New York. A clause was inserted in the articles of corporation, binding Young Israel to the National Council: "That at said meeting it was duly decided that Young Israel of Syracuse will conform in all its proceedings to the constitution, by-laws, rules and regulations of the Council of Young Israel and Young Israel Synagogue organizations; otherwise this corporation and its powers shall cease and be of no further effect."

The certificate of corporation was executed on February 28, 1945, and signed by J. Leo Feigenbaum, William Reisman, and Hyman Levine.[32]

In 1948 they purchased the property on the corner of East Genesee and Allen Streets. In the same year they opened the Hebrew Academy of Syracuse, the first Hebrew day school in the community. Rabbi Israel Fink served as the first rabbi of Young Israel. In 1954 the original building of Young Israel was destroyed by fire, and High Holiday services were conducted in the Westcott Theater. The Hebrew Academy was discontinued after the fire.

The construction of a new synagogue was planned in 1955 for the same location. It was built during 1956 and dedicated in 1957. The building consists of about 4,200 square feet, containing a synagogue, which is also used as a meeting hall, and a small kitchen.

In 1961 Rabbi Stanley Wexler was engaged as the spiritual leader. Under Rabbi Wexler's leadership, the facilities of Young Israel were greatly expanded: a new addition to the building was constructed, containing a social hall, classrooms, a chapel, and a *mikvah*. In 1963 Young Israel cooperated with the Hillel Foundation to bring kosher dining facilities to Jewish students at Syracuse University.

Rabbi Wexler remained with Young Israel for five years. Both he and his wife served the congregation with great devotion and were active in all Jewish community projects. Mrs. Wexler was an accomplished person and was principal of the Hebrew Day School.

J. Leo Feigenbaum, the initiator of the Young Israel movement in

Syracuse, passed away on February 9, 1956, just before the new synagogue was completed. A resident of Syracuse for twenty-five years, he was a strong believer in and an ardent worker for all Jewish causes. His wife Evelyn and his family moved back to Cleveland after his death.[33]

Rabbi Wexler was succeeded by Rabbi Irwin S. Borvick in 1967. Rabbi Borvick received the Bachelor of Arts degree from Yeshiva College and was ordained by Yeshiva University in 1960. After two years of service as a chaplain in the United States Army, in 1962 he became the spiritual leader of Congregation Degal Israel in Lancaster, Pennsylvania, a post which he occupied until he came to Syracuse. He is the author of several articles in *Jewish Life* and *Young Israel Viewpoint*.[34]

NEW TRENDS IN SYNAGOGUES

The problem which confronts all Jewish communities is whether to increase the size of the established synagogues, or to organize smaller congregations in various sections of the city and suburbs to which Jewish families have moved. It is well to note that, although the Jewish population in Syracuse has spread into suburban areas, it has not increased appreciably in numbers. The 1967 *American Jewish Year Book* estimates that the Jewish population of Syracuse is 11,000, which is in accordance with the figure arrived at by the Syracuse Jewish Welfare Federation. This is about the same estimate arrived at in 1922 and 1944, according to surveys made in those years. While the Jewish community has remained nearly the same in numbers, there has been a considerable increase in temple and synagogue affiliations since World War II.

The membership of the two largest temples has increased to the point that one (Adath Yeshurun) now holds High Holiday services in the War Memorial Auditorium, while the other (the Temple of Concord) holds two identical services in order to accommodate all its congregants and their families. Temple Beth El has, of course, greatly enlarged its previous seating capacity.

The Suburban Jewish Center in North Syracuse

North of the city, where large industrial plants are located, live many Jewish professional men employed by the General Electric Company, Carrier Corporation, and Bristol Laboratories. These families were very much concerned about their children's religious education, and a number of the families in North Syracuse, headed by Elihu Cohen, Gustave Pearlman, and Marvin Barish, organized a religious school in 1955. Major Emanuel Abramson, stationed at nearby Hancock Field Air Base, arranged for this group to use the Air Base Chapel for Friday evening Sabbath services. In 1960 they formally organized the Suburban Jewish Center. Dr. Jesse Ross, director of adult education in the Syracuse public school system and an ordained rabbi, guides the young congregation and administers the Sunday school, assisted by David Altfield. The congregation adheres to the Conservative form of worship.

In 1963 the need of a building of their own became apparent, and a site was purchased on Vine Street in the town of Clay. They raised enough funds within their own group to build a temple, to be known as the Suburban Jewish Center. It was completed and dedicated in early 1968. It now has a membership of forty families, with sixty children enrolled in the Sunday school.[35]

Beth Sholom in Dewitt

The trend of the general population has been more toward the east, so that now Dewitt and Fayetteville, which adjoin Syracuse in that direction, have a considerable number of Jewish residents. Most of these are young families with small children.

Dewitt's new Congregation Beth Sholom (House of Peace) is another example of the new generation of Jews in action. Those who organized Beth Sholom were pioneers with courage and vision in the same sense as the Jews who started congregations in the early years of Syracuse.

Beth Sholom began with an informal get-together of twelve families at the home of the Herbert Alperts in July of 1962. This was a group of young Jewish couples, among them Mr. and Mrs. Herbert Alpert, Dr. and Mrs. Arthur Stockman, Dr. and Mrs. Seymour Dushay, Dr. and Mrs. Myron Schaffer, Mr. and Mrs. Bruce Rumaner, and Mr. and Mrs. Saul Braverman, to name a few.

In 1963 they held their first High Holiday services in the Pebble Hill Presbyterian Church. A religious school was organized under the leadership of Mrs. David Yaffee. The teachers were women of their own congregation. The first school was a combined nursery school, kindergarten, and first grade. An adult education program was inaugurated. The group met semi-monthly to study and explore Jewish history, Jewish philosophy, and something of the Talmud.

In a truly ecumenical spirit, the Dewitt Community Church offered them the use of its edifice for the 1964 High Holiday services. The relationship between this church and Congregation Beth Sholom is of the finest. For several years the two groups have held a number of programs and fund-raising projects together.

In the beginning, services were led by volunteer members of the congregation. For the High Holidays they secured a senior student-rabbi from the Jewish Theological Seminary in New York City. Later, they made arrangements for the student-rabbi to come to Syracuse once a month to lead the Friday evening and Saturday morning prayers. Having a strong belief in the value of the Jewish religion, they raised enough money to build their own temple on Jamesville Road in Dewitt in 1965. They now possess a complete religious institution, with an active men's club, an effective sisterhood, a youth group for teenagers, a religious school with professional teachers, and a full-time leader, Rabbi Harvey Goldscheider. He is a young man with a great deal of promise, a graduate of Yeshiva University and the Jewish Theological Seminary of America. The congregation is affiliated with the United Synagogue of America.[36]

DISSOLUTION AND AMALGAMATION

We have accounted for and recorded the history of the temples and synagogues now in existence. There have been more, perhaps two or three times the number we have now. Most of them were organized during the days of the large immigration. To start an Orthodox congregation was not a big undertaking. All that was needed was a *min-*

yan. Unlike other religious groups, it is not necessary to have the authority of a higher body. They did not even need a rabbi or a *hazzan;* any male over 13 years of age who can read Hebrew may lead a congregation in prayer. A *minyan* or congregation was usually started when there were enough men from one European province who desired to worship together. In some instances a new congregation was formed when an aspirant for the presidency in one congregation was not elected; he then would take a few of his supporters with him and form a new *minyan.* So it was in Syracuse: through the years a number of small congregations met in rented halls or vacant stores, hoping some day to be able to build a *shul.*

Now, the small congregations are practically all gone. As the more progressive congregations built larger temples in the newer neighborhoods, they drew members away from the older Orthodox synagogues. When the second and third generation grew to maturity, they required better classrooms and more efficient teachers for their children. The newer temples supplied the need. The Reform Temple of Concord membership consists of approximately seven hundred families, and Adath Yeshurun, the Conservative temple, claims well over a thousand.[37]

The Orthodox congregations are making a strong effort to retain their younger members and perhaps regain some of their lost membership. Beth El, the merger of Beth Israel and Poiley Tzedeck, has built a new, large synagogue. It is not quite as Orthodox as it was; it now has mixed seating and fine, up-to-date Sunday and Hebrew schools. The services are not what they were when Beth Israel was on Grape Street in the old nieghborhood. It now wants to be known not as an Orthodox but as a "Traditional" synagogue.

Young Israel still retains the Orthodoxy of the old school. The ladies sit separately, but on the same floor, divided from the men only by a short transparent curtain.

In all of Syracuse hardly any of the old-style Orthodox synagogues remain—the kind that were a carry-over from the Old Country, where a man would rush in early in the morning to say his prayers before he started out on his day's work. They have moved or disappeared, together with the old Jewish neighborhood, and the Urban Renewal Project has speeded them on their way.

CHAPTER X

The Community and the World Wars

THE FIRST WORLD WAR

On June 28, 1914, the Archduke of Austria and his consort were assassinated in Serbia. Austria's stiff demands for satisfaction would have all but wiped out that little country, but, backed by Russia, Serbia balked. Austria thereupon declared war on Serbia. In a rapid succession of events, Russia mobilized; Germany, allied with Austria, declared war on Russia and France; and England, joining France and Russia, declared war on Germany and Austria. In a period of about thirty days the First World War engulfed all of Europe.

The German armies, taking the offensive against Russia, marched toward the East. Poland, Latvia, and Lithuania were the first to fall, the three countries in Europe that contained the largest concentrations of Jews. In 1915 the Germans started their submarine warfare. The United States warned Germany that she would be held to strict account for any American losses. On April 25, Germany torpedoed an American tanker. On May 7, a German submarine sank the *Lusitania*, and 124 American lives were lost. In 1917 Germany began unrestricted submarine warfare.

The United States broke off diplomatic relations and declared war on Germany on February 28. Troop "D" of Syracuse of the New York National Guard was mobilized for service in France on May 14, and President Woodrow Wilson directed that the New York State Fair Grounds at Syracuse be turned into a training camp.

Relief societies were hastily formed on the local and national level to meet the needs caused by the war. A "War Chest" was started in Syracuse for the aid of families whose men were in the armed forces. The Jewish community contributed generously. At the time war broke out, the Syracuse Jewish Welfare Federation was in its formative stage, and the call for overseas help and the dramatic impact of the Balfour Declaration of November 2, 1917, added another dimension, Palestine, to the needs of the Jewish people and stimulated contributions to the Federation. The Federation has since become the mainstay and source for all Jewish philanthropic endeavors in Syracuse.[1]

Of the twelve to fifteen thousand men who went into service from Syracuse and Onondaga County, 5.8 percent were Jewish. Among the Jewish personnel were two majors, three captains, nineteen lieutenants, and one ensign. Seventy-two percent of the Jewish men were in combat units. Colonel Joseph Bondy was active in recruiting for the Officer's Training Corps. Five men from Syracuse went to Canada and enlisted in the Jewish Legion, serving with the British Army in Palestine. Many Jewish men and women participated actively in the civilian effort supporting the war.

The following Jewish men from Syracuse were killed or died while on active duty in the war:

Asher Yaffee, killed in action at Chateau-Thierry on July 15, 1918.
Manuel Prowda, died in France on February 17, 1919.
Joseph Livshin, died in France on August 3, 1918.
David Freeman, wounded at St. Mihiel on September 17, 1918; died of wounds December 3, 1918.[2]

The Armistice was declared on November 11, 1918, and the First World War was over. When the news reached Syracuse, the principal stores and factories closed. People gathered and danced in the streets, impromptu parades were formed, and strangers embraced and congratulated each other.

The people believed in what Woodrow Wilson had said: "The world must be made safe for democracy." President Wilson went to the Peace Conference in Paris to stress his Fourteen Points for peace among nations. He did not achieve all that he went after, but he did accomplish the acceptance of the plan for a League of Nations. However, while the peace treaty was being written in Paris, the isolationist movement gained a strong hold in the United States, including the Congress. Senator Henry Cabot Lodge of Massachusetts led the Republican opposition, and the United States did not join the League of Nations.

The war had a unifying effect on the Jews of Syracuse. They recognized their obligations to their brothers who were left in distress after the war in Europe and the Balfour Declaration of 1917 aroused an interest in the support of Palestine. As a result, the United Charities was founded. The name was later changed to the Syracuse Jewish Welfare Federation. The Federation proved its worth when, in 1933, Hitler and the Nazi Party gained control in Germany and World War II was on its way.

WORLD WAR II

The First World War seemed to happen suddenly and unexpectedly, but the Second World War could be foreseen years in advance. Each year it became more apparent that another war was inevitable, for Adolph Hitler, a crafty genius, had so aroused the German people that they followed him blindly, seeking revenge for their defeat in World War I.

When Hitler became head of the National Socialists (Nazi Party), he and his followers were not satisfied only with instilling their vindictive ideas in the people of Germany, but zealously spread their cause among Germans everywhere. In the United States, groups of German-Americans in most of the large cities formed Bunds in order to help their mother country. It was rumored that such a Bund existed in Syracuse, drilling and goose-stepping like the Storm Troopers. The American Legion decided to investigate and formed a "raiding party." Led by Daniel Kelly and Wesley Markson, they invaded the Bund headquarters and found, according to the *Syracuse Herald* of October 17, 1938, a group of men dressed in Nazi uniforms, complete with Sam Browne belts. The raiding party took samples of their literature, and later requested that the Bund be investigated by the proper authorities. After the investigation the Bund went underground.

Hitler and his "master race" were determined not only to conquer the world but first to annihilate all the Jews—those whose families had lived in Germany for a thousand years, and also those living in every country he conquered. He succeeded in destroying six million souls—about one-third of all the Jews in the world.

The only Jews left in any number and substance were in America. The Jews of America rose, united as never before, to succor the Jewish remnant left in the concentration camps and those who came out of hiding.

The Jews of Syracuse did their share of philanthropic work through their agencies: the Welfare Federation, which raised the funds, and the Jewish Family Service Bureau, which assisted the refugees settling in Syracuse.

Syracuse Jews also did their share in the military services; young men volunteered and were drafted. Those who were too old or exempt from direct service participated in many areas of the war effort.

Many Syracuse Jews received citations and decorations for distinguished service in the war. Those so recognized included fifty-three officers and ninety-nine enlisted men. Seventy-eight were awarded the Purple Heart for combat injuries or death. Others earned such coveted medals as the Silver Star, the Distinguished Flying Cross, the Distinguished Service Medal, and the French Croix de Guerre. Among the most decorated men from this Jewish community were Major Paul Schwartz, 1st Lt. Bruce Sabine, 1st Lt. Maurice Spector, and Sgt. Jerome Hoffman.

Thirty-two of these Jewish servicemen from Syracuse lost their lives while on active duty during the war. Those who made the supreme sacrifice for their country were: [3]

Killed in Action

Abramson, Robert S., Capt.
Belmont, Albert, Pvt.
Black, Julius M., S/Sgt.
Glass, Richard, PFC
Golde, Allan, 2d Lt.
Gordon, Alfred G., Pvt.
Grody, William H., 2d Lt.
Kantor, Morris, 1st Lt.
Kessel, Bernard, PFC
Lavine, Harry, S/Sgt.
Lavine, Sanford, 1st Lt.
Lazaroff, Martin, PFC
Margolis, Arthur G., Cpl.

Marshall, Sidney, PO2/c
Menter, Marvin, 2d Lt.
Pierson, Robert M., 1st Lt.
Posner, Solomon, PFC
Rubenstein, Samuel, I., Maj.
Ruffine, Barney, PFC
Sasson, Ellis, 1st Lt.
Weiner, Samuel, PFC
Weltmann, Jacob S., PFC
Weltmann, Samuel J., PFC
Wolfe, Lester L., PFC
Zaleon, Myron, Cpl.
Zutrauen, Rudolph

Non-Combat Deaths

Ginsburg, Irving, S2/c	Rubenstein, Morton D., Pvt.
Hodis, Jacob, Cpl.	Spivak, Irving, Ens.
Hodiss, Meyer, 2d Lt.	Tecler, Bruce E., AS

SURVIVORS COME TO SYRACUSE

When the war was over, refugees began to come to America in larger numbers. It is estimated that about 200 families arrived in Syracuse between 1945 and 1955. Syracuse was hard put to find homes and jobs for the new arrivals. The Jewish Family Service Bureau estimated that it expended an average of $600 from the time a refugee family arrived until they were settled and could take care of themselves.

Fifteen families arrived from Salonika, Greece, between 1949 and 1960. Salonika was the only city in Greece that had a proportionately large percentage of Jews. The Nazis took 20,000 Jews out of that city to concentration and labor camps. Only 2,000 returned, according to the survivors who reached Syracuse.

In 1956, when the Hungarian revolt against Soviet domination took place, Jews and others had the opportunity to escape. Ten Hungarian families were received in Syracuse.[4]

THE CHRONICLE OF A REFUGEE FAMILY

The following story, told by a surviving member of one refugee family, is typical of what happened to many Jewish families during World War II.[5]

My name is Ben Choroser. My father and mother, Maurice and Rachel Choroser, left the city of Warsaw, Poland, in 1917 with one child and traveled to Paris, France, because they felt there was less anti-Semitism in France. They lived in Paris twenty-five years where they had a small shoe factory, employing ten people, and a retail shoe store. We were not rich people but lived comfortably. Nine children were born in Paris.

I was nine years old when the war started. I knew nothing about Nazis until they marched into Paris in 1940. They made all Jews register. We had to put a sign in the window of our store and sew the Star of David on all of our clothing to show that we were Jews. My father and mother, sensing what was happening, sent my three younger brothers and two younger sisters to a farm about fifty miles outside of Paris in 1942. The Germans came to our house and took my parents, my oldest sister (age twenty-one), two brothers (ages twenty and seventeen), and a baby sister, one year old, to a concentration camp in Germany. I was in the house that day, too, but my mother told me to climb the roof of the house and run away. I joined my other brothers and sisters living on the farm. Later I was forced to work for the Germans in an airplane factory until we were liberated by the American armies in 1944. When I returned to Paris at age fourteen I found that everything had been taken by the Germans. At the Jewish Joint Distribution Center where I made inquiries about my family I learned that nothing could be done until the war ended. In 1945 when the war stopped and news started coming back about people in the concentration camps, I was informed that my brother Bernard, age seventeen, was coming back. His health was so bad that the French government sent him to a convalescent home where he remained for almost two years. At the time of his return we also learned that our parents, my oldest sister, one brother and the baby had been exterminated in the Auschwitz, Poland, concentration camp. When Bernard was completely recovered we reopened our shoe business in Paris, which we operated until 1948.

My brother Bernard and myself were not able to take care of our brothers and sisters, so they were sent to a camp for war-orphaned children supported by the United Jewish Appeal.

We had no family left in France—no relatives—but my brother Bernard remembered that our mother used to write to an aunt in America before the war. We knew only that her last name was Meyers and that she lived near Syracuse, New York. We went to the HIAS [The Hebrew Immigrant Aid Society] organization, which located her in Liverpool, New York. We wrote to her for help. She and her cousins, Mr. and Mrs. Abe Menter, signed the necessary affidavits to bring us to America. Because my aunt was quite old and unable to take care of the seven of us we decided to let our younger brothers and sisters be adopted by other families. My two sisters, Renee and Therese, were adopted by Mr. and Mrs. Melvin Rudolph; my youngest brother, Jacques, by Mr. and Mrs. Harold J. Shure. The rest of us, Bernard, Simon, Joseph, and myself, either went to school or enlisted in the armed forces. We are all married now, with children of our own.

The following letter from Choroser provides a sequel to the above account:

Syracuse, New York
September 19, 1967

Dear Mr. Rudolph:

Here is the additional information you requested. The farm where we stayed during the war was a small, self-supporting farm located near the town of Meulan about fifty miles from Paris. The people knew we were Jewish. They were not paid until I started working in the airplane factory, and then they received all my pay to support my brothers and sisters. The airplane factory was also located near Meulan.

The names and ages of the children taken with my father and mother are as follows: Suzanna, age 21; David, age 20; and Marie, age 1. All three did not return. I'm sorry I don't have any photographs of those days.

The names, ages, etc. of my other brothers and sisters are as follows:

Bernard, age 39, lives in St. Louis, Missouri, where he is Branch Manager for Metropolitan Life Insurance Company. He is married—the father of three daughters.

Simon, age 35, is an electrical engineer. He lives near Los Angeles with his wife and one son and one daughter.

Joseph, age 33, works in advertising in Los Angeles where he lives with his wife, two daughters and one son.

Renee, age 31, lives in Schenectady, New York. She is married, the mother of two daughters and one son.

Therese, age 29, lives in Syracuse with her husband and family—one daughter and one son.

Jacques, age 27, is a businessman in Syracuse.

Benjamin, age 37, is a purchasing agent for an insurance company in Syracuse, the father of four sons and one daughter.

Jewish citizens of Syracuse and the Jewish Family Service Bureau played a part in helping to bring the Choroser children to this country and caring for them until they were self-sufficient.

How the Choroser Family Came to Syracuse

When Mrs. Meyers, their aunt, received word from France that seven of the children were alive and had the proper visas and affidavits to be brought to the United States, she consulted Max Stolz, who was president of the Jewish Family Service Bureau and who acted as her attorney. They decided to send for only the boys at first. When they arrived on March 18, 1949, all seven children appeared. Their aunt was in no position to take care of the children, physically or financially. The boys ranged in age from seven to twenty and the two girls were eight and nine. Max Stolz took the two little girls home with him, and Mrs. Abe Menter temporarily took care of the other children. The girls had been with the Stolz family six weeks when Mrs. Stolz, who had two children of her own, was forced to go to a hospital for treatment. Mr. and Mrs. Melvin Rudolph, who had three children of about the same ages, volunteered to care for the girls. The Melvin Rudolphs brought them up as their own and educated them along with their own children. One attended Syracuse University. They lived as one family until both girls married two fine young men.

The youngest, Jacques, did not take long to become Americanized in the Shure home. Besides being a good student, he was an exceptionally fine athlete. He participated in every one of the three major sports while he was in high school—basketball, baseball, and football. He was president of his senior class, and at graduation received a scholarship to Dartmouth. He played on the Dartmouth baseball team for four years and was a member of two honorary societies when he graduated. Bernard, the oldest, joined the U.S. Army, and the two other boys were cared for in foster homes and received college educations.

It is estimated that in addition to previous refugees, nearly one hundred families arrived in Syracuse between 1955 and 1965. Not all remained here, but enough stayed so that there are now former-refugee groups of German, Polish, Hungarian, and Greek Jews in Syracuse.

WOMEN OF VALOR

Jewish women of Syracuse played a very substantial role in every endeavor of religious and charitable institutions. The Councils, the Auxiliaries, and the Sisterhoods contributed greatly to each synagogue and temple and their respective Sunday schools. They not only supported but initiated movements, and it was through their encouragement that men undertook the building of important institutions of lasting worth. One such example is the Ladies' Auxiliary of Temple of Concord, which initiated and provided the impetus to start the new building at Madison Street and University Avenue. The old saying, "Never underestimate the power of a woman" is as valid today as it was in the years gone by.

ETHEL OBERDORFER (1883–1946). In no congregation in Syracuse did a Sisterhood play a bigger role than it did at Temple of Concord, and in no Sisterhood was there a woman whose strong leadership played a larger part than that of Mrs. Jonas (Ethel) Oberdorfer. For twenty-seven years she was the president and keystone of the Sisterhood. From the time when it was still called the Ladies' Auxiliary, she ruled the Sisterhood with vigor and wisdom. Her intense interest in the temple stemmed from her forebears on both sides of the family, the Oberdorfers and the Thalheimers, who were among the original founders of the Temple of Concord. Her father, Gates Thalheimer, was president of the Temple of Concord for almost as many years as she was president of the Sisterhood. Although her principal interest was the Sisterhood, she found time for many other worthwhile organizations. She served on the boards of the Council of Jewish Women, Memorial Hospital, and the Onondaga County Sanitarium, as well as being active as a board member of Hadassah in the years before that society was popular in her circle.[6]

CARRIE GAIS (1874–1961). As a young girl Carrie Manson Gais had the urge to help others. At the age of fourteen, she was instrumental in forming a young ladies' auxiliary for the purpose of raising funds for the Western New York Orphan Asylum. Carrie Gais attributed her devotion to charity and love of Israel to her rigid, traditional Jewish upbringing.

When Carrie Manson married Mark Gais, she married a man who equally adhered to the Orthodox way of Jewish life. The Manson and Gais families were staunch members of Beth Israel *shul*. Individually and together, they gave of their time, energy, and possessions to all worthy causes.

In 1915 Mrs. Carrie Gais joined with Mrs. Samuel D. (Henrietta) Solomon, a staunch Zionist, to form the first Syracuse chapter of Hadassah. Mrs. Gais was elected president eight times, and remained active in the Hadassah movement all her life. Today there are three chapters in Syracuse, one of which is named in memory of Carrie Gais.

She did not confine herself entirely to Hadassah. She was also very much interested in the Council of Jewish Women, which she served as president for five terms. Mark Gais, her husband, was one of the founders of the Home for the Aged, and Carrie's interest in the home led her to form a Ladies' Auxiliary. This Auxiliary has done noble work for the institution, which is now the Jewish Home of Central New York.

Never experiencing the happiness of having children of their own, Carrie and Mark were foster-parents to two daughters. Carrie Gais was a little woman, not over five feet tall and weighing hardly a hundred pounds. How she managed to do so much is hard to understand. Perhaps she gave the explanation on her eighty-fifth birthday when she said, "I had a strict father and mother, but they acted with great love, so important to character building." [7]

BERTHA FRENSDORF (1864–1962). Bertha Frensdorf lived to be ninety-eight and, when she passed away on June 24, 1962, she was the last of a large family of Frensdorfs who had contributed greatly to civic and Jewish institutions in Syracuse.

Bertha was born April 2, 1864, at 403 Harrison Street, just around the corner from the old Temple of Concord that stood for sixty years at the corner of Harrison and State Streets. After graduating from high school and business school, she worked as a secretary at the Gray Brothers' Shoe Company, on the corner of Franklin and Walton Streets, retiring after twenty-seven years. The remainder of her long life was devoted to charity and other worthy causes. At one time she was on the boards of more than twenty organizations, many of which she had helped to found. Among these organizations were Camp Bradley Brook, the Onondaga County Sanitarium, the Jewish Community Center, the Jewish Home of Central New York, Temple of Concord, and the Syracuse Day Nursery. Miss Frensdorf also cooperated with T. Aaron Levy in forming the Americanization League, and contributed substantially to Camp Fren-Le. The camp combined the names of Frensdorf and Levy in honor of these two worthy Jewish citizens.

Of the many organizations in which she was active, the Council of Jewish Women was her major interest. She brought the Council to Syracuse, nourished and loved it, was familiar with every little detail concerning it, took care of the budget, and served for many years as secretary and president.[8]

What Ethel Oberdorfer was to the Sisterhood of Temple of Concord, what Carrie Gais was to the Syracuse Chapter of Hadassah, Bertha Frensdorf was to the Syracuse Council of Jewish Women.

There have been many more Jewish women native to Syracuse who have labored long and lovingly in all good causes, for both civic and Jewish betterment. They, too, are worthy of special mention, but to attempt to name them all would take too much space and would be unfair to some who might unwittingly be omitted.

HENRIETTA SOLOMON AND HADASSAH

HENRIETTA SOLOMON (1888–1962) came from Louisville, Kentucky. Her father, Simon Shapinsky, was a leader in the Jewish community of Louisville and an ardent follower of Theodore Herzl's political Zionism. He attended the Second World Zionist Congress in Basle, Switzerland. Henrietta's mother died at an early age, so that she was very close to her father. She participated in the organizations in which her father was interested and often accompanied him to their national conventions.

At the American Zionist Convention in Pittsburgh, Pennsylvania in 1910, she met Samuel D. Solomon, a delegate from Syracuse. There was quite a difference in their ages; Henrietta was twenty-two and Sam Solomon was forty-two, but they shared a strong interest in communal Jewish life and world problems. They were married in the Shapinsky home in Louisville, Kentucky, on June 6, 1911.

When Henrietta came to live in Syracuse, she brought the spirit of Zionism and her interest in organizational work with her. She had met Henrietta Szold, the founder of Hadassah, at her father's home in Louisville. In Syracuse she found a worthy helpmate in Carrie Gais, and together they organized a Hadassah chapter in 1914. It was hard going at first; most of the leaders among the women were from the Reform temple and shied away from Hadassah. The following ten women are believed to have been the charter members and present at the first meeting: Henrietta Solomon, Carrie Gais, Tillie Kaletzki, Lee Alperin, Rose Sarason, Etta Klein, Annie Jacobs, Bessie Elman, Rose Algase Cohen, and Sophia Silverman.

During the First World War, Hadassah women were actively engaged in working with Red Cross knitting, sewing, and rolling bandages. After the announcement of the Balfour Declaration and the end of the war, Hadassah found its true aspirations, "To heal and succor the poor and the sick, Jew and Arab alike." This appealed strongly to womanly instincts, and the membership grew rapidly.

New chapters were springing up, and in 1927 the upper New York State region was formed. The Syracuse chapter took a leading part in organizing this region, and three of its members have been presidents of the chapter: Henrietta Solomon, Ann Shulman, and Sally Pliskin.

The establishment of the state of Israel brought forth another flurry of activity. "Youth Aliyah" was formed, and thousands of orphaned children were taken out of the concentration camps, and from Christian homes where the parents had left them for safe-keeping, and were brought to Israel by Hadassah.

The Syracuse chapter continued to grow, and two more chapters were added. There are now three: the original Henrietta Szold, the Stephen Wise, and the Theodor Herzl chapters.

The Syracuse Hadassah Women organizations had approximately one thousand members in 1967. The spirit and inspiration left by Henrietta Solomon and Carrie Gais still prevail in the Syracuse chapters of Hadassah.[9]

From Peddlers to Professionals

In reading the history of any Jewish community in America one discovers that the pioneers, with few exceptions, started out as peddlers. There are several reasons why this was so. It is safe to say that the principal one was that, as a peddler, a man was his own master and could observe the Sabbath if he so desired without having to ask someone else's permission. Also, having been long excluded from agriculture in other countries, the Jew turned to trading and merchandising in which he had some experience.

With changes in the American economy and trade, there followed changes in types of peddling. The first newcomers were predominantly peddlers of notions and dry goods, with packs on their backs and baskets on their arms, traveling on foot. When they had saved enough to buy a horse and wagon, they not only could cover greater distances but could also carry a larger variety of stock, adding household goods and kitchenware. Some added readymade clothing.

The Jewish immigrants who came later looked for new fields. They found that America had become industrialized and that the factories needed old paper and rags for making paper, scrap iron for making steel, old bottles to make into new glassware. Thus, many immigrants became what was known as "junk" peddlers. They could be seen on the streets of practically every city, driving a horse and wagon with a string of cowbells stretched across the back, crying out, "rags, bottles, iron." With industry growing ever larger, these East European junk peddlers soon began to deal directly with manufacturing plants, buying up their waste material, sorting it, and selling and shipping to other plants in need of such material. The scrap and iron yards became big business. In Syracuse there were and still are a number of these merchants who came up from peddling and amassed considerable wealth.

THE HURWITZ BROTHERS. Louis and Morris Hurwitz were among the first large-scale scrap metal dealers in Syracuse who did business directly with manufacturing plants. Louis came to Syracuse from Odessa, Russia, in 1881, followed a few years later by his younger brother Morris. Odessa is a large seaport city on the Black Sea. It contained a thriving Jewish community, considered more progressive than those in other parts of Russia in the nineteenth century. It was the home of a number of well-known Yiddish and Hebrew writers and poets. The father of Morris and Louis was himself an author and translator. The two young men were probably better educated than the average immigrants of those days.

They both started out as peddlers, selling and canvassing from door to door. Morris went to Rochester, where he entered into the scrap iron business with Joseph Allen. He learned the business well, and came back to Syracuse about 1900 to form a partnership with his brother Louis. They opened a scrap iron yard at West Onondaga and

Clinton Streets and were successful from the start. Just before and during the First World War, there was a big demand for scrap iron; prices were high, and during those years the Hurwitz Brothers amassed considerable wealth.

Both Louis and Morris had strong Jewish attachments and became leaders in the Jewish community. Louis was a founder and assisted in planning and building Poiley Tzedeck Synagogue on Orange Street in 1896. When his family was growing up he joined the Temple of Concord and took an active part in that congregation. Louis was a "joiner." He belonged to practically every civic and Jewish organization, from the Hebrew Free School to LaFayette Country Club. Morris was a bit more reserved. He belonged to Temple Adath Yeshurun, and his outstanding achievement was his chairmanship of the building committee which erected the new temple on the corner of Harrison Street and Crouse Avenue in 1920. It was a heavy undertaking to raise the money, plan, and look after the construction of the largest Jewish house of worship in the city. He was ably assisted by Israel Kaplan, the president of the congregation, and Isaac Markson.

When the Hurwitz children were grown and some had married, the two brothers decided to separate as business partners. Louis retained the scrap iron business, and Morris took as his share the real estate holdings, which were considerable in downtown Syracuse. Morris was elected a member of the Board of Directors of the City Bank Trust Company (later merged with the First Trust and Deposit Company). Morris died not long after their separation, on May 19, 1934, at the age of sixty-three. Louis lived to be eighty-five.[10]

PHILIP ROTH, PEDDLER TO PHILANTHROPIST. Philip Roth and his brother Samuel came to Syracuse at the turn of the century. They started out peddling junk with a horse and wagon. Before long they opened a scrap iron yard at a point on Grape Street where it was crossed by the railroad tracks. By hard work and close attention to their business, over a period of years they expanded into three large establishments, Roth Brothers Metal Company, Inc., Roth Steel Company, Inc., and the Roth Smelting Company, Inc., in which they reduce non-ferrous metals into ingots. As soon as his business was well established, Philip started making contributions to deserving charitable agencies. He was a strong Zionist and supported the movement liberally. Immediately after the Second World War, he made several trips to Russia and Poland in search of surviving relatives. It is estimated that he made it possible for at least twenty-five families to come to this country. In 1951 he and his wife took a trip to his beloved Israel. On their return trip, when only a day away from New York harbor, he suffered a severe stroke and never fully recovered. He died in 1960.[11] His brother Samuel and the sons of both brothers carry on the business, and the sons have followed in the steps of their parents. Other Syracusans who were successful as scrap iron dealers are Abe Cooper, Jack and Emanuel Rubenstein, and Hyman Matlow.

Following the junk and dry goods peddlers, the fruit and vegetable hucksters prospered and then moved into the produce markets as wholesale dealers. The cattle dealers, who went around the country roads buying up cattle, became meat packers.

Among the first to abandon peddling were the pack peddlers who sold notions and dry goods. They opened stores in small towns that were expanding into big cities as America grew. In Syracuse, S. Rosenbloom and Sons operated one of the large department stores as early as 1900. Paul and Albert Flah, who came to Syracuse from Syria when they were in their teens and peddled laces from door to door, now have one of the finest ladies' specialty stores in central New York, with branches in Rochester and Albany.

THE MARKSON BROTHERS. Abraham and Isaac Markson[12] came to Syracuse from Honesdale, Pennsylvania, and sold clothes wringers and religious pictures from house to house. In 1905 they opened a hole-in-the-wall on North Salina Street, and in fifty-four years built up the largest instalment furniture business in central New York. They branched out into four surrounding cities. They had to—Abraham had eleven children, Isaac had two. All their sons and sons-in-law were put to work. Abraham and Isaac became leaders in the community. Isaac was president of Temple Adath Yeshurun for twenty-five years.

THE GOLDBERG BROTHERS. Barney and Moe Goldberg followed in the steps of the Marksons. Their father, Meyer Goldberg, had a little store on South State Street from which he sold coal at retail by the bag. He delivered many a bag of coal weighing fifty or seventy-five pounds, often carrying them up three flights of stairs. Later he stocked coal stoves and other household goods. From that little store grew one of the largest retail furniture businesses in this area. Meyer's grand-son, Leonard (Skippy), is now the top executive of the firm.

FLEISCHMAN. Then there are the three Fleischmans—Jacob, Gabriel, and Pierce. Their father, Isaac, came to Syracuse in the late 1880's. He was a carpenter and cabinetmaker, and opened his own little furniture store on East Genesee Street. The three sons are now considered to be among the wealthiest Jewish families in Syracuse.

There were also some successes in the needle trade. Besides the Danziger brothers, whom we have mentioned previously, the Amdur-skys and the Belloffs also manufactured clothing. Sam Shopiro started in a small tailor shop in the Jewish neighborhood and built up a prosperous manufacturing business specializing in men's pants. Shopiro constructed a large factory building on North State Street, where he could secure Italian female help. He branched out into real estate, became prosperous, and was a man-about-town. He left the city as a wealthy man, moving to California. Another successful clothing manufacturer was Sam Elman, who started as a contractor making vests for Woodhull, Goodel, and Bull. He branched out on his own and built a large plant on West Genesee Street near the Polish neighborhood, where he could get women workers. He also gave employment to many Jewish immigrants.

Among other manufacturing concerns, we recall the Oberdorfer Brass Company, manufacturers of brass and aluminum castings, which has been mentioned previously, and the Syracuse Ornamental Company, manufacturers of molded wood products.

ADOLPH M. HOLSTEIN, the founder of this business, arrived in Syracuse in the late 1880's with a wife and two children. Back in the old country he was a cabinetmaker. Here he worked for others for a while and then opened his own cabinetmaking shop. He soon developed a new product of molded wood, trademarked "Syroco." It was a completely new concept of making wood ornaments. The business was a success from the start. His three sons, David, Alexander, and Philip, entered the business and, when his daughter Martha married Moses Winkelstein, he also became a partner. The Holsteins became one of the leading Jewish families in Syracuse. Adolph, the father, was one of the kindest and most charitable of men, always ready to contribute to all good causes. He started a fresh air camp for underprivileged children on Cazenovia Lake. This later developed into a large overnight camp, Bradley Brook, which was sponsored by the Holstein family. David, the eldest son, was elected president of the Temple of Concord. Alex, the next oldest, is a great humanitarian. He was president of the Syracuse Jewish Welfare Federation for a number of years and still takes a leading role in numerous civic and Jewish agencies. Philip, the youngest, was for many years the leader of the Luncheonaires club, which stages the annual charity ball, the proceeds of which go to various local children's camps.

The men named here are mentioned not only because they were successful in business, but mainly because when they succeeded in accumulating some wealth, they shared it with others. The Community Chest, the Welfare Federation, the Home for the Aged, the synagogues and temples all benefited from their generosity—and with it all, most of them found time to personally participate in all worthwhile causes for the community.

The second generation of Eastern European Jews started graduating from the colleges at the turn of the century. The first Jewish professional men appeared and hung out their shingles as doctors and lawyers. Even before the early 1900's there were young Jewish men in the professions; some of those names have been mentioned previously —men like Henry Elsner and Nathan Jacobson in medicine, Louis Marshall and Joseph Bondy in law. More were appearing rapidly. A few of the early doctors were I. Harris Levy and his brother, Jacob, and Mark Heiman and his cousin, Jesse. Early lawyers were Samuel D. Solomon, Will Rubin, William Gerber, David Sugarman, and Judge Nathan Abelson.

Great indeed have been the changes in the United States, from the pioneering days when the principal vocation was farming, to the present economy of manufacturing and industrial growth. And so was the change in the vocations of the Jews, from pack peddling to the learned professions and sciences.

In our attempt to account for the number of Jewish men in the professions, we have relied on the latest lists published by professional organizations. The Onondaga County Bar Association year book of 1966 recorded 850 lawyers, of whom 150 were Jewish. The Onondaga County Medical Society year book of 1966 listed 650 medical practioners, of whom 132 were Jewish. Of 230 dentists, 47 were Jewish. There were 275 pharmacists in the county, 65 of them Jewish. Most professional men are located in Syracuse, the largest center of population in the county.

Since the advent of large industrial plants in Syracuse—General Electric Company, the Carrier Corporation, General Motors, Chrysler, and others—it is estimated that approximately 1,000 engineers are employed by industry in Syracuse. Probably more than 100 of these are Jewish. Similarly, the post-war years brought to Syracuse University an increasing number of Jewish teachers and scientists.

CHAPTER XI

Syracuse University and the Jewish Community

In 1867 the city fathers attempted to have Genesee College moved from Lima, New York, to Syracuse. The attempt failed, but the idea of establishing an institution of higher learning in Syracuse remained.

It was not until 1870, when the Methodist Episcopal Church convention was held in Syracuse, that another opportunity arose.[1] Through the influence of educational and church leaders from Syracuse, the convention passed a resolution calling for $500,000 to be raised for the purpose of establishing a non-sectarian, coeducational university in Syracuse. The same year the New York State Legislature passed an act chartering a university in Syracuse, and the city agreed to donate $100,000 towards the cost.

The search for an appropriate site in Syracuse ended with the decision to purchase fifty acres of farmland from Gerorge F. Comstock, one of the early leaders in the drive for a university in Syracuse. The site selected was a fortunate one for the Jewish residents, since the area chosen was within walking distance from what was known as the "Jewish Neighborhood."

Syracuse University brought fame and culture to the city of Syracuse. To the Jews, the University meant that their sons and daughters could receive a college education at a relatively low cost. Proximity to the University and the ancient quest for learning among the Jewish people made the newly established school seem like manna from heaven.

The University, though founded and funded mainly by Methodists,

238

was non-sectarian from its inception. At no time did it impose a quota on the number of Jews who could attend, as was the common practice at many other colleges and universities. Jewish names are intertwined with the history of the University from its very beginning. In the early days, however, most Jewish boys and girls had to work to augment the family income, and not many who wanted to were able to take advantage of this educational opportunity.

The first class of the University consisted of forty-one students and five teachers and met in temporary quarters downtown in the Myers Block.[2] The University grew at a rapid pace. In 1873 the Hall of Languages, the first building on the campus, was completed. In 1872 the Geneva Medical School, originally a part of Hobart College, moved to Syracuse as a division of the University. In 1889 the John Crouse College of Fine Arts was established, and in the same year football was organized as a regular sport. James Roscoe Day became chancellor in 1893, and from that year Syracuse University started to move rapidly. Chancellor Day had a way of getting to large donors. Mrs. Russell Sage established the Slocum Teachers College (now the School of Education), and John D. Archbold of Standard Oil donated the gymnasium and stadium.

Situated approximately in the center of the state, Syracuse likes to be known as "Central City," a slogan which has been taken over by many local industrial firms. Since the founding of the University in 1870, the city's convenient location has attracted large numbers of students from the entire state of New York, as well as from the nearby areas of Pennsylvania, New Jersey, and Ohio. Although New York City is 300 miles away, it is easily accessible to Syracuse by plane and train, and can be reached in less than six hours by automobile. Syracuse, therefore, has been a favorite out-of-town university for New York City Jewish youth and has been particularly acceptable to parents who do not want their children too far from home.

JEWISH STUDENTS

The first Jewish student on record at Syracuse University was Nathan Jacobson, a native Syracusan, who entered in the class of 1873 and was graduated from the medical school in 1877. Carrie Ida Shevelson, class of 1881, was the first Jewish woman to graduate from the University. In 1885, there were two Jewish graduates, Jesse Lincoln Bronner and Ida Esther Goldman. There are no records of any Jewish graduates from 1886 to 1889. In 1890 there were two, Henry Danziger, Jr., and I. Harris Levy. Between 1900 and 1910 there were fourteen, and from then on the number grew steadily.[3] By 1930, 11 percent of those receiving undergraduate degreees were Jewish. In 1960 the proportion rose to 18 percent, and in 1968 over 20 percent of the University graduates were Jewish.

The rabbis and other leaders of the Jewish community have always been concerned with the welfare of the Jewish students on "The Hill." Out-of-town students are often invited to Jewish homes on the High Holidays, and the rabbis welcome them at the temples and synagogues. In 1917, Rabbi Guttman, in an attempt to shepherd these students, organized a Jewish Student Fellowship Club at the Temple of Concord. Three local students, A. Clement Silverman, Jesse Cantor, and Isadore Belloff, were leaders of the group of about twenty-five members.[4] The club met regularly on Friday afternoons in the temple's social hall, and some of the students remained for the Sabbath services. This organization flourished for some years, until the Jewish Greek-letter societies became popular at the University.

Two other Jewish organizations functioned at the University in the early years of this century. The Jewish Collegiate Society and the Syracuse Menorah Society met in the years before World War I. The two groups merged into the Menorah Society in 1919. Both groups often met and held social functions at the Temple of Concord.

In the late 1930's, Jewish students, feeling the pressure of world events, combined in a new Zionist society, Avukah, part of a national collegiate movement which aimed "to bring the Jewish students on the campus closer together, to help solve their problems, and to provide social and cultural functions for them, and to foster and spread Zionism." [5]

The history of Jewish fraternities on the campus dates back to 1911, when the local chapter of Zeta Beta Tau received its charter.[6] Sigma Alpha Mu organized a chapter in 1913, Phi Epsilon Pi in 1917, and Tau Epsilon Phi in 1922. Other Jewish fraternities still active in the University are Alpha Epsilon Pi, Beta Sigma Rho, Tau Delta Phi, and Phi Sigma Delta. The girls, too, formed societies. The earliest Jewish sororities were Alpha Epsilon Phi (1914) and Phi Sigma Sigma (1927). The sorority list now includes Alpha Sigma Tau, Iota Alpha Pi, Delta Phi Epsilon, and Sigma Delta Tau. In addition, approximately half the members of Alpha Xi Delta are Jewish, and some of the so-called "Christian" chapters have increasingly admitted Jewish students since World War II.

At the outset, the Jewish fraternal societies, national and local, were organized because virtually all other Greek-letter fraternities and sororities were closed to Jews. At that time—probably more so than at present—it was a mark of social status to belong to a national fraternity and to live in the chapter house. Jewish societies followed in the steps of their Christian counterparts—the Jewish fraternity, too, was a symbol of superior social standing. Students from wealthy families were "rushed" first. There was very little, if any, Judaism in the religious sense connected with these houses. All it seemed to mean was that Jewish students lived together and looked down on those who were not selected, those who did not wish to join, and those who could not afford to join. There was little rapport between these "Greek" houses and other Jewish organizations on the Hill. In later years, individual fraternities and sororities started to take an interest in Jewish life on campus and in the community. Through representation in the chapel program, many developed a continuing concern for Judaism. For instance, Rabbi Earl Stone has said that his first interest in becoming a rabbi developed when he was appointed the Zeta Beta Tau representative to Hendricks Chapel. His association with Dean William Powers and, later, with the rabbis of the community led him to study for the rabbinate.

The Founding of the Jewish Student Fellowship

In 1945, when Jewish enrollment passed the thousand mark, the time had come to provide a more structured organization for Jewish religious observance on campus.[7] The University invited the local Jewish community to sponsor a formal program for Jewish students. The Syracuse Jewish Welfare Federation, interested friends, and alumni met to discuss the University's request. The group included Dr. A. Clement Silverman, who had been active many years earlier as a student, Alexander Holstein, Milton Macht, Theodore Pierson, Aaron

Rose, Judge Jesse Cantor, T. Aaron Levy, and Jesse Silverman, among others. Included also were Rabbis Benjamin Friedman, Irwin Hyman, and Samuel Yalow, representing the three major religious groups in Syracuse—the Reform, Conservative, and Orthodox, respectively.

Discussion centered on whether to join the national Hillel Foundation or to start a local organization. Since at that time Hillel activities on other campuses were generally based on a Hillel house, and since many of the students were interested in preserving their close relationship with other faith groups within Hendricks Chapel, the decision was made to start on a local basis, with the establishment of the Jewish Student Fellowship Foundation. Local rabbis gave invaluable help and sympathetic faculty members provided leadership. Dr. Milton Barron of the Sociology Department served as the first director. He was succeeded by the first full-time leader, Rabbi Leopold Wallach. Later, Rabbi Earl Stone, a former student whose activity in Hendricks Chapel had led him into the rabbinate, returned to Syracuse as assistant rabbi at Temple of Concord and adviser to the Student Fellowship. Theodore Pierson, one of the founders, continued his active interest and support.

Rabbi William Schwartz, a former military chaplain, became director of the Student Fellowship in 1948, and greatly expanded the program. Finding the football weekends almost impossible competition for Friday evening services, he established the famous "Colgate Eve Brotherhood Service." This plan brought an outstanding Christian minister to Syracuse each year with a service that filled the chapel amid the social activity on the Friday evening preceding the Colgate game. This tradition continued with great success until the Syracuse-Colgate rivalry ended. The intercollegiate Zionist Federation (1947–49) established a chapter on the Syracuse campus during this period.[8]

Many Jewish traditions on the Syracuse campus originated during those years. Rabbi Schwartz obtained community support to properly equip the Fellowship, including a Torah presented by B. G. Rudolph and his brother, Max, in honor of their parents. This Torah is still used in the services. It became traditional to build a *Sukkah* on campus, and for the local temples to cooperate in providing facilities for Passover meals and the traditional *seder*.

In 1953 Rabbi Hyman was appointed chaplain, and Dr. Fred Krinsky of the Political Science Department took over active leadership of the program on campus.

START OF A HILLEL PROGRAM

Because a separate building was no longer considered essential, new pressure arose for the start of a Hillel program.[9] In 1959 Rabbi Louis Neimand came to Syracuse as the first Hillel Foundation rabbi. He was succeeded in 1963 by Rabbi Louis Jordan, who helped to increase membership to over 500 in his one year on campus.

Rabbi Milton Elefant arrived in 1964. An enlightened Orthodox rabbi, he has vigorously emphasized religion and Jewish tradition in Hillel activities. Under his leadership, membership was increased to over a thousand during the 1967–1968 school year, making it one of the largest groups among the Hillel Foundations in the country. Friday evening services are held regularly in Hendricks Chapel, followed by an *Oneg Shabbat*. A trained student choir participates in the services and gives concerts at community functions. Hillel holds supper dances and other social events. It has established a Kosher Dining Club, which is recognized by the University through permission for students to pay their compulsory board contracts directly to the Hillel office. The Hillel Graduate Society and the Hillel Faculty Society hold Sunday morning brunches and meet to hear outstanding speakers. The rabbi-chaplains have advanced the cause of Jewish education by offering non-credit courses in ancient and modern Hebrew, Jewish history, literature, and religious thought. In such ways the Hillel Foundation prepares students to take their place in the Jewish community after graduation.

THE FACULTY

The Syracuse University faculty [10] has been studded with Jewish names almost from its beginning. The early names were primarily associated with the College of Medicine.

The University medical school in the early years, around the turn of the century, ranked fourteenth in enrollment in the country. Until 1948 it was a part of Syracuse University. Entering classes numbered between forty and fifty students, of whom an average of five or six were Jewish. In 1948, the University of the State of New York took over the medical school and absorbed it into the state educational system. Class sizes have increased to about 100, and Jewish students make up a large percent of each class. The number of Jewish faculty members and clinical professors has increased accordingly.

Dr. Henry L. Elsner, one of the earliest and most beloved professors in the College of Medicine, was appointed to a full professorship in 1884. Though he had a large practice in Syracuse and was often called out of the city for consultations, he fulfilled his teaching obligations until his death in 1916. His students' fondness for him as a person and teacher was such that, after his passing, they organized "The Henry L. Elsner Association."

In 1886, Dr. Nathan Jacobson, the first Jewish alumnus of the University, was appointed Instructor of Surgery and later Professor of Clinical Surgery. It is worthy of note that he was one of the first Jews in America to hold such a high position in a medical college. Elsner and Jacobson have been gone for more than half a century, but their memories linger on, and their names have become a legend in the history of the medical college.

Other Jewish men in the medical profession in Syracuse have left their mark as teachers and professors. Among the very earliest were I. Harris Levy, Joseph Wiseman, and A. Clement Silverman. Dr. Levy was Professor of Medicine throughout his long medical career. Dr. Wiseman, son-in-law of Dr. Nathan Jacobson, taught for many years at the College. Dr. Silverman entered Syracuse University as a freshman in 1908. He attended the University on a clergyman's scholarship, because his father was a functionary in one of the synagogues. During his student years he was active in promoting the Jewish Student Fellowship Society. He later became Professor of Pediatrics, and in 1923 the city of Syracuse appointed him director of the Department of Communicable Diseases. He served the city in that capacity for forty-two years and retired in 1965. The city of Syracuse has honored him by changing the name of the City Hospital to the A. C. Silverman Hospital.

Medical Societies in Syracuse

Doctors of medicine have their own professional clubs and societies. These groups serve to advance the science of medicine and to safeguard the interests of their members and the profession.

The Onondaga County Medical Association, affiliated with state and national medical societies, includes virtually every practitioner as a member. Jewish doctors have taken an active part in this group. The following have served as president: [11]

Henry Elsner	1888
Nathan Jacobson	1891
I. Harris Levy	1914
Joseph R. Wiseman	1937
Irving L. Ershler	1952
William D. Kopel	1959
Aaron Burman	1961
Daniel Burdick	1964

There are also several private medical societies into which Jewish physicians have not been invited. To balance such discrimination, a group of Jewish doctors formed the Lancet Society in 1925.[12] Among the founders were A. C. Silverman, H. Henry Haft, Harry Rubenstein, Philip Rosenberg, Max Newer, Alexander Mason, Mandell Shimberg, Mark Heiman, Morris Levine, and Arnold Kauffman. The main objective was to advance the science of medicine, and when the society was small it also served as a social group. They met once a month in a member's home.

Another Jewish medical club was started in 1930, named the Elsner-Jacobson Society.[13] Among its founders were I. Harris Levy, Joseph Wiseman, Jacob R. Levy, Bertram Levinson, Monroe Rosenbloom, Abe Levin, Philip Rakov, and Ephraim Goldman. Each of these clubs now has over fifty members.

Jewish men have been associated with other departments of the University from an early date. Since 1895, when the Reverend Dr. Guttman served briefly as Professor of Semitic Languages, Syracuse rabbis have actively participated in the life of the University. They have been students, invited lecturers, and advisers to Jewish students. Rabbi Benjamin Friedman has the degree of Doctor of Sacred Theology from the University, while Rabbi Irwin Hyman, Rabbi Samuel Yalow, and Rabbi Theodore Levy have at different times been associated with the University as counselors and guest lecturers.

SAMUEL D. SARASON, one of the early Jewish professors at the University, joined the faculty in 1910 as an instructor of Civil Engineering. He immediately became active in the Jewish community. His wife, Rose, taught in the Sunday school of the Temple of Concord. Sarason founded the first Boy Scout Troop, #58, at Temple of Concord and acted as the scoutmaster for many years. Professor Sarason served for thirty-eight years as head of the Civil Engineering Department. The Sarason family continues to be connected with the University. Samuel's son, Ernest, is Associate Professor of Surgery in the Upstate Medical Center in Syracuse.[14]

ISMAR JOHN PERITZ, a convert from Judaism to Christianity, came to Syracuse in 1895 to be an instructor of Semitics.[15] Born in Breslau, Germany, he had acquired a traditional Jewish education. At the age of eighteen, while studying in Berlin, he experienced a change of faith. The next year he went to London and attended the Jewish Mission Institute. The missionary society sent him to America to do evangelistic work among Jews in New York. Very soon he entered Drew Theological Seminary in Madison, New Jersey. Later he took a doctorate at Harvard.

Professor Peritz did much to advance the study of religion at Syracuse University. An outstanding scholar and author, he wrote a number of books on the Bible and contributed many articles to religious magazines. He was a founder of *The Journal of Bible and Religion* and of the National Association of Biblical Instructors. He was well acquainted with some of the rabbis in Syracuse. Rabbi Joseph Hertz took a course in the Arabic language under him.[16] He had many long discussions about the Bible with Rabbi Guttman. Rabbi Friedman said that he would occasionally come to his temple on Friday evening. Peritz once told Rabbi Yalow: "I am still a Jew and will remain a Jew, even though I am a converted Christian." [17] It is known that he would frequently go down to a Jewish grocery store to purchase some favorite Jewish edibles, such as marinated herring, corned beef, and rye bread.

Professor Peritz was a member of the Syracuse faculty for thirty-eight years, and retired as Professor Emeritus of Biblical Literature at the age of seventy. He had held the position of Willard Ives Professor of the Bible. After retirement he returned several times a year to deliver lectures. He was an ordained Methodist minister and very active in the Methodist conferences and Methodist churches in and around Syracuse. He died at the age of eighty-nine at Winter Haven, Florida, and was buried in Oakwood Cemetery in Syracuse.

The Faculty after World War II

Until the outbreak of World War II,[18] Syracuse had comparatively few Jewish professors. Like most colleges with denominational ties, it had earlier tended to select persons of Christian background for its faculty.

During William P. Tolley's administration, which began in 1942, Syracuse University opened its doors to scholars of all creeds and races. Many of the German-Jewish refugee scholars and American Jews with degrees and qualifications, who previously found it difficult to secure a position on the faculty of many of our universities, were now acceptable. This open-door policy was necessitated by the great influx into the student body of ex-service men who were subsidized by the government. The enrollment at the University immediately following the war was about double the figure of 1940. By 1967–68 the faculty of Syracuse University approximated 1,100, including more than 100 Jewish men. Among these were 3 heads of departments, 49 full professors, 39 associate professors, 13 assistant professors, and about 10 in other instructional and research positions.

Professors, to be sure, are a sophisticated and cosmopolitan group, highly individualistic and often not much interested in organized religion or even secular Jewish activities. Some have held themselves aloof from the Jewish community. However, there are others who are mindful of their Jewish heritage, and the Syracuse Jewish community has benefited by the presence of these learned men, many of whom have been here for many years. They have joined the temples and social clubs; they contribute to the Jewish Welfare Federation and have given support to local Jewish causes. Thus, a number of the outstanding scholars and scientists deserve mention in a history of Syracuse's Jewish community.

Three Jewish scholars now head departments of the University. Dr. Nathan Ginsburg became Chairman of the Department of Physics in 1966, the first Jew to hold such a high post in this institution. Other

Jewish chairmen at present are Dr. Myron Lichtblau in Romance Languages, and Dr. Salamon Eskinazi in Mechanical and Aero Space Engineering.

In the Physics Department there are such distinguished men as Dr. Peter G. Bergmann, who was a research associate and scientific collaborator of Albert Einstein at the Institute for Advanced Study in Princeton; Dr. Nahmin Horwitz, whose specialty is cosmic ray physics; and Professor Joshua N. Goldberg, internationally known for his work in relativity theory.

In economics there are Dr. Sidney C. Sufrin, Professor of Economics and Business Administration, who has been at the University since 1946, and Dr. Irving Swerdlow, Professor of Economics and Associate Dean of Overseas Operations and Research in the Maxwell School.

Several are prominent in music and fine arts. Louis Krasner, Professor of Violin and Chamber Music, was formerly concertmaster of the Minneapolis Symphony Orchestra under Dimitri Metropoulos, and a violin soloist with the Boston Symphony, the New York Philharmonic, and the Cleveland, Chicago, and other symphony orchestras. As the conductor of the Syracuse University Orchestra and concertmaster of the Syracuse Symphony Orchestra, he is as well known in the city as he is on the Hill. Abraham Veinus is Professor of Musicology and Fine Arts, an author and composer, and an authority on Hebrew liturgical music. For a number of years he directed music at Temple Adath Yeshurun and is still a consultant to the choir of that temple. Professor Murray Bernthal is mentioned elsewhere in this book.

In the College of Law, there is Professor Robert F. Koretz, a native Syracusan who has been with the University since 1946. A specialist in labor relations, he is a member of the New York Board of Mediation and has arbitrated more than 200 disputes since 1949. His parents were, and he still is, active members of the Temple of Concord. Victor Levine was a professor in the College of Law, beginning in 1927, for a period of twenty-three years. He is now a practicing attorney and considered a "lawyer's lawyer" in the community.

Martin Edward Barzelay has been Professor of Mechanical Engineering with Syracuse University since 1947. His specialty is aerodynamics, structure, and aeroplane design. Professor Barzelay has been active as a political leader in the Democratic party, and has worked with the Syracuse Jewish Welfare Federation in the annual campaign for funds.

Many other Jewish members of the faculty have achieved distinction in their profession and are worthy of mention here, but they are too numerous to be named individually.

JEWISH ATHLETES AT SYRACUSE UNIVERSITY

Athletics has always been an important feature of student life at Syracuse.[19] The University's first organized football team played in college competition as early as 1889.

Two local Jewish students, Harry Kallet and Joe Alexander, added glory to themselves and Syracuse University in the sport of football.

Harry Kallet entered Syracuse University as a special student. The first time he tried out for the football team he was considered too light to play in the rugged game. The second year he went out weighing 145 pounds, which was enough for him to play, and therefore to stay in school. The next year he played often enough to earn a varsity letter. In 1910 the season's first big game was against Yale. Kallet's play was so spectacular that he was described as the most outstanding player on the team. From then on he was a regular, and was selected as a member of Walter Camp's All-American team in his senior year. His classmates elected him president of the senior class, and he was chosen national vice-president of the Zeta Beta Tau Fraternity. Upon graduation from the Medical College he interned in the Memorial Hospital and served as coach of the freshman football team.

When Kallet began his medical practice he offered his services as football coach at the Manlius School, a military academy near Syracuse. During his coaching years there he endeared himself to the faculty and students, besides turning out the best football teams in the history of the Manlius school up to that time. In appreciation of his services the school named its football stadium, "Kallet Athletic Field."

Joseph A. Alexander received his lumps and bumps playing football with other Jewish boys on the Jackson Flats. He played football in high school and earned a varsity letter. In 1915 he entered Syracuse

University. During his freshman year he was a substitute on the varsity football team. For the next three years he played regularly, first as a guard and then as a center. In 1919 he was elected captain of the team. The following year he was selected as a guard on Walter Camp's All-American team. In 1921 he made the All-American second team as a center.

He graduated in 1921 as a physician. During his internship at Bellevue Hospital in New York City he played professional football on weekends. In 1925 he signed with the New York Giants as a center for $3,000 a season. In 1927 he took a job as coach but, finding that it interfered too much with his duties at Bellevue Hospital, he resigned.

Dr. Joseph Alexander said "football taught me sportsmanship, fellowship, and decency; football is a way of life." In 1937 the *New York Telegram* placed him on its All-Time All-American College Football Team, and he has been chosen as a member of the College Football Hall of Fame in New Brunswick, New Jersey.

Paul Steinberg, although he did not attend Syracuse University, was a Syracuse Jewish athlete of renown. Born in New York in 1880, he came to Syracuse as a small boy. He enlisted in the Spanish-American War at the age of sixteen and was in action with Teddy Roosevelt at San Juan Hill.

Steinberg loved athletics and competitive sports. He excelled in all three standard American games—baseball, football, and basketball. In 1902 he signed with Connie Mack's Philadelphia Athletics as a utility catcher. Later he played professional football. Dr. Henry March, the father of professional football, had this to say about Steinberg's career: "He was one of the fastest and most elusive backs in the country, and one of the cleanest players." At the time he was five feet eleven, and weighed 210 pounds. After he gave up professional football he was invited to be basketball coach at Cornell Univeristy. While at Cornell he earned a degree in physiotherapy. He returned to Syracuse and practiced his profession.

Another Jewish student who received recognition and achieved a measure of success on the football and basketball teams at Syracuse University was John Barsha. He was captain of the 1918 basketball team, which won sixteen games and lost one, and that by only one point in the last game of the season, to the University of Pennsylvania.

Another excellent basketball player was Sol Bloom of Norwich,

New York. He was later a distinguished physician in Binghamton, New York. Dr. Bloom was very much interested in Syracuse University athletics and sent many fine high school players to Syracuse.

Dr. Louis Alkoff was an outstanding basketball player on Syracuse University teams, and was captain of the 1934–35 varsity. Alkoff also played football with the 1934 team. That team was notable for having four Jewish players: Lou Stark, fullback; Milt Singer, center; Walter Singer, end; and Lou Alkoff, substitute center. Dr. Alkoff married a Syracuse girl, Rachel Lerman, and remained to practice medicine in Syracuse.

One of the early athletes who brought fame to Syracuse University was a native of Syracuse, Myer Prinstein. His outstanding athletic achievement was setting a world record in the running broad jump in 1900. He participated in the third modern Olympic games in St. Louis, Missouri, in 1904, and the fourth Olympic games in Athens, Greece, in 1906. He won a gold medal in the running broad jump at both meets.[20]

Harvey Levy, a local boy, attracted considerable attention playing football and basketball while still in high school. He entered Syracuse University in 1936 and participated in lacrosse, boxing, and football. He was a star guard on the football team during his college years. After graduation from the College of Law, he assisted Vic Hanson in coaching the football team at Syracuse University.

Martin ("Marty") Glickman, from Brooklyn, was a track and football star at Syracuse University from 1935 to 1939, and set numerous records in the sprints while running on the track team. In 1936 he was a member of the United States Olympic team which went to Berlin, and in that same year he was a member of the American 400-meter relay team, which included Jesse Owens, that established a new world's record in London.

In addition to the notable athletes mentioned here, many other Jewish students participated in sports at Syracuse University at different times.

A Child Prodigy Attends Syracuse University

Moses Finkelstein, a native Syracusan, graduated from high school at the age of eleven and was admitted to Syracuse University. He was the object of admiration on the campus and the talk of the town. His father was an engineer at the Solvay Process Company, and the family belonged to Temple Adath Yeshurun. At his Bar Mitzvah, Moses conducted the entire service of the day, including the delivery of a scholarly sermon on the philosophy of Judaism. He received the B.A. degree from Syracuse University at the age of fifteen and went on to Columbia University as a graduate student. The following is an item that appeared in the *Syracuse Post Standard* in 1927:

SYRACUSE GRADUATE GAINS M.S. DEGREE AT
AGE OF SIXTEEN. MOSES FINKELSTEIN, CHILD
PRODIGY, GETS AWARD FROM COLUMBIA.

A child prodigy in the form of Moses Finkelstein has just been awarded the degree of Master of Arts from Columbia University. Finkelstein has accomplished this feat at the age of 16 years.

He was awarded a Bachelor of Arts degree from Syracuse University at the age of fifteen, after having been graduated from high school at the age of eleven. His record is considered phenomenal, and educators who are authorities on the subject claim that this is the first known record of a person obtaining a Master's Degree at that early age.

His thesis was based on the subject, "The Opinion of United States Supreme Court Justices on Due Process of Law." Finkelstein is a member of Phi Beta Kappa and Phi Kappa Phi honorary societies.

Finkelstein is now a Fellow and Professor of Philosophy at Cambridge University in England. He is the author of a number of books on early Greek life and thought. He has legally changed his name to Finley and has become a naturalized British subject.[21]

Dr. Samuel Rosen Receives the George Arents Pioneer Medal

A world-famous otologist and the developer of the *stapes* operation (this operation restores hearing to many people who otherwise would have remained deaf), Sam Rosen, a native Syracusan and son of George and Ella Rosen who owned a crockery store on Grape Street, was born April 19, 1897. He was one of five brothers. The other four helped to pay for his education at Syracuse University.

On June 6, 1964, his alma mater awarded him the George Arents Pioneer Medal for Excellence in Medicine, the highest alumni award of the University. Presenting the award, Chancellor William P. Tolley read the following citation: [22]

SAMUEL ROSEN, a native Syracusan, product of the Madison School and Central High School, you began your studies at the University in January 1915. Attracted by the field of Law, you had a full year in the Law School before yielding to the greater attraction of medicine. Making up the premedical requirements, you took your degree in Liberal Arts in 1918 and your Doctor of Medicine degree in 1921. At Mount Sinai Hospital in New York, where you still serve, you began one of the world's greatest careers in otolaryngology and medicine.

In 1952, you perfected a new operation to restore hearing in otosclerotic deafness. Since that time you have returned thousands upon thousands of patients to the world of sound by personally teaching and performing your Stapes mobilization procedure literally all over the world and at your own expense. In 1956 the American Medical Association gave you its highest citation for original work in medicine, the Hektoen Gold Medal. A year later you received the quadrennial Pietro Caliceti Award from the University of Bologna for the most significant and original published work in the field of otolaryngology.

Consulting Otologist at Mount Sinai Hospital, Chief of the Stapes Mobilization Clinic there, clinical professor of otolaryngology at the Columbia University College of Physicians and Surgeons, a giver of hearing and medical skill to the world, we are proud to claim you as a son of Syracuse and to award you the George Arents Pioneer Medal for Excellence in Medicine.

Dr. Rosen has taken time out from a busy medical practice to travel extensively, at his own expense, to demonstrate his ear operation.[23] President Nasser of the United Arab Republic thanked him personally for the demonstration he gave at the Cairo Medical College. At the start of their ninety-minute talk, Nasser said, "I am very grateful to you for coming here to help my people." "Thank you," said the Doctor, "but I'm surprised I was invited. I am Jewish, you know." "We know that, too," Nasser said, "but your work is above race or country; actually you doctors are the best diplomats." [24]

In 1960, on his second trip to Israel, where he taught his method again, he was summoned by Prime Minister David Ben-Gurion. Ben-Gurion said: "I am very pleased that you went to the Arab countries to teach them as you did us; this is very good for everyone." [25]

Dr. Rosen was invited to Russia and was unanimously elected a member of the Soviet Medical Academy. He is one of the few foreign scientists to be so honored. His latest travels have taken him to the Sudan in Africa, where he spent a month among the tribesmen of Mabaan to determine why this tribe has such a keen sense of hearing and very little, if any, hearing loss due to old age. He read a paper on his findings to the 1967 American Medical Association Convention.[26]

JEWISH CONTRIBUTORS TO THE UNIVERSITY

The advantages the Jewish community derived from the presence of Syracuse University were not all one-sided. Jewish students and members of the faculty have contributed to the scholastic standing of the University, and Jewish alumni and friends of the University have contributed generously to relieve its financial needs.

It is well to list here a few of the donors who have made notable contributions: [27] Samuel I. Newhouse, Arnold Grant, Mr. and Mrs. Joe Lowe, Mr. and Mrs. Morris Haft, and J. Robert Rubin. Samuel I. Newhouse made the largest single gift to the University in its history. This gift was $15,000,000 for the Newhouse Communications Center. The first building, for the School of Journalism, was dedicated on August 5, 1964. President Lyndon B. Johnson and Mrs. Johnson came from Washington, D.C., for the dedication ceremonies at which the President made the principal address. The Center will eventually have two additional buildings: one for the Radio-Television Department, and the other for the Department of Instructional Communications and a library.

In addition to the new construction, Newhouse's gift will endow the Center and provide scholarships for students. Newhouse, who did not attend college, received an honorary degree from Syracuse University in 1955. He is a permanent member of the University Board of Trustees, and both his sons, Donald and Samuel I., Jr., attended Syracuse University. Newhouse is known for his prominence in the field of journalism. Through his corporations he owns the *Syracuse Herald-Journal* and *Post Standard*.

Mr. Arnold Grant, a graduate of Syracuse University, class of 1927, has been a University trustee for many years and is active in all types of alumni programs, primarily fund raising. His major financial contribution to Syracuse University was $900,000 for the Arnold Grant Law School Auditorium. In addition, he has made numerous other gifts of substantial amounts.

Joe and Emily Lowe for years had a major interest in the Fine Arts program at Syracuse University. The Lowes contributed $170,000 towards the construction of the Joe and Emily Lowe Art Center. The building is the major fine arts exhibit area of the University, and also provides a number of classrooms and art studios. The Lowes have also made gifts for scholarships and other purposes related to the School of Art.

Mr. and Mrs. Morris H. Haft donated approximately $60,000, making possible the construction of the Morris Haft Co-operative Dormitory. The Hafts did not attend Syracuse University, but their daughter graduated here.

J. Robert Rubin, one of the early Jewish graduates from Syracuse, was for years very active in programs related to the University, particularly fund-raising. A lawyer, he took a great interest in the Law School and the Drama Department. Robert Rubin died in 1958 and bequeathed the University approximately $250,000 for the Drama Department. This money was used for remodeling the Regent Theater on East Genesee Street. Besides this major bequest, Mr. Rubin made a number of substantial gifts to the College of Law. He graduated from Syracuse University in 1904 and from the Law School in 1909.

In 1963 the B. G. Rudolph Lectures in Judaic Studies were established at the University. This series has brought some eminent Jewish scholars to the campus, including Moshe Davis, Lou Silberman, Robert Gordis, Leo W. Schwarz, Maurice Samuel, Jacob Marcus, and Jacob Neusner. These lectures are published by the University and distributed with the assistance of the American Jewish Historical Society.

There are, of course, many more men and women of the Jewish faith, both alumni and friends, who have, from time to time, made substantial gifts to the University.

CHAPTER XII

Expanding Vistas

INTERFAITH—CHRISTIANS AND JEWS

For well over a century the Jews of Syracuse have enjoyed cordial relations with their Christian neighbors. Although no community is ever completely free of various kinds of prejudice, Syracuse has fortunately never been the scene of serious conflicts between religious and ethnic groups. In 1969, something more than a polite mutual tolerance prevails between Jews and Christians in this city—they are united in every major civic activity, and the spirit of religious brotherhood grows steadily stronger.

Instances of interfaith friendliness are recorded as early as 1871, when the Temple of Concord issued an expression of condolence and eulogy on the death of Dr. Samuel J. May, pastor of the Unitarian Church, which resolved, "that this Society, in a body, attend the funeral obsequies of the lamented departed." [1] A few years later, in 1874, the Reverend Isaac Cohen, spiritual leader of Concord, addressed an audience composed of representatives of nearly every church in the city at a meeting in Plymouth Chapel. He lectured on the ancient Tabernacle, and the *Syracuse Journal* concluded its account of the event with the question: "Who shall say that the world does not move when a Jewish Rabbi instructs Christian Sunday School teachers?" [2] Later in the same year, Cohen exchanged pulpits with the Reverend Ezekiel W. Mundy of the Independent Church. Each man conducted the service of worship in his own sanctuary, with the other delivering the sermon. [3]

Dr. Adolph Guttman fostered this ecumenical spirit throughout his

256

long tenure at Concord. In 1886, *The American Israelite*[4] reported
that he had invited the Reverend Charles J. Little of Syracuse University to lecture in the temple. Dr. Samuel Calthrop preached at Concord on several occasions, and the Unitarian Church extended the
same courtesy to Dr. Guttman.[5] The latter also began a series of
union Thanksgiving services with the Unitarian and Universalist
churches. This custom was later adopted by other churches in the
downtown area, and today the rabbis of Concord and Adath Yeshurun
regularly join in interdenominational Thanksgiving services with Christian ministers in Plymouth Church on East Onondaga Street. Rabbi
Guttman always encouraged such joint endeavors, at a time when the
gulf between Jews and Christians was much wider than it is now, and
the present cordial interfaith relations owe much to his initiative.

In 1919 Rabbi Benjamin Friedman came to Syracuse fresh from his
experience as an Army chaplain, in which he had served with chaplains
of other faiths. He immediately began to build more bridges between
the temples and the churches. His invitation to preach at the Civic
Lenten Series in 1921 was a landmark in local religious history. The
following year, 1922, at the suggestion of Rabbi Friedman, the downtown Lenten service featured a distinguished rabbi from New York,
Stephen S. Wise.[6] This was not Rabbi Wise's first introduction to Syracuse. In 1900 he had spoken at the New York State Zionist Convention. That appearance was in itself somewhat unusual, since at that
time Zionism was considered a movement of Yiddish-speaking Eastern
Jews, and Wise was a Reform rabbi of Hungarian extraction, with an
eloquent command of English. He returned to Syracuse often after
1900, but he is perhaps best remembered here for his annual engagements as a preacher during Lent over a period of thirteen years.

Rabbi Friedman later had this to say about Rabbi Wise's impact
on this city: "His annual visits to Syracuse brought out the largest audiences in the series. Hundreds of Jews flocked to hear him. It was said
that on the day of Dr. Wise's preaching the collection plates were
filled to overflowing. 'Stephen Wise Day' during Lent was a sort of
Yom Tov for the Jewish people, who took pride in having a rabbi represent them before the Christian community. It was the beginning of
a Syracuse Ecumenical Movement." Christians were no less eager to
hear the famous rabbi, and his incomparable oratory filled Keith
Theater, the largest in Syracuse, to the uppermost gallery.

After thirteen annual visits, Rabbi Wise was not again asked to participate in the Lenten services, nor was any other rabbi. Some time later, when Dr. Wise asked why the invitations were no longer extended, Rabbi Friedman gave one explanation. "Dr. Wise," he said, "we all know that you have a superb sense of humor, but it proved your undoing at the last service. You could not resist playing on the name of the presiding minister who introduced you. His name was Reverend Golightly. The name evidently amused you, for you kept harping on 'Go lightly.' Christianity was guilty of 'going lightly.' Everything you said for five minutes emphasized 'go lightly.' After those five minutes you lost the respect of the Civic Lenten Committee and embarrassed many Jews and Christians, who wished they could have yelled from the audience, 'Rabbi Wise, go lightly yourself.'"

In 1935 Rabbi Wise was invited to speak at a combined Sisterhood and Brotherhood dinner at the Temple of Concord. Many Christian notables of the city were invited to this event, which was termed the "Brotherhood of Faiths" dinner. In 1935 Father Coughlin was at his height in popularity. He was addressing radio audiences every Sunday on a national hook-up and he would malign the "International Jewish Bankers" and make other anti-Semitic utterances. It was also the period of the rise of Adolph Hitler. The two gave Rabbi Wise a made-to-order subject for his speech. His talk was so outstanding that it was quoted in full by the local papers,[7] and parts of it were picked up by leading papers in other cities. Of Father Coughlin, he said, "If he were here I would tell him that I do not pretend to be an economist or an expert on government, but I do know something of America and of the Jews, and of the spirit and idealism of American democracy. Perhaps I have addressed more Christians in Christian churches than any Jew in history." Of Hitler, he said, "There must be no compromise with Hitler until civilization is returned to Naziland. There is a deeper depth to be reached and we will be overwhelmed by it if we make peace. You may not know it, but Hitler says that the Jewish problem is now solved. I would rather see every Jew in Germany dead, every Jew on earth dead, than to make peace with that Attila-like scourge, providing he is nice to us. Sir John Simon, British Minister of Foreign Affairs, will soon confer with Hitler. God help England and civilization, if she gives up one ship or one soldier, after listening to the lies of Hitler and Goering." Considering that Rabbi Wise made this address in 1935, it sounds like the words of a "Prophet in Israel."

In 1924 the Temple of Concord held its first annual Clergy Institute for all Catholic priests and Protestant ministers of the city.[8] For more than forty years the Institute has brought a succession of outstanding Jewish scholars and rabbis to interpret Judaism to their Christian colleagues. Until quite recently it was the only organized effort to promote religious understanding at a high intellectual level between the faiths in this community. The lecturers have included professors from the Hebrew Union College and the Jewish Theological Seminary of America, as well as distinguished rabbis, and the cause of religious harmony has been greatly advanced.

On February 27, 1966, the old religious barriers were further broken down when a Catholic-Jewish Symposium was held at LeMoyne College. This occasion was sponsored by the Jesuit college and B'nai B'rith, in cooperation with the Jewish Welfare Federation and the Roman Catholic Diocese of Syracuse.[9] Planning was done by a committee of thirteen Catholics and Jews, among whom were President William L. Reilly, S.J., and Father William A. Scott, S.J., of LeMoyne, and Rabbi Theodore S. Levy, Norman Edell, A. Solomon Menter, and Donald J. Ball. The subject of the symposium was "Agreeing and Disagreeing in a Democratic Society." Major addresses were delivered by Dr. Joseph Lichten, National Director of Intercultural Affairs and representative at Vatican II of the Anti-Defamation League of B'nai B'rith, and Dr. Samuel Sandmel, at that time Provost of the Hebrew Union College–Jewish Institute of Religion. The kosher dinner meeting was held in Temple Beth El. Both clergy and laymen joined in discussion groups, which considered such topics as "The Impact of Religion on Contemporary Social Problems" and "Church–State Relations." This was undoubtedly one of the most stimulating meetings of its kind ever held in Syracuse.

In 1967 the Symposium became a tri-faith affair,[10] when the Syracuse Council of Churches was invited to participate, and The Reverend Howard Horn of the Danforth United Church gave the main address. The 1968 Symposium was led by two outstanding scholars: Dr. J. Coert Rylaarsdam, Professor of Old Testament at the University of Chicago, and Professor A. Roy Eckardt of Lehigh University, who has contributed several books to the contemporary dialogue between Judaism and Christianity.

The urban and race problems of the 1960's brought Jews and Christians together in programs of grave concern to the city. In 1960 the Syracuse Interfaith Committee on Religion and Race was formed, composed of twenty representatives of five major religious groups: Protestant, Roman Catholic, Jewish, Eastern Orthodox, and Unitarian. These groups promised "to proceed together to face realistically the urgent problems in racial relations existing among us." [11] Over the years since 1963 this committee has worked for racial and religious harmony by issuing policy statements, consulting with the Mayor and civil rights groups, and sponsoring a limited low-cost housing program for disadvantaged families. Rabbi Theodore Levy was the first representative of the Syracuse Rabbinical Council on this body, and he has continued to play a leading role in its activities. In a similar endeavor, Rabbi Irwin I. Hyman has served as chairman of the Mayor's Human Rights Commission for several years.

One last example of the new spirit of religious brotherhood deserves notice. In the course of an address at the Temple of Concord in May of 1967,[12] The Very Reverend William J. Reilly, S.J. (the first priest to preach at Concord in its 128-year history) announced the appointment of Rabbi Theodore Levy to the faculty of LeMoyne College.[13] Since the fall term of 1967–68, Rabbi Levy has lectured on Judaism in a course carrying academic credit. The predominantly Catholic students of LeMoyne have responded to this course with great enthusiasm. A similar course on Judaism was introduced at Syracuse University by Dr. A. Leland Jamison, Willard Ives Professor of the Bible, and local rabbis have been invited to give frequent lectures to the students.

THE 1967 CRISIS

Fully a month before the Arab-Israeli war started on June 5, 1967, the air was heavy with foreboding. The Arab threats of annihilation for Israel sounded ominous. Their claims that they were prepared for war appeared to have more weight than in the past. It had been known for some time that the Soviet Union was supplying their latest arms and planes to the Arab countries, particularly Egypt and Syria.

On May 23, President Nasser of Egypt demanded the removal of the United Nations forces from the Gaza Strip and the Gulf of Aqaba and proclaimed, "The Israeli flag shall not go through the Gulf of Aqaba." This was tantamount to a declaration of war.

In a television address President Johnson reaffirmed the 1957 commitment that the Gulf of Aqaba must be kept open for Israel and all maritime countries. Unwilling to act alone, the United States was seeking support from other powers, but no country came forward.

President Nasser massed 100,000 troops in the Sinai and moved them up to the Israeli border. On June 3, the surrounding Arab countries—Jordan, Iraq, and Syria—were poised for the kill. On the same day, the Egyptian commander of the Sinai frontier addressed his forces, saying, "The eyes of the whole world are upon you in your most successful war against imperialist Israel. . . ." The Israeli Army, consisting mostly of reserve forces, was mobilized. Moshe Dayan had been called back into the Cabinet two weeks before and given the post of Minister of Defense.

In the meantime, the Jews of Syracuse were mobilizing with the only weapon at their disposal—money. The United Jewish Appeal declared an emergency campaign for funds in America, seeking not pledges, but cash. The Council of Jewish Federations and Welfare Funds called for an extraordinary meeting of the presidents and executives from every Welfare Federation in the country to meet in New York City the weekend of June 2d. Norman Edell, the executive director of the Syracuse Jewish Welfare Federation, left early on that Friday to be there for the opening. He was joined by the president, Herman Dubnoff, on Sunday.

Urgency was the salient point of the entire emergency conclave. The need for dollars was immediate. "The Government of Israel," they said, "must pour its people and resources completely into protecting its existence as a nation. It faces enormous economic losses of industries trying to operate without the workers who have been called up, loss of income from tourists, of unharvested crops." A figure of $300,-000,000 was mentioned as needed. When Norman Edell, a veteran of fund-raising campaigns, returned to Syracuse he said that he "had never been so moved by the sense of urgency and the significance of the moment."

The Six-Day War

On Monday, June 5, the shooting started. The Jews of the world held their breath. How could the little country of Israel withstand the onslaught of all the Arab countries? Additional help for the Arabs was already on the way from Algeria, Iraq, Saudi Arabia, Libya, and the Sudan. Monday evening in Syracuse (which is seven hours later than the time zone in the Middle East) word came via television news broadcasts that, although the fighting was intense, it appeared that Israel had been victorious in the first brush with the Egyptian Air Force. There was hope.

Herman Dubnoff and Norman Edell immediately called for a special meeting of the board of directors of the Federation. An emergency meeting was held in Joseph Roth's home on that very Monday evening, June fifth. $125,000 was raised then and there, with money, checks, and stock certificates laid right on the table.

The next day Rabbi Theodore Levy, Solomon Menter, and B. G. Rudolph left for Washington to attend a mass rally.[14] On Wednesday they went to visit their Congressman and their Senators. Fortunately, our representatives in Washington—Senators Jacob Javits and Robert Kennedy, and Congressman James Hanley—were all on the Israeli side. The Syracuse delegation received a very cordial greeting from their fellow Syracusan, Congressman Hanley. They thanked him for the position he had taken on Israel, for he had already signed a petition favorable to Israel that was circulated on the floor of the House, and he had also made a speech on the floor a few days previously, urging that the United States should honor its commitment to Israel.

The news that Israel was victorious on the battlefield against every one of its Arab foes was coming in rapidly. The mass meeting at the Shoreham Hotel that night, and the open-air meeting in LaFayette Park, opposite the White House, the next noon appeared to be anticlimactic. When the delegation of Syracusans returned from Washington on Friday, the war was over.

In Syracuse, the meetings and the campaigns for funds were progressing well. By the end of the first ten days Syracuse had raised $500,000, and in two weeks that sum had increased to $630,000.

Herman Dubnoff, president of the Federation, performed an extraordinary task, working night and day, attending every meeting. There were no out-of-town speakers, all local talent. Jay B. Rudolph, Harry Slater, William Smith, and others did a commendable job.

After six days of war, Israel had taken all of the Sinai Peninsula, including the left bank of the Suez Canal, had driven out the Egyptian forces, and reopened the Gulf of Aqaba for Israeli ships, pushed back the Jordanians to the east bank of the Jordan River, and conquered the Golan Heights in Syria from which the Syrians had for almost twenty years harassed the Israeli towns along the border.

The war was over. A cease-fire was accepted by Egypt, Jordan, and Syria. The Jews of America had raised more than the $300,000,000 needed to help Israel over this critical struggle, and the Jews of Syracuse raised over $600,000 as their share.

Even though the Jews of Syracuse were gravely concerned with the life-and-death struggle in Israel, the interest of the community in local progress was not forgotten. In 1965 Congregation Beth El made its momentous move from the old neighborhood and constructed a modern edifice on the eastern boundary of the city. This move was necessitated by the shift of the center of Jewish population. While the location was questioned by many at first, when the temple was completed, it was enthusiastically received and gave a lift in morale to the entire Jewish community.

In 1967 the Adath Yeshurun congregation decided that it must move away from its old location on the corner of Harrison Street and Crouse Avenue, toward the newer residential section of the city. At its one hundredth anniversary celebration, the congregation announced the plan to build a new sanctuary on Kimber Road.

A $2,500,000 ANNIVERSARY CELEBRATION

On February 5, 1967, a banquet to celebrate the one hundredth anniversary of the Congregation Adath Yeshurun was held in the Grand Ballroom of the Syracuse Hotel. To commemorate this event, the plans to build a new $2,500,000 temple were unfolded. The plans had been many years in the making. The idea of a new temple, started in 1963 when Asher Markson was president, was further developed during Sidney Grossman's administration, and was brought to fruition when Melvin R. Rudolph was elected president in 1967.[15]

Never in the history of Syracuse was such a costly plan to build a new temple so eagerly accepted and approved by its membership. Saul North, a proven campaigner, was appointed chairman of the fund-raising committee; William Smith, the former chairman of the board and a well-known public accountant, was chosen to be chairman of the special gifts division; [16] and Melvin Rudolph became chairman of the building committee.

The reasons for a new structure were explained as: (1) the present temple is where the Jews are not (in a census conducted in 1967 it was found that 98 percent of the members do not live within convenient distance of the temple); (2) Urban Renewal (the city of Syracuse plans to turn Harrison Street into a six-lane highway); (3) the University Hill Development Plan (Syracuse University has an extensive program of expansion which will turn Crouse Avenue into a commercial street to service the University community). These were the most obviously pressing reasons.

Other statements in justification of the plan were that the congregation is now forced to transfer the High Holiday services to the War Memorial auditorium in order to find room for all the members and their families, as well as others who desire to worship with Temple Adath Yeshurun. Also, the neighborhood is now run-down and was recently the scene of racial disturbances within a few blocks of the temple, and finally, there is a lack of parking space for automobiles in the present location.

Such considerations led the congregation to purchase a thirteen-and-a-half acre plot of ground in the Bradford Hills section, facing Kimber Road, together with the beautiful L. W. Singer home that faces Brookford Road, for $175,000. One of the first contributions, and perhaps the largest, was made by Abe Cooper in the amount of the purchase price of the lot.

The plans for the new Adath Yeshurun Temple have been prepared by Percival Goodman of New York, one of the foremost designers of synagogue buildings in America. Professor Goodman teaches at the Graduate School of Architecture at Columbia University. A few of the outstanding temples he has designed in recent years are the Shaarey Zedeck Temple in Detroit, one of the largest synagogues in America; Temple Beth El in Rochester, New York; and the Temple Beth El of Springfield, Massachusetts.

The local architectural firm who will assist in the planning is Quinlivan, Pierik and Krause. The building is to be of non-combustible construction, with brick facing and a stainless steel roof over the sanctuary and chapel. The sanctuary, chapel, administrative offices, and social halls will all be air-conditioned. The sanctuary will seat 750, and expand for the High Holy Days to a seating capacity of 2,700. The social hall, which includes a modern stage and a kosher kitchen, will have a seating capacity of 750. Through the use of folding walls, it will be divisible into three units so that three separate affairs can be held at the same time. The school wing will include twenty-four classrooms, two kindergartens, a youth lounge, and school administrative offices. Each schoolroom will accommodate thirty students.

The building will house a large memorial library designed for community use. The lobby will face a landscaped court and is also designed as a memorial hall. There is to be parking for over 250 cars. It is planned that it will be completed and ready for the High Holiday services of 1970.

Our story starts with the first *minyan* which met in the back of a peddlers supply store in 1839 and ends, in 1969, with the breaking of ground for a $2,500,000 temple complex. In the century and a quarter that lies between these two events, we have portrayed the growth of the community and the achievements of the men and women who have shaped the history of the Jews of Syracuse, New York.

"History is the essence of innumerable biographies," said Thomas Carlyle.

Addenda

JEWISH COMMUNITIES ADJACENT TO SYRACUSE

Auburn and Oswego, though thirty and forty miles from Syracuse, respectively, were considered more or less as parts of the Syracuse Jewish Community. In the early days they were almost completely dependent on Syracuse for their association with things Jewish.

When a male child was born, the *mohel* from Syracuse was called to perform the circumcision. Their dead were buried in Syracuse Jewish cemeteries. Before they built synagogues of their own, they came to Syracuse for the High Holidays, and quite a number became regular members of Syracuse congregations.

Many would drive in on a Sunday (and still do) to visit a Jewish meat market for kosher meat and to pick up some groceries and delicatessen to take home. While they now have synagogues of their own, they are not as dependent on Syracuse as they were in the early days. The close relationship still exists, however, so that the histories of these communities are worth recording in this book.

THE CITY OF OSWEGO, NEW YORK

Oswego was incorporated as a city in 1848, the very same year that the neighboring city of Syracuse received its charter. Many people speculated that Oswego, situated on Lake Ontario, with a natural harbor, would soon outstrip Syracuse.

In the early 1840's, when the population of the city was a scant 1000, the few Jews of Oswego would travel to Syracuse for the High

Holidays. It is recorded in the minute book of the Beth Israel Synagogue of Syracuse that a Mr. Abram Levy from Oswego was elected as a member on September 4, 1854.[1]

In 1858 there were enough Jews in Oswego to form their own congregation. On January sixth, Congregation Berith Sholom was founded. The officers elected were A. S. Garson, president; M. Rypinsky, vice-president; S. Goldberg, treasurer; and M. I. Garson, secretary. The Reverend Weiland was their first congregational functionary.

In 1860 the population of Oswego reached 16,000. By comparison, the city of Syracuse had a population of 28,000.

Services were maintained regularly at different members' homes. No house of worship was built, but in 1864 Berith Sholom felt that land for burial purposes was necessary, and they purchased a plot for $250. The first and second recorded burials, respectively, were those of Mrs. Sarah Wendel on November 24, 1864, and Mrs. F. Hess on November 15, 1865. Later in 1864 the congregation secured the services of Rev. Marcus Rubin, who remained in Oswego for five years, until he was called to Syracuse to become the spiritual leader at Beth Israel Congregation.

In 1876, Congregation Berith Sholom was reactivated after a period of quiescence and elected the following:

Rabbi—Rev. Rehfelt
President—Garson Meyer
Vice-President—R. Eliken
Treasurer—Jacob David
Secretary—A. Freundlich

Other well-known men of that period were Emil David, Henry Freundlich, and Mr. Ould of Ould's Clothing Store. Beyond their names, little is now recalled of these once-prominent citizens of Oswego's early Jewish population. In 1898 Dr. Alex Calish, the first Jewish physician in the city, settled in Oswego. Even though 1900 brought an influx of more Jewish immigrants into Oswego, services were still being held in local homes. Some more names, without the desired accompanying information, pop up at this juncture—Kapron, Meyers, Weiner, Cohen, Rosenthal, and Arnosky.

In 1910 the High Holiday services were held in the upper floor of

the Lannon Hotel between East Bridge Street and East Cayuga
Street, and in 1911 a site over Horn's between East First and East Cayuga Streets was used for Jewish services.

On August 7, 1911, a new congregation, Temple Adath Israel, was
legally incorporated under the laws of the State of New York. The
first president was Abraham Abrams. From 1914 to 1916, services were
held at Moose Hall on East First Street between Bridge and Oneida
Streets. At that point, the congregation moved to quarters over the Oswego County Savings Bank. For many years Aaron Cohen served as
president. He was the father of Dr. Milton Kogan and Clarence
Kogan. In that same year, 1916, a $300 burial plot was purchased near
Riverside Cemetery, but was later resold for the same amount when it
was deemed undesirable. This sum became the nucleus for the purchase of the present house of worship.

On May 9, 1927, the congregation realized their dream, and Helen
M. Couch was given a down-payment of $1,750 on the purchase price
of $5,750 for the present site of the temple, and the congregation had
a mortgage of $4,000 to repay. On June 5 of that year, an additional
mortgage was secured from Oswego City Savings Bank for $6,500. The
building was completely remodeled at a cost of $10,000. Julius Karch
(father of Mrs. H. B. Lasky) worked very diligently, giving his time
and funds to make it a complete success. Officers at that time were:
Max Gover, president; Jacob Shapiro, vice-president; Sam Rosenberg,
secretary; Max Shapiro, treasurer; and Aaron Cohen, Jacob Shapiro, Max Gover, and M. Mesnich, trustees. Others on the committee
were I. H. Shapiro, H. B. Lasky, B. N. Shapiro, Sam Rosenberg, Joseph Cohen, and Morris Rakov.

The Sisterhood was organized in November, 1927, and took on the
responsibility for paying off the mortgage. Mrs. Abe Cohn was the
first president, and Mrs. Max Gover succeeded her and remained the
leader of the Sisterhood for nineteen years, from 1929 to 1948. A drive
for funds in 1927 yielded between five and six thousand dollars. The
rabbi was Rev. Mr. Wachnin.

After the death of Joseph Arnosky (father of Benjamin Arnold of
Syracuse), Mr. Kapron, last survivor of the original Berith Sholem,
joined Adath Israel and gave all rights to the cemetery previously
owned by Berith Sholem and the *Sefer Torah* to Adath Israel.

A fire partially destroyed the synagogue in 1935, but under the leadership of J. Shapiro, chairman of the building committee, it was immediately rebuilt. He was the father of Ralph Shapiro, Oswego's present mayor.

From 1945 to 1948 there was no rabbi. In 1948 Mr. Harry B. Lasky was elected president, assisted by Sam Rosenberg as vice-president; William White, secretary; and David Brien, treasurer. Max Gover and Jacob Shapiro were elected honorary presidents in recognition of their untiring loyalty to the synagogue. Harry Lasky, together with Sam Rosenberg and I. H. Shapiro, members of the house committee, worked endlessly in rehabilitating the synagogue, making it a house of beauty in readiness for the fortieth anniversary celebration. The men were assisted by Mrs. H. B. Lasky and Mrs. M. W. Kogan of the Sisterhood.

Officers of the Sisterhood were: president, Mrs. H. Lasky; vice-president, Mrs. Leonard Shapiro; treasurer, Mrs. M. W. Kogan; secretary, Mrs. William White. Mrs. Max Gover was made honorary president for her unceasing loyalty to the Sisterhood. Rabbi J. Sivowich was engaged to lead the congregation in 1948.

In 1955 a campaign was undertaken to raise funds to remodel the outside of the synagogue. It was successful, and on completion in 1959 the Golden Anniversary Dedication and dinner dance was held at the Frederick Leighton School on Hillside Avenue on April 12. Mr. Arthur Shapiro was dinner chairman. Max Karch was president of the synagogue, and Harry Lasky was remodeling chairman. The building now is very imposing. It has a red brick colonial front with white trim.

The Oswego Jewish community, although small in numbers (about 35 families), and mindful of its own heritage, has contributed leadership to the larger community.

The outstanding civic leader in the community is Mayor Ralph Shapiro. Among the professional men are Milton W. Kogan, M.D.; Benjamin Sidenberg, M.D.; and Julius Weinreb, D.D.S. Leonard Amdursky and his son, Robert, are attorneys at law. Prominent businessmen are: Bernard Shapiro, vice-president of the Oswego Hospital Board of Trustees; Charles N. Goldstein (now deceased), who was president of the Retail Merchants Association of New York State and a prominent businessman; and Harry B. Lasky, warehouse operator and executive in Oswego and Syracuse.

Prominent women are Mrs. Milton W. Kogan, former president of the medical auxiliary of New York State, and Mrs. Harry B. Lasky, president of the auxiliary of the Oswego Hospital and member of the board of trustees.

Fort Ontario—Oswego

In 1944 Oswego, New York, became host to 1,000 refugees. They were sheltered at the abandoned camp at Fort Ontario just outside the city of Oswego. The small Jewish community of Oswego measured up to their responsibility and, under the leadership of Harry Lasky, formed citizens' committees to aid and succor these refugees who had escaped Nazi extermination.

"Motivated by the European conflict, a special meeting of the Intergovernmental Committee on Refugees, formed to continue and develop the work of the Evian Conference, was called at the White House on October 17, 1939." President Roosevelt's concern for the thousands of persons left homeless from this war was in evidence when he stated, "This problem involves no race group—no religious faith. It is the problem of all groups and all faiths. It is not enough to indulge in horrified humanitarianism, empty resolutions, golden rhetoric, and pious words. We must face it actively if the democratic principle based on respect and human dignity is to survive—if world order, which rests on security of the individual, is to be restored. . . ." As a direct result of the President's efforts, Fort Ontario near Oswego, was declared the first "free port," which eliminated the legal immigration restrictions.[2]

President Roosevelt announced that the United States would accept 1,000 refugees from Italy, who should be brought immediately to this country (regardless of the usual immigration regulations) and sent to "an emergency refugee shelter" at Fort Ontario, there to stay until the war's end. "Preference was to be given to those for whom no other havens are at present available, and the selection and procedure of bringing them here is to be as simple and expeditious as possible, . . ."[3]

Harry B. Lasky, who was responsible for helping at the Oswego end of this project, reports that refugees arrived at Fort Ontario in April of 1944. Their first reaction upon arrival at Fort Ontario was that they felt as if they were prisoners of war because they were kept inside an inclosure which surrounded the Fort. Later they had permission to come and go more freely.

The total number of the group was 999, which included men, women, and children. Only ninety-nine of the individuals were single, the rest were families.

Among these were many outstanding professional people—artists, actors, musicians, writers and movie producers—none of whom stayed long enough in Oswego to become well-known to the local residents.

National service organizations were very much interested and helped considerably by giving moral and financial aid to the refugees. Many agencies looked at the Fort Ontario refugee camp as an experiment, hoping that more refugees would be permitted to come out of Europe in the same manner.

Among the agencies that were active in this venture were: the National Refugee Service, Inc. (Mr. Gomberg was the representative of this agency in Oswego, assisted by Harry Lasky); the Hebrew Sheltering Immigrant Aid Society, Isaac Asofsky, executive director; the American Jewish Congress, Rabbi Stephen S. Wise, president; the National Council of Jewish Women, represented by Mrs. Esther Kaunitz, head of the department of service to foreign-born. The B'nai B'rith of Syracuse equipped a recreation center at the camp, and the Syracuse rabbis were frequent visitors.

Considering the Army rules that governed the fort, everything that could be done to supply the refugees with kosher food and other Jewish amenities was effected; even a *mikvah* was provided.

Some refugees remained in Oswego for twenty months. One or two families stayed on for a couple of years after they were granted their release, but the majority left at once and none are now in Oswego.

Two significant things happened to Oswego Jewry during the 1960's: first, Ralph Shapiro, son of one of the early settlers, was elected mayor and served with honor and distinction for eight consecutive years; second, the synagogue at 163 East Third Street which served as a house of worship for over forty years has been sold, and the Baptist church (a much larger edifice in a better neighborhood) was purchased. It is now in the process of renovation at a cost of $50,000, and completion is expected in time for the High Holiday services of 1969.

It has been recognized for some time that the smaller communities are losing much of their population to the larger cities, and this is particularly true of the Jewish people, who look for better opportunities in metropolitan centers. Oswego has been more fortunate in this respect. The Oswego Normal School has been taken over by the New York State University College, whose enrollment is growing rapidly, and many among the young student teachers and professors who have come from out of town are Jewish. The president of the congregation Adath Israel is Dr. Kenneth Sipser, supervisor of secondary mathematics at State University College of Oswego.

THE CITY OF AUBURN, NEW YORK

The city of Auburn, in Cayuga County, is located thirty miles west of Syracuse. Situated in the center of good, fertile land which provides a solid base for its economic life, it was settled mostly by New Englanders and Easterners. In early days, grain, cattle, sheep, and poultry were raised in large quantities. Because of lack of transportation, little of these products found their way to outside markets. Some of the surplus grain was disposed of at the forty or more distilleries around the countryside, and was manufactured into over 80,000 gallons of spirits each year. The clergy greatly deplored this industry. Wool obtained from the sheep kept several thousand looms in and around Auburn busy turning out over 340,000 yards of woolen, cotton, linen, and mixed cloth per year. In addition, there were numerous tanneries, carding machines, cloth factories, and earthenware plants.

Log-house schoolrooms were established as early as 1800. In 1806 a group of men met in Daniel Avery's Tavern and formed the Cayuga County Medical Society. Dr. Fredrick Delano of Aurora was chosen president. A newspaper, *The Western Federalist,* came to Auburn in 1808. A Literary Library was established in 1812. Thus it was that Auburn was developed in industry and culture several years before Syracuse.[4]

As in most Jewish communities, the first recorded history starts with the establishment of a congregation. During the 1880's and 1890's, when immigrants from Eastern Europe started coming to the United States in large numbers, a few found their way to Auburn. They started as peddlers, shoemakers, tailors, and cigar makers, and there was one umbrella mender; these were lowly trades but it was a way of eking out a living. Some moved on to larger communities and some remained.

In 1890, a rabbi arrived in Auburn and set up his residence in that city. That was before they had established a regular congregation. Rabbi Jaffe busied himself as a *shohet* (one who butchers chickens and other kosher animals according to Jewish ritual and law).

On March 24, 1903, the hopes of the small group of Jews in Auburn were crystallized in the formation of the first congregation and they named it *B'nai Israel* (Children of Israel). The following is a listing of the twenty-six men who were the charter members of the congregation: president, Moses Saperstein; vice-president, Louis Bernson; secretary, Lewis Gardner. The other charter members were: A. Kalet, I. M. Liberman, Isidore Blumberg, Eli Cohen, Israel Goldman, Joe Kaletski, Max Blumberg, Herman Zuckerman, Louis Denison, Louis Lipsitz, Barney Gardner, Samuel Podworsky, Jacob Blume, George Davis, J. S. Hurwitz, M. Cooper, J. Cooper, A. Cooper, T. Pfifer, S. J. Blumberg, Sol Podworsky, R. D. Louis, and I. S. Black.

Rabbi Jaffe was retained as spiritual leader at a salary of $20 per month. Supplementing his income by his ritual slaughtering business and by his teaching, the rabbi remained for about a year after the young congregation was established. A series of Orthodox rabbis followed him, and continued to draw the same salary and to augment their meager income by the same means as the first rabbi.

The congregation met in various halls and homes before voting to purchase a house for worship.

In 1911, its members voted to purchase a house at 18 Seminary Avenue for $3500 as a home for the Rabbi and as the site for the daily worship service, the Hebrew school and for meetings. It was not large enough to accommodate the crowds at the High Holidays, and thus the Rosh Hashana and Yom Kippur services remained at Woodman's (Hall) until 1921. . . . A few years later plans were made to construct a synagogue at the Seminary Avenue location. Fund raising activities were undertaken almost immediately.[5]

Another milestone was passed when, in 1915, Rabbi Tamaris was engaged as the congregation's first full-time spiritual leader. Personal tragedy brought his stay to an early close, and Rabbi Levine followed him to the pulpit. Both men were paid a salary of $30 per month.

In 1920, Samuel Schwartz was elected president of the Congregation and he determined to follow through with the building of the long-planned, much talked about synagogue. Oldtimers still vividly recall his bringing Rabbi Yalow down from Syracuse one cold winter evening to spur the lagging fund drive. Rabbi Yalow must have been a good talker, too, because $7,000 was pledged that night.[6]

A series of fund raising drives resulted in a treasury of $17,500 by the end of that year. The funds were matched by taking out a loan, and the dreamed-of synagogue was shortly a reality. Architect Carl Tallman of Auburn designed the synagogue, and Ross and Co. of Syracuse were given the building contract.

The Auburn Citizen describes the new synagogue as

. . . a small edifice, it is claimed that for beauty and grace of interior structure it cannot be rivaled by any other Synagogue in the country. The assembly proper is lined on each side with graceful arches, supported by columns and the altar and sanctuary are built in accordance with the specifications laid down in the Mosaic Law.

All interior woodwork is of selected oak and the lighting is profuse and artistic.[7]

The first spiritual leader to serve the new synagogue was Rabbi Reuthberg. He was followed by Rabbis Simon, Wallace, Pogeralsky, and Shappo in quick succession, and all were Orthodox.

The Younger Element Takes Over

From the glories of the first quarter of the twentieth century, matters took a turn for the worse. The depression of the 1930's almost wrecked B'nai Israel; by 1935 membership had dwindled to forty families. Samuel Schwartz, president at the time, took a drastic step. He sent a letter to the past and present membership stating that in his opinion the congregation should be dissolved. The fear of losing all the effort and money which went into the building of B'nai Israel awoke the Auburn Jews. At the next regular meeting it was voted to continue the synagogue, but changes had to be made. The second generation took over. They insisted that services be modernized and that strict Orthodoxy be abandoned in favor of Conservative Judaism. B'nai Israel affiliated with United Synagogue of America and elected Rabbi Eleazer Levi as their spiritual leader.

Rabbi Levi brought new life to the congregation. Very personable and popular, his Conservative services had a wide appeal, and the membership started to grow.

In 1936 the Goldman family erected a bronze tablet in memory of their wife and mother, Bella. Names of other deceased members were added to the tablet as a fund-raising project by the congregation. When Hitler rose to power in 1938, Rabbi Levi and Dr. Ralph Philbrook, the minister of St. Luke's Evangelical Church, inaugurated the American Way Assemblies which are held each year during Brotherhood Week. As part of the observance, Rabbi Levi and Rev. Philbrook exchanged pulpits. After a stay of six years, Rabbi Levi resigned in 1940. During the period of the 1940's the rabbis changed frequently.

Fifty-eight Jewish men and women of Auburn participated in the Second World War effort. In 1950, through the efforts of Harry Tecler, president of the congregation, arrangements were made with Fort Hill Cemetery for a B'nai Israel burial section.

As B'nai Israel approached its fiftieth anniversary in 1953, it could look back at its early history and see how the Auburn Jewish community had prospered.

The Early Settlers

Little is known about the very early Jewish settlers of Auburn. We do know that there was one named Jacob Levi, a Civil War veteran who owned a clothing store. It is believed that he was the first permanent Jewish settler in Auburn. In the 1870's two prominent families took up residence in the city, the Marshalls and the Krafts. Both of these families had their roots in Syracuse. Joseph Marshall was a brother of Jacob Marshall of Syracuse, and the Krafts were from a large family of Syracusans. Marshall operated Marshall's Clothing Store, a forerunner of the present store of the same name, still located at 131 Genesee Street and operated by Milton Marshall, son of the founder. Julius Kraft operated a leather and hides business and, as it was with the Marshalls, the business remained a family enterprise.

The history of a Jewish community can best be understood through the lives of the men and women who founded the synagogues and other institutions and those who have maintained them over the years.

The same thing was true in New England. When the Puritans arrived, one of the first things they did was to build a house of prayer, and to this day, if we want to know the history of a New England town, we can go to the church register where will be found the names of the original founders and their deeds for many years thereafter. This is just as valid for the Jewish community of Auburn. Look up the names of the charter members, follow through to their descendants, and there lies the history of the community.

We cannot here give a full account of all the charter members; some left Auburn shortly after the synagogue was started, others passed on without leaving descendants who remained in Auburn. We give a report only of those families whose descendants remained and continue to take an active party in the synagogue and community.[8]

THE LIBERMAN FAMILY. When Isaac Liberman arrived in America from Neustadt, Poland, he was still in his teens. He came to Syracuse, where he found family and friends from his native town. At the age of 16, he started peddling in and around Cayuga County. He married Etta Blumberg and continued to live in Syracuse until 1890, when he moved to Auburn. There he opened a jewelry store in partnership with his brother-in-law, Meyer Blumberg, on State Street. The partnership broke up in 1896. The firm continued to operate under the ownership of Isaac Liberman and his son-in-law in the same location for over 70 years.

Isaac was a charter member of B'nai Israel and his wife was a charter member of the Sisterhood. They took a deep interest in the Jewish community throughout their lives. Isaac and Etta had three children—Isidor, the eldest, Rosylyn, and Lorraine. Isidor became a successful businessman and took an active interest in the community and B'nai Israel.

THE ABRAHAM KALET FAMILY. Another early settler in the Auburn Jewish community was Abraham Kalet. He arrived in Syracuse about 1880, where there were already a number of Kalets who had arrived earlier. As was the case with other immigrants, he was fitted out with a pack of dry goods and sent forth. From then on he was on his own. He looked for new territory and went beyond Auburn into Seneca County. His experiences were like those of most peddlers. He married a girl from one of the Kalet families in Syracuse, opened a little store in Seneca Falls, and settled down to raise a family. Though he was getting along quite well in Seneca Falls, Abraham and his wife decided to move to Auburn which was larger and had a few Jewish families, since they thought it would be a better place to raise their children. This was about 1890, and they opened a store at 78 State Street. The Kalets took an active part in the organization of a congregation, and Abraham was made treasurer of B'nai Israel. They raised a family of five children. Abraham has passed on; two of his sons carry on the business—one of the leading ladies' apparel shops in Auburn—and both are active in the community at large and in Temple B'nai Israel.

MOSES SAPERSTEIN and his wife Rachel were pioneers of the Jewish community of Auburn. They arrived in Auburn before the turn of the century and immediately began to agitate for the formation of a congregation. Auburn had only a small, poor Jewish community at this time, and it took a lot of work to arouse interest and raise the necessary money. Moses Saperstein was the first president of B'nai Israel, and his wife was president of the ladies' auxiliary. During those years they brought up a fine family of three sons and three daughters. Moses and Rachel passed on many years ago, but the children who remained in Auburn continued an active life in the Jewish Community. Their son Gerald took over the presidency of B'nai Israel when it was about to go under. The services were changed from Orthodoxy to Conservative, and the congregation was revitalized. Gerald, a lawyer, is now judge of the Surrogate Court in Auburn.

WETZLER. Among the early Jewish settlers were Solomon Wetzler and his wife Bella. Both were pillars of strength in congregation B'nai Israel. He was president when the temple was built. Their son, Benjamin Wetzler, entered politics and for many years has been secretary of the Democratic party of the State of New York.

ELI AND MINNIE COHEN came to Auburn in 1896. They became stalwarts in this community and were among the builders of the congregation of B'nai Israel.

ISRAEL AND BELLA GOLDMAN came to Auburn in 1902. Israel and Bella were among the hard-working pioneers of this community. They are both gone now, but they left a family of 10 children, each of whom carried on the Jewish tradition as did their parents before them. Charles Goldman is a leader in the community at large, and Samuel has given of his time and energy to the small Jewish community. His contribution of articles to the Temple bulletin of B'nai Israel is the foundation on which this story of Auburn has been written.

THE JACOB HURWITZ FAMILY. Jacob Hurwitz was a learned man in Hebrew and the Talmud. He attended a *yeshiva* in Lithuania before he came to this country. They were among the early Jewish arrivals in Auburn where, as did other pioneers, they engaged in peddling or were owners of small stores. Jacob Hurwitz was not a merchant, and he chose to repair umbrellas. You could see him on the streets of Auburn, carrying a number of old umbrellas on his back and crying out, "Umbrellas to mend."

SAMUEL SCHWARTZ arrived in Auburn from Lithuania the year the congregation B'nai Israel was founded, in 1903. In the small town in Lithuania he was a *yeshiva boher* (a student in the *yeshiva*), where he devoted himself to studying the Talmud. He married and had three children before he left his small town, and came to America without a trade or any skills. He therefore did the usual thing for an immigrant to do, go peddling. His brother-in-law Isaac Cohen, who had been established in Auburn for a number of years, staked him to a horse and wagon, and Samuel Schwartz, the student of the Talmud, went out looking for waste materials. He saved up enough to send for his wife and three children, who joined him in 1905. Mrs. Schwartz was a typical Jewish mother devoted to her family, and her home was open to the stranger and wayfarer. She was considered the best cook of Jewish dishes in Auburn. All the children attended the Auburn elementary and high schools. Young Maurice helped to augment the family income by selling papers on the corner of Genesee and North Streets. Business improved for the Schwartzes during the 1920's, and Mr. Schwartz purchased the Crane junk yard. Maurice was sent to attend Syracuse University. After leaving the University, Morrey, as he was known by all Auburnites, joined his father's business.

Samuel Schwartz was able to take things easier and began to take a greater interest in B'nai Israel Synagogue. He was elected president and retained that position for twelve years. Just as the Schwartz family arrived at the height of prosperity and well-being, both Bertha and

Samuel Schwartz passed away in the year 1944, within six months of one another. Morrey and his brother Herman continued the business and branched out into real estate and other investments. Morrey became one of the popular young men in Auburn. He married the daughter of Israel Goldman, one of the influential families of the Jewish community. He was elected to the presidency of B'nai Israel and was made a member of the Board of Education, the first Jew to attain this position. He held that office for twelve years. Maurice Schwartz went on and on in his public life and occupied many responsible positions, until he was elected to the highest office, as mayor of Auburn, in 1959. He served with honor and distinction and was elected for a second term. No doubt he would have gone further in politics, but suddenly, while on a business trip to Rochester, he died of a heart attack on December 8, 1967. His loss was a great tragedy to the city of Auburn and to the Jewish community.

The many tributes paid to Maurice Schwartz stressed two outstanding traits: his dedication to the city where he lived and which he served so faithfully, and his deep sense of charity and compassion.

Governor Nelson A. Rockefeller wrote, "I was deeply shocked to learn of the most untimely death of my dear friend Maurice Schwartz. His outstanding service to the people of his community will long be remembered by his fellow New Yorkers."

Leaders of the opposition political party praised him as if he were one of their own. William H. McKeon, Country Democratic Chairman, and Edward T. Boyle, the Democratic candidate for mayor, paid him just tribute.

When a Jew is elected mayor of a city, no further proof is needed that there is very little, if any, anti-Semitism in the community and that the Jews are well integrated in the business and cultural activities of the city.

We may mention a few more personalities who are part of the Jewish community and also serving the city, state and federal government: George Michaels is a representative of the district that includes Auburn in the New York State Assembly; Gerald Saperstein is Surrogate Judge of Cayuga County; Edmund Port is District Federal Judge; Max Goldman is a trustee of Auburn Community College; Charles

Goldman is a director of the Marine Midland Trust Company; and Herman Schwartz is a director of the National Bank of Auburn.

Rabbi Michael Kurz has been the spiritual leader of Congregation B'nai Israel for the past seven years. He is a graduate of the class of 1939 of the Jewish Theological Seminary of America.

Congregation Beth Sholom on Jamesville Road,
DeWitt, New York, dedicated December, 1965.
(*Courtesy of Beth Sholom*)

**Congregation Young Israel was founded in 1945. This
building on the corner of Allen and East Genesee
Streets was built in 1957.   (*Courtesy of Young Israel*)**

The Suburban Jewish Center, North Syracuse, was
founded in 1955, and this synagogue on Vine
Street was dedicated in April 1968.
(*Courtesy of Marvin Barish*)

Rabbi Stephen S. Wise, speaker at the Lenten Services during the 1930's
in Syracuse. Left to right, Rabbi Irwin Hyman, Asher Markson, Rabbi Wise,
and Rabbi Benjamin Friedman.　(*Courtesy of Asher Markson*)

Syracuse delegates, American Zionist Convention at Atlantic City, New Jersey. Left to right, Rabbi Stuart Rosenberg, Bernard S. Cohen, the Reverend Max Wechsler, B. G. Rudolph, and Dr. Aaron Burman. (*Courtesy of Mrs. Louis Nesbit*)

The founders of the Bureau of Jewish Education at a dinner October 22, 1950, in honor of Professor Salo W. Baron. Standing, left to right: Ben Zion Miller, Hyman Poltenson, Hayyim Margalit. Seated: Donald J. Ball, Professor Baron, and Judge Albert Orenstein. (*Courtesy of Bureau of Jewish Education*)

The Luncheonaires and guests at Testimonial Dinner for Asher Markson on November 29, 1955. (Courtesy of Asher Markson)

The Hall of Languages, the first permanent building on the Syracuse University campus. (*Courtesy of Onondaga Historical Society*)

Sabbath Evening Services at Hendricks Chapel, Syracuse University. (*Courtesy of Hillel Foundation*)

Joseph Alexander, member of the
Syracuse University football
team, 1918-21, named to Walter
Camp's All-America team in 1920.
Selected as guard on All-Time,
All-Star Eastern College
Athletic Conference team in 1969.
(*Syracuse University Archives*)

Harry Kallet, member of the
Syracuse University football
team, 1908-11, and named to
Walter Camp's All-American
team in his senior year.
(*Courtesy Richard Kallet*)

Rabbi Emeritus Benjamin Friedman, retired in 1969 after fifty years of continuous service as rabbi of Temple of Concord. (*Courtesy of Temple of Concord*)

Irwin I. Hyman, rabbi of Temple Adath Yeshurun (Conservative) since 1935. (*Courtesy of Temple Adath Yeshurun*)

Jacob H. Epstein, rabbi of
Temple Beth El (Traditional)
since 1965; previously served
Congregation Beth Israel Syracuse
from 1950 until 1965.
(*Photo by Bergan and Klineberg*)

Theodore Levy, rabbi of
Temple of Concord (Reform)
since 1962.
(*Courtesy of Temple of
Concord, photo by Sarkin*)

Harvey Goldscheider, first
permanent rabbi of Congregation
Beth Sholom (Conservative),
DeWitt, New York.
(*Photo by Bergan and Klineberg*)

Samuel Yalow, rabbi of Ahavath Achim (Orthodox)
for over fifty years, now retired.
(*Courtesy of Aaron Yalow*)

Three generations of the Marshall family. Jacob Marshall (seated), **Louis Marshall, and Clara Marshall** [Bronner].   (*Hebrew Standard*)

Harold Lerner, cantor and
musicologist at Temple
Adath Yeshurun since 1953.
(*Photo by Sarkin*)

The Reverend Moses J. Braude,
cantor of Beth Israel
(Orthodox) from 1900 to 1957.
(*Courtesy of Beth Israel*)

Ralph Shapiro, Mayor of Oswego, New York, from 1959-67.

Congregation Adath Israel, Oswego, New York, dedicated in 1925 and occupied until 1969.

Congregation Adath Israel, Oswego, New York, dedicated in 1969.

Maurice Schwartz, Mayor of Auburn, New York, from 1959 until his death in office on December 8, 1967.

Congregation B'nai Israel, Auburn, New York, founded in 1903. The synagogue was dedicated in the early 1920's.

Appendices

APPENDIX A

The following list is a record of the years of Solomon Rosenbloom, his wife, seven sons, and one daughter. All but the parents were born and spent their entire lives in Syracuse.

	Born	Died
Solomon	November 20, 1822	January 20, 1896
Hannah (wife)	January 27, 1827	September 2, 1884
Marcus	June 11, 1849	April 2, 1919
Daniel	January 2, 1851	August 27, 1905
Simon	February 22, 1853	February 6, 1923
Hannah (daughter)	March 31, 1855	May 17, 1912
Moses	January 6, 1860	September 27, 1917
Isaac	January 4, 1862	March 18, 1954
Henry	February 14, 1865	May 22, 1933
Abraham	April 9, 1867	April 9, 1947

APPENDIX B

REVEREND WECHSLER'S BAR MITZVAH BOYS

The following is a partial listing, divided into professional categories.

Business and Civic Leaders

Irving Berman
Philip Holstein
Dave Lerman
Harold Lerman
Gilbert Matlow
Melvin Rudolph
Raymond Rudolph
Solomon Rosenbloom
Hiram Weisberg
Gordon Alderman
Herbert Kaletski

Judges

Hon. Nathan Abelson
Hon. Arnold Blumberg
Hon. Jacob Serling

Attorneys

Bernard Cohen
Earl Freshman
Sanford Engel
Herman Lipstein
Sidney Grossman
Harold Weisenberg
Warren Winkelstein
Sol Menter
Morris Berman
Irving Lessen

Dentists

Leon Harris
Lester Isaacs
Theodore Katz

Doctors

David Ball
Leon Berman
Sidney Berman
Daniel Burdick
Louis Bragman
Isadore Cohen
Elmer Gais
Kenneth Goldstein
Hilbert Harris
David Horwich
Harry Kallet
Arnold Kauffman
Isadore Levy
Frederic Nesbit
Fred Roberts
George Roberts
Abe Serby
Jesse Serby
Emanuel J. Wexler
Asher Winkelstein

APPENDIX C

Syracuse School Teachers

From 1861 to 1891

Name	Date	Place
Strause, Simon	1861–64	Townsend, Montgomery
Silberman, Mary	1869–76	Putnam
Strause, Sophia	1872–74	Genesee
Goldstein, Marilla	1874–84	
Lowe, Bessie	1874–90	High School
Loomis, Yetta R.	1875–78	Seymour
Shevelson, Carrie L.	1881–88	High School
Rosenthal, Belle	1885–92	Clinton
Isaacs, Abby	1885–92	Clinton, Vine
Ettleson, Dora	1885–87	Montgomery
Bondy, Yetta E.	1885–86	High School
Goldman, Ida E.	1886–87	High School
Levy, Julia	1886–92	Montgomery
Metzger, Lizzie	1888–92	Madison
Levy, Clara	1888–92	Madison
Levi, Etta	1888–92	Putnam
Shevelson, Rachel	1889–92	High School
Finkelstein, Brinna	1888–92	Irving, Madison
Ettleson, Etta	1890–92	Putnam
Bloom, Sophia	1891–92	High School

After 1891

Kaufman, Birdie
Kaufman, Ceil
Kaufman, Ray
Kaufman, Miriam
Weisberg, Goldie (Harris)
Lowe, Tracy
Bloom, Stella (Goldwater)
Schreiber, Rachel (Mendelsohn)
Amdursky, Sadie
Amdursky, Birdie (Macht)
Liberman, Anna Rae (Kaletski)
Tumin, Sara

Levi, Deborah
Cohen, Gertrude
Oberdorfer, Rena (Bronner)
Shapiro, Ida (Ferguson)
Rosenthal, Martha
Lopsitz, Lottie
Heiman, Rose (Grody)
Volinsky, Rebekkah
Volinsky, Sarah (Murphy)
Friendly, Fannie
Sobalovage, Sarah
Tumin, Bessie (Katz)
Ross, Lottie

APPENDIX D

Presidents of the
Syracuse Jewish Welfare Federation

1918–32 Benjamin Stolz
1932–37 Moses Winkelstein
1937–42 Rabbi Benjamin Friedman
1943–45 Alexander E. Holstein Sr.
1945–47 David Lerman
1948–50 B. G. Rudolph
1950–51 Ives Jacobs
1951–52 Tracy Ferguson
1952–53 Malcolm Sutton
1954–57 Samuel Greene
1958–62 Lewis Goldner
1963–65 Louis Yaffee
1966–   Herman Dubnoff

APPENDIX E

A Recent Membership Roster
of the Luncheonaires

William Aberson *
Saul H. Alderman
Howard Aronson
Benjamin S. Arnold †
Samuel Bragman †
Abe Cohen
Tracy Ferguson
Paul Flah †
Charles Gilbert *
Leopold E. Goldberg
Harold C. Greenstein
Lionel O. Grossman
Sidney L. Grossman
Alexander E. Holstein
Philip M. Holstein
Ives Jacobs
Milton Macht

Emanuel Manheim *
Asher S. Markson
Harry Marley
Hon. Albert Orenstein
Ernest Rambar
Bernard G. Rudolph
Hon. Jacob Serling
Irving Shimberg
Jack Simmons *
Samuel Singer
Harry G. Slater
William Smith †
Malcolm A. Sutton
Harold M. Weisenberg
Jerome M. Wilson
Isaiah Wolfson
Louis Young

* Moved to other cities.   † Deceased in past twelve months.

Notes to Chapters

INTRODUCTION

1. *The Authorized Daily Prayer Book,* revised edition, Hebrew text, English translation with commentary and notes by Dr. Joseph H. Hertz, the late Chief Rabbi of the British Empire (New York: Bloch Publishing Co., 5717–1957), p. 644.

2. On American Jewish local and regional history, see the *Proceedings of the Joint Session of the American Historical Association and the American Jewish Historical Society,* December 30, 1959, at the Conrad Hilton Hotel, Chicago, Illinois, *Publication of the American Jewish Historical Society,* XLIX, no. 4C (June, 1960), pp. 213–64; and in particular, the article by Abraham G. Ducker, "An Evaluation of Achievement in American Jewish Local Historical Writing," *ibid.,* pp. 215–63. In commenting on Dr. Ducker's paper, Professor Selig Adler of the University of Buffalo made this observation:

> Obviously, few graduate students trained in secular institutions will specialize in this area. Our recruits will have to come from the Jewish sponsored universities in the purely theological schools all of which, it is hoped, will henceforth pay increasing attention to our discipline. . . . For the immediate future, however, we will be largely dependent upon the labor of rabbis, dedicated laymen, and men of letters who are not primarily historians. (*Ibid.,* p. 254.)

Some of the histories published in this field, have been the following: Charles Reznikoff, *The Jews of Charleston: A History of an American Jewish Community,* with the collaboration of Uriah Z. Engelman (Philadelphia: Jewish Publication Society of America, 1950); Selig Adler and Thomas E. Connolly, *From Ararat to Suburbia: The History of the Jewish Community of Buffalo* (Philadelphia: Jewish Publication Society of America, 1960); Louis J. Swichkow and Lloyd P. Gartner, *The History of the Jews of Milwaukee* (Philadelphia: Jewish Publication Society of America, 1963); Stuart E. Rosenberg, *The Jewish Community in Rochester, 1843–1924* (New York: Columbia University Press, 1954); S. Joshua Kohn, *The Jewish Community of Utica, New York 1847–1948* (New York: American Jewish Historical Society, 1959); W. Gunther Plaut, *The Jews in Minnesota: The First Seventy-five Years* (New York: American Jewish Historical Society, 1959); Leon

L. Watters, *The Pioneer Jews of Utah* (New York: American Jewish Historical Society, 1952); and on Minneapolis, Albert I. Gordon, *Jews in Transition* (Minneapolis: University of Minnesota Press, 1949). In the preface to his book, Gordon discusses the role of the participant observer in the writing of a community history. The prognosis by Professor Adler as to who the potential writers of local Jewish history may be is borne out in large measure by the aforementioned titles. The work on Syracuse is by a dedicated layman, and the most recent one, *"Nothing Left to Commemorate": The Story of the Pioneer Jews of Jackson, Amador County, California,* by Dr. I. Harold Sharfman (Glendale, California: The Arthur H. Clark Co., 1969), is that of a rabbi.

3. See Moshe Davis and Isidore S. Meyer, editors, *The Writing of American Jewish History* (New York: American Jewish Historical Society, 1957), particularly the section on "Local and Regional History," pp. 11–61, reprinted from the *Publication of the Amercan Jewish Historical Society,* XLVI, no. 3 (March, 1957), pp. 143–93; and *Local History: How to Gather It, Write It, and Publish It,* by Donald Dean Parker, revised and edited by Bertha E. Josephson (New York: Social Science Research Council, 1944). In recent years the theme of "American Jewish History Week," sponsored annually by the American Jewish Historical Society, has been "Discover Your Community." In the furtherance thereof the Society has published some guidance pamphlets such as: *Preserving and Understanding Your Local Jewish Heritage: The Objectives of a Local Jewish Historical Society* (Waltham, Mass.: American Jewish Historical Society, 1968); and earlier, Bernard Postal, *Touring Your Jewish Community* (New York: American Jewish Historical Society, 1963). For those interested in pursuing work in this field, see also the *Technical Leaflets Series* published by the American Association for State and Local History, and Jacob R. Marcus, *How to Write the History of an American Jewish Community* (Cincinnati: American Jewish Archives, 1953).

4. See the "Proceedings of the Joint Session of the American Jewish Historical Society and the American Historical Association (December 28, 1966)," held in New York City at the New York Hilton Hotel, *American Jewish Historical Quarterly,* LVI, no. 3 (March, 1967), pp. 268–82. Dr. Shipton's address is found *ibid.,* pp. 271–82. On the Puritan version of the Hebraic contribution, see *ibid.,* p. 273.

5. *Ibid.,* p. 279.

6. *Ibid.,* p. 277.

7. *Ibid.,* p. 273.

8. Bernard G. Rudolph, *Tell Me More* (Syracuse: Senehi's Originals, 1966).

CHAPTER I

1. Benjamin Friedman, "The Days of Our Years: A History of the Society of Concord," *Society of Concord: One Hundredth Anniversary 1839–1939* (Syracuse, N.Y., 1939), p. 9.

2. Dwight H. Bruce, *Memorial History of Syracuse* (Syracuse, N.Y., 1891), pp. 523–26.

3. *Ibid.*

4. Miscellaneous Book "G" (1840–58), Onondaga County Clerk's Office, pp. 60–61.

5. *Onondaga Standard,* November 30, 1842.

6. Friedman, *Society of Concord,* p. 10.

7. David Philipson, "Isaac Mayer Wise," *The Jewish Encyclopedia,* XII (New York & London, 1907), pp. 541–42.

8. Isaac Mayer, *Reminiscences,* trans. and ed. by David Philipson (Centenary Edition, New York, 1945), pp. 36–40.

9. The description of Syracuse in 1839 was compiled from many sources. Most useful are W. M. Beauchamp, *Past and Present of Syracuse and Onondaga County* (New York, 1908); Dwight Bruce, *Memorial History* (already cited); and Franklin H. Chase, *Syracuse and Its Environs: A History* (New York, 1924). Photographs of Syracuse in the 1830's can be found in the files of the Onondaga Historical Association.

10. *Syracuse Journal,* Centennial Edition, March 20, 1939.

11. Ronald E. Shaw, *Erie Water West: A History of the Erie Canal, 1792–1854* (Lexington, Kentucky, 1966), *passim.*

12. *New York Tribune,* June 6, 1851.

13. Information on the Schloss family provided to the author in 1967–68 by Tracy Ferguson, a direct descendant.

14. *Syracuse Standard,* September 5, 1854.

15. Also listed as "Bonta" and "Bondi" in *Winsor's Syracuse City Directory for 1857–8* (Syracuse, 1857).

16. Information on Gabriel Bondy was supplied to the author by Arline B. Davis, a granddaughter, in letters dated August 26 and September 2, 1966.

17. Joseph and Sarah Wiseman are listed in the United States Census of 1840.

18. Temple of Concord's incorporation papers list Joseph Wiseman as a trustee.

19. Obituary in the *Syracuse Standard,* April 6, 1880.

20. Information on Meyer Weisman and his family was supplied by Ruby Marks, a direct descendant, in a letter dated February 20, 1967, addressed to the author.

21. Some recollections by Jonas L. Oberdorfer, dated April 25, 1935, have been Xeroxed by Tracy Ferguson and presented to the author for his files.

22. Obituary in the *Syracuse Sunday Times,* October 19, 1890.

23. Oscar Handlin, "Introduction," in *Louis Marshall: Champion of Liberty. Selected Papers and Addresses,* Charles Reznikoff, ed., I (Philadelphia, 1957), pp. ix–xliii.

24. Obituary in *Syracuse Standard,* September 22, 1851.

25. Friedman, *op. cit.,* p. 13.

26. *Rochester Democrat,* February 29, 1872.

27. *Hebrew Standard,* November 15, 1907.

28. *Daily Journal City Register & Directory for 1851–52.*

29. Early records of the Merchants National Bank.

30. *Syracuse Standard,* September 22, 1851.

31. *Ibid.,* September 11, 1852.

32. *New York Tribune,* November 17, 1856.

33. Abstract of will, *New York Tribune,* January 31, 1857. The original of the very long will is on file at the Onondaga County Courthouse, and a copy of it is recorded at the Onondaga Historical Association's office.

34. From records copied by WPA Book "I," p. 157, at the Onondaga County Clerk's Office.

35. *Winsor's Syracuse City Directory for 1857–8* (Syracuse, 1857).

36. *The Occident and American Jewish Advocate,* IX (September 1851).

37. *Daily Journal City Register & Directory for 1851–52* (Syracuse, 1851).

38. The name of Aaron Henochsburg is so recorded on a tablet in the Temple of Concord, Madison Street and University Avenue.

39. *Syracuse Post Standard,* January 1, 1927.

40. Information provided to the author by Mrs. David Brodsky, a grand-daughter, in 1967.

41. Richard H. Brown, "Nathan Adler Stops at the Bahams," *New York Folklore Quarterly,* XXIV (March 1968), pp. 27–43.

42. W. Lee Provol, *The Pack Peddler* (Philadelphia, 1937), pp. 67–80.

CHAPTER II

1. *The Occident and American Jewish Advocate,* IX (October, 1851).

2. *The Israelite,* I (October, 1854).

3. Population figures for the early years in Syracuse (data received from United States Census Reports)

        1830— 2,500
        1840—11,074
        1850—22,271
        1860—28,119

4. The lists were compiled from *Boyd's Syracuse Directory 1874–5,* and from *Winsor's Syracuse City Directory for 1857–8.*

5. Records of the Syracuse Savings Bank, Main Office, Clinton Square, Syracuse, N.Y.

6. "Consecration of the New Synagogue, Kenesseth Shalom, at Syracuse, New York," *The Occident and American Jewish Advocate,* IX (September, 1851), pp. 373–80.

7. Information on the builder and architect were taken from the dedicatory tablet of the old temple.

8. Quoted in Friedman, *op. cit.,* pp. 11–12.

9. *Ibid.,* p. 12.

10. "Consecration of Kenesseth Shalom," *Occident, op. cit.,* pp. 373–80.

11. *Ibid.*

12. *Ibid.*

13. *The Israelite,* September 29, 1854.

14. Original Minutes Book of New Beth Israel Synagogue on file at Temple Beth El, Syracuse, N.Y.

15. *Ibid.*

16. *Ibid.*

17. S. Joshua Kohn, *The Jewish Community of Utica, New York 1847–1948* (New York, 1959), p. 12.

18. Stuart E. Rosenberg, *The Jewish Community in Rochester 1843–1925* (New York, 1954), p. 36.

19. *Syracuse Courier,* September 3, 1881.

20. *The Israelite,* May 3, 1861.

21. *Hebrew Standard,* November 15, 1907.

22. *Ibid.*

23. Personal interview by the author in 1966 with Louis Stolz, son of Jacob Stolz.

24. W. Freeman Galpin, *Central New York: An Inland Empire* (New York, 1941), I, *passim.*

CHAPTER III

1. Franklin H. Chase, *op. cit.,* Vol. I, pp. 335–41.

2. *The Israelite,* September 19, 1862.

3. The following sources were used for the material on the Civil War affecting Jewish participation: data from Adjutant-General's *Annual Report* for 1904 (Assembly Doc. No. 13, part 3, Albany, 1906); Moses Summers, *Sword and Pen,* in *Syracuse Standard* 1862–65; Captain George K. Collins *Memoirs of 149th Regt.* (Syracuse, 1891); Frederick Phisterer, *New York in the War of the Rebellion* (Albany, 1912).

4. *The Israelite,* October 31, 1862.

5. *Syracuse Standard,* January 1, 1892.

6. Original Minutes Book of Beth Israel, Syracuse, N.Y. Entry dated July 6, 1884. Information also provided in 1966 by Mrs. Ralph Shulman, a descendant of the Manson family.

7. Tracy Ferguson, a direct descendant, gave information to the author in the years 1966 through 1969.

8. Biographical sketches of the Rubin family are from Franklin Chase, *op. cit.,* Vol. II, p. 139, and Vol. III, p. 393. Also, the November 15, 1907, issue of the *Hebrew Standard* on Moses and William Rubin. J. Robert Rubin in the *Syracuse Post Standard,* July 26, 1959.

9. *The Israelite,* April 12, 1861.

10. Friedman, *op. cit.,* pp. 14–15.

11. Miscellaneous Book "I," p. 14, Onondaga County Clerk's Office.

12. *Hebrew Standard,* November 15, 1907.

13. *The American Israelite,* September 2, 1887.

14. *Syracuse Daily Journal,* August 26, 1887.

15. Friedman, *op. cit.,* p. 23.

16. The author was provided additional information by two daughters, Beatrice Rosenbloom Silverman and her sister, Helen Rosenbloom Harris, wife of Dr. Hilbert Harris.

CHAPTER IV

1. *Winsor's Directory, op. cit.,* p. 248.

2. In a letter dated December 18, 1968, the Texas State Library in Austin, Texas, furnished the author with information on "Dan Dopplemyer." Notice difference in spelling of Doppelmayer.

3. Information on the Weismans, Exsteins, Wolfs, Doppelmayers, etc., was pro-

vided by Ruby Marks, already cited in Chapter I, note 20. Mrs. Charles Beehm, secretary of the Museum and Historical Society, Marshall, Texas, furnished additional facts in a letter to the author. The *Marshall News Messenger* of October 9, 1966, ran a special section in celebration of the ninetieth anniversary of the founding of the Weisman department store.

4. *National Cyclopedia of American Biography,* IX (New York, 1899), pp. 520–21.

5. *The Universal Jewish Encyclopedia,* VI (New York, 1939), p. 572.

6. *The Red Book of Syracuse and Onondaga County,* Ray Smith, ed. (Syracuse, 1923), pp. 66–67.

7. *Ibid.*

8. Frieda Gates Friedman, a granddaughter of George Freeman, provided the author with family history.

9. *Syracuse Herald,* May 25, 1932.

10. Mrs. Jacob (Frances) Moss, a descendant, provided the author with family history.

11. "In Retrospect," *1930 Yearbook, Temple Adath Yeshurun* (Syracuse, 1930), pp. 4–6.

12. *Ibid.,* pp. 4–6.

13. Letter to author from Harold Greenstein, a past student of Rebbe Levy, dated November 4, 1966. Rebbe Levy is mentioned in *The Pack Peddler, passim.*

14. Mrs. Ben Ross, a descendant, provided information to the author in 1966 and 1967.

15. Information provided to the author in a letter dated October 31, 1966, by Mrs. Esther Nesbit, a daughter, of Syracuse.

16. Obituary in *Syracuse Herald-Journal,* March 1, 1954.

17. Stuart Rosenberg, *op. cit.,* pp. 133–35.

18. *Ibid.,* p. 274.

19. *Syracuse Courier,* October 5, 1880.

20. Rosenberg, *op. cit.,* pp. 223–24.

21. Bertram Wallace Korn, *American Jewry and the Civil War* (Philadelphia, 1951), pp. 84–86.

CHAPTER V

1. U.S. Census (1870), and U.S. Census (1890).

2. *Alumni News—Syracuse University,* Vol. VIII, no. 5 (January, 1927).

3. *Memorial Services in Honor of Louis Marshall,* a brochure published by Temple Emanu-El, New York City (November 10, 1929).

4. *American Hebrew and Jewish Tribune,* "Louis Marshall Memorial Issue," September 14, 1934.

5. The author used *The Universal Jewish Encyclopedia* and the *Dictionary of American Biography* for much of the information on Marshall. He is indebted to the Local History Room of the Syracuse Public Library for their bound scrapbook of local newspaper clippings on Marshall, as well as their pamphlets cited in footnotes 3 and 4 and a biographical sketch, *Louis Marshall,* by Cyrus Adler, published by the American Jewish Committee in 1931. Syracuse University made

available to the author copies of the *Alumni News* of January, 1927, October, 1929, and April, 1933, relating to Marshall. Charles Reznikoff's book has already been cited in Chapter I, note 23.

6. *The Pack Peddler*, pp. 67–80.

7. Obituary in *Syracuse Herald-Journal*, December 21, 1945.

8. Information on Joseph Bondy and his wife, Frances Elias Bondy, was provided by their daughter, Mrs. Arline Davis, in letters to the author dated August 26 and September 2, 1966.

9. Ethel Thalheimer Oberdorfer's obituary appeared in the *Syracuse Herald-Journal*, June 10, 1946, and Jonas Oberdorfer's appeared in the same paper on July 31, 1938. Additional information has been cited in note 21, Chapter I. Gates Thalheimer's obituary appeared in the *Syracuse Post Standard*, December 22, 1928.

10. Henry L. Elsner, "The Prognosis of Internal Diseases," *Monographic Medicine*, V (New York, 1916).

11. *The Syracusan*, March 1, 1916. It is the official publication of the Alumni Association of Syracuse University.

12. *Hebrew Standard*, November 15, 1907.

13. *The Syracusan*, October 1, 1913.

14. Personal knowledge of author as friend. Additional information provided by Solomon's daughter, Mrs. Sol (Molly) Levy, of Syracuse, in 1966 and 1967.

15. *Americanization in Syracuse and Onondaga County* (Syracuse, 1920), pamphlet published by The Americanization League of Syracuse and Onondaga County.

16. T. Aaron Levy, *Lincoln, the Politician* (Boston, 1918).

17. The late Dr. Bertram Levinson, of Syracuse, provided the author with familial history in a letter dated January 22, 1967. Obituary of T. Aaron Levy appeared in the *Rochester Jewish Ledger*, January 14, 1955. Obituary also in the *Syracuse Post Standard*, January 6, 1955. Letter from the then Executive Secretary, the late Alice E. Murphy, dated April 5, 1967, provided further information on T. Aaron Levy and The Americanization League.

18. *Syracuse Post Standard* of May 29, 1937, and *Syracuse Herald* of May 29, 1937, contained obituaries.

19. Personal interview by the author in 1966 and again a few months prior to his death in January, 1969, with Louis Stolz at his home.

20. Information and lists of early Jewish schoolteachers was provided by Mrs. Carolyn B. Wright of the Onondaga Historical Association and in a letter from Mrs. Dorothy Brodsky, daughter of Mrs. Stella Bloom Goldwater, an early teacher. Also, Smith's *History of Syracuse Schools* (Syracuse, 1893), pp. 269–90.

21. *Rochester Jewish Tidings*, April 4, 1890.

CHAPTER VI

1. *The Jewish Encyclopedia*, IX (New York & London, 1909), p. 260.

2. *The Occident and American Jewish Advocate*, IX (October, 1851).

3. From records at the Onondaga County Clerk's Office, Book "H," p. 307.

4. From records at the Onondaga County Clerk's Office, Book "I," p. 249.

5. Louis Swichkow and Lloyd Gartner, *The History of the Jews of Milwaukee* (The Jewish Publication Society of America, 1963), pp. 70–83.

6. Book of Minutes of the United Jewish Charities.

7. *Seventeenth Annual Report of the United Jewish Charities* (Syracuse, 1915), pamphlet of 8 un-numbered pages.

8. *Ibid.*

9. The material in the following pages on the Syracuse Jewish Welfare Federation was taken from Minute Books and Annual Reports of the agency generously lent to the author.

10. The author had access to the Annual Reports of the Jewish Family Service Bureau for information which he used in writing the section on the agency.

CHAPTER VII

1. Israel Cohen, *The Zionist Movement* (New York, 1946), *passim.*

2. Personal reminiscences of the author.

3. Additional information was recorded in a letter to the author from Morris Margulies, secretary of B'rith Rishonim of the United States, dated December 1, 1966, and a letter from Dr. Aaron Burman, dated February 28, 1967, as well as Xeroxed clippings from the *Rochester Jewish Ledger* on Zionism.

4. Interviews by the author with members of Ben Zion Miller's family.

5. The book of Minutes of The Jewish Home for the Aged was lent to the author while he was writing the history of the Home. Also in the author's files on the Home are brochures of the Dedication Programme (June 7, 1914) and annual reports for 1926 and 1938, lent by Mrs. Reuben Lavine, daughter of Moses Braude, who also provided family history.

6. A copy of the Jacobson letter was lent to the author by Mrs. Levine and is in the author's files.

7. Brochure of The Jessie and Harry Kaplan Annex of The Jewish Home of Central New York is in the author's files.

8. Franklin Chase, *op. cit.*, gives a description of the early theaters and performers in his book.

9. Frieda Gates Friedman provided information to the author.

10. "The Shuberts of Syracuse," a bound volume of newspaper clippings on the Shubert family is available in the Local History Room of the Syracuse Public Library. *The Brothers Shubert*, by Jerry Stagg (New York, 1968), is very critical of the Shuberts.

11. Obituary in *Syracuse Herald-Journal*, September 10, 1957.

12. Personal knowledge of the author.

13. Personal knowledge of the author.

14. Letter addressed to author from Myron Kallet.

15. Personal knowledge of the author.

16. Biographical data supplied by Syracuse University Alumni Association.

17. *The Red Book of Syracuse and Onondaga County*, Ray B. Smith, ed. (Syracuse, 1923), pp. 66–71.

18. The Syracuse Board of Education sent the author information regarding the Board of Education members.

19. All information and dates up to 1923 were taken from *The Red Book of Syracuse and Onondaga County, op. cit.*

20. Records at City Hall and the Onondaga County Courthouse were available to the author for dates after 1923. Judge Albert Orenstein provided the author with additional information on judgeships.

21. *Hebrew Standard*, November 15, 1907.

CHAPTER VIII

1. Photocopy of the original handwritten report of the twenty-fifth annual meeting of the Hebrew Free School is in the author's possession.

2. Photostat of the original typewritten report of September 15, 1904, is in the author's files.

3. Personal knowledge of the author.

4. Minute Book of the Syracuse Jewish Welfare Federation, 1945.

5. Temple Adath Yeshurun, *1930 Year Book* (Syracuse, 1930).

6. Interview with Rabbi Irwin I. Hyman by the author.

7. Interviews with Rabbi Benjamin Friedman and Rabbi Theodore Levy by the author.

8. Personal knowledge of the author, who participated in the activities of the Bureau of Jewish Education from 1945 through the balance of its existence.

9. Samuel Eber, Rabbi William Shimansky, and Rabbi Moshe Alon provided information to the author on the Syracuse Hebrew Day School in 1969.

10. Interview with Myron Small and the late Max Rosenbloom by the author in 1967.

11. Myron Small has generously lent to the author all of his mementoes, such as dance programs, old snapshots, etc., from which the author has chosen to cite the ones appearing in this book.

12. *Ibid.*

13. Information was gathered by the author from Minutes of the Syracuse Jewish Welfare Federation.

14. Since the Federation was intimately involved in the growth and development of the Jewish Community Center, the author used the Minutes of the Federation for information.

15. *The 75th Anniversary of Lessing Lodge* (Syracuse, 1926). The celebration was held at Poiley Tzedeck's community building on October 10, 1926. The brochure printed for the occasion provides a history of the origin of the lodge.

16. Obituary in *Syracuse Post Standard*, June 1, 1929.

17. *Centennial History of Salt Springs Lodge No. 520, F. & A.M.* (Syracuse, 1962), p. 72.

18. *By-Laws with Historical Sketch Mount Sinai Lodge, No. 864* (Syracuse, 1948).

19. *Syracuse Journal*, December 31, 1872.

20. *Syracuse Journal*, December 14, 1936.

21. The author has in his files copies of newspaper clippings dealing with these now defunct organizations.

22. The *Rochester Jewish Tidings,* Syracuse Section, reported on the various activities and meetings of The Standard Club.

23. Irving Shimberg, in a letter to the author dated February 14, 1967, provided additional information about the early social clubs. The Standard, for example, was located in Mr. Shimberg's grandfather's house on Grape Street.

24. *Syracuse Journal,* Feb. 16, 1875.

25. Letter of Irving Shimberg cited above.

26. As told to the author by Lionel Grossman, an early participant.

27. As told to the author by early members and founders. Since 1925 the author has personal knowledge.

CHAPTER IX

1. Friedman, *Society of Concord,* p. 19.

2. *Ibid.,* p. 22.

3. *The Concord Cook Book* (Syracuse, 1915), compiled by Mrs. Adolph Guttman and Mrs. Levi Oppenheimer, is in the possession of Estelle Rosenthal Kushner and was lent to the author.

4. All of the foregoing information was taken from the One Hundredth Anniversary (1839–1939) brochure of *Society of Concord,* already cited frequently in prior footnotes.

5. Early seating plans of Temple of Concord are in the author's files, diagrammed from memory by Louis Stolz, son of Jacob Stolz.

6. Friedman, *op. cit.,* p. 16.

7. *Ibid.,* p. 17.

8. *The American Israelite,* August 6, 1887.

9. The *Rochester Jewish Tidings* reported the sermons of Dr. Guttman almost weekly in the Syracuse section of the newspaper, which gave the flavor of his personality and scholarship.

10. Personal interview with Rabbi Benjamin Friedman by the author.

11. Personal interview with Rabbi Theodore Levy by the author.

12. Friedman, *op. cit.,* pp. 24–25.

13. *Ibid.,* pp. 25–26.

14. Temple Adath Yeshurun, *1930 Year Book* (Syracuse, 1930).

15. *Commemorating Twenty-Five Years: Rabbi Irwin I. Hyman, Temple Adath Yeshurun 1935–1960* (Syracuse, 1960).

16. Personal interview with Rabbi Hyman by the author.

17. Obituary in *Syracuse Journal,* September 23, 1924.

18. Personal knowledge of the author.

19. Interview with Cantor Harold Lerner by the author.

20. *Syracuse Herald-Journal,* May 15, 1963.

21. Personal interview with David Altfield by the author.

22. A brief history of Temple Beth Israel was published in 1954 on the occasion of the 100th anniversary, "Historical Sketch of Congregation New Beth Israel," *Souvenir Journal of Temple Beth Israel* (Syracuse, 1954).

23. Personal interview with Rabbi Jacob Epstein by the author.

24. Papers of incorporation are to be found in the Onondaga County Clerk's

Office, Book "N," p. 88. Additional information on history can be found in the November 15, 1907, issue of the *Hebrew Standard*.

25. *1965–5726 Dedication Temple Beth El, Syracuse, New York* (Syracuse, 1965). Additional information provided by Rabbi Epstein in interviews with the author during 1968–69.

26. In 1937 Finette Edwards, a reporter for the *Syracuse Herald* did a series on Syracuse churches and synagogues. On May 1, 1937, she wrote an article on the history of Ahavath Achim.

27. *Who's Who in World Jewry* (New York, 1965), p. 1067.

28. Personal interviews with Rabbi Samuel Yalow by the author.

29. Obituary in *Syracuse Herald-Journal*, October 20, 1968.

30. Mrs. Maurice Agronin, secretary of Anshe Sfard, provided information on the history of the synagogue in a letter addressed to the author.

31. *Syracuse Post Standard*, September 28, 1968, reports on activities of the new group of Jews from the Middle East. Author also received additional information from Rabbi Jacob Epstein.

32. *Young Israel of Syracuse, 20th Anniversary Dinner, March 28, 1965* (Syracuse, 1965). The booklet provided a historical background.

33. Obituary in *Syracuse Herald-Journal*, February 9, 1956.

34. Letter from Rabbi Borvick to the author.

35. Personal interview with member Marvin Barish, who lent newspaper clippings, etc., to the author for use in writing about the Suburban Jewish Center.

36. Personal letter to the author from Rabbi Goldscheider. Interview and written data, scrapbook of clippings on Beth Sholom lent to the author by Myron Schaffer, a former president of the congregation.

37. These membership figures were provided by the secretaries of the synagogues to the author.

CHAPTER X

1. Information gathered from Minutes of the Syracuse Jewish Welfare Federation, formerly called the United Jewish Charities.

2. From records on file at the Onondaga County Veterans' Service Agency, 110 Cedar Street, Syracuse.

3. I. Kaufman, *American Jews in World War II*, II (New York, 1947). The Syracuse veterans were identified from the list of New York State Jewish veterans, comprising 218 pages. Martin Birnbaum was also helpful in reviewing the list for omissions.

4. Information provided to the author by the Syracuse Jewish Family Service Bureau.

5. The letters from Ben Choroser are in the files of the author. The author also held interviews with Mr. Choroser.

6. *Syracuse Herald-Journal*, June 10, 1946.

7. *Syracuse Post Standard*, July 5, 1953; *Syracuse Herald-Journal*, March 20, 1953; *Syracuse Post Standard*, March 20, 1953.

8. A Xerox copy of a handwritten letter dated July 8, 1950, by Bertha Frensdorf to her cousin, Herman Salinger, is in the possession of the author, along with

a letter (also Xeroxed) addressed to Albert Orenstein by Herman Salinger, dated July 10, 1962. *Syracuse Post Standard,* June 26, 1962; *Syracuse Herald-Journal,* April 1, 1954.

9. Molly and Minnie Solomon, daughters of Henrietta Solomon, provided material on their mother to the author in letters dated April 9 and April 24, 1968.

10. Information on the Hurwitz brothers was provided by their children to the author.

11. Seymour and Lewis Roth, sons of Philip Roth, provided information on their father to the author.

12. The other men mentioned in this section were known personally by the author.

CHAPTER XI

1. Franklin Chase's *Syracuse and Its Environs* was used for the background material on Syracuse University.

2. W. Freeman Galpin's *Central New York: An Inland Empire,* already cited, was also used for the historical background on Syracuse University. Dr. Galpin was in the Department of History at the University.

3. Information on early Jewish graduates of Syracuse University was provided to the author by the University.

4. Friedman, *Society of Concord,* p. 18.

5. From the Archives at Syracuse University.

6. Sidney Grossman provided the author with historical background on the Jewish fraternities at the University.

7. Date of charter from Syracuse University Archives. Rabbi Friedman and Theodore Pierson provided historical background on the Jewish Student Fellowship.

8. The date of the charter was taken from the Archives of Syracuse University. Fred Krinsky of the Maxwell School was faculty adviser. It lasted until 1949.

9. The monthly publication of Hillel, *The Sage,* provided background on Hillel, and additional information was provided by Rabbi Milton Elefant, the present director of the Hillel program.

10. Syracuse University provided biographical material to the author.

11. The list of Jewish presidents has been taken from the sesquicentennial publication of the *Onondaga County Medical Society 1906–1956* (Syracuse, 1956).

12. Dr. A. Clement Silverman provided information about The Lancet Society.

13. Prior to his death in 1969, Dr. Bertram Levinson provided information about the Elsner-Jacobson Society to the author.

14. Samuel Sarason's son, Dr. Ernest Sarason, provided information on the family to the author.

15. Biographical material on Dr. Peritz was obtained through James K. Owens, in charge of the Archives branch of the Syracuse University Library.

16. D. B. Robertson, *History of the Department of Religion,* Syracuse University (Syracuse, 1968), p. 13.

17. The anecdote reported was told to the author by Rabbi Samuel Yalow.

18. Biographical material on the faculty was provided by Syracuse University.

19. Information on Jewish athletes was gathered by the author from the files at Syracuse University.

20. Pestal, Silver & Silver, *Encyclopedia of Jews in Sports* (Bloch, New York, 1965), p. 480.

21. M. I. Finley, *The Ancient Greeks* (New York, 1963). The dust jacket gives a brief account of the author.

22. *Syracuse University Alumni News, Commencement 1964,* pp. 15–16.

23. *The Octagonian of Sigma Alpha Mu,* LI (May, 1963), pp. 2–3 and cover photograph.

24. *New York Mirror,* June 26, 1960.

25. *Ibid.*

26. *Time,* June 30, 1967, 47.

27. Syracuse University provided information on donors mentioned in the text.

CHAPTER XII

1. *Syracuse Journal,* July 7, 1871.

2. *Syracuse Journal,* April 24, 1874.

3. *Syracuse Journal,* October 12, 1874.

4. *The American Israelite,* April 30, 1886, and May 3, 1886.

5. The *Rochester Jewish Tidings* reported almost weekly on the Temple of Concord in its Syracuse section during the 1880's and 1890's, when the interfaith meetings were developing.

6. Rabbi Friedman gave the author a typed account of his reminiscences and contacts with Rabbi Stephen S. Wise.

7. *Syracuse Herald,* March 14, 1935.

8. Material provided by Rabbi Friedman.

9. *The Heights, The LeMoyne College Magazine,* "A Catholic-Jewish Symposium," 4 (May, 1966), pp. 30–47.

10. *The Heights, The LeMoyne College Magazine,* "Breaking the Barrier," 5 (Summer, 1967), p. 35–36.

11. "Fact Sheet" (mimeographed), September 15, 1963, of The Interfaith Committee on Race and Religion.

12. *Syracuse Post Standard,* May 6, 1967.

13. *Syracuse Herald-Journal,* May 6, 1967.

14. The author participated in the events related in this section.

15. The brochure, *To Chart a Destiny,* issued in 1968, provides the "10 Reasons Why." The brochure, *Your New and Greater Temple Adath Yeshurun,* gives layouts and descriptions, as well as sketches, of the new edifice. Melvin Rudolph, president of Temple Adath Yeshurun and chairman of the building committee, provided additional information to the author.

16. During the fund-raising campaign for the newest Adath Yeshurun an unfortunate automobile accident occurred on September 8, 1968, in which both Mr. and Mrs. William Smith lost their lives.

ADDENDA

1. We are deeply indebted to Mrs. Harry B. Lasky (Margaret Karch) for most of the material and information recorded here. Mrs. Lasky is descended from one of the early Oswego Jewish families, and Harry has lived in Oswego over forty years. They contributed much from their personal recollections.

2. *American Jewish Yearbook 1946*, 47 (New York, 1945–46), p. 44.

3. *American Jewish Yearbook 1945*, 46 (New York, 1944–45), p. 154.

4. W. Freeman Galpin, *Central New York: An Inland Empire* (New York, 1941), I, pp. 279–92 on Cayuga County.

5. *Golden Jubilee Journal B'nai Israel* (Auburn, N.Y., 1953), p. 10.

6. *Ibid.*

7. *Ibid.*, p. 12.

8. We gratefully acknowledge the assistance of Samuel Goldman, who supplied the printed material and his personal recollections which made the chapter on Auburn, New York, possible.

Index

Oswego

Auburn

FIFTEENTH
WARD

*The Old Jewish Neighborhood
at the Turn of the Twentieth Century*